THE PAGEANT

OF AMERICA

R.K.

Independence Edition

VOLUME XI

THE PAGEANT OF AMERICA

A PICTORIAL HISTORY OF THE UNITED STATES

RALPH HENRY GABRIEL

EDITOR

HENRY JONES FORD HARRY MORGAN AYRES

ASSOCIATE EDITORS

OLIVER McKEE

ASSISTANT EDITOR

CHARLES M. ANDREWS
HERBERT E. BOLTON
IRVING N. COUNTRYMAN
WILLIAM E. DODD
DIXON RYAN FOX
ALLEN JOHNSON
WILLIAM BENNETT MUNRO
VICTOR H. PALTSITS
ARTHUR M. SCHLESINGER
NATHANIEL WRIGHT STEPHENSON

ADVISORY EDITORS

DAVID M. MATTESON

INDEXER

After the daguerreotype in The Players' Club, New York

EDGAR ALLAN POE

THE
AMERICAN SPIRIT
IN LETTERS

BY

STANLEY THOMAS WILLIAMS

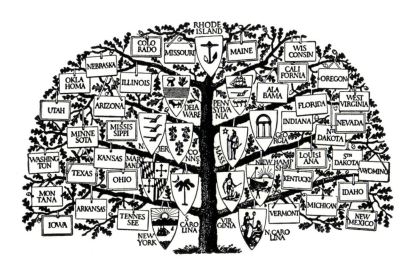

NEW YORK
UNITED STATES PUBLISHERS ASSOCIATION
TORONTO · GLASGOW, BROOK & CO.

TABLE OF CONTENTS

THE AMERICAN SPIRIT IN LETTERS

AMERICAN writing, like the literature of any people, is the outgrowth of the contacts with life and thought that the national writers have had the fortune to experience. In a sense literature is the expression, though not the only expression, of the life experience of a people. The Greeks, in their dramas and their poetry, mirrored the civilization which arose at the eastern end of the Mediterranean and suggested the forces which helped to shape it. The Latin writers make clear the debt which Rome owed to Athens. In the same way American writings reflect the struggles, the aspirations, the ideals and the cynicism of the people who have lived during the last three centuries within the limits of the United States on the continent of North America. The literature of the New World is under heavy obligation to that of the Old, yet it is not mere imitation. To understand American writing as it has steadily become emancipated from the tutelage of Europe one must understand the larger forces that have shaped American character.

When Englishmen and Dutchmen first built their rough habitations in Virginia, New England and New Amsterdam, they cast their lot within the shadow of the forest. Into the forest also plunged the Germans and the Scotch-Irish who crossed the Atlantic in the eighteenth century. They were all north Europeans whose forbears not many centuries back had likewise lived in the forest. A part of the race heritage of the first American pioneers was the memory of the barbarian tribes who had halted the advance of the Roman legions and had finally overrun the decadent empire. Ten centuries had passed since the old nature gods, Odin and Balder, had called those ancient forest warriors to the banquet of the strong and brave in Valhalla. During this time many of the forests of Europe had melted away and broad manor farms had taken their place. A new god was worshiped in the stone cathedrals that lifted their spires above the huddled dwellings of the walled towns. The rough, primitive life of the tribal village gave place to the refinements and artificialities of civilization. When, early in the seventeenth century, the *Sarah Constant* and the *Mayflower* left their adventurers in America, a handful of north Europeans entered again into the wilderness. They walked backward along the path of experience. In their hearts stirred old, half-forgotten impulses.

This contact with the wilderness was to be a factor in American life until the passing of the frontier at the end of the nineteenth century. For two centuries and a half Americans were continually extending their culture to the forests of Ohio and of Oregon, to the valleys of the western mountains and to the treeless plains. For the frontiersman the wilderness was one of the ugly facts of life. He did not sentimentalize about it; he fought it. Life reverted at times to a primitive struggle for existence. Yet with all its dangers and hardships the wild country had a fascination for many of those who came to live in it. Boone, abandoning Kentucky and moving west when the settlements grew thick around him, was but one of a number who would not give up the wild, free life of the forest. It demanded that the pioneer forget some of his civilization and learn the age-old virtues, strength, resourcefulness, perseverance, fidelity, courage. It unloosed race impulses long chained by law and custom. It brought the white man face to face with the hostile and embittered Indian.

The white learned many things from the Indian and imitated some of his ways. A few fine friendships between the races illumine the records of the past but, in the main, the story is one of relentless aggression. The stronger people pushed back the weaker, despoiled them of their hunting grounds and desecrated the graves of ancestors whose spirits still lived in the familiar forests. The American refused either to blend or to compromise with the redskin. The instincts of a primitive fight between race and race proved stronger than the precepts of the Teacher of ancient Palestine to whom the white men looked for guidance. A God-fearing Puritan, confident in the belief that the red man stood in the way of the Divine will, could write of the smoking ruins of a Pequot town, where lay the charred bodies of scores of warriors side by side with those of their women and children, that God, by His special providence, had brought into the village an unusually large number of Indians on the night of the attack. To understand the American of the eighteenth, nineteenth, and even the twentieth centuries, one must understand this recrudescence of the jungle spirit. The rough strength born of the forests of northern Europe was born again in the wilderness of America.

The volume of writings that sprang directly from the frontier is not large. Here and there is a description of the wild country and the settlements in it. More common is the straightforward narrative of personal adventure. In the nineteenth century men of letters like Cooper, who knew the forest, re-created its life for their readers. Later Bret Harte wrote of the California mining camps. But more important than all of these is the impress which the frontier left on American character. Here were first seen the distinctive traits of the new country, personal independence, individualism and aggressive advance. Here also was found the intellectual stagnation which was the inevitable result of complete isolation from the world of thought.

The boundless virgin forest has largely passed away and the frontier has disappeared. But still an instinct for the out-of-doors takes the people of the nation, covered now with towns and cities, to the woods, the lakes and the rugged mountain valleys. To the sons of the pioneers for whom the forest was a challenge the wild country offers rest and recreation. As a result of the knowledge that scientific men have gathered, the wilderness makes a new impress on the spirits of men. The crude, manlike gods of an earlier day have disappeared, and men feel themselves in contact with a Power that baffles speech. There are some, like Burroughs, who say: "I cannot tell what the simple apparition of earth and sky mean to me; I think at rare intervals one sees that they have immense spiritual meaning, altogether unspeakable, and that they are the great helps after all." A majestic wilderness still aids in the molding of American character. Among the writers of latter-day America here and there may be found one who reflects the feeling of this companionship with nature.

At the eastern edge of the forest lay the sea. It has called to American shore dwellers of all generations. The Indians were landsmen rarely venturing their canoes on the ocean. But the blood of the Vikings was in the veins of the English who settled along the desolate New England coast. Very early, sturdy smacks from the shore hamlets of Massachusetts Bay were cutting their way eastward to the Grand Banks. Later New England mariners followed the sea lanes to the West Indies and to Europe and Africa. As the years passed, they rounded Cape Horn and learned the contour of the Pacific coast. In the nineteenth century the encompassment of the world became a commonplace. Packet ships and clipper ships made the flag of the United States familiar on all oceans. Whalers sought their prey amid the ice floes of the north and on the off-shore whaling grounds of the tropics. The sea bred a sturdy race. Men of the frontier like Daniel Boone, Jim Bridger and Kit Carson found their counterpart in the captains who pioneered the way to China, and in the whalers who faced in the day's work the dangers of the ocean and the perils of the whale chase. The sea beckoned from ocean to ocean, to mysterious islands and strange coasts. The mariner made contacts with all the races of the earth. Yet he remained an American, most commonly a New Englander whose outlook upon American affairs was limited by that of the section where, from time to time, he returned to the family who daily prayed for his safety. The hardships and triumphs of life on the old sea-going sailing ship have their place in the literature of America, and the appeal of the old salt's yarn never lessens.

The Atlantic called the first American cities into being, Boston, New York, Philadelphia, Charleston. The sea trade brought to America its first important accumulations of capital other than land. It made possible a social life lifted above the immediate hand-to-hand encounter with nature. In New England, commerce supported the stiff-necked Federalist aristocracy. There were merchant gentlemen in all the cities of the coast. Many American men and women in these small commercial cities of the eighteenth and early nineteenth centuries found leisure to make contact with the world of European thought. Tiny peripheral centers of thought appeared in these American commercial towns. In the sea-born communities of early America began the breakdown of the deadening isolation of the forest which had restricted men's minds to the insistent problem of mere existence. From New York and the towns of New England came a large part of the writing of the first half of the nineteenth century, the first important literary epoch of the United States. Like the forest, the sea has been a part of the life experience of the nation, its influence reaching even to the broad plains of the interior where, as the trees were cleared away, fields of grain appeared.

Behind the westward-moving frontier lay an ever-widening countryside. In the forty-five years between 1803 and 1848 the United States acquired a stupendous area of practically unoccupied land whose western boundary was the Pacific. In less than a century the frontier had crossed this area and had vanished. Behind the frontiersman into the broad valley of the Mississippi and the lesser valleys of the Pacific coast came the husband-man. For two centuries and more America was, for the most part, a nation of farmers. In the South appeared an aristocracy of planters based on slavery. The traveler through the North and West, in the days when Lincoln was debating Douglas in the villages of Illinois, would ride for days over dusty roads bordered by the simple houses and roughly fenced fields of small farms. The men who worked on these acres were out of touch with the quickening life of the commercial centers, out of touch with the great current of world thought, out of touch, for the most part, with the people over the ridge in the next county. The isolation of the frontier was inherited by the farm which followed it. A few wealthy southern planters escaped it but most American farmers, north and south, east and west, found their lives bounded by the interests of the small neighborhoods of which they were a part. Yet on these same farms occurred some of the most striking developments of nineteenth-century America.

Beneath the calm exterior of the mid-nineteenth-century countryside, human life ran as deep as among men anywhere. Human relationships were simple; there was little of the complexity and artificiality of a highly developed civilization. Life lay exposed in all its rough beauty and irregularities like rock strata brought to the surface by ages of erosion. Born and reared in the midst of great spaces, farm folk were impressed by the primitive bigness of things. Their moral code was founded on the primitive rightness of things. They were uncultured and childishly boastful of their communities and their country. Foreign visitors to America in the decades just before the Civil War found in the rural districts a dead level of sameness, a population spread thinly over a vast area as uninteresting as the rolling prairies which stretched without change to the horizon. Yet the uncultivated farm folk of the nineteenth century played a part in shaping the destinies of the nation.

The husbandman who depended upon his own brain and muscles to wrest from nature a living for himself and family was, inevitably, an individualist. Outside the Cotton Kingdom and the commercial cities there was little wealth and little poverty, and men were instinctively democrats. The farm home, where the family gathered in the evening about the fireplace or the chunk stove, was the one important social and economic unit in vast areas of America. The figure of the mother became the symbol of the love and pain, the hope and sacrifice that went into the making of this fundamental institution. Yet the American home differed from the patriarchal group that is the foundation of the ancient civilization of China. In the Celestial Kingdom the son's family looks to the father for guidance and the father bows in worship at the altar of his ancestors. The American did not look to his ancestors; his first thought was for his children. His opportunities for education and training had been limited; theirs should be the best that he could provide. He had struggled against a stubborn environment when the country was young; they should build on his labors and begin where he left off. The plain folk of the farms had shared in a great conquest. With confidence they dreamed great dreams for their children.

Out of this background came many of the greatest Americans of the nineteenth century. Andrew Jackson and Abraham Lincoln are classic examples of farm boys who achieved political eminence. The farms were constantly sending their best blood to the cities to recruit all the callings of life. Some of these sons, like Bryant, became men of letters. Others, like Whittier, never cast their lot with the city. American men of letters have left a lasting picture of the characteristics and ideals of the old farm life which has now well-nigh passed away. Even before the end of the Civil War a rising industrial revolution was wrenching the nation into a new form.

It chanced that America was possessed of unmeasured natural wealth. When this knowledge was brought home to men generally and when the economic organization of the nation had been developed to a point where exploitation was profitable, a struggle developed in the United States scarcely less primitive than the ancient conflict with the forest and its inhabitants. Vast, formless urban centers sprawled out at the meeting of the highways of commerce. New industrial cities, noisy with the clatter of machines and black with the smoke of chimneys, rose in a generation. The factories, the houses, and the streets were ugly. There was no time to give regard to beauty. The old ruthlessness of the marauding Northmen reappeared in the contest for wealth that lay stored up under the soil of America. Power went to him who could grasp it. Giants rose in a decade and towered above their fellows. A stark materialism was loosed and Mammon was worshiped by the descendants of those who had prayed to Odin and Thor.

Into this struggle for power was drawn, during the latter half of the nineteenth century, the best blood and brains of the nation. American thought took shape in masonry and steel. Men trained in the school of self-reliant individualism were caught in the iron discipline of industry and there learned the difficult art of coöperation. Yet the fundamental ideals of the old America passed over into the new. If equality disappeared in the face of mounting fortunes, there was roughly equal opportunity for all. That humble origin did not block the way to the achievement of greatness was proved again and again in the years following the Civil War. Power that was often gained in ruthless conflict was also often used with wise statesmanship. If Americans became the wealthiest people in the world, their discriminating generosity reached to the farthest corners of the earth. Out of the simple ideas of right and wrong that had made up the codes of the farm and the sea have come larger concepts of responsibility and the ideal of stewardship. A new code to fit the needs of the new industrial civilization is now in the beginnings of development and it has gone far enough to give grounds for the belief that the sudden acquisition of power has not impaired the moral fiber of the nation. Yet the new order has been built at tremendous human cost.

In the congested urban districts where dwell the less fortunate in the struggle for existence, living conditions unfamiliar to the old America have developed. The filth and misery of the slum have bred antagonism between the weak and the strong. At times this has flamed into open conflict as labor has slowly and painfully organized and advanced against the strongholds of capital. In the city the peculiar American institution of the home has lost some of its old significance. The harnessing of men and women to the automatic machine where the passing days bring nothing but endless repetition of the same simple task has dulled the vigor and enterprise that were the outgrowth of life in the forest and on the farm and sea. This same intricate, almost human machine which is the proud achievement of the enterprise and freedom of the leaders of the new era has become a blight stunting the growth of the led. Here lie the seeds of possible class hatreds and class wars in the future.

The thoughts and emotions of industrial America are only now becoming articulate. As a people, we have been too absorbed in building railroads, factories and commercial enterprises to pause to consider the significance of what we are doing. Moreover, the wealth and power which industrialism has engendered has made possible a civilization of almost infinite complexity. No poet can sing of the new day in the simple refrains that Whittier or Riley used in describing the life of the old farm. Perhaps the literature of the new America is at hand. There are many who think so. But as yet it is a literature of localities, of neighborhoods, and of classes. Interesting and sometimes significant vignettes of portions of America are being produced. Perhaps they are the harbingers of a national intellectual awakening. With industrialism has come the full maturity of the nation. But industrialism is not the last of the factors that have contributed to the molding of American character.

To say that America is the result of the expansion of Europe and that American civilization is essentially European civilization modified by a different environment is to repeat a well-worn truism. American life, like that of Europe, is set against the classical background of Greece and Rome. The influence of Europe has increased with the passing decades. But, though America lies midway between the East and the West, in Europe and the Near East American cultural traditions come practically to an end. The older civilizations of India, China and Japan have contributed but little. Nor is the Indian in any real sense a part of the cultural background of the people of the United States. Yet America lost by the obliteration of the redskin. The shapely monuments of the Mississippi valley, the vigorous drawings on the skin-covered tipis of the Great Plains, the delicate tracery of the relics of ancient Mexico and the jungle-covered ruins of the Maya temples in Yucatan and Guatemala suggest, on the part of the red man, an artistic sense that the world could ill afford to lose. But the Indian, like the forest, stood in the way of the Anglo-Saxon, and the two melted away together. North of the Rio Grande there is but the faintest trace of native influence in American culture. The United States looks only to Europe and itself for its culture, and shares to the full the gigantic provincialism of that western civilization which has, for the time being, usurped the hegemony of the world.

In the sense in which the anthropologist uses the term, the United States and Europe have become part of the same culture area. America, three hundred years ago on the periphery of this area, has, in the twentieth century, become a part of its dynamic center. The period of isolation and of tutelage has passed. As never before in our national history, the forces that are molding the development of Europe are molding also the life of the transatlantic republic. Industrialism, Socialism and Christianity are but a few of the forces common to the peoples of the western world. Americans are becoming conscious of their new world situation and of the international character of many of the factors with which they have to reckon. They are making adjustments to these new conditions. As yet American literature of the twentieth century seems to be largely national and, since the World War, iconoclastic. It has been in harmony with a trend toward an intense national consciousness that has been an outstanding characteristic of twentieth-century America. Perhaps it is too soon for men of letters to grapple with the implications of the fact that America is one of the small group of very powerful nations. American writers, in the main, seem content to display the pettiness, the credulities, and the absurdities of Americans. They have declared their intention that American literature shall stand on its own feet. So speaks the nationalist in almost every country of the world. The American movement has its counterpart in many other lands. He would be a bold man who would undertake to prophesy what will come of all this nationalism and industrialism. There are some who see a little way ahead limitless opportunities for development and, for America, increasing power. Others cannot escape the haunting specter of a world debacle. With anticipation mingled with apprehension we push forward into the unknown.

RALPH H. GABRIEL

CHAPTER I

WRITINGS OF THE PIONEERS

TO the student of literature the copy of the *Bay Psalm Book* on exhibition in the Bodleian Library at Oxford stimulates meditation. This book, the first published in America, was a gloomy promise of New England literature of the seventeenth century, a literature laden with theology, and sweetened, as John Cotton would have described it, by the morsels of John Calvin. In the New England of Puritan theocracy, literature, for at least a century, became the handmaid of Calvinistic religion. We hear the manly narratives of John Smith or the mockery of Thomas Morton, but their voices sound faint compared with those of the "New England saints," as, turning their pulpit hourglasses, they repeat the doctrines of the Fall of Man, his damnation and his problematical redemption — taking care to give to their sermons the immortality of print. The religious tradition is the fiber of New England literature of the seventeenth century.

The severe views of life taught by English Puritanism were intensified by the realities of the frontier. Famine, disease, and warfare breathe new life into such worn phrases as "God's Protecting Providence." Cotton Mather's tales of "wonderful deliverances" express the universal feeling of a people that had called upon God, and had received help from Him. Their spiritual life, however, like the vast wilderness about them, was a battle field, and God did not intervene lightly. The true Puritan in America kept his musket ready for the Indian, and his soul tense with the struggle to know and enjoy Jehovah. "It is," says Thomas Shepard, "a Tough Work, a wonderful hard Matter to be saved." "Jesus Christ," he declares, "is not got with a wet finger."

The other-worldliness of New England produced in this early epoch great divines and theologians, and, years later, philosophers. Moreover, when the Puritans felled the forests for fire, tilled their farms, and set their straggling huts by the shore, they began the shaping of that frontier around which, as it thrust its way westward or daringly put to sea, so much of the literature of later America was to gather. Their respect for learning founded our universities, and so indirectly the more cultivated, if more imitative, American literature; and from their center, named in affection after the little Lincolnshire town of Boston, arose the cities, or many of them, which were to mold a new literature. No one can say that the civilization of the Puritans was the only factor in orienting our early literature. At this very time in Virginia powerful traditions were growing up, in some respects quite unlike those of the North. Yet New England men and women, who were not, as Bradford said quietly, easily discouraged, and who, as Edwards said of himself, made salvation their business in life, laid the foundations of America's character and of its literature. In our story we shall recur again and again to the early Puritan civilization.

Besides the discourses, the meditations, and the raptures of the religious zealot, there were also events in the life of the colonies which were chronicled in records, histories, and

diaries. The records range from cool statements to England of the colonies' needs in
supplies and men to impassioned appeals for justice. The histories describe the planting
of corn, the building of stockades, the converting or the conquering of the Indians. Sometimes they rise into biblical eloquence as some mighty Indian stronghold is overthrown by
fire and sword. But more often, when they are not merely dull, their virtue lies in racy
anecdote, a vigorous and homely style, a clear story, moving from its very simplicity.
"But out we must go," says Mary Rowlandson, as, a child in her arms, she is driven from her
house, "the fire increasing, and coming along behind us, roaring, and the Indians gaping
before us with their Guns, Spears and Hatchets to devour us." The journals of Bradford
and Winslow; the histories of Hubbard, Church, and Johnson; the diary of Sewall; the
letters of the Winthrops; the narratives of John Smith, Strachey, and Stith; all are alike
in this: they reveal a powerful people engaged in a soul-testing enterprise. We picture the
Virginia coast in spring, the redskin, the vast sweep of lakes, rivers, and forests which so
stirred James Fenimore Cooper and we think as we read this matter-of-fact prose: "Was
there no romance in this people?" Then we think of the New England wilderness in
winter, of King Philip, "that doleful, great, naked dirty beast," and we understand why
this literature clings to hard fact. Men who spend their days in acting romance have
less time to write it.

For like reasons the verse written in America before 1700 is both religious and practical,
but is seldom transported on wings of viewless poesy. Its bleak Muses are John Calvin
or Francis Quarles; its themes are the necessity of man's intolerance in this world, and the
certainty of God's in the next; its manner and meter are those of the theologian and
poetaster. "Let groans inspire my quill," was the invocation of one clergyman. In the
poetry of John Rogers, Urian Oakes, John Norton, and especially in that of Nicholas
Noyes may be found the influence of the English metaphysical school — gone to seed.
Anne Bradstreet, our first American poetess, save in one or two poems, turns from the
pageant of nature about her to write of the thrush and the nightingale; Du Bartas,
Greek and Roman history; and "bloody, Popish, hellish miscreants." Indeed the most
effective verse of the century is that which, abandoning the conventions, and succumbing
to the mood of the age gives us the clear essence of Calvin in wild doggerel. Such poetry
is that of Michael Wigglesworth; its pictures of hell may still stir the old ancestral fear.
What if, after all, Wigglesworth were right about the next world?

It would be confusing to consider the American writers of the seventeenth century in
their chronological order, and there would be little point in grouping them by colonies.
The basic conditions of life were alike in all the settlements along the Atlantic coast.
Whether in Virginia or Pennsylvania or New England, Englishmen, with the cultural
background of the times of James I, Cromwell, and Charles II, were attempting to plant
homes in a difficult environment. Most of the elements influencing American life were
here: the sea, the forest, the Indian, and the civilization of Europe. So the writers, without emphasis upon place, are considered as historians of colonial enterprise, narrators
of personal adventure, expounders of theology, and poets.

Newes from Virginia

OF THE HAPPY A

riuall of that famous & worthy
knight Sir Thomas Gates and well
reputed and valiant Captaine
Newport into England.

IT is no idle fabulous tale,
  nor is it fayned newes:
For *Truth* herselfe is heere arriu'd,
  becaufe you fhould not mufe.
With her, both Gates and *Newport* come,
  to tell *Report* doth lye :
Which did deuulge vnto the world,
  that they at Sea did dye.

Tis true that Eleauen monthes and more,
  thefe gallant worthy wights :
Was in the Shippe (*Sea-venture* nam'd)
  depriu'd *Virginia's* fight.
And brauely did they glyde the maine,
  till *Neptune* gan to frowne:
As if a Courfer prowdly backt,
  would throwe his ryder downe.

                                    The

A

1   From *Newes from Virginia*, London, 1610, a poem by Robert Rich. Only known copy in America in the Henry E. Huntington Library, San Gabriel, Cal.

SHIPS FOR VIRGINIA

THE earliest literature in America was narrative and history. The voyagers wrote of their fearful sea journeys. In Virginia the pioneers struggled against starvation, fever, and the wilderness. Even in the midst of their distresses, artless historians set down their adventures in clear, matter-of-fact prose. Amid perilous seas and strange lands, they bent themselves to the task of telling a plain tale. They described the new kingdom which extended from Cape Charles to the Appomattox River.

JOHN SMITH'S OWN STORY OF HIS ADVENTURES

THE first of these, and the greatest, was Captain John Smith (1579?–1631) of Virginia. He had had many stirring experiences in Europe before embarking for America. Wounded in battle, captured by the Turks, Smith was sold to a gentlewoman in Constantinople. Her angered brother stripped him of his clothes and shaved his head. Smith killed the brother and fled. So runs Smith's tale. His first book, *A True Relation*, published in 1608, is a vivid record of the first year of the colony, a book in which Smith himself played no small part. It is full of lively adventures such as his capture by the redskins. Sixty miles up the Chickahominy he heard the "halooing of Indians." To the amazement of his two hundred assailants and the delight of all his readers he made his Indian guide his "barricado," and so saved his own life.

2   From a copy of the original engraving in the University Library, Cambridge, England

3   From John Smith, *Generall Historie of Virginia, New-England, and the Summer Isles,* London, 1624

JOHN SMITH AND POWHATAN

In narrating later the famous sequel to his capture by the savages, perhaps Smith smiled, fancying that in at least one story he would rival the chronicles of Hakluyt or Mandeville. It was after a long pilgrimage that he beheld the barbaric chieftain, Powhatan, magnificent in pearls and raccoon skins, surrounded by his court. This dignitary had, Smith declares in apparent sincerity, "such a grave and Majesticall countenance, as drave me into admiration to see such state in a naked Salvage." True or not, through stories like this of his rescue by the princess Pocahontas from Powhatan's decree of execution Smith won a considerable portion of his fame. To his intrepid spirit the unbroken frontier was a challenge. He explored New England and Virginia, and fought the Indians long before the arrival of the Pilgrims.

SMITH AS A HISTORIAN OF VIRGINIA

Nevertheless, Smith's loving praise of the lusty soil of Virginia and the "glistering tinctures" of its rivers is only an aside in his valuable book, *The Generall Historie of Virginia, New-England, and the Summer Isles,* first published in 1624. In this volume, one may discover the Smith who was the friend of George Wither and Samuel Purchas — "brave Smith," John Donne called him. He extols his fair Virginia and scolds the mother country for her misjudgments; he describes the Indians; he names rivers and forests; and he recounts his adventures in terse, masculine English. He is the first of our many American men of action who have written forceful literature. Even to-day his words seem alive. "Who can desire more content . . . than to tread, and plant that ground he hath purchased by the hazard of his life? If he have but the taste of virtue, and magnanimitie, what to such a minde can bee more pleasant, than planting and building a foundation for his Posteritie, gotte from the rude earth, by God's blessing and his owne industry . . . ? If he have any graine of faith or zeale in Religion, what can he doe lesse hurtfull to any: or more agreeable to God than to seeke to convert those poore Salvages to know Christ, and humanitie, whose labors with discretion will tripple requite thy charge and paines?"

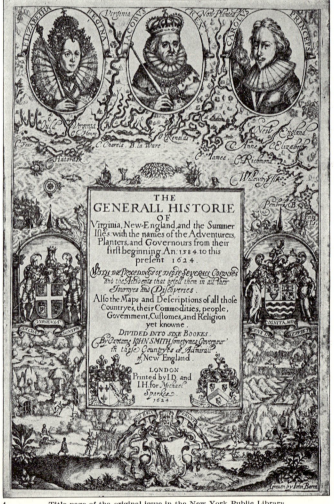

4   Title-page of the original issue in the New York Public Library

GEORGE PERCY AND RALPH HAMOR ON VIRGINIA

Darker pictures of the sufferings of the early Virginians are found in a fragment of a history called *Discourse of the Plantations of the Southerne Colonie in Virginia by the English*, 1606, by Master George Percy. The extant six pages of this work are contained in *Purchas his Pilgrimes*, 1625. The last events chronicled occurred in September, 1607. "There were never Englishmen," Percy cries out in a kind of anguish, "left in a foreign country in such misery as we were, in this new discovered Virginia." Ralph Hamor carries his story of Virginia to June, 1614.

SOMERS' VOYAGE TO THE BERMUDAS

The early historians of America furnished material for literature. William Strachey set out for Virginia with Sir Thomas Gates, later secretary of the colony. Driven off its course by a violent storm, the fleet was wrecked on the Bermudas. Here the explorers built crude ships and continued the voyage to Jamestown. The entire journey occupied nearly a year. Shakespeare perhaps read, in William Strachey's *True Reportory of the Wracke and Redemption of Sir Thomas Gates, Knight*, 1610, of the wreck off Bermuda. Ariel in *The Tempest* says:

> Now on the beak,
> Now in the waist, the deck, in every cabin, I flam'd amazment.

A TRVE
DISCOVRSE OF THE
PRESENT ESTATE OF VIR-
GINIA, and the successe of the affaires
there till the 18 of *Iune*, 1614.

TOGETHER.

WITH A RELATION OF THE
seuerall English Townes and forts, the assured hopes of that countrie and the peace
concluded with the Indians.

The Christening of *Powhatans* daughter
and her mariage with an English-man.

Written by RAPHE HAMOR the yon-
ger, late Secretarie in that Colony.

Alget, qui non ardet.

Printed at London by JOHN BEALE for WIL-
LIAM WELBY dwelling at the signe of the
Swanne in Pauls Church yard.1615.

5   Title-page of original issue of Ralph Hamor, *A True Discourse*, etc., in the New York Public Library

In Strachey's powerful description of the storm near "the still-vexed Bermoothes," Sir George Somers sees the blaze of St. Elmo's fire. Strachey's account describes also the colony, but is chiefly remarkable as a record of the adventurers' sufferings at sea.

6   From *The Tempest*, Act I, Scene I, engraving after the painting by George Romney (1734–1802)

LEAH and RACHEL,
OR,
the Two Fruitfull Sisters
VIRGINIA,
AND
MARY-LAND:
Their Present Condition, Im-
partially stated and related.

WITH
A Removall of such Imputations as are scandalously
cast on those Countries, whereby many deceived
Souls, chose rather to Beg, Steal, rot in Prison,
and come to shamefull deaths, then to better their being
by going thither, wherein is plenty of all things
necessary for Humane subsistance.

By *John* Hammond.

Ecclef. 11. v. 8.
*If children live honestly and have wherewith, they shall put away the
shame of their Parents.*

LONDON,
Printed by *T. Mabb,* and are
to be sold by *Nich. Bourn,* neer the Royall
Exchange, 1 6 5 6.

7   Title-page of the original issue, in the John Carter
     Brown Library, Providence, R. I.

A DEFENSE OF THE NEW LAND

YET in spite of hardships John Hammond (*fl.* 1655), after twenty-one years in Virginia and the new colony of Maryland, writes from England that he longs for America. There, he says, "I desire to spend the remnant of my days." Hammond's affection for America was outraged by the slanders on her name which he encountered in England. He determined to check these "black-mouthed babblers," who described Virginia and Maryland as a land of "dissolute and rooking persons." He published, accordingly, in 1656, in London, *Leah and Rachel, or, the Two Fruitfull Sisters Virginia, and Mary-land*, an ardent defense of the communities of the New World. Hammond was among the first to urge emigration to America, thinking it evil for so many souls to "follow desperate and miserable courses in England than to engage in so honourable an undertaking as to travel . . . there."

GEORGE   ALSOP.

*View here the Shadow whose Ingenious Hand
Hath drawne exact the Province Mary Land
Display'd her Glory in such Scenes of Wit
That those that read must fall in Love with it
For which his Labour hee deserves the praise
As well as Poets doe the wreath of Bays.*

Anno Do: 1666. *Ætatis Suæ* 28.   H.W.

8   From George Alsop, *A Character of the Province
     of Maryland,* London, 1666, in the New York
     Public Library

AN OBSERVER IN MARYLAND

NINE years later Maryland had its own representative in history in George Alsop (1638–?), a merry and eccentric *raconteur* in both prose and verse, who had escaped to Maryland to avoid the triumph of Oliver Cromwell. In his *A Character of the Province of Maryland,* 1666, he describes the Indians, their "absurdities, and religion." He marvels at the vast forests, and at the herds of animals, as numerous, he characteristically adds, as the cuckolds in London. The book is an amusing mixture of sense and fantastic nonsense.

HISTORIANS OF A STERNER TEMPER

IN New England, as in the southern colonies, almost from the landing of the first boat, these American pioneers recorded their rugged life in plain-dealing histories. But here, as in their lives, the mood is more austere. The lighter vein, as in George Alsop, is rare; the events chronicled are closely knit with the providences of God. The cast of these histories is gloomier, and their writers are, for the most part, learned, God-fearing men. Their defect is lack of high spirits, so different from many of the Virginian historians; their virtue is a deep earnestness.

From many writers of history such as Nathaniel Morton and Francis Higginson one turns to the early Puritan historians whose names still stand for what was strong and enduring in the early life of New England. These men are both historians and diarists. Bradford, Winslow, Winthrop, and Sewall write in the heat of the event: in the cabin of the *Mayflower;* after a battle with Indians; during a trial of the witches.

9   Pilgrims Discovering Indian Corn, from J. W. Barber, *Interesting
     Events in the History of the United States,* New Haven, 1831

WILLIAM WOOD, d. 1639

BEFORE studying the sterner historians we stay a moment over the genial writing in William Wood's *New Englands Prospect*, 1634. In a small way Wood was a naturalist, an ethnologist, and a poet, and he lightens his topography with snatches of verse and shrewd, ironic observation. He likes Massachusetts Bay because it is "free from such cockling seas as run upon the coast of Ireland, and in the channels of England." In his list of trees he includes "the ruddy Cherry and the jetty Plum," and among his animals "the grim-faced Ounce, and ravenous, howling Wolf." He has heard of a lion not six leagues from Boston, though he is not sure that this might not be a devil. He feels respect for porcupines and "Humbirds," and almost veneration for the Indian sagamore. *New Englands Prospect* is a history with a touch of tarragon.

EDWARD WINSLOW, 1595–1655

A MORE serious document is the journal kept by William Bradford and Edward Winslow from the ninth of November, 1620, when the *Mayflower* first sighted America, through the terrible year of 1621. This is the book now known as Mourt's *Relation* (see Vol I, No. 424). In this direct prose we wander again with the Pilgrims about Cape Cod; see the first clash with the Indians, or the meeting with Massasoit; and watch the founding of the colony. "About midnight," says the *Relation*, "we heard a great and hideous cry, and our Sentinell called, *Arme, arme.* So we bestirred ourselves and shot off a couple of Muskets, and noyse ceased."

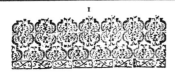

GOOD NEWES
FROM
New-England.

THE Good Ship called the *Fortune*, which in the Moneth of *Nouemb.* 1621. (bleſſed be God) brought vs a new ſupply of 35. perſons, was not long departed our Coaſt, ere the Great people of *Nanohigganſet*, which are reported to be many thouſands ſtrong, began to breath forth many threats againſt vs, notwithſtanding their deſired and obtained peace with vs in the fore-going ſummer. Inſomuch as the common talke of our neighbour *Indians* on all ſides was of the preparation they made to come againſt vs. In reaſon a man would thinke they ſhould haue now more cauſe to feare vs than before our ſupply came: but though none of them were preſent, yet vnderſtanding

B derſtanding

Chap. 6.   *New Englands Proſpect.*   23

good wives Hen rooſt, to fill their Paunch: ſome of theſe be blacke; their furre is of much eſteeme.

The Ounce or the wilde Cat, is as big as a mungrell dog, this creature is by nature feirce, and more dangerous to bee met withall than any other creature, not fearing eyther dogge or man; he uſeth to kill Deare, which hee thus effecteth: Knowing the Deares tracts, hee will lye lurking in long weedes, the Deare paſſing by he ſuddenly leapes upon his backe, from thence gets to his necke, and ſcratcheth out his throate; he hath likewiſe a deviſe to get Geeſe, for being much of the colour of a Gooſe he will place himſelfe cloſe by the water, holding us his bob taile, which is like a Gooſe necke; the Geeſe ſeeing this counterfet Gooſe, approach nigh to viſit him, who with a ſuddaine jerke apprehends his miſtruſtleſſe prey. The *Engliſh* kill many of theſe, accounting them very good meate. Their ſkinnes be a very deepe kind of Furre, ſpotted white and black on the belly. The Woolves bee in ſome reſpect different from them of other countries; it was never knowne yet that a Woolfe ever ſet upon a man or woman. Neyther do they trouble horſes or cowes; but ſwine, goates and red calves which they take for Deare, be often deſtroyed by them, ſo that a red calfe is cheaper than a blacke one in that regard; in Autumne and the beginning of the Spring, theſe ravenous rangers doe moſt frequent our *Engliſh* habitations, following the Deare which come downe at that time to thoſe parts. They be made much like a Mungrell, being big boned, lanke paunched, deepe breaſted, having a thicke necke, and head, pricke eares, and long ſnoute, with dangerous teeth, long ſtaring haire, and a great buſh taile; it is thought of many, that our *Engliſh* Maſtiffes might be too hard for them; but it is no ſuch matter, for they care no, more for an ordinary Maſtiffe, than an ordinary Maſtiffe cares for a Curre; many good Dogges have beene ſpoyled with them. Once a faire Grayhound hearing them at their howlings run out to chide them, who was torne in peeces before he could be reſcued, One of them makes no more bones to runne away with a Pigge, than a Dogge to runne away with a Marrow bone.

It

10   From William Wood, *New Englands Prospect*, London, 1634

GOOD NEWES FROM NEW-ENGLAND

LATER Winslow carried on the narrative to September, 1623, in his *Good Newes from New-England*, 1624. This version of our early history is not only a personal revelation of intense interest, but is invaluable as a source for later historians. For Bradford and Winslow can describe modes of government, or life at a humble frontier outpost.

amongst them, and was sleghted by ye meanest servants. Haveing continued ther [159]
some time, and not finding things to answer their expectations, nor profits to arise
as they looked for. Captaine Wollaston takes a great part of ye servants, and transports
them to Virginia, wher he puts them of at good rates, seling their time to other
men; and writs back to one mr Rasdall (one of his cheefe partners, and a
counteth their marchant) to bring another parte of them to Virginia like=
wise, yntending to put them of ther as he had done ye rest. And he (not
ye consente of ye said Rasdall) appointed one fitcher to be his livetenante,
and gouerne ye remaines of ye plantation, till he or Rasdall return=
ed to take further order therabouts. But this Morton abousaid haue=
ing more craft, then honestie, (who had been a kind of petie fogger, of
furnefolls ynne) yn ye others absence, watches an oppertunitie (com=
mons being but hard amongst them) and gott some strong drinck
& other Junkats, & made them a foust; and after they were merie
the bogans to tell them, he would giue them good counsell; you see
(saith he) that many of your fellows are carried to Virginia; and
yf you stay till this Rasdall returne, you will also be carried away
and sould for slaues with ye rest. Therfore y would aduise you, to
thrust oute this Leuetenant fitcher; and y having a parte in the
plantation, will receiue you as my partners, and consocials so may
you be free from seruice, and we will conuerse, trade plante & liue togeather
as equalls, & suppoit, & protecte one another, or to like effecte.
This counsell was easily receiued, so they tooke oppertunitie, and thrust
Leuetenant fitcher out a dores, and would suffer him to come no
more amongst them; but forct him to seeke bread to eate, and o=
ther releefe from his neigbours, till he could gett passage for Eng=
land. After this they fell to great licenciousnes, and led a dissolute life, poor=
ing out them selues into all profanenes; And Morton became Lord of misrule,
and maintained (as it were) a schoole of Athisme. And after they had gott
some goods into their hands, and gott much by trading with ye yndeans,
they spent it as vainly, yn quaffing, & drinking; both wine, & strong waters
yn great excess, (and as some reported) 10li worth in a morning. They allso
set up a may-pole, drinking and dancing aboute it many days togeather,
ynuiting the yndean women for their consorts, dancing and frisking togither
(like so many fairies, or furies rather) and worse practises. As if they had
celebrated
anew reuiued, the feasts of ye roman goddes flora; or ye beasly practises
of ye madd Bacchinalians; Morton likwise (to shew his poetrie) com=
posed sundry rimes, & verses, some tending to lasciuiousnes, and
others to ye detraction, & scandall of some persons, which he affixed
to this y , or ydoll may-polle. They chainged also the name of
their place, and in stead of calling it mounte Wollaston; they call it merie
mounte

13 Facsimile page from the Ms. of William Bradford, *History of Plimoth Plantation*, in the Massachusetts State Library, Boston

BRADFORD'S *HISTORY OF PLIMOTH PLANTATION*

WILLIAM BRADFORD (1588–1657) was the author, likewise, of a *History of Plimoth Plantation*, concerned with the Pilgrims from 1608 to 1647. This manuscript has had a romantic history. It was entrusted to later distinguished historians; it was lost; and it was rediscovered. In content and tone it is a just monument to Bradford who, beginning as a youthful member of the Separatist group at Scrooby, was many times governor of Plymouth Colony. The page reproduced recounts the scandalous affair at Merry Mount (No. 26).

JOHN WINTHROP, 1588–1649

THE *History of New England from 1630 to 1649*, by John Winthrop, begun on shipboard (originally his *Journal* and published as such in 1790), is perhaps more matter-of-fact than Bradford's. It contains, notwithstanding, a swiftly moving procession of incident. How the governor passed the night in the forest at Sagamore John's; how Vane was disciplined; how Captain John Underhill did penance in foul linen cap, with much blubbering; or how the father of the child drowned in the well did acknowledge in this "the righteous hand of God" — such are the events that make up the first act of the New England drama.

LETTERS OF JOHN AND MARGARET WINTHROP

"DEARE in my thougts," begins a letter to Winthrop from his wife; but Margaret Winthrop's tenderness is not less than his toward her.

Throughout Winthrop's writing one may discover evidences of the sympathy and affection which were such strong elements in his nature. The letters of this husband and wife reflect a side of Puritan life that merits more emphasis.

JOURNAL

Of the TRANSACTIONS and OCCURRENCES in the settlement of Massachusetts and the other New-England Colonies, from the year 1630 to 1644:

WRITTEN BY

JOHN WINTHROP, Esq.

First Governor of Massachusetts:

And now first published from a correct copy of the original Manuscript.

Utcumque erit, juvabit tamen, rerum gestarum memoria, ipsum consuluisse.

Tit. Liv. Præf.

HARTFORD: PRINTED
By ELISHA BABCOCK.
M,DCC,XC.

14 Title-page of the original issue, in the New York Public Library

15 Facsimile of a letter from Margaret Winthrop to her husband, Boston, 1637, in the Massachusetts Historical Society

THE WONDER–WORKING PROVIDENCE OF SION'S SAVIOUR IN NEW ENGLAND

ON the ship which brought John Winthrop to America was Edward Johnson (1599–1672), later town clerk, farmer, Indian-fighter, and founder of the Massachusetts town of Woburn. His crude but vigorous history, *The Wonder-Working Providence of Sion's Saviour in New England*, 1654, with its symbolistic picture of America as a female Indian warrior (at this time a popular personification),

AMERICA.
'Tis J, in tempting divers, for to try
By sundry meanes, t'obtaine me, caus'd the them dye
And, last discouer'd, vndiscouer'd am:
For, men, to treade my Soyle, as yet, are lame.

16 From *Gorges Tracts* (*America Painted to the Life*, etc., London, 1659) in the Massachusetts Historical Society, Boston, which contains a reprint of *The Wonder-Working Providence*

declares that the founding of New England is an expression of Christ's purpose to exhibit his divine power by the establishment of a pure church. The language of the militant Puritan, often fantastic and pompous, occasionally achieves a biblical splendor: "And as for you who are called to sound forth his silver trumpets, blow loud and shrill to this chiefest treble tune — for the armies of the great Jehovah are at hand."

17   From the mural painting *New Amsterdam, 1664*, by Barry Faulkner (1881–) in the Washington Irving High School, New York

THE DUTCH SETTLEMENTS

REAL histories of the other colonies, apart from New England, do not appear during the seventeenth century, but we have an interesting glimpse, through early narrations, of the beginnings of the Dutch community which was eventually to become the city of New York. The Dutch, unlike the Puritans, were not fleeing from difficulties at home. They were men of action, seeking profit by agriculture and the fur trade.

THE FIRST HISTORIAN OF NEW YORK

IN his little book, *A Brief Description of New York*, 1670, Daniel Denton (*d.* before March, 1696), the first, but not the last son of a Connecticut minister to become a New York landowner and politician, speaks respectfully of the "hideous roaring" of Hell-Gate and of the military significance of Sandy Hook; and offers a charming vignette of early New York a few years after the English had taken possession of the Dutch trading post at the mouth of the Hudson.

18   Title-page of the original issue in the Columbia
University Library, New York

CAPTAIN MASON AND THE PEQUOT WAR

NARRATIVES like those of William Hubbard and John Mason in the seventeenth century, and Captain Thomas Church's in the eighteenth, were all part of a definite, if minor tradition among the colonial historians. A piece of writing which has the ring of Old Testament narrative, as a soldier describes the vengeance of the Lord, is Captain John Mason's thirty-three page book, *A Brief History of the Pequot War*, 1677. Who has not, passing along the Connecti-

19   From Barber & Barber, *Historical, Poetical and Pictorial
American Scenes*, Boston, *ca.* 1850

cut and Rhode Island coast, thought of the "Mystic swamp fight?" The simplicity of this early prose was well suited to such a tale: "Thus," says Mason, "did the Lord judge among the heathen. . . . In little more than one hour's space was their impregnable fort, with themselves, utterly destroyed."

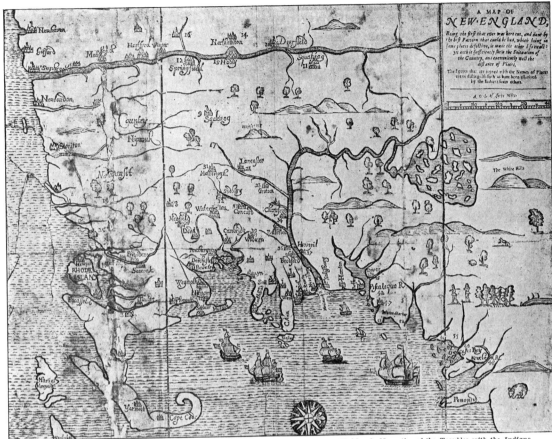

20   Map of New England engraved on wood by John Foster in 1677, from William Hubbard, *Narrative of the Troubles with the Indians in New England*, Boston, 1677

HUBBARD'S HISTORY OF THE INDIAN WARS

PERHAPS the most sustained narrative of fierce conflict with the Indians came from "the impartial Pen of that Worthy Divine William Hubbard" (1621–1704), in his *Narrative of the Troubles with the Indians in New England*, 1677. Hubbard's long story is as absorbing as a novel by Cooper. Well might it seem to the anxious soldiers awaiting the attack that the eclipse of the moon resembled a scalp or an Indian bow. This is a record of merciless swamp fighting. "It is," says Hubbard, "ill fighting with a wild Beast in his own Den."

MRS. ROWLANDSON'S *NARRATIVE OF THE CAPTIVITY AND RESTORATION*

THE dreadful moment — so often recurring in New England life — when all that was gentle and lovely in it was blasted by all that was ugly in savage barbarism is nowhere arrested so vividly as in Mary Rowlandson's *Narrative of the Captivity and Restoration*, 1682. Driven from her home, her friends slaughtered, she knew torture at the hands of the redskins. She sets it all down in artless writing.

21   From W. A. Crafts, *Pioneers in the Settlement of America*, Boston, 1876, after the drawing by F. O. C. Darley (1822–88)

SONG.

1. Of worthy Captain LOVEWELL, I purpose now to sing,
How valiantly he served his country and his King;
He and his valiant soldiers, did range the woods full wide,
And hardships they endured to quell the Indian's pride.

2. 'Twas nigh unto Pigwacket, on the eighth day of May,
They spied a rebel Indian soon after break of day;
He on a bank was walking, upon a neck of land,
Which leads into a pond as we're made to understand.

3. Our men resolv'd to have him, and travell'd two miles round,
Until they met the Indian, who boldly stood his ground;
Then speaks up Captain LOVEWELL, "take you good heed," says he,
"This rogue is to decoy us, I very plainly see.

4. "The Indians lie in ambush, in some place nigh at hand,
"In order to surround us upon this neck of land;
"Therefore we'll march in order, and each man leave his pack,
"That we may briskly fight them when they make their attack."

5. They came unto this Indian, who did them thus defy,
As soon as they came nigh him, two guns he did let fly,
Which wounded Capt'n LOVEWELL, and likewise one man more,
But when this rogue was running, they laid him in his gore.

6. Then having scalp'd the Indian, they went back to the spot, [not,
Where they had laid their packs down, but there they found them
For the Indians having spy'd them, when they them down did lay,
Did seize them for their plunder, and carry them away.

7. These rebels lay in ambush, this very place hard by,
So that an English soldier did one of them espy,
And cried out, "here's an Indian," with that they started out,
As fiercely as old lions, and hideously did shout.

8. With that our valiant English, all gave a loud huzza,
To shew the rebel Indians they fear'd them not a straw:
So now the fight began, and as fiercely as could be,
The Indians ran up to them, but soon were forced to flee.

22   The first known appearance in print of the ballad *Lovewell's Fight*. From J. Farmer and J. B. Moore, *Historical Collections of New Hampshire*, Concord, 1822–24

INDIAN WARS AND AMBUSCADES

THE histories of the development of the colonies themselves include the record of the endless struggles with the race whose subjugation made that development possible. Prose like John Smith's or John Winthrop's is never long silent concerning the Indian menace. Other annalists, usually military men themselves, chronicle battles and ambuscades for their own sake. From the histories of these wars grew up among the settlers traditions of bitter conquest. Every one, for example, knew the story of "Lovewell's Fight," 1725.

GOD'S PROTECTING PROVIDENCE

STORIES of escapes from the Indians are not confined to New England. Late in the century Jonathan Dickenson (*d.* 1722), a Quaker, confronted "the inhumane cannibals of Florida." The story of his shipwreck and deliverance from the Indians is told in his *God's Protecting Providence*, 1699. Dickenson was an English Quaker, and tells of his adventures in quiet, straightforward writing. He later became Chief Justice of Pennsylvania.

23   From a Dutch translation, Leyden, 1700, of Jonathan Dickenson, *God's Protecting Providence*

THE APOSTLE OF VIRGINIA

BESIDES those pioneers who conceived the wilderness to be the realm of the devil and the Indians as his true liegemen, were others who preached patience to the settlers and salvation to the redskins. Among such missionaries was Alexander Whitaker (1585–1617?), "the apostle of Virginia," who prayed in these early days of the colony for the welfare of the savages. His *Good Newes from Virginia*, which appeared in the year of his death, reflects his zeal as a preacher among the Indians.

JOHN ELIOT, 1604–90, APOSTLE TO THE INDIANS

JOHN ELIOT'S influence was of larger scope, witness his title, "Apostle to the Indians." His work was done chiefly near Natick, though he says that "Westward the Cords of Christ's Tents are more enlarged." Much of his writing is lost or scattered. What is left, as he writes solemnly of Indians who inquire "What is sack?" or

25 From the mural painting by H. O. Walker (1843–) in the State House, Boston. © Curtis and Cameron

GOOD NEWES
FROM VIRGINIA.

ECCLESIASTES 11.1.
Caft thy bread vpon the waters : for after many daies thou fha't finde it.
Aude hofpes contemnere opes & te quoq; dignum Finge Deo——

24 First page of Alexander Whitaker, *Good Newes from Virginia*, London, 1613

ask how they may be saved, betrays slight literary merit. He is remembered for his Bible in the Indian tongue, and for his *Brief Narrative of the Progress of the Gospel Among the Indians of New England*, 1671.

Daniel Gookin, the associate of Eliot, and the friend of Oliver Cromwell, wrote two treatises on the Indians. Both breathe piety, tenderness, and reflect the unusual capacity of Gookin as a man of affairs, without in the least becoming literature. The prose of New England was more adapted for narratives of action than for tepid records of missionary achievement.

REVELS AT MERRY MOUNT

PERHAPS every energetic community needs a scandal. New England's was supplied by a waggish adventurer, Thomas Morton (?–1646), who not only endangered the settlers by selling powder and shot to the Indians and training them to shoot, but also made his libertine festivals so picturesque as to figure in many a Puritan history. Even to-day these stand out in the dull prose like the scarlet color in a somber Corot. Morton set up at Merry Mount, near Wollaston, that ancient emblem of free-living, the Maypole, and though Miles Standish and the shocked Puritans tore it down, and shipped Morton back to England, the echo of his derisive laughter at the godly sounded through the colony. It was as if Cotton Mather's four-hour sermons should be interrupted by the merriest of Cavalier roundelays. Morton, however, was more than a jester. He fiercely attacked Massachusetts, and he nearly succeeded in his attempt to destroy her charter.

26 From W. A. Crafts, *Pioneers in the Settlement of America*, Boston, 1876, after the drawing by W. L. Sheppard (1833–1912)

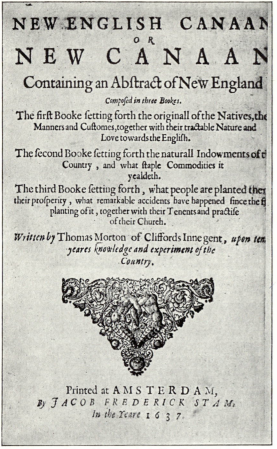

27   Title-page of the original issue, in the New York Public Library

MORTON'S *NEW ENGLISH CANAAN*

BRADFORD's account of the fairies "or furies" who danced in beaver coats about the Maypole may be found in the reproduced page of his *History of Plimoth Plantation* (No. 13). But Thomas Morton's own *New English Canaan*, Amsterdam, 1637, that "infamouse and scurrillous booke" tells with contagious glee of "the good liquor," and how "the setting up of his Maypole was a lamentable spectacle to the precise seperatists [*sic*]." The *New English Canaan* is a garrulous, careless book, but it makes us laugh to-day, which is more than can be said for some of Morton's contemners.

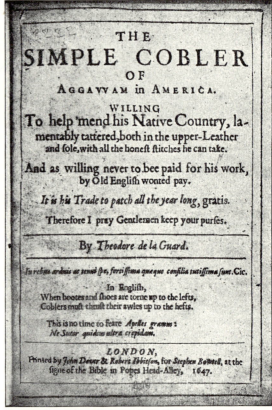

28   Title-page of the original issue, in the New York Public Library

THE SIMPLE COBLER OF AGGAWAM

BESIDES the secular literature or history of the colonies or diaries or histories of the Indian wars or records of missionary labors, two or three works emerge as extraordinary either in subject or point of view, or by reason of a certain manner of writing. Thus Thomas Morton is a historian, but a singularly profane one; Nathaniel Ward is orthodox, but in his fanaticism on a single subject hardly falls into the usual categories; and John Josselyn is the author of our first book of natural history.

It is suggestive to compare the license of a man like Morton, of whom there were many in Virginia, and some in New England, with the tireless intolerance of the vigorous Nathaniel Ward (1579?-1652?), who undertook in *The Simple Cobler of Aggawam*, 1647, to mend his lamentably tattered native country. Ward writes with the gusto of a Carlyle. He never modulates his voice, damning with equal vehemence ungodliness or fashion in women's dress, and always with a boundless self-confidence. "I dare," he says, "take upon me, to be the Herauld of New England"; "I hold myself bound to set up a Beacon." The woman who cares what the Queen wears is "the very gizzard of a trifle, the product of a quarter of a cypher." He makes a list of "pernicious Hereticks who are making a hell above ground," and declares that the man who will tolerate an unsound opinion will presently "hang God's Bible at the Devil's girdle." Ward is a fiery, breathless writer. He arrived in New England in 1634, and for the next two years was assistant pastor at Ipswich. Here he aided in writing an early code of laws, *The Body of Liberties*, 1641. Soon after 1647 there followed three other amended editions of *The Simple Cobler*. It also reappeared in 1713 and, in 1843, in Boston.

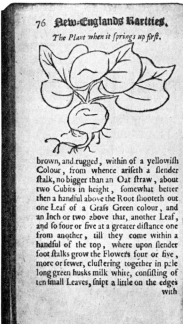

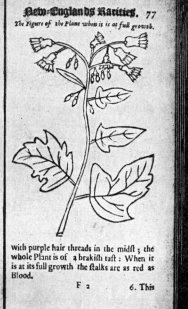

29   Two pages of John Josselyn, *New England's Rarities*, London, 1672

OTHERS in New England were untouched by polemical tempests. John Josselyn made two voyages to America, and studied the "Birds, Beasts, Fishes, Serpents, and Plants of the Country." In *New England's Rarities*, 1672, he quotes Lucian and Du Bartas, and notes that there are three hundred kinds of fish in this strange land, as against only one hundred and forty-four mentioned in Pliny and Isidore. But then, he adds, "I suppose *America* was not known to *Pliny* and *Isadore* [*sic*]."

JOHN COTTON, 1585–1652

THE first, though not the greatest, of the Mather dynasty was John Cotton. He had been vicar of St. Botolph's Church in Boston, Lincolnshire (1612–33), and it was in his honor that Shawmut was renamed Boston. In learning, righteousness, and dynamic moral force Cotton was a giant, and his prodigious powers encouraged legends, some of which were not free from absurdity. The common metaphor concerning him, used both by his contemporaries and by posterity, was that of a bright light in the darkness. Nathaniel Morton, indeed, on the night of Cotton's death saw in the heavens a great comet, which God had set there to symbolize the great theologian's life. Centuries later Longfellow speaks of him as one who came

> To be a burning and a
> shining light
> Here in the wilderness.

Yet some have ventured to say that Roger Williams, whom Cotton honored with the dispute of *The Bloudy Tenent*, 1647, was not wholly serious when he quoted Massachusetts people as saying that "they could hardly believe that God would suffer Mr. Cotton to err." To-day Cotton's writings seem an unredeemable morass of learning and theology, but for nineteen years (1633–52) he was the undefeated master of the Puritan theocracy.

30   St. Botolph's Church, Boston, Lincolnshire, England, from a photograph in the Massachusetts Historical Society

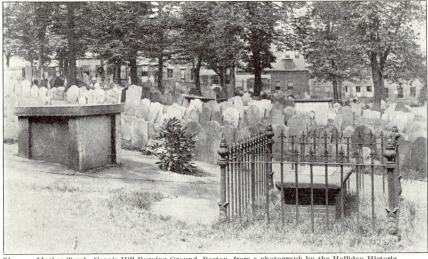

31   Mather Tomb, Copp's Hill Burying Ground, Boston, from a photograph by the Halliday Historic
                                    Photograph Co.

THE MATHER DYNASTY

IF, indeed, we consider American literature as a whole prior to 1700, the most marked bias is religious. The group of powerful intellectuals who dominated New England in the seventeenth, and well into the eighteenth century, were expressions of this tendency. The leaders of this religious thought were the Mather dynasty.

INCREASE MATHER, 1639–1723

THE most distinguished son of the distinguished Richard Mather, who was a founder of the Mather succession, was Increase Mather (No. 32), whose activity is attested by the fact that he was for some years both president of Harvard College and pastor of North Church, in Boston. He upheld the family traditions in scholarship and religion, and was distinctly a man of the world, serving his country for four years abroad. His "scholar's day" of sixteen hours, for nearly threescore years, produced an appalling flow of prose. This often attains a majestic simplicity.

32   From the portrait, 1688, by John Vanderspritt in the
                    Massachusetts Historical Society

COTTON MATHER, 1663–1728

THE flower of this remarkable family was Cotton (No. 33), the grandson of John Cotton and Richard Mather. He outlived the peak of the Puritan theocracy, but, with the exception of Jonathan Edwards, was its most marvellous product. In learning and spiritual effort he excelled his forbears, but in him the old rough Puritan vigor was somewhat tamed. His mood is more often that of the mystic. He was intensely active in the community and his published works were famous.

33   From the portrait, 1727, by Peter Pelham (1684–1751) in the
                    American Antiquarian Society

COTTON MATHER'S TEMPERAMENT

COTTON MATHER'S weaknesses are those of the man who is by temperament an ascetic, and Robert Calef's robust objections to his principles in the witchcraft persecution disclose the Puritan leader's somewhat feminine sensibility. Beneath these surface faults there burned in Mather a pure and aspiring spirit, evident in his writings on the soul and its relations with God. In his old age he incurred many disappointments; defeat for the presidency of Harvard, loss of influence, and bereavement.

Magnalia Christi Americana:

OR, THE

Ecclesiastical History

OF

NEVV-ENGLAND,

FROM

Its First Planting in the Year 1620. unto the Year of our LORD, 1698.

In Seven BOOKS.

I. Antiquities: In Seven Chapters. With an Appendix.
II. Containing the Lives of the Governours, and Names of the Magistrates of *New-England*: In Thirteen Chapters. With an Appendix.
III. The Lives of Sixty Famous Divines, by whose Ministry the Churches of *New-England* have been Planted and Continued.
IV. An Account of the University of *Cambridge* in *New-England*; in Two Parts. The First contains the Laws, the Benefactors, and Vicissitudes of *Harvard College*; with Remarks upon it. The Second Part contains the Lives of some Eminent Persons Educated in it.
V. Acts and Monuments of the Faith and Order in the Churches of *New-England*, passed in their Synods; with Historical Remarks upon those Venerable Assemblies; and a great Variety of Church-Cases occurring, and resolved by the Synods of those Churches: In Four Parts.
VI. A Faithful Record of many Illustrious, Wonderful Providences, both of Mercies and Judgments, on divers Persons in *New-England*: In Eight Chapters.
VII. *The Wars of the Lord*. Being an History of the Manifold Afflictions and Disturbances of the Churches in *New-England*, from their Various Adversaries, and the Wonderful Methods and Mercies of God in their Deliverance: In Six Chapters: To which is subjoined, An Appendix of Remarkable Occurrences which *New-England* had in the Wars with the *Indian* Salvages, from the Year 1688, to the Year 1698.

By the Reverend and Learned *COTTON MATHER*, M. A.
And Pastor of the North Church in *Boston, New-England*.

LONDON.

Printed for *Thomas Parkhurst*, at the *Bible* and *Three Crowns* in *Cheapside*. MDCCII.

35 Title-page of the original issue, London, 1702, in the New York Public Library

34 From Cotton Mather, *Essays To Do Good*, new editon, Glasgow, 1825, after an engraving by W. H. Lizars

HIS *MAGNALIA CHRISTI AMERICANA*

"BE brief"; and again, "be fruitful," wrote Cotton Mather. The first injunction was apparently for others; the second for himself. One of his works survives, partly by sheer size, partly by merit: *Magnalia Christi Americana*, an indispensable source book. In spite of pedantry, superstition, and an incurable interest in Harvard College, Mather can tell a good story, as various New England writers of the nineteenth century discovered. Had he known this, he would doubtless have thought it further proof of his "vileness." He is unique in showing us the cumulative force of Hebrism — in Matthew Arnold's sense — in successive generations, and so proving once more that "strictness of conscience" can contribute only one element in human development. This principle the Mather family realized, it would seem, to its fullest potentialities.

THE

Clear Sun-shine of the Gospel

BREAKING FORTH

UPON THE

INDIANS

IN

NEVV-ENGLAND.

OR,

An Historicall Narration of Gods Wonderfull Workings upon sundry of the INDIANS, both chief Governors and Common-people, in bringing them to a willing and desired submission to the Ordinances of the Gospel; and framing their hearts to an earnest inquirie after the knowledge of God the Father, and of Jesus Christ the Saviour of the World.

By Mr. THOMAS SHEPARD Minister of the Gospel of Jesus Christ at *Cambridge* in *New-England*.

Isaiah 2, 2, 3. *And it shall come to passe in the last dayes, that the mountain of the Lords house shall bee established in the top of the mountains, and shall bee exalted above the hills, and all Nations shall flow unto it. And many people shall go and say, Come ye and let us goe up to the mountain of the Lord, to the house of the God of Jacob, and he will teach us of his wayes, and we will walk in his paths: for out of Zion shall goe forth the Law, and the word of the Lord from Jerusalem.*

London, Printed by R.Cotes for *John Bellamy* at the three golden Lions in *Cornhill* near the Royall Exchange, 1648.

36 Title-page of the original issue, in the New York Public Library

THOMAS SHEPARD, 1605–49

THOMAS SHEPARD, a minister at Cambridge, with a moral interest in the Indians, suffered the mystic's longing for the ineffable, with despairs and ecstasies; he finds constantly that his heart is "more sweetly drawn close to God." Yet he believes man to be as full of poison as a toad, and his pictures of the Last Judgment are as searing as those of Jonathan Edwards, whose spiritual forbear he was.

37 From the statue by Charles H. Niehaus (1855–) in the Connecticut state capitol, Hartford

THOMAS HOOKER, 1586–1647

AMONG the powerful associates of John Cotton was Thomas Hooker, whose independence won him the much-quoted phrase that while doing his Master's work he "would put a king in his pocket." He possessed indeed a sense of civil liberty that must have seemed out of joint with theocratic government. "After Mr. Hooker's coming over," remarks Hubbard, "it was observed that many of the freemen grew to be very jealous of their liberties." Hooker's sermon, in 1638, before the General Court on this subject sounds like the preliminary roll of a Revolutionary drum, with its talk of "free consent of the people." In 1636 Hooker made his way through the forest, and founded Connecticut.

ROGER WILLIAMS, 1604?–84

JOHN COTTON's theocracy was challenged by Roger Williams, who refused to believe in its jurisdiction over the individual conscience. The *Bloudy Tenent* of Williams was an arrow sharp, if heavy, and Cotton's replies and Williams' rejoinders cloud the sky as in the fiercest battles of the Persians. In this, as in his missions to the Indians, his founding of Rhode Island, and in all that he did, Williams was on the humane side, and also on the side of good writing. There are sentences in this pioneer as militant as any in his friend Milton. As he says, he fears not iron and steel, but only the Most High.

38   Statue of Roger Williams, at Providence, R. I., by Franklin Simmons (1839–1913)

Mr Cottons
LETTER
Lately Printed,
EXAMINED
AND
ANSVVERED:

By *Roger Williams* of *Providence*
In
NEW-ENGLAND.

LONDON,
Imprinted in the yeere 1644.

39   Title-page of the original issue in the John Carter Brown Library, Providence

40   Roger Williams Landing at Providence, from *The New Mirror*, 1844, after the drawing by T. F. Hoppin

41 From the painting *Bellman Reading Thanksgiving Day Proclamation*, by Stanley M. Arthurs (1877–) in his possession

THE EFFECT OF THE FRONTIER ON POETRY

On seventeenth-century poetry also rests the chill of Calvinism. After the historians, diarists, and theologians, we hope in vain to discover some work of pure literature, perhaps a genuine poem. Poetry as a form of æsthetic expression the colonists, consciously or unconsciously, denied themselves; their emotional natures found expression in communal prayer and praise, such as that of Thanksgiving Day. In them was love of beauty, but at the end of the picturesque village street was the wilderness with its travail. To conquer this and to make real the unseen world were their dearest cares. Never has American poetry been more imitative, less indigenous, though never so with better reason. The grim frontier did not smile on poetry. Thus in these years it either imitates the English fantastical school, or shallows away into learned epitaphs and elegies; or, abandoning its models, becomes Calvinism in doggerel. Urian Oakes wishes that his pen could distil "rare conceits," and Michael Wigglesworth sings merrily, if rather unevenly:

> But who can tell the plagues of Hell,
> and torments exquisite?

THE *BAY PSALM BOOK*

At this point in their history New Englanders were capable only of such poetry as *The Whole Book of Psalms*, or the *Bay Psalm Book*, 1640, published within two years of Milton's *Lycidas* and Thomas Browne's *Religio Medici*, and in the very year of the printing of Thomas Carew's *Poems*. The editors of this popular work were Richard Mather, Thomas Welde, and John Eliot. In the preface these worthies remark (with the assent of posterity) that they have been concerned with "Conscience rather than Elegance, fidelity rather than poetry." This version of the twenty-third psalm is representative.

42   Two pages of the *Bay Psalm Book*, Cambridge, 1640, in the New York Public Library

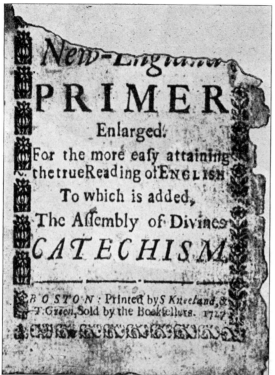

43 Title-page of earliest extant edition of *The New-England Primer*, Boston, 1727, printed by S. Kneeland & T. Green, in the New York Public Library

THE NEW-ENGLAND PRIMER

WHILE the elders chanted these verses their children drew their first impressions of life from *The New-England Primer*, one of the most curious and popular books of the seventeenth and eighteenth centuries, first referred to in an almanac of 1691. In its first form, now not available, it must have been about four inches in length and three in width. The earliest complete version of the *Primer* now extant was published in Boston in 1727. After the title-page appear the "Easy Syllables for Children," and later "Words of six Syllables," the whole "Adorn'd with Cutts."

A CALVINISTIC A B C

ON this miniature volume of the current theology, the "little vipers," to use a term of the Calvinists, were nourished. The alphabet in verse brings the book within our category. Indeed its fusion of sound theology and unsound meter makes it typical of the time. Most of all, *The New-England Primer* is a commentary on the age in its amazing confusion of hard common sense, relentless dogma, and gloomy æsthetics. That any child should have taken seriously this "*Lion* bold" or grandiose cock (see No. 44), both of which were probably carved by some Puritan's dull knife, is not more strange than the blurred view of life which they represent.

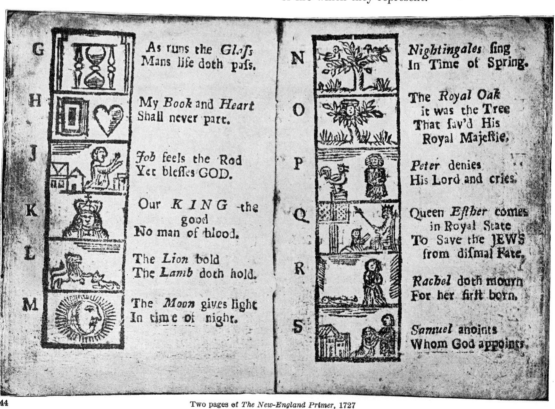

44 Two pages of *The New-England Primer*, 1727

GEORGE SANDYS' TRANSLATION OF OVID

ASIDE from such oddities as the *Primer*, the first New England poem was probably the *Nova Anglia* of William Morrell, written in 1625. Yet in this time of Englishmen writing in America, we may claim George Sandys (1577–1644), traveler and scholar, a son of Edwin Sandys, Archbishop of York, whom Dryden considered the best versifier of the age. "Let's see what lines Virginia will produce," wrote Michael Drayton to Sandys after the latter had come to the new colony. And in spite of the Indian massacre of 1622, Sandys completed in Virginia his translation of Ovid's *Metamorphosis*, 1626.

45 Title-page of the original issue in the New York Public Library

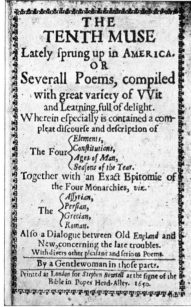

46 Title-page of the original issue in the New York Public Library

ANNE BRADSTREET, 1612–72

THAT poetry flourished with difficulty is shown in Anne Bradstreet, the daughter of one governor, Thomas Dudley, and wife of another, Simon Bradstreet — a woman of culture, and poetic feeling. Her gifts were repressed by Puritan tradition, and the contemporary literary ideals of England.

ANNE BRADSTREET'S HOME, NORTH ANDOVER, MASS.

THE FOUR MONARCHIES, 1650, and similar poems show the influence of Governor Bradstreet's relatively huge library of sixty volumes; the models of the poetess were Quarles, Wither, and — all too seldom — Spenser. Only in *Contemplations*, 1650, and in a few other lyrics do our weary eyes look through the narrow panes of her library at the Merrimac country.

47 From *The Work of Anne Bradstreet in Prose and Verse*, Charlestown, Mass., 1867, after the engraving by Henry Marsh

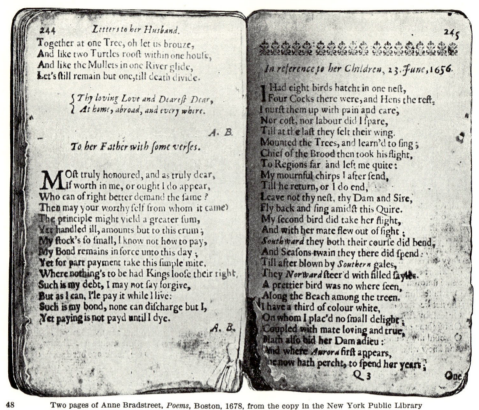

48   Two pages of Anne Bradstreet, *Poems*, Boston, 1678, from the copy in the New York Public Library

A PURITAN POETESS

YET *The Tenth Muse lately sprung up in America*, 1650, is a revelation of New England life. Here is the Puritan mother, with her "eight birds hatcht in one nest," touched with the maladies of conscience, superstition, and loneliness for England, yet a lover of literature, even a wonderer before nature. She pours out her heart in yearning over her son on his voyage to England, or her husband in absence; and during illness and anxiety strives to express in the highest medium of thought the longings of her soul for the beatific vision — an early and Puritan Christina Rossetti, brought to the very edge of the wilderness.

The Day of Doom:
OR, A
DESCRIPTION
Of the Great and Laft
Judgment.
WITH
A SHORT DISCOURSE
ABOUT
ETERNITY.

Ecclef. 12. 14.

*For God fhall bring every work into Judgment
with every fecret thing, whether it be good
or whether it be evil.*

LONDON,

Printed by *W. G.* for *John Sims*, at the *Kings-
Head* at *Sweetings-Alley-end* in *Cornhill*,
next Houfe to the *Royal-Exchange*, 1673.

49   Title-page of the second edition in the New York Public Library

MICHAEL WIGGLESWORTH, 1631–1705

THE human voice, however, is silent in the poetry of Michael Wigglesworth, a graduate of Harvard, and a minister in Malden. In *The Day of Doom*, 1662, Christ the Avenger executes his judgment upon vile mankind without mercy, save that the infants, in the famous stanza, secure "the easiest room" in hell. Hawthorne was fond of imagining the scene before the Puritan hearths when this poem was read aloud by the light of blazing fagots. As one conjures up the serious faces in semi-darkness, lighted by the gleams from the pine wood, prefiguring the darker fires of hell, one recalls James Mill's cool remark two centuries later: "Think," he used to say, "of a being who would make a Hell — who would create the human race with the infallible foreknowledge . . . that the great majority of them were to be consigned to horrible and everlasting torment." Such a voice this stern people had never heard, or else reckoned it blasphemy.

The Day of Doom.

54 The Day of Doom.

CLXXVIII.
If upon one what's due to none
I frankly shall bestow,
And on the rest shall not think best
compassions skirt to throw,
Whom injure I? will you envy,
and grudge at others weal?
Or me accuse, who do refuse
your selves to help and heal?

CLXXIX.
Am I alone of what's my own
no Master or no Lord?
Or if I am, how can you claim
what I to some afford?
Will you demand Grace at my hand,
and challenge what is mine?
Will you teach me whom to set free,
and thus my Grace confine?

CLXXX.
You sinners are, and such a share
as sinners may expect,
Such you shall have, for I do save
none but mine own elect.
Yet to compare your sin with their
who liv'd a longer time,
I do confess yours is much less
though ev'ry sin's a crime:

CLXXXI.
A crime it is; therefore in bliss
you may not hope to dwell:
But

The Day of Doom. 55

But unto you I shall allow
the easiest room in hell.
The glorious King thus answering,
they cease, and plead no longer:
Their consciences must needs confess
his Reasons are the stronger.

CLXXXII.
Thus all mens plea's, the Judge with ease
doth answer and confute,
Until that all both great and small,
are silenced and mute.
Vain hopes are cropt, all mouths are stopt,
sinners have nought to say,
But that 'tis just, and equal most
they should be damn'd for ay.

CLXXXIII.
Now what remains, but that to pains
and everlasting smart
Christ should condemn the sons of men,
which is their just desert?
Oh ruful plights of sinful wights!
Oh wretches all forlorn!
That happy been they ne're had seen
the Sun, or not been born.

CLXXXIV.
Yea, now it would be good they could
themselves annihilate,
And cease to be, themselves to free
from such a fearful state.
Oh happy Dogs, and Swine, and Frogs!
yea, Serpents generation! Who

50   Two pages of Wigglesworth, *The Day of Doom*, 1673

THE DAY OF DOOM

THE poet, indeed, gives himself to his awful dream with an intense abandon, that is not without sublimity. The tortures and the screams of torment are real. Indeed, if we laugh at this poem, we laugh as if awakened from some childish nightmare. It is not true, but it was for the readers of *The Day of Doom*, and the dark imaginings of the Puritan clergyman cloud for the moment our own sunlight. This is the reply of Christ to the plea of the infants:

You sinners are, and such a share as sinners may expect,
Such you shall have, for I do save none but mine own elect.
Yet to compare your sin with their who liv'd a longer time,
I do confess yours is much less though ev'ry sin's a crime:

A crime it is; therefore in bliss you may not hope to dwell;
But unto you I shall allow the easiest room in hell.

URIAN OAKES, 1631?–81

A POET of similar mood was Urian Oakes, pastor of the church at Cambridge and president of Harvard College. In spite of many effusions Oakes, who, Cotton Mather thought, was a light of the church, has come down to us as a single-poem man. His *Elegie upon the Death of the Reverend Mr. Thomas Shepard*, 1677, is, in spite of the crudest of verse, a moving expression of manly sorrow.

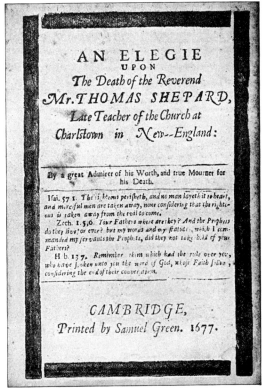

AN ELEGIE
UPON
The Death of the Reverend
Mr. THOMAS SHEPARD,
Late Teacher of the Church at
Charlstown in New--England:

By a great Admirer of his Worth, and true Mourner for his Death.

CAMBRIDGE,
Printed by Samuel Green. 1677.

51   Title-page of the original issue in the Massachusetts Historical Society

SEVENTEENTH–CENTURY SATIRE

THERE is force in the seventeenth-century satirists, Peter Folger (1617–90), and Benjamin Tompson. Folger was surveyor of Nantucket, and a worthy grandfather of the hard-headed Benjamin Franklin. In *A Looking-Glass for the Times*, 1675, he urges the old plea for intolerance. He makes the usual New England choice between sincerity and meter; the two seem never to be conjoined before the Revolution. The *Looking-Glass* is a straightforward poem, and as stiff as whipcord.

(9)

The Rulers in the Country I
  do own them in the Lord ;
And such as are for Government,
  with them I do accord.
But that which I intend hereby,
  is that they would keep bound,
And meddle not with God's Worship,
  for which they have no ground.
And I am not alone herein,
  there's many hundreds more
That have for many Years ago
  spake much upon that Score.
Indeed I really believe
  it's not your Business
To meddle with the Church of Christ,
  in Matters more or less.
There's work enough to do besides,
  to judge in *mine* and *thine,*
To succour Poor and Fatherless,
  that is the Work in fine.
And I do think that now you find
  enough of that to do ;
Much more at such a Time as this,
  as there is War also.
Indeed I count it very low,
  for People in these Days,
To ask the Rulers for their leave
  to serve God in his Ways.
I count it worse in Magistrates
  to use the Iron Sword,
To do that Work which Christ alone
  will do by his own Word.
The Church may now go stay at home,
  there's nothing for to do ;
              B   Their

52   Page of Peter Folger, *A Looking-Glass for the Times,* second edition, 1763, from the copy in the John Carter Brown Library, Providence

BENJAMIN TOMPSON, 1642–1714

BENJAMIN TOMPSON, author of *New England's Crisis,* 1675, is a poet of the same school. His best work is rough and vigorous satire. Certain minor pieces show his allegiance to the fantastics. Such, then, was the stark muse of the Puritans. As we survey the poetry of New England from William Morrell, with the first known poem written in New England (*Nova Anglia,* 1625) through Wigglesworth and the others, there are evident the repressive forces of Puritanism toward art itself. In all this poetry one may detect the learning and the severe training in the classics; the influence of English seventeenth-century poetry; and spiritual intensity. But the learning does not express itself, as in Milton, in new beauty; the metaphysical influences of the seventeenth century are at their worst here; and the spiritual aspiration is straitened by theology. This Puritan poetry lacked genius or even unusual talent. It is difficult to believe that the same race produced, even after two hundred years, the poets of the Concord and Cambridge groups.

53   Broadside by Benjamin Tompson, *A Neighbor's Tears,* 1710, in the Boston Public Library

CHAPTER II

THE LITERATURE OF EIGHTEENTH–CENTURY AMERICA

THE year 1700 suggests conveniently a significant change in the tone of colonial literature. The history of Thomas Church, indeed, and the sermons of Benjamin Colman and the rhymes of Nicholas Noyes continue the story of Puritan New England, just as William Byrd and William Stith show us the later generations of adventurous, semi-feudal Virginia gentlemen. Yet America, though perhaps still a province of seventeenth-century England in outlook upon life, and though still producing histories of settlements, diaries, accounts of the Indians, sermons, and verse groaning with piety, begins to be less unlike the rest of the world. Although John Williams' anguished story is like Mary Rowlandson's, it is among the last of the Indian narratives of this sort in New England. The frontier is receding. Although the Puritan theocracy offers its most brilliant product in Jonathan Edwards, it is dying. Even in the conventional American poetry of the eighteenth century there is more vitality. Perhaps there is meaning, too, in the appearance, in 1741, in Philadelphia, of the first American magazine, Franklin's *General Magazine and Historical Chronicle*, and Bradford's *American, or a Monthly View*.

This, then, is the change: an increased sense of life in this world, a world in some measure freed from the Calvinistic menace, a world from which has been lifted the threat of famine and the Indian. The country was now more than a century old. Philadelphia, for a great part of the eighteenth century, was more important than Boston. The "fruitfull sisters," Virginia and Maryland, ruled from their scattered settlements a small empire. Meanwhile New York, city and province, and New Jersey grew before 1765 to be significant factors in commerce, government, and even in literature. Communication was difficult, but populations shifted, and horizons widened. Ships from New England and New York were hurrying to the West Indies, to England, to France, and Africa. In Maryland, Virginia, and the Carolinas a planter aristocracy was developing a social and intellectual life that compared favorably with that of the landed gentry of England. Germans were coming to Pennsylvania and New York, followed soon by the Scotch Irish. Most of the newcomers passed through the older settlements and built their habitations on the frontier from the Mohawk to the Yadkin River. The mingling of peoples, so typical of America, had begun.

Gradually but emphatically this wider life stamped itself upon the colonial literature of the eighteenth century. Histories now concern themselves with problems of internal government. They show the beginnings and development of natural science. They describe different climates and different ways of dealing with the Indians. They hint at the individual peculiarities of the several colonies: William Byrd of Virginia sneers at the fanatical New Englanders and the lazy Carolinians. Most of all they reveal a growing self-reliance. This was a generation born, for the most part, in America, and more indifferent to England. Surviving journals indicate the increase in material prosperity, the appearance of a social consciousness, and of personalities which even now might be called American. Samuel Sewall is under the influence of the Mather dynasty, but he does public penance for his share in the witchcraft persecution, and his gossip is of a community well-established and bound closely to the interests of this world. Sarah Kemble Knight journeys from Boston to New York, observing, like a kind of Puritan blue-stocking, the shrewd, practical traits of her countrymen. She feels much at home everywhere, and concedes that the inhabitants of Connecticut are "a good, Sociable people."

If secular literature betrays the decline of Calvinistic and purely pioneer states of mind, this change is evidenced also by the marked decline in the number of theological works. The very perfection to which Jonathan Edwards had brought Puritanism as a system heralded its decline. "The Great Awakening," for which he was responsible, carried within it seeds of decay. The first straw in the wind of liberalism had been perhaps the banishment of Roger Williams to Rhode Island for liberty of conscience. The retreat of Hooker to Connecticut was not without significance. The religious extremism which was to thrive in the eighteenth century was to be the passive enthusiasm of the Quakers. To this age they gave, under the very shadow of Jonathan Edwards' Calvinism, a great statesman, William Penn, and a great religious leader, John Woolman. If we think of the century as a whole, Edwards seems belated. Woolman is a more natural representative of the kind of enthusiasm which stood alone against the robust forces of rationalism typified by Benjamin Franklin.

Things were not yet favorable for pure letters, but the indifference of most of these Americans to such a point of view as Cotton Mather's was on the whole better for literature. There would not be another *Day of Doom*. The other hindrances were as potent as ever: the practical work of developing the country and the lack of culture. Yet it is not surprising that here and there sprang up a versifier who might be called an able follower of Pope. We hear also with less surprise that Thomas Godfrey, steeped in Chaucer, Spenser, and Shakespeare, and caring only for art and literature, dares to write the first American play. Slight as they are, these are the beginnings in America of literature as an art.

54   Great Snow in 1717, from J. W. Barber, *Interesting Events in the History of the United States*, New Haven, 1831

55   From Robert Beverley, *History of the Present State of Virginia*, London, 1705, after engraving by T. de Bry,
in *Grand Voyages*, Part I, 1591, from original sketch by John White, 1585

ROBERT BEVERLEY, 1675?–1716?

A SENSE of solidity and security is felt distinctly in the *History of Virginia*, 1705, 1722, by Robert Beverley. He knows the evil that is said of Virginia, but he believes in her; in her climate, her government, and her resources. Virginia is one of the greatest tobacco-producing areas in the world. Beverley has none of the earlier writers' anxiety to justify Virginia before England. She has endured without the mother country for a century, and he expects for her even greater felicity. Such also was the expectation of the prosperous planter aristocracy. Part II of the *History* deals with "The natural Productions and Conveniences of the Country, Suited to Trade and Improvement."

56   From Robert Beverley, *History of the Present State of Virginia*, London, 1705, after
engraving by T. de Bry, 1591, from original sketch by John White, 1585

HUGH JONES, 1669–1760

BEVERLEY's businesslike respect for the future of Virginia has academic sanction in Hugh Jones, possibly the first professor (at William and Mary) to write American history. Jones in *The Present State of Virginia*, 1724, admits liberally that North Carolina may be "the refuge of runaways, and South Carolina the delight of buccaneers and pirates,"

THE
PRESENT STATE
OF
VIRGINIA.

GIVING

A particular and short Account of the *Indian*, *English*, and *Negroe* Inhabitants of that Colony.

Shewing their Religion, Manners, Government, Trade, Way of Living, &c. with a Description of the Country.

From whence is inferred a short VIEW of

MARYLAND *and* NORTH CAROLINA.

To which are added,

Schemes and Propositions for the better Promotion of Learning, Religion, Inventions, Manufactures, and Trade in *Virginia*, and the other *Plantations*.

For the Information of the *Curious*, and for the Service of such as are engaged in the *Propagation of the Gospel* and *Advancement of Learning*, and for the Use of all Persons concerned in the

Virginia Trade *and* Plantation.

GEN. ix. 27.

God shall enlarge JAPHETH, *and he shall dwell in the Tents of* SHEM, *and* CANAAN *shall be his Servant.*

By *HUGH JONES*, A. M. Chaplain to the Honourable Assembly, and lately Minister of *James-Town*, &c. in *Virginia*.

LONDON:

Printed for J. CLARKE, at the *Bible* under the *Royal Exchange*. M DCC XXIV.

57   Title-page of the original issue in the New York Public Library

58   From the painting *The Meet in Old Virginia*, by Thure de Thulstrup (1848–)
in the possession of James Barnes, Princeton, N. J.

WILLIAM BYRD, 1674–1744

EASILY the most brilliant figure of early eighteenth-century Virginia was Colonel William Byrd, director from his estate at Westover of many acres of land; a wit, and a lover of books. His library numbers four thousand volumes. He can quote from *Hudibras*, and when the first copy of *The Beggar's Opera* appears in America, he reads it aloud to a clever lady, a neighbor of his. Like others in his distinguished family, he was a man of affairs in the colony. He managed its interests and his own with energy and with a distinctive grace. Byrd, though real enough, stands out from the heterogeneous population of Virginia as a romantic leader. He is the true English aristocrat in a freer environment.

"TRUE BRITONS AND TRUE CHURCHMEN"

JONES' Virginians may exercise only in horse racing and cockfighting, or may even be "climate-struck." Yet when all is said, "Virginia may be justly esteemed the happy retreat of true Britons and true Churchmen."

59   From the portrait at Shirley, Va., attributed to Sir Godfrey Kneller
(1646–1723)

WESTOVER, THE HOME OF A LITERARY VIRGINIA GENTLEMAN

THE spirit of Byrd's mind may be found in his *History of the Dividing Line*, written in 1729, a record of the establishment of the boundary between Virginia and North Carolina. Byrd leaves his fields of "that bewitching vegetable, Tobacco," and plunges into the "Great Dismal," where he sleeps out of doors, coquets with rattlesnakes and bears, and lives generally as a gay and fearless frontiersman. Byrd sees, however, the wilderness through the eyes of a man of the world, and his writing has an ironic twist. He could love the Indian girls, with "a little less dirt"; he names a stream Matrimony Creek, because it is "so noisy and impetuous"; and to North Carolina he refers gravely as "lubberland." The entire book is animated and delightful. In the same year in which John Bulkeley is writing a history of the "Anti-pedo Baptists" and Samuel Mather produces his life of Cotton Mather, Byrd laughs from Westover at "kill-Devil" New England rum, and the "New England saints,"

60   From a photograph. © Detroit Publishing Co,

WILLIAM STITH, 1689–1755, VIRGINIA HISTORIAN

WILLIAM STITH, president of William and Mary College, and the last important historian of Virginia before the Revolution, who thought the "materials" of Captain John Smith excellent but confused, was himself judged by Thomas Jefferson to be "inelegant." *The History of the First Discovery and Settlement of Virginia*, 1747, is scholarly, but lacks the quality of the other histories of Virginia.

62   From John Lawson, *A New Voyage to Carolina*, London, 1709

JOHN LAWSON, ?–1712

SOUTH of Byrd's "Great Dismal," John Lawson, a young Englishman, paddled a canoe through the wilds of North Carolina. Escaping from alligators and brisk young Indian girls, he at last perished ignominiously at the hands of the natives. His *A New Voyage to Carolina*, 1709, gave him at least a local fame.

JOHN ARCHDALE, d. before 1709

JOHN ARCHDALE, with his *A New Description of that Fertile and Pleasant Province of Carolina*, 1707, is an early historian of these new demesnes. Archdale had formerly been governor of the colony. His book has now only an antiquarian interest.

THE

HISTORY

OF THE

First DISCOVERY

AND

SETTLEMENT

OF

VIRGINIA:

BEING

An ESSAY towards a General HISTORY of this COLONY.

By WILLIAM STITH. *A. M.*
Rector of *Henrico* Parish, and one of the Governors of *William* and *Mary* COLLEGE.

Tantæ molis erat ✳✳✳ condere gentem.   Virg.

WILLIAMSBURG:
Printed by WILLIAM PARKS, M,DCC,XLVII.

61   Title-page of the original issue in the New York Public Library

A NEW

DESCRIPTION

OF THAT

Fertile and Pleasant · Province

OF

CAROLINA:

WITH A

BRIEF ACCOUNT

OF ITS

Difcovery, Settling,

AND THE

GOVERNMENT

Thereof to this Time.

With feveral Remarkable Paffages of *Divine Providence* during my Time.

By *JOHN ARCHDALE:* Late *Governour of the fame.*

LONDON:
Printed for *John Wyat,* at the *Rofe* in St. *Paul's Church-Yard.* 1707.

63   Title-page of the original issue in the New York Public Library

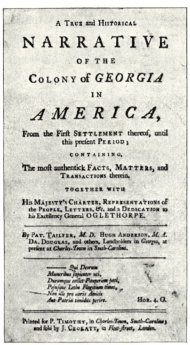

64   Title-page of the original issue in the New York Public Library

A COLONIAL LITERARY CENTER, PHILADELPHIA

THE southern states of the Carolinas and Georgia were the fringe of co-lonial literary life. One center during the eighteenth century was to be in the middle states. "This noble spot of earth," said Gabriel Thomas of Pennsylvania, a Quaker, "will thrive exceedingly."

PATRICK TAILFER, FIRST HISTORIAN OF GEORGIA

ONE early piece of Georgian literature must have delighted, if he saw it, the satirical Byrd, in spite of its democratic tendency. This was *A True and Historical Narrative of the Colony of Georgia*, 1741, by Patrick Tailfer, in collaboration with others. In a dispute which has never been finally settled Tailfer carves to bits the founder of the colony, Governor Oglethorpe. The work is brief, but is armed with a stinging dedication to Oglethorpe; its tone is poised but venomous. Certainly no other statesman, Tailfer declares, was ever so successful as Oglethorpe in making "such a copious jumble of power and politics."

65   Penn's Landing at Essex House, Chester, from John Fanning Watson, *Annals of Philadelphia*, Philadelphia, 1830

WILLIAM PENN, 1644–1718

WILLIAM PENN himself founded schools and encouraged the life of the intellect for its own sake. He wrote letters which, although not strictly literature, are a mirror of his serene spirit. One letter in particular, written in 1683 to the Free Society of Traders, depicts the Indians whom Penn served so wisely.

66   From the painting *The Road to Penn's Manor, 1701,* by J. L. G. Ferris (1863–) in Independence Hall, Philadelphia

From the beginning Pennsylvania numbered persons of culture among its settlers. Penn himself was a gentleman born and capable of setting forth his lofty Quaker principles in clear and effective prose. His adjutant and "true friend," James Logan, shown conversing with Penn's daughter, Letitia, was a scholar and wrote his comrades in Latin and Greek. He produced no creative literature, but left a translation of Cicero's *De Senectute*, 1744, and also *Cato's Moral Distichs Englished in Couplets*, 1735.

WILLIAM SMITH, 1727–1803, OF PENNSYLVANIA

UNDER such patronage a lively, though not inspired, literary culture flourished in Philadelphia. We hear of Franklin's interest in James Ralph, George Webb, and other youthful writers. They, together with Henry Brooke and Aquila Rose, wrote poetry, and a genuine, if humble worship of letters grew up. The ideals in literature and education of these Quaker writers found a natural expression in William Smith's *A General Idea of the College of Mirania*, 1753. Smith was a clergyman, an educator, a historian, and a representative of this intellectual society. His book anticipates later ideas in education, in the form of a Utopian romance. A work from his versatile pen which is and will continue to be a source book is *An Historical Account of the Expedition against the Ohio Indians, . . .* , Philadelphia, 1766.

68   From the miniature *ca.* 1760?, by H. Stubble in the New York Historical Society

AN HISTORICAL ACCOUNT
OF THE EXPEDITION
AGAINST THE OHIO INDIANS,
IN THE YEAR MDCCLXIV.
UNDER THE COMMAND OF
HENRY BOUQUET, ESQ.
COLONEL OF FOOT, AND NOW BRIGADIER GENERAL IN AMERICA.

Including his Transactions with the INDIANS,
Relative to the DELIVERY of their PRISONERS,
And the PRELIMINARIES of PEACE.

With an INTRODUCTORY ACCOUNT of the Preceding CAMPAIGN,
And BATTLE at BUSHY-RUN.

To which are annexed
MILITARY PAPERS,
CONTAINING

Reflections on the War with the Savages; a Method of forming Frontier Settlements; some Account of the INDIAN Country; with a List of Nations, Fighting Men, Towns, Distances, and different Routs.

The whole illustrated with a MAP and COPPER-PLATES.

Published, from authentic Documents, by a Lover of his Country.

PHILADELPHIA, PRINTED:
LONDON, Re-printed for T. JEFFERIES, Geographer to his MAJESTY, at Charing Cross. MDCCLXVI.

67   Title-page of the original issue in the New York Public Library

WILLIAM SMITH, 1728–93, HISTORIAN OF NEW YORK

ANOTHER William Smith, as passionate a New Yorker as if he had trod Broadway, sketched interestingly the early society of the little village. Smith, a graduate of Yale in 1745, was a lawyer and politician, and his *History of New York, from the First Discovery to the Year 1732*, published in 1757, reminds one of a conscientious thesis, with its documents and collections of facts. It presents a contrast to the Quaker Smith's romance, published four years earlier, and even to his history.

CADWALLADER COLDEN, 1688–1776, HISTORIAN OF THE FIVE NATIONS

IN spite of its "facts," Smith's book was accused of dishonesty by Cadwallader Colden. All the histories of early New York are far too silent about the more romantic aspects of the society which had its beginnings in the Dutch adventurers. It is to Colden himself that we must turn as the most important colonial historian of old New York.

Colden, like Smith, was a Tory, and was Lieutenant Governor of New York at the outbreak of the Revolution. When allowances are made for this foible, for his irritability, and one or two other absurdities, it must be concluded that he was a great man; and, in many ways, a distinguished American of the eighteenth century. Colden was self-made. Beginning as a young Scotch physician, he became a skillful botanist, an experimenter in natural science, a successful business man, and an official who served the colony for fifty-eight years. His *History of the Five Nations*, 1727, though derived partly from secondary sources, is authoritative concerning the Iroquois.

69   From the portrait, 1772, by Matthew Pratt (1734–1805) in the Chamber of Commerce of the State of New York

70   From the portrait by Nathaniel Emmons (1703–40) in the Massachusetts Historical Society

SAMUEL SEWALL, 1652–1730

IN New England the secular writings of the early eighteenth century are still pietistic, but some of them speak out more freely. Samuel Sewall belonged to the Mather dynasty, but his *Diary* extends well on into the eighteenth century (1674–1729). It differs from the records of Bradford, Winslow, and Winthrop in its racy gossip about daily life in New England. Sewall reads sermons and psalms without provocation, but he has an intense interest in the business, food, and love-making about him. He was a weighty person, practical, and fortunate in a rare endowment of common sense.

SEWALL'S *DIARY*

THE delightful *Diary* is as candid as Franklin's *Autobiography*. Sewall is a kind of Puritan Pepys. He jots down fears for his soul. He also manifests equal concern about his digestive system. He jumps up from an exposition of Habakkuk with alacrity, as he hears the guns which announce the arrival of the new governor. Who does not love his courtship of Madame Winthrop? He is so much in earnest; so naïvely matter-of-fact. Love does not blind him so much that he does not notice that his lady's dress has lost its freshness. Madame Winthrop, then in the fourth year of her widowhood, could be marvelously cool, and Sewall puts it all down in the *Diary*. "Offer'd me no Wine," he says after a discouraging evening, "that I remember. I rose up at 11 a-clock to come away, saying that I would put on my Coat. She offer'd not to help me. I pray'd her that Juno might light me home, she open'd the Shutter, and said twas pretty light abroad; Juno was weary and gon to bed. So I came home by Star-light as well as I could." These pages of the diary contain Sewall's famous apology for his part in the Salem witchcraft tragedy.

71   A page of Samuel Sewall's *Diary*, from the original Ms. in the Massachusetts Historical Society

72   A page of Samuel Sewall's *Diary*, from the original Ms. in the Massachusetts Historical Society

THE *JOURNALS* OF SARAH KEMBLE KNIGHT, 1666–1727

SEWALL entertains us unconsciously. Another personal record is as mirthful as the wit and fancy of a shrewd New England woman can make it. The *Journals* of Sarah Kemble Knight, 1825, relate her adventures during a journey from Boston to New York in 1704. As an ingenuous, half-satirical, and merry sketch of contemporary manners in the colonies this paper is priceless. Traders, Indians, the citizens of New London or New Haven, the roisterers at taverns — all have a place in this graphic prose or humorous verse. Kept awake at an inn by topers in the next room, Mrs. Knight props herself on her elbow, and by the dim light of a candle, invokes in verse "potent Rum" to come to her aid by thoroughly intoxicating the rascals.

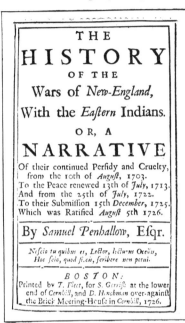

74   Title-page of Penhallow's *History of the Wars of New-England*, Boston, 1726, in the New York Public Library

73   Title-page of the original issue in the New York Public Library

LIBERAL TENDENCIES

THE journals and histories of the eighteenth century are obviously affected by democratic tendencies of the time; they are far more liberal in tone than those written under the influence of the Puritan theocracy. John Callender, of Rhode Island, in *An Historical Discourse*, 1738, writes feelingly of liberty of conscience; William Douglass in his *A Summary, Historical and Political*, 1747, praises rationalism and natural religion; and Samuel Penhallow, in describing the horrible scenes among the Indians, finds time to quote from the ancients, and to make us aware that he himself is a peaceful colonial gentleman living upon a great estate. His *The History of the Wars of New-England with the Eastern Indians* was published in 1726. Liberalism in religion and politics points forward to significant events in Boston and Philadelphia.

THOMAS PRINCE, 1687–1758

AN amusing instance of historical ambition was Thomas Prince's *Chronological History of New England*, 1736. Prince possessed the true scholar's breadth of view, his passion for accuracy, and his devotion to history for its own sake. He began with Adam, on the first day, a method which left him too little time for the worthies of New England; this history was not brought beyond the year 1630. He told the story rigidly, literally, in the form of succinct *Annals*, without imaginative interpretation. The meaning of it all we must deduce for ourselves. Yet as a feat of scholarship the book is impressive. Of all early New England writers Prince had the clearest vision of the historian's task.

75   From the portrait, artist unknown, in the American Antiquarian Society

76   Goffe, the Regicide, Leads the Defense Against the Indian Attack at Hadley, Mass., from a print after the
engraving by John McRae, about 1870

NARRATIVES OF ENCOUNTERS WITH THE INDIANS

EVEN as Thomas Prince wrote, accounts of the bitter fighting with the Indians during the latter part of the seventeenth and the first years of the eighteenth centuries were read at New England firesides as reminders of the dreadful past. To many readers, perhaps, they prophesied scenes in the coming French and Indian wars. The best of these are told by the participants, and do not differ appreciably from the narratives of Hubbard or Church.

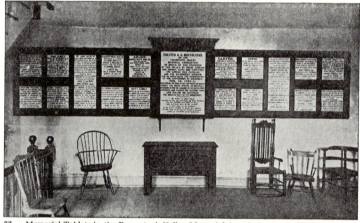

77   Memorial Tablets in the Pocumtuck Valley Memorial Association to the Victims of
the Deerfield Massacre, from a photograph by Frances and Mary Allen

78   From Benjamin Church, *The Entertaining History of King Philip's War*, Newport, 1772, after the engraving by Paul Revere (1735-1818)

ENTERTAINING PASSAGES RELATING TO PHILIP'S WAR

SOME two score years after the Pequot horror, Captain Benjamin Church (1639–1718) relentlessly pursued the terrible King Philip, until the chief turned at bay. It is probable that Philip was slain by one of his own race, though Church's version says that a soldier "sent one Musket Bullet thro' his heart, and another not above two inches from it; he fell upon his face in the Mud & Water with his Gun under him." His blunt narrative the Captain gave in the form of notes to his son, Thomas Church. It was published in 1716 as *Entertaining Passages Relating to Philip's War*.

THE REDEEMED CAPTIVE RETURNING TO ZION

IT is difficult to say which is more graphic, the tale of the capture of Philip, that "great, naked, dirty beast," by merciless men or other stories of heartless murder of women by the redskins. The Reverend John Williams (1644–1729), in *The Redeemed Captive returning to Zion*, 1707, re-creates the dreadful night of February 28, 1704, that of the Deerfield massacre. He describes also the later terrible march into Canada and how "four women were tired, and then slain by them who led them captive."

79   From John Williams, *The Redeemed Captive Returning to Zion*, New York, 1833

THE WILLIAMS HOUSE, DEERFIELD, MASSACHUSETTS

JUST before dawn Williams hears the axes at the windows, and almost instantly the painted faces are at his bedside. Two of his children are killed, and he, with the rest of his family, is taken captive. Then follows the story of his wanderings and ultimate return. No art is needed in such a record; the fearful truth and simplicity are enough to make it literature.

80   From a photograph by the Halliday Historic Photograph Co.

THEOLOGICAL LIBERALISM

ALTHOUGH Jonathan Edwards' stern Puritanism is wholly of the eighteenth century, New England divines of this period show signs of more liberal views. The age of the mighty Mathers is past. John Wise (1652–1725), a democrat, a fighter in the church and in the field, does not consider man a viper, but "the most august animal in the world." *A Vindication of the Government of New-England Churches*, 1717, is based on the theory that man owes homage only to God.

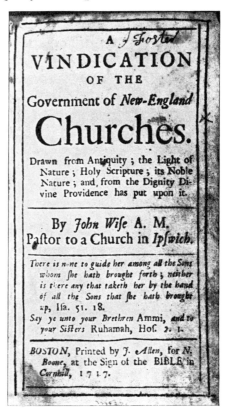

81   Title-page of the original issue in the New York Public Library

82   From the portrait by John Smibert (1684–1751)
         in Memorial Hall, Cambridge, Mass.

GROWTH OF DEMOCRACY

EDWARDS' preaching on the elect and the
nonelect does not suggest democracy, but
the eighteenth century in America beheld
the development of this doctrine. Natural,
then, was the approval toward the tolerant
Quakers, especially from men who had not
fallen wholly under the sway of rationalism.

84   From a drawing by Robert Smith, probably from
memory, by permission of George Vaux, Jr., the owner,
and of Mrs. Amelia Gummere

BENJAMIN COLMAN, 1673–1747

"IT is indeed best," says Benjamin Colman, "to err on the
charitable side." Colman's sermons are orthodox, but gentle
in tone. He professes that he himself hardly dares to judge men;
he cannot believe in "confining the Church of Christ to a narrow
compass." Critics have not been slow to note that in temper and
in manner of writing Colman is like Joseph Addison.

83   Quakers Going to Church in Wilmington, Del., from *Harper's Monthly*, Jan., 1881,
after a drawing by Howard Pyle (1853–1911), by permission of Harper & Brothers

JOHN WOOLMAN, 1720–72

THE Quakers' most remarkable — though unconsciously so —
man of letters was John Woolman of New Jersey. The tributes
of Lamb and Whittier to the *Journal* are well known, and men
so different from
Woolman as Henry
Crabb Robinson and
George Macaulay
Trevelyan were fond
of this Quaker diary.
"Beyond compari-
son," said Channing to
Whittier, "the sweet-
est and purest auto-
biography in the lan-
guage." The *Journal*
differs from the Puri-
tan diaries, even from
that of Edwards, not
so much in unworld-

liness as in utter self-forgetfulness and tenderness for others. It
must not be forgotten that Woolman was uneducated; the beauty
of his thought and writing seems not the result of training, but
inherent in the natural man.

85   Woolman's Shop, 47 Mill Street, Mount Holly, N. J.,
from a photograph, by permission of Mrs. Amelia
Gummere

SAMUEL JOHNSON, 1696-1772, FIRST PRESIDENT OF KING'S COLLEGE

A DISTINGUISHED theologian of the eighteenth century was the American Samuel Johnson, the first president of King's College (Columbia), the friend of Berkeley, and himself a philosopher. In him, too, is increased freedom of thought.

JONATHAN EDWARDS, 1703-58

THE mood of liberalism appears in Jonathan Edwards only in his ideas on church government and in his conception of Congregationalism. In other respects he is New England Calvinism itself, though after him its power was exhausted. Born in 1703, he manifested in youth the two interests of his mind, extreme Calvinism and mysticism. A "pillar tutor" at Yale (1716-20), he penetrated even then deep into metaphysics, in these early years reading Locke through and through. He has recorded in his *Diary* his experience of the sweet excellency of Christ. Walking in the fields he wept as he became conscious of the luminous presence of that self-evident Being, his Creator. Soon after taking the pastorate at North-

86   From the portrait by Laurence Kilburn in the collection of Columbia University

ampton he married Sarah Pierpont, so well known to later generations as that "young lady in New Haven, who is beloved of that Great Being who made and rules the world," and who, in heaven, "is to dwell with him, and to be ravished with his love and delight forever."

87   From the portrait, 1740, possibly by John Smibert, in the possession of Eugene P. Edwards, Stonington, Conn.

88   Sarah Pierpont Edwards, from a portrait, 1740, possibly by John Smibert, in the possession of Eugene P. Edwards

89   First page of Jonathan Edwards' notes for the sermon, "Sinners in the Hands of an Angry God," preached at Enfield, July 8, 1741, in the Yale University Library

"SINNERS IN THE HANDS OF AN ANGRY GOD"

Edwards' pastorate at Northampton lasted twenty-three years. It is there that we think of him, rather than at Stockbridge with the Indians, or, at the end of his life, as president of Princeton College.

Resting his head upon his hand (legend says) he preaches, as at Enfield, quietly, but with the exactitude of a mathematical demonstration, telling sobbing women and terrified men, that at that moment over the furnace of wrath "you hang by a slender thread, with the flames of divine wrath flashing about it." Or, in the last sermon before his eviction, which resulted in part from his severe views concerning admission to the Lord's Supper, he pictures the settlement of their disagreement before God. "Oh," he calls out, "let not this be the last parting."

EDWARDS AND THE "GREAT AWAKENING"

Edwards was an Augustinian in his conviction concerning the absolute reality of God. "I made," he says, "seeking salvation the main business of my life." His belief in his own mystical communion with Christ was evident in his toleration of the strange psychological phenomena of the "Great Awakening," when some hearers became hysterical and many swooned. He possessed powers almost unparalleled — in America — for sustained abstract thought. He was discussed by Boswell and Dr. Johnson. Leslie Stephen thought him a strange admixture of logic and supernaturalism.

He clothes his sharply-defined thought, as in the sermons, in simple, even colloquial language. His *Freedom of the Will*, 1754, is still an enduring philosophical monument. As a thinker and writer he stands like a peak between two ages. In one pure, strong mind met all the ideals, all the aspiration of Puritan New England.

Edwards is, in the broadest sense of the term, the supreme Puritan. He also looks forward. No one can read Edwards' passages on the unseen world without feeling that he is causative. For, strip from him his system of Calvinism, and he is a transcendentalist. Other men were to come after him, very like him in mind, even in face and expression, who had brushed aside Calvinism, but who saw life, like Edwards, as a show, a film on eternity.

90   Singing Procession in 1740, from John W. Barber, *History and Antiquities of New England, New York, New Jersey, and Pennsylvania*, Hartford, 1856

COLONIAL POETRY

COLONIAL poetry for the half century prior to the Revolution was still fettered by religion and convention. Like other forms of literature, however, it was less under the dominance of bigotry. During the French and Indian wars a few battle lyrics appeared, such as the *Song of Braddock's Men* or *The Death of the Brave General Wolf.*

THE SOT-WEED FACTOR

A SURVIVAL of the cruder type of jingle is Ebenezer Cook's *The Sot-Weed Factor*, 1708. Cook, who was describing a visit to Maryland, wrote, says a biographer, "printed, published and sold [the poem] in London for sixpence sterling, and then disappeared forever." In this unfortunate tobacco transaction Cook met dogs, cats, frogs, rattlesnakes, dubious ladies of Maryland, and "a *Quaker, Yea* and *Nay*; a Pious Conscientious Rogue" (see No. 92), all of whom he cursed heartily in rough, humorous couplets. Cook may possibly have written *Sotweed Redivivus; or the Planters Looking-Glass*, published in 1730.

92 Page of Ebenezer Cook, *The Sot-Weed Factor; or A Voyage to Maryland. A Satyr*, London, 1708

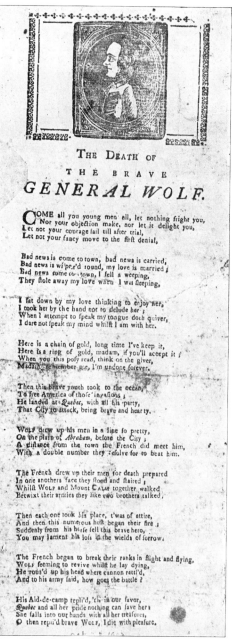

91   From a broadside in the Boston Public Library

ELIZABETH GRAEME FERGUSSON,
1739–1801

THE southern and middle colonies may claim most of the verse written between 1700 and the Revolution. At Graeme Park, near Philadelphia, lived Elizabeth Fergusson, a talented woman with a flair for light verse. In tune with the conventions of the age she imitated Pope, her gayest lines, *The Country Parson*, being a parody on lines in *Eloisa to Abelard.*

93 Graeme Park, the Home of Mrs. Fergusson, built by Sir William Keith in 1722; from the painting by Isaac L. Williams, about 1755, in the Historical Society of Pennsylvania

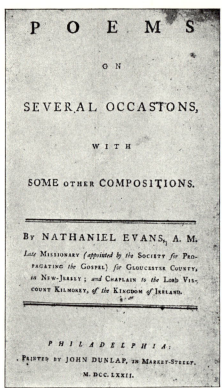

POEMS

ON

SEVERAL OCCASIONS,

WITH

SOME OTHER COMPOSITIONS.

By NATHANIEL EVANS, A. M.

Late MISSIONARY (appointed by the SOCIETY for PRO-
PAGATING the GOSPEL) for GLOUCESTER COUNTY,
in NEW-JERSEY; and CHAPLAIN to the LORD VIS-
COUNT KILMOREY, of the KINGDOM of IRELAND.

PHILADELPHIA:

Printed by JOHN DUNLAP, in MARKET-STREET.
M. DCC. LXXII.

94   Title-page of original issue, in the New York
Public Library

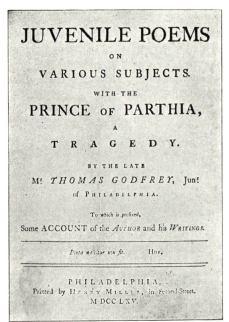

JUVENILE POEMS

ON

VARIOUS SUBJECTS.

WITH THE

PRINCE OF PARTHIA,

A

T R A G E D Y.

BY THE LATE

Mr. *THOMAS GODFREY,* Junr.

of PHILADELPHIA.

To which is prefixed,

Some ACCOUNT of the *AUTHOR* and his *WRITINGS.*

Poeta nascitur non fit. Hor.

PHILADELPHIA,
Printed by HENRY MILLER, in Second-Street.
M DCC LXV.

97   Title-page of original issue, in the New York
Public Library

NATHANIEL EVANS, 1742–67

How happy is the country parson's lot! —
Forgetting bishops, as by them forgot.

So ran the opening lines of *The Country Parson* addressed by
Mrs. Fergusson to her friend Nathaniel Evans, a clergyman in
the Episcopal Church. Evans died at the age of twenty-five leaving the memory of a fine character, and verse of some slight value.

WILLIAM LIVINGSTON, 1723–90

THE influence of Pope on this young generation of American poets was especially evident in the work of William Livingston. This Scotchman, lawyer and statesman, was in the thick of Revolutionary affairs. When a young man, he wrote a poem called *Philosophic Solitude*, 1747.

95   From Theodore Sedgwick, Jr.,
*Memoir of the Life of William
Livingston,* New York, 1833

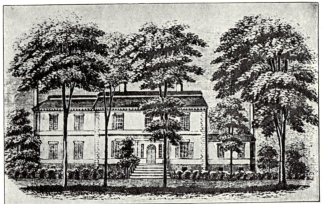

96   Liberty Hall, Livingston's Home, Elizabethtown, N. J., from Barber and
Howe, *Historical Collections of New Jersey,* New York, 1845

PHILOSOPHIC SOLITUDE

THIS poem was indeed the only taste of solitude Livingston had,
or, probably, wished. The seven hundred lines, ushered into
the world with the subtitle "The Choice of a Rural Life," and
the benevolent explanatory phrase: "by a gentleman educated
at Yale College," are as smooth and insincere as any devotee of
Pope could wish.

THOMAS GODFREY, 1736–63

A FRIEND of Nathaniel Evans was Thomas Godfrey whose *Juvenile Poems on Various Subjects* appeared in 1765. Godfrey
was the son of a mathematician. He had studied the trade of
watchmaking. There is romance in observing the struggles of Evans and Godfrey against poverty and the
repressive influences of a community in which emulators of Franklin could make progress more easily than
literary men. The poems themselves are graceful trifles. *The Wish* has achieved the reputation of having
inspired the later poem of the same name by Oliver Wendell Holmes.

THE PRINCE OF PARTHIA

GODFREY, however, was a pioneer in American creative literature. It is well-nigh impossible to accuse him of religiosity, or of having written, like so many in the eighteenth century, as an avocation. He wrote because he loved books, and a list of those masterpieces which left their stamp upon him would be long. Moved by the literature of the past, he wrote *The Prince of Parthia* (acted 1767), which, to give it its due in the familiar phrases, was the first tragedy written by a native American produced on the stage in America. As a play it is bookish and reminiscent, but as a landmark it cannot be disregarded.

By *Authority.*
NEVER PERFORMED BEFORE.
By the AMERICAN COMPANY,
At the NEW THEATRE, in *Southwark,*
On *FRIDAY,* the *Twenty-Fourth* of *April,* will be
presented, A TRAGEDY written by the late ingenious
Mr. *Thomas Godfrey,* of this city, called the
PRINCE of PARTHIA.
The PRINCIPAL CHARACTERS by Mr. HALLAM,
Mr. DOUGLASS, Mr. WALL, Mr. MORRIS,
Mr. ALLYN, Mr. TOMLINSON, Mr. BROAD-
BELT, Mr. GREVILLE, Mrs. DOUGLASS,
Mrs. MORRIS, Miss WAINWRIGHT, and
Miss CHEER.
To which will be added, A *Ballad Opera* called
The CONTRIVANCES.
To begin exactly at *Seven* o'Clock.---*Vivant Rex & Regina.*

98   Announcement of performance of *The Prince of Parthia,* from the *Pennsylvania Journal,* April 23, 1767

MY Old Companion! and my Friend!
I cannot Come, and therefore send.
Some pity should be shown to One
That's heavy laden with the Stone;
That's wearied out with fits of pain
Returning like Clouds after Rain.
Alas! my Brother, what can I
Do for thee, more than Pray and Cry,
To Counsel, and to comfort try,
And bear a part by Sympathy?
Excuse me, though I Write in Verse,
It's usual on a Dead mans Hearse:
Thou many a Death hast under-gone,
And Elegies made of thine own.
Our Saviours Funeral Obsequies,
One Celebrates before His eyes;
And He the Oyntment kindly takes,
That for His Burial she makes.
Two Saints array'd in glorious dress,
Appear, and talk of His Decease;
Whose Death from thine did take the Sting,
And wholsome make that Poyson thing.
And I have seen thine hand, and Pen,
Play on that Cockatrices den
In measur'd Lines, as if inspir'd,
And *Paroxisms* had only fir'd
An holy Soul with flaming zeal,
That flesh-pains it could scarcely feel.
What, in one breath, both Live and Dye,
Groan, Laugh, Sigh, Smile, cry, Versifie
Is this the Stone? are these the pains,
Of that Disease that plagues the Reins?
That slyly steals into the bladder?
Then bites, and stings like to the Adder.

99   From the broadside by Nicholas Noyes, *Poem to Mr. James Bayley,* 1706, in the Boston Public Library

NICHOLAS NOYES, 1647–1717

THE old school of the fantastics did not die without a murmur. The eighteenth century was well along when Nicholas Noyes wrote the most crabbed of his verse and the most eccentric of his puns. Let others imitate Dryden and Pope! Noyes had resolved not to forsake Donne, Herbert, and Wither. In his consolatory poem dedicated to Cotton Mather, at the death of his wife, he assures his friend that

> Her soul took wing and soared higher;
> But left choice ashes here behind.

Or, abandoning metaphor, he describes John Higginson, who died in 1708, at an advanced age:

> At ninety-three had comely face
> Adorned with majesty and grace;
> Before he went among the dead
> He children's children's children had.

MATHER BYLES, 1707–88

YET in New England were many henchmen of Dryden and Pope. The greatest of these was Mather Byles, a descendant of Richard Mather and of John Cotton. Byles was known generally as the famous Boston Tory preacher, poet, and wit. A preacher he was, and a sound one. His verse, too, did not discredit his master, Pope, any more than his preaching did his ancestry. As we think of him at dinner among the scarlet coats of King George, we feel that he was a genial companion. How, nevertheless, he become known as a wit will to some remain a mystery. To say when his study had received a coat of dun paint that he was in "a brown study" will not kindle Homeric laughter among posterity, though Cotton Mather may guffaw in heaven at this side-splitting pun. Byles as a divine, as a poet, and as a man of the world illustrates, in his way, the tendencies of this first half of the century.

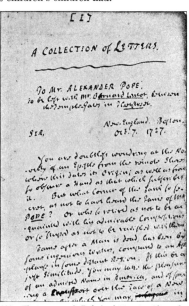

100   First page of Byles's letter to Alexander Pope, October 7, 1727, in the New England Historic-Genealogical Society, Boston

CHAPTER III

THE REVOLUTION: SATIRE AND CONTROVERSY

BENJAMIN FRANKLIN was the most distinguished of many thoughtful Americans, during the decade before the Revolution, who appreciated the power of the colonial empire and, more particularly, the problem of its loyalty to England. At this time the real unity of the scattered colonies resided in their affection for the mother country. Communication was difficult. Religious ideas differed. Local pride flourished. Jealousies were in the air. Yet from Georgia to Maine men considered themselves Englishmen. John Adams warns Americans against mistaking the unworthy policies of the King and his ministers for the spirit of England, and James Otis thinks the British constitution "the wisest and best in the world."

Accordingly, when the break came, the anguish of this new America was intense. As the word "Independence" is hurled across the Atlantic to Parliament, the patriots are not free from a stern despair. Nothing but defiance is possible to manhood. But the defiance carries with it the wrench of broken family ties, and disillusionment of an old ideal. It must not be forgotten that the years from 1765 to 1789, and later, were years of spiritual confusion. The American nation did not rise full-formed. The colonies' first bonds were of those fighting a common enemy and of a new and rather terrifying ideal of freedom. What Franklin said later was true now: they must indeed hang together or hang separately.

Two factors intensified the turmoil. The first of these was the division within America herself. American histories have often been inclined to underrate the strength and particularly the moral idealism of the Loyalists. The American Revolution was in part a civil war; brother smote brother. The character of such Tories as Seabury, Odell, Byles, and others precludes the easy disposition of this party as mere reactionaries or tufthunters. The wealth, dignity, and force of this group disturbed the patriots and blurred the sharpness of the issue with England. A second way in which the perplexity of these years increased was in the protraction and the bitterness of the struggle. Ridicule of the British regulars after Lexington was a transient mood; there were terrible years of defeat and hardship; and, finally, when peace came, the depression of the years before the framing of the Constitution.

It has already been observed that the writer of American literature was not a cloistered soul in pursuit of its fugitive virtues. He tended rather to be a man of action who wrote when he could. In the midst of alarms, Crèvecœur cries out: "I am a lover of peace, what must I do? . . . I was happy before this unfortunate Revolution. I feel that I am no longer so; therefore I regret the change." As for the others, Freneau or Barlow, their muses became the handmaids of Mars. Meanwhile from the men of action who could write — and already America had excelled in this practical kind of writing — poured the broadsides of oration, pamphlet, satire. The literature of the Revolution was a literature of excitement.

Out of the Revolution came enough writing to make a paper bridge to hostile England. Students of the unsigned reviews in the English quarterlies have a nicer problem in America, to determine the parentage of the endless essays, pamphlets, speeches, and letters which appeared in the new American press. In this litter are masterpieces of political prose. The first state papers, to consider but one phase of this writing, are admirable. "When your lordships," said Lord Chatham in 1775, "look at the papers transmitted us from America, when you consider their decency, firmness, and wisdom, you cannot but respect their cause, and wish to make it your own." Then, after a comparison with Thucydides and allusions to their "solidity of reasoning, force of sagacity, and wisdom of conclusion," Lord Chatham ends: "I trust it is obvious to your lordships, that all attempts to impose servitude upon such men, to establish despotism over such a mighty continental nation, must be vain, must be fatal."

What survives of Revolutionary literature seems to us too forensic. We wonder at the expansive gestures, tire under the elaborate periods, and detect the source of many a later Fourth of July speech by the rocket's red glare. The words of the orators echo faintly through the passage of the years, but Samuel Adams of Massachusetts, James Otis, of the same state, and Patrick Henry of Virginia are still mighty. In eloquence they are the brothers of Burke and the spiritual progenitors of Webster. "Otis," declares John Adams, "was a flame of fire!" Samuel Adams' essays stung, we are told, like horned snakes. His pamphleteering antedated the Revolution. Thomas Paine's reckless and effective writing during the first years of the struggle increased the general wrath, and after its close Jay, Madison, and Hamilton made the essay their weapon, in *The Federalist*, to uphold the new Constitution. All this appears far from literature, and savors of a bout at quarterstaff. In much of this writing, however, are visible American literary characteristics: enthusiasm for ideas and nervous, forceful expression.

This last quality is apparent, too, in the narratives of contemporary life which now supplant the memoirs of Indian warfare. Histories like Ramsay's and Gordon's are conventional. Not so are the first accounts of experiences with the redcoats. The same race which coolly set down stories of torture by the Indians, now recounts the horrors of war with mercenaries, or of the prison ship. In the barracks at Montreal, Colonel Prescott taunts Ethan Allen. "I told him," said Allen in reply, "he would do well not to cane me — for I was not accustomed to it — and shook my fist at him, telling him that was the beetle of mortality for him if he offered to strike." "I saw no Bible," so Andros writes of the "Old Jersey" prison ship, "heard no prayer, no religious conversation; no clergyman visited us, though no set of afflicted men more needed the light and consolation of religion." Good writing, this, in its fearlessness and sincerity.

How great was the cataclysm is best realized if we turn to personal letters, or look for pure literature. We find, to be sure, the so-called *Letters* of Crèvecœur with their love of nature, and we may read an occasional gentle essay in the *Pennsylvania Magazine* or *The American Museum*. (Between 1741 and the end of the century almost all of the forty-five pioneer magazines proved to be ephemeral.) But most of the wine has turned to vinegar. In verse the "Connecticut Wits," and Philip Freneau, Jonathan Odell, and others are writing satire or partisan poetry. Lyrics have become battle songs, and the drama stages the cruelty of the Grenadiers or the absurdity of rebels who are uniformed like Falstaff's army. What injury the war did our literature may be guessed from Scott's admiration for Freneau's few peaceful lyrics, or from the innate power in the writings of Hugh Henry Brackenridge. Some have transferred Odell's scornful words concerning the rebels to the entire literature of the time: "Since creation's dawn earth never yet produced so vile a spawn." Yet if the acid of the Revolution entered in, it at least gave bite to many a ballad. Of Freneau's satires or Trumbull's *M'Fingal* no American need be ashamed.

It is difficult to conceive that under all this unrest the old currents of life were flowing. Yet it was so. The democratic rationalism of Franklin, the radicalism of the unkempt corset-maker, Paine, the frontier spirit of Ethan Allen were all products of the earlier age, and they were to be creators of thought in the next century, both in life and in literature.

101   Reduced facsimile of the engrossed copy in the Library of Congress

THE DECLARATION OF INDEPENDENCE

THE most profound as well as the most moving of the Revolutionary state papers is The Declaration of Independence, the creation of Thomas Jefferson (1743–1826), part statesman, part philosopher, but basically an imaginative idealist. At this document the vultures of criticism have pecked unceasingly. They have declared it sentimental, rhetorical, and illogical, but to reread it now is to feel its strength, its serenity. It lives because it deals not with tea or taxation, but with "the unalienable Rights" of mankind.

The Manner in which the American Colonies Declared themselves INDEPENDANT of the King of ENGLAND, throughout the different Provinces, on July 4. 1776.

102 From Edward Barnard, *New, Comprehensive, Impartial, and Complete History of England*, London, 1790?, from the engraving by Noble after the drawing by Hamilton

JAMES OTIS, 1725–83

THE passionate resolution which lay behind the Declaration of Independence was the result of agitation through political essay and oratory. The firebrand of the North was James Otis. He was a Harvard graduate, and a criminal lawyer in Boston. His *The Rudiments of Latin Prosody* appeared in 1760. A year later he made his memorable speech on the Writs of Assistance. Otis was, John Adams thought, "Isaiah and Ezekiel united." His speeches were intensely forceful, and his reasoning on the relations of the colonies to Great Britain was always logical. In the *Vindication*, 1762, are the chief arguments against taxation, and the seeds of greater books. In the *Vindication* Otis took part in the dispute between the governor and assembly, which asserted that the former had violated principles of legislative power. "How many volumes," John Adams said, "are concentrated in this little fugitive pamphlet."

A REFLECTION OF AMERICAN THOUGHT

FOR students of literature the Declaration of Independence is interesting twice over: first, because it is a revelation of Thomas Jefferson, and, second, because it is the most perfect representation within a single paper of the moral temper of the American people at the end of the third quarter of the eighteenth century. It was Jefferson himself who directed what his epitaph should be. It read in part: "Here was buried Thomas Jefferson, author of the Declaration of Independence." The recognition by the colonies, in spite of dissenting voices, that independence was the only possible issue of the long struggle attests that through Jefferson spoke the people themselves. Perhaps one of its salient characteristics is its concern not with "historic precedent," as was the case with so many Revolutionary documents, but with abstract thought and principles, suggesting Jefferson's debt to French thought. He was considered in his own time a "philosopher," and the Declaration has the tone which is found in much European writing of the late eighteenth century. It made articulate in grandiose phrase the latent thought of many Americans.

103 From the portrait, about 1760, by Joseph Blackburn, in the Museum of Fine Arts, Boston, courtesy of Mrs. Charles F. Russell, Boston

The Rev.ᵈ JONATHAN MAYHEW. D.D.
Paſtor of the Weſt Church. BOSTON. N.E.
OBᵗ JULY. 9ᵗʰ 1766. Æ 48

104   From the engraving by Paul Revere, in the New York Public Library

JONATHAN MAYHEW, 1720–66

In this decade before the Revolution angry, pleading voices were everywhere: in the assembly, the town meeting, and the pulpit. At the West Church, in Boston, Jonathan Mayhew declares the issue of the state that also of the church: "The Son of God came down from heaven to make us 'free indeed'." Mayhew was a rationalist in religion, a thorough democrat, an intellectual. In the crowd of statesmen he is an early and minor figure, but he reflects the mind of conservative New England before the Revolution.

105   From the posthumous portrait, 1815, by Thomas Sully (1783–1872) in possession of Charles L. Hamilton, Philadelphia

PATRICK HENRY, 1736–99

Comparable with James Otis' speech against the Writs of Assistance in 1761 is that of Patrick Henry in the Virginia Convention at Richmond, in 1775. Patrick Henry was no statesman; much of his writing has moods of melodrama, but his demagogic power over men is typical of what Professor Barrett Wendell calls the explosive temper of the time. His voice is sometimes shrill but it is magnetic with passion as he sweeps his hearers along with him. In spite of repetitions and travesties, one remembers the tremendous climax. "Forbid it, Almighty God!—I know not what course others may take, but as for me, give me liberty, or give me death!"

106   From the statue at Richmond, Va., by Thomas Crawford (1814–57)

SAMUEL ADAMS, 1722–1803

SAMUEL ADAMS, cousin of John Adams, was the relentless and volumi-
nous enemy of the Tories. Far into the night his candle burned, so
said the passers-by, as he damned the enemies of his country in essay
and pamphlet. Whether he was "Samuel the Publican" or "the
Cromwell of New England," he was a dangerous patriot, not less so
that his writing was anonymous and disinterested.

107   From the statue of Samuel Adams, 1875,
by Martin Millmore (1844–83) in the Town Hall,
Lexington, Mass.

108   From the miniature painted in Philadelphia, 1792, by John
Trumbull (1756–1843) in the Yale School of Fine Arts

JOHN ADAMS, 1735–1826

LESS fiery than either Otis or Mayhew, John
Adams was destined by his solid qualities of
mind for statesmanship and for the second presidency of the United States. He, too, like earlier New
Englanders, jots down youthful resolutions, and the reflections of a young lawyer on life. His ten volumes
sum up the wisdom of a well-balanced nature. He is a patriot, but he is thoughtful as well as patriotic:
"Yesterday," he quietly writes his wife, after the passage of the Declaration, "the greatest question was
decided, which ever was debated in America, and a greater, perhaps, never was nor will be decided among
men." Meeting Francis Hopkinson, the poet, in 1776, we find him saying wistfully: "I wish I had leisure
and tranquillity of mind
to amuse myself with
those elegant and ingen-
ious arts of painting,
statuary, architecture,
and music. But I have
not." One wonders if
they would really have
pleased him, these arts.
Late in life he wrote
excellent personal letters.
Yet there is a burr about
him, a truculence of tem-
per, which bespeaks not
the man of letters, but
the maker of a nation.

109   Birthplace of John Adams, Quincy, Mass.   © The Halliday Historic
Photograph Co.

THE ORIGIN

OF THE

AMERICAN CONTEST

WITH

GREAT-BRITAIN,

OR

The prefent political State of the
Maffachufetts-Bay, in general,

AND

The Town of Bofton in particular.

Exhibiting the Rife and Progrefs of the difor-
dered State of that Country, in a feries of
weekly Effays, publifhed at Bofton, under
the Signature of

MASSACHUSETTENSIS,

A Native of New-England.

Mr Sewell, attorney General at Bos

NEW-YORK:

Printed by JAMES RIVINGTON, 1775.

110 Title-page of original issue of the pamphlet by Daniel Leonard,
in the New York Public Library

JUST PUBLISHED.
Printed on a large Type, and fine Paper,
And to be fold at the LONDON BOOK-STORE,
North Side of King-ftreet.

LETTERS

FROM

A FARMER in *PENNSYLVANIA,*
To the INHABITANTS of the
BRITISH COLONIES.

(Price two Piftareens.)
Among all the WRITERS in favour of the COLONIES,
the FARMER fhines unrivalled, for ftrength of A gument,
Elegance of Diction, Knowledge in the Laws of Great Britain, and the true intereft of the COLONIES: A pathetic
and perfuafive Eloquence runs through the whole of thefe
Letters: They have been printed in every Colony from Florida to Nova-Scotia; and the univerfal applaufe, fo juftly
beftowed on the AUTHOR, hath fully teftified the GRA-
TITUDE of the PEOPLE of AMERICA, for fuch an able
Advifer, and affectionate Friend.

112   Advertisement of an early edition, from the
Boston Chronicle, March 14, 1768

VOICES OF THE LOYALISTS

THE strength of the colonies' attachment for Britain was shown in their joy at the repeal of the Stamp Act, in 1766. The pamphleteers laid aside their pens with a sense of accomplishment. Britain had come to her senses. Alas, it was but a breathing spell. New duties followed, and with them new and stronger resistance. In 1764 Martin Howard, a Newport Tory, had written *A Letter from a Gentleman at Halifax to His Friend in Rhode Island*, pointing out that American representation in Parliament was hardly less than that of many Englishmen living in England. Howard, for his pains, lost all his property, and was forced to flee. His mode of warfare, however, after the resumption of the paper battle, became popular. Samuel Seabury, "the Westchester Farmer" (No. 111), and Daniel Leonard, "Massachusettsensis" (No. 110), proclaimed every ideal of the discontented, raising a hurricane in the country, and about his own ears. Already Americans were making ready for "Independence Hall."

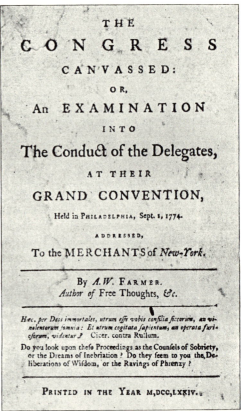

THE

CONGRESS

CANVASSED:

OR,

An EXAMINATION

INTO

The Conduct of the Delegates,

AT THEIR

GRAND CONVENTION,

Held in PHILADELPHIA, Sept. 1, 1774.

ADDRESSED,

To the MERCHANTS of New-York.

By A.W. FARMER.
Author of Free Thoughts, &c.

*Hæc, per Deos immortales, utrum effe vobis confilia ficcorum, an vi-
nolentorum fomnia: Et utrum cogitata fapientum, an operata furi-
eforum, videntur?* Cicer. contra Rullum.

Do you look upon thefe Proceedings as the Counfels of Sobriety,
or the Dreams of Inebriation? Do they feem to you the De-
liberations of Wifdom, or the Ravings of Phrenzy?

PRINTED IN THE YEAR M,DCC,LXXIV.

111   Title-page of original issue of the pamphlet by
Samuel Seabury, in the New York Public Library

LETTERS FROM A FARMER

THE most able of these controversialists was John Dickinson, admired by Burke, Voltaire, and Franklin, and decorated with the grandiose title of "Penman of the American Revolution." Dickinson was an able lawyer. The text of his remonstrance to Americans is temperance. To the colonies, hoping against all evidence for a reconciliation, these letters were soothing.

JOHN DICKINSON, 1732–1808, THE "PATRIOTIC AMERICAN FARMER"

THERE is sense in this. It is only when the beloved parent is made concrete in the persons of a willful, myopic ministry, that the sentiment melts into thin air. In these very years, while Dickinson breathes his pious hopes, Lord Hillsborough keeps Franklin waiting in his antechamber, and censures the doctrines of "the Farmer" as "extremely wild." In literary form the letters are excellent; direct, forceful, and readable even now.

THE WAR

SUCH voices as Dickinson's seemed to be silenced by the rattle of musketry at Lexington and at Bunker Hill. The fashionable Tories laughed at the haste with which boys seized their guns, and plunged into the half-drilled throngs of patriots. It was a war in which many farmers expected to take up their arms for a few weeks, and then return to the fields to finish a summer's haying. There were some brave spirits who sensed the full gravity of the struggle and who set out for war not simply because of the enthusiasm of a moment, but determined to see it through to the bitter close. Such were the men who formed the nucleus of Washington's often defeated but, in the end, successful army.

THE PATRIOTIC AMERICAN FARMER. J-N D-K-NS---N Esqr. BARRISTER at LAW.

113 From a copy in the New York Public Library of the original engraving in the Library Company of Philadelphia

114   From the painting *The Spirit of '76.* © John Ward Dunsmore (1856-), in his possession

THOMAS PAINE, 1737–1809

YET the archpamphleteer's winged words were to be heard above the drums and shouting — nay, were actually read aloud to the despairing soldiers at Valley Forge. "These are the times that try men's souls — " was a sentence to brace not only Washington himself but many a patriot. Their author was Thomas Paine, "rebellious stay-maker," tobacconist, exciseman, poet, soldier, and adventurer. Paine's real life began in 1774 with his advent in America. His mental naturalization was instantaneous and complete. "Our great title," he said with his gift of felicitous phrase, "is Americans — our inferior one varies with the place." Paine was among the first to speak the words: "The United States of America." "Tyranny," he says (*The Crisis*), "like hell, is not easily conquered; yet we have this consolation with us, that the harder the conflict, the more glorious the triumph."

115   From the engraving by William Sharp, after the portrait, 1792, by George Romney (1734–1802)

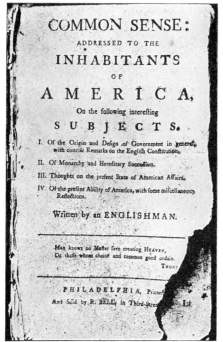

116   Title-page of original issue, 1776, in the Thomas Paine National Museum, New Rochelle, N. Y.

PAINE'S *COMMON SENSE*

AT one with Americans in resentment of tyranny and beyond them in daring, he advocated the break with England. A very "ingenious young man" indeed, as Franklin said. "Where liberty is," Franklin had declared, "there is my country." Paine had replied: "Where liberty is not, there is mine." Once established in America, largely through a connection with the *Pennsylvania Magazine*, Paine brought out in January, 1776, his *Common Sense*, a crude, slashing, brilliant exhortation for liberty, full of satire, pleading, and ardent glimpses into the future.

COMMON SENSE.   29

Nation and set it together by the ears. A pretty business indeed for a man to be allowed eight hundred thousand sterling a year for, and worshipped into the bargain! Of more worth is one honest man to society and in the sight of God, than all the crowned Ruffians that ever lived.

THOUGHTS, *on the present* STATE *of* AMERICAN AFFAIRS.

IN the following pages I offer nothing more than simple facts, plain arguments, and common sense: and have no other preliminaries to settle with the Reader, than that he will divest himself of prejudice and prepossession, and suffer his reason and his feelings to determine for themselves: that he will put *on* or rather that he will not put *off* the true character of a man, and generously enlarge his views beyond the present day.

Volumes have been written on the subject of the struggle between England and America. Men of all ranks have embarked in the controversy, from different motives, and with various designs; but all have been ineffectual,

117   From the issue, 1776, in the New York Public Library

A PAGE OF *COMMON SENSE*

"A GREATER absurdity," Paine declares, "cannot be conceived of, than three millions of people running to their seacoast every time a ship arrives from London, to know what portion of liberty they should enjoy." Or in dithyrambic vein, glowing phrases tumble over one another: "Ye that tell us of harmony and reconciliation . . . The last cord now is broken . . . Ye that love mankind . . ." And so on. In three months the publishers sold one hundred and twenty thousand copies of *Common Sense*. Its effect, thought Franklin, was prodigious.

PAINE'S ROMANTIC LIFE

No one can repeat all the stories of Paine which make him, in the rise and fall of his fortunes, so like a romantic hero, dying friendless and in poverty. In America his fame was recognized by Congress. In England he was fêted by the liberals. In France he sat in the Convention during the Revolution. But he was imprisoned in the Luxembourg, and he lived to be

118   Paine's Home, New Rochelle, N. Y., from a photograph

tried in England for sedition, and to lose some part of his fame in America. He attacked Washington for indifference to his imprisonments. Returning home he found many Americans hostile. In the *Rights of Man*, 1791–92, written in reply to Burke's *Reflections*, may be found the good and the evil in him: his intense love of liberty, his honesty in religion, his gusto, but also his rhetoric, his superficiality, and his coarseness.

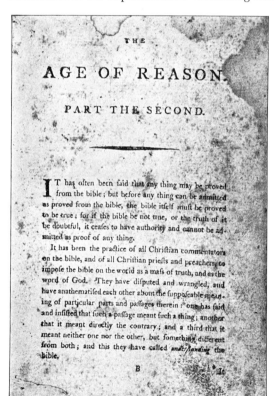

119   First page of Thomas Paine, *The Age of Reason*, Part II, 1795

THE AGE OF REASON

THE AGE OF REASON, 1794–95, the other work of his later life, although full of smart writing, shows him at his worst. His reputation as an atheist is an absurd relic of the age which first read him. But he attempts to cast clear sunshine on the mysteries of religion, and succeeds in showing how impotent he is before any interpretation of spiritual things. Paine could not get far beyond the evidences of his own five senses; he was a brutal literalist. So he fumbles at symbolism in a way which could have pleased only the coarsest of cracker-barrel philosophers. In the last analysis his offenses are less against religion than against taste.

A FEARLESS REBEL

LATER Paine admitted that he tackled these questions without the Bible at hand, and for fun. In his nature were wide shallows; his entire life suggests a certain naïveté. Yet he was, in the deepest sense, a rebel. His place is secure as a crystallizer and creator of American thought. He was fearless, and, most of all, he loved his fellow men. If he is now but a name, and his works unread, it is because his work is done; the best of his thought is assimilated. To-day Paine's best known work is *Common Sense*.

120   Paine's Death Mask by John Wesley Jarvis (1780–1840), courtesy of the Paine National Historical Association

THE

FEDERALIST:

ADDRESSED TO THE

PEOPLE OF THE STATE OF
NEW-YORK.

NUMBER I.

Introduction.

AFTER an unequivocal experience of the ineffi-
cacy of the subsisting federal government, you
are called upon to deliberate on a new constitution for
the United States of America. The subject speaks its
own importance; comprehending in its consequences,
nothing less than the existence of the UNION, the
safety and welfare of the parts of which it is composed, the fate of an empire, in many respects, the
most interesting in the world. It has been frequently
remarked, that it seems to have been reserved to the
people of this country, by their conduct and example,
to decide the important question, whether societies of
men are really capable or not, of establishing good
government from reflection and choice, or whether
they are forever destined to depend, for their political
constitutions, on accident and force. If there be any
truth in the remark, the crisis, at which we are arrived,
may with propriety be regarded as the æra in which
A   that

121   Page of *The Federalist*, first collected edition,
New York, 1788

MINOR HISTORIANS

ALTHOUGH Paine and others brought the
pamphlet to a high degree of effectiveness,
an impression remains that it scattered

ALEXANDER HAMILTON, 1757–1804

THE American political essay was an instrument capable of many
tunes. After the war and in the struggle to found a stable
government, Alexander Hamilton, with Jay and Madison, made
it in *The Federalist*, unlike Paine's diatribes, a medium for dispassionate, reasoned thought. The letters, written by "Publius,"
which make up *The Federalist* are strong, intellectual appeals for
support of the Constitution of 1787. Of most of these Hamilton
was the author. His career was versatile. Early in the Revolution he had won his literary spurs in *The Farmer Refuted*. As aide
to the commander-in-chief during many years of the struggle,
he had composed large numbers of those able letters which bear
the signature of George Washington. He had opposed Patrick
Henry, opponent of the Constitution, in convincing speeches;
and later, as Secretary of the Treasury under Washington,
was a pioneer in American finance. He met death in a duel with
Aaron Burr, the grandson — it is irrelevant but suggestive — of
Jonathan Edwards.

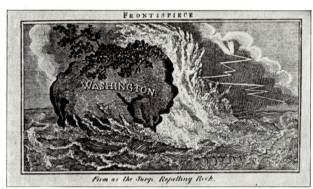

FRONTISPIECE

WASHINGTON

Firm as the Surge Repelling Rock.

122   From David Ramsay, *The Life of George Washington*, Baltimore, 1818

our literary power. The ponderous old histories of the earlier age were, after all, monuments of learning,
patience, and concentration. The repose of such a work as Thomas Prince's *Chronological History of New
England* makes *Common Sense* seem staccato. The
literature of excitement included very few histories.
After the tension of the war had passed, David Ramsay
(1749–1815), a South Carolina physician, compiled a
History of the American Revolution, 1789, and a *Life of
Washington*, 1807. Both books lack power.

JEFFERSON'S *NOTES ON VIRGINIA*

IN 1785 Thomas Jefferson had published his *Notes on
Virginia*, hardly a history, but a book lightened occasionally by the sympathy of its author. The conception of Jefferson obtained from the *Declaration of
Independence* should be supplemented by his *Autobiography*, his letters, and his memorial to Virginia.
Jefferson, like Washington, represents in his tolerance
and liberal ideals an American type peculiar at this
time to Virginia. He believed in what Matthew Arnold
liked to call "a harmonious expansion of our humanity,"
and was far from the Puritan view of life. Fond of
learning and universities, a disciple of French thinkers,
he possessed, in addition, a fine literary sense.

123   The Old Plantation School, Tuckahoe, Va., where Jefferson and
Randolph went to school, from a photograph by H. P. Cook

THOMAS HUTCHINSON'S *HISTORY OF THE PROVINCE OF MASSACHUSETTS-BAY*

ONE of the best early histories of colonial America was written during the Revolution by Thomas Hutchinson (1711–80), governor of Massachusetts, and later an exile for his loyalty to George III. Manuscript sheets of the second volume of the *History of the Province of Massachusetts-Bay*, Boston, 1764, tell the story of Hutchinson's loyalty to the crown. The paper is torn by the trampling of horses and men, and defaced by the mud of the street, into which it was thrown by a patriot mob that broke into his house. The history is brought down to the year 1774, though not published in its entirety till many years later (1764; 1767; 1828). Hutchinson was a scholar. His fault as a historian was lack of imagination. He tells the story of the events of the years leading up to the Revolution from the point of view of an American who was profoundly convinced that the best interests of his fellow countrymen would be served by remaining within the British empire.

ETHAN ALLEN, 1737–89

THE journals, diaries, and narratives of the actors, humble or otherwise, in the Revolution, bear the seal of reality. To-day at Ticonderoga they are sceptical about Ethan Allen's Olympic command to open "in the name of Jehovah and the Continental Congress." There is some of King Cambyses' vein, too, in Allen's account of his imprisonment and adventures in England, *A Narrative of Colonel Ethan Allen's Captivity*. True American brag, this, but no one can question the robust patriotism of Allen's narrative. This book was first published at Philadelphia in 1779, and since this date has often reappeared.

124 Page from the original Ms. (soiled by the mob), in the Massachusetts State Archives, Boston

Its most valuable characteristic is in Allen's frank statements of opinions, furnishing us with a genuine portrait of him as a man.

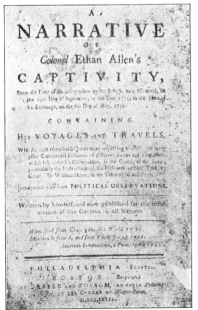

CAPTURE OF TICONDEROGA.

126 From Ethan Allen, *Allen's Captivity*, Boston, 1845

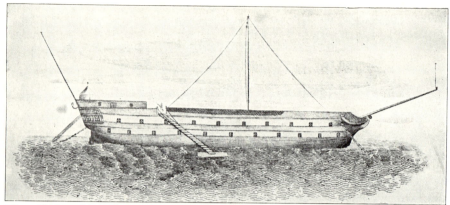

127   The Jersey Prison Ship, from Thomas Dring, *Recollections of the Jersey Prison Ship*, Providence, 1829

RECORDS OF AMERICAN PRISONERS

THE spirit of the times is apparent also in the records of Americans in British prisons. Henry Laurens in the Tower merely asks for a book or desires to have his cane mended. He remarks quietly: "God Almighty sent me here for some purpose. I am determined to see the end of it." Or the farmer's lad from Connecticut may be heard in *The Old Jersey Captive, or, a Narrative of the Captivity of Thomas Andros*, 1823. Andros was confined on the "Old Jersey" prison ship, but escaped. "Disease and death," he says, "were wrought into her very timbers." The story of Andros is a memorable bit of realism.

128   From David Humphreys, *Essay on the Life of the Honorable Major-General Israel Putnam*, Middletown, 1794, after the engraving by Alexander Anderson (1775–1870)

DAVID HUMPHREYS, 1752–1818

VIGOROUS writing of the same kind occurs in the *Essay on the Life of the Honorable Major-General Israel Putnam*, 1788, by David Humphreys, aide-de-camp to Washington and first minister to Portugal. One famous passage in the *Essay* describes Putnam's descent into the cave, a rope attached to his foot. With his gun he put an end to the marauding wolf. Humphreys won a local reputation as a poet. His brief verses, *On Life*, in his *Miscellaneous Works*, 1804, have grace and feeling. His longer poems, such as *The Armies of the United States*, 1780, and *The Industry of the United States*, 1794, are very nearly absurd.

ABIGAIL ADAMS, 1744–1818

BESIDES these somewhat rough narratives there appeared occasionally letters and journals of a gentler temper. Abigail Smith Adams was the wife of John Adams and the mother of John Quincy Adams, both presidents of the United States, but her letters are merely those of a gracious, intelligent matron of the eighteenth century. She gives us vivacious glimpses of Madame Helvetius in France crying out, "Hélas! Franklin," and giving the Doctor a double kiss; of the Ambassadors' Ball at St. James'; and of the city of Washington in the second presidency.

129   From the portrait, 1800, by Gilbert Stuart, in the possession of the Adams family, Boston

J. HECTOR ST. JOHN DE CRÈVECŒUR,
1731–1813

AN extraordinary book of the period is the *Letters from an American Farmer*, 1782, by J. Hector St. John de Crèvecœur, a Frenchman by birth, who had been educated for a short time in England, and who was American chiefly because of his passionate faith in her future. For a score of years (1759?–79) he was "an American Farmer." The letters, really essays, describe, as in *What is an American?*, conditions preceding and during the Revolution; or the life on Nantucket with its perilous forays on the deep; or slavery in the South; or such themes as a battle between snakes, and the habits of bees and birds. Crèvecœur is in a random way a naturalist, and has been called "an eighteenth-century Thoreau." There is a romantic strain in this Frenchman. When he contemplates his family and his fireside, he cries out: "I cannot describe the various emotions of love, of gratitude, of conscious pride which thrill my heart, and often over-flow in involuntary tears." Yet this aspect of Crèvecœur has been exaggerated. Newly-discovered letters, *Sketches of Eighteenth-Century America*, 1925, show him as realist in his pictures of frontier life. He tells with exact care how to build a wagon or mend a fence or keep off mosquitoes. Moreover, he is now revealed as a staunch Tory. In *Landscapes*, one of the earliest attempts in America to write drama, he satirizes bitterly the persecutions of Loyalists by patriot committees. Crèvecœur is one of the most original and powerful writers of the era of the Revolution.

130   From St. John de Crèvecœur, *Sa Vie et ses Ouvrages*, Paris, 1883, after the original portrait, 1786, in the possession of Countess Marie de Crèvecœur, Paris

BENJAMIN FRANKLIN, 1706–90

IN his thrift Benjamin Franklin was, perhaps, as Carlyle said, the "Father of all Yankees," but deeper qualities explain his amazing career, which really begins when he leaves Yankeeland and breathes the freer air of Pennsylvania; and which ends when the poor printer's devil becomes a European statesman and a friend of kings. Franklin's forceful and versatile nature was a concentration of that American rationalistic democracy which had undermined Puritanism. Its watchword was the free play of thought; it encouraged science, practiced success, and created literature in the image of common sense.

131   From the bas-relief *The Reception of Franklin by Louis XVI in 1778*, executed by Frederic Brou, on the Franklin statue, Paris

132 Franklin the Student, from Benjamin
Franklin, *Autobiography*, New York, 1849,
drawing by J. G. Chapman (1808–89)

THE YOUTHFUL FRANKLIN

"O POWERFUL goodness!" Franklin prayed in his youth, in the country of the Mathers, ". . . Increase in me that wisdom which discovers my truest interest." This interest, he early determined, did not reside in polemical divinity or in his copy of *Pilgrim's Progress*, which he sold. On signing the indentures as a printer's apprentice, he rejoiced that he now had access to "better books." At evening he borrowed a book; he read far into the night; and at dawn he returned it. All this reading was "useful." The descendant of Northamptonshire blacksmiths never dreamed of entering the world of Jonathan Edwards — or of Dante or Shakespeare, neither of whom he mentions.

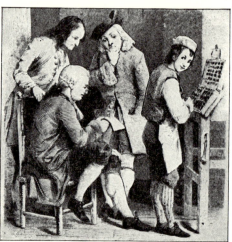

133   From Benjamin Franklin, *Autobiography*, 1849,
drawing by J. G. Chapman

ATTEMPTS AT LITERATURE

FRANKLIN quotes Pope, and imitates Addison, on whose writing he thought, with a characteristic touch of complacency, he occasionally improved. To imagine him slipping an anonymous paper under the printing-office door of his brother's *New England Courant*, and hearing later the favorable comments of the editors, suggests the maiden aspiration of a man of letters. But Franklin was ambitious of becoming "a tolerable English writer," not for the fame which raises the clear spirit. He did it precisely as he "put on the humble inquirer and doubter," or mastered Cocker's *Arithmetic*. He is grateful that he escaped being a wretched poet, and says that "prose-writing has been of great use to me in the course of my life, and was a principal means of my advancement." During his lifetime Franklin poured out vast quantities of this utilitarian prose: on baths, balloons, chess, chimneys, government, religion, and scores of other subjects. The undistinguished *Busybody Papers*, 1728–29, are favorable examples of his writing in these early years. Franklin would doubtless be surprised to find posterity taking him seriously as a man of letters. He is another in a long list of American men of action who have written acceptable prose in hours of leisure. His virtues as a writer were, at this time, those of the exemplary schoolboy: brevity, clarity, force, simplicity.

No. 474.

THE
AMERICAN
Weekly Mercury,

From TUESDAY *January* 28th, to TUESDAY *February* 4th, 1728-9.

Mr. ANDREW BRADFORD,

134   Facsimile of first *Busybody Paper* in *The American Weekly Mercury*,
January 28, 1728, in the Historical Society of Pennsylvania

POOR RICHARD'S ALMANACK

YET Franklin had something to say. He was the embodiment of
the useful virtues, and his pithy style lent itself pleasantly to hard
maxims about life which have worn well. In 1733 he began *Poor
Richard's Almanack*, a handbook of practical prudence which attained
immense popularity. For a long time ten thousand issues were sold
annually. Franklin was indebted partly to the vogue of the almanac
in the American home and partly to European aphorists whose
subtler dishes, when necessary, he boiled down to good, homely
porridge.

PROVERBS OF COMMON SENSE

SUCH gospel, and its expression in epigram, were natural to Franklin.
Like Lincoln, his knowledge of life slides easily into anecdote. Nor
must we forget how ready this materialistic age was for such texts
of philosophy. The sneer to-day at "Honesty is the best policy"
is a proof of the widespread assimilation of "Poor Richard." Such
sayings as "Creditors have better memories than debtors"; "Three
removes are as good as a fire," or "A small leak will sink a great
ship" have lost none of their truth. "Human felicity," says Franklin
in the *Autobiography*, "is produced not so much by great pieces of
good fortune, that seldom happen, as by little advantages that occur
every day; thus, if you teach a poor young man to shave himself and
keep his razor in order, you may contribute more to the happiness
of his life than in giving him a thousand guineas."

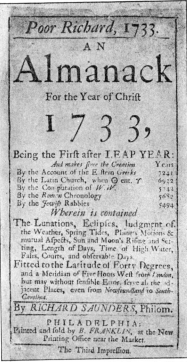

135 Title-page of the first (third impression) issue,
from the unique copy in the Historical Society of
Pennsylvania

136 From *Poor Richard Illustrated*, 1868, after the engravings by O. Pelton

137   From the painting *Franklin's Book Shop* by J. L. G. Ferris
in Independence Hall, Philadelphia

STATESMAN AND MAN OF LETTERS

A NARRATIVE concerning Franklin's successes belongs to history and not to literature, but we may guess at his position from Hume's remark when Franklin sailed for England in 1764 as the representative of Pennsylvania: "the first philosopher and indeed the first great man of letters" from America. From

FRANKLIN IN PHILADELPHIA

FRANKLIN's association with Philadelphia is almost a perfect realization of "Poor Richard's" ideals. His printing shop, his bookstore, and his own writings soon gave him the character of a local celebrity. Yet these achievements are by-products compared with his services to the growing city in science and government.

138   From the portrait, 1778, by Joseph Siffrein Duplessis
(1725–1802) in the Boston Public Library

now until the end of the Revolution Franklin, though a guiding spirit of the new nation, was in America little more than two years, spending, before his death in America in 1790, approximately a decade each in England and France. In both countries, he assumed easily the rôle of statesman and man of letters.

139   From the engraving *Mirabeau Arrive aux Champs Elisées*, by Masquelier
after the drawing by J. M. Moreau (1741–1814)

FRANKLIN IN EUROPE

FRANKLIN's successes as a diplomat, as one who stood before four kings, as an urbane ornament to French society, and his prodigious quantity of writing on the Revolution and on life, have given these years abroad an almost legendary charm. Pictures and anecdotes depict him at the tomb of Voltaire; with Madame Helvetius; or crowning Mirabeau upon the latter's arrival in the Elysian fields,

AN EIGHTEENTH–CENTURY AMERICAN

HISTORY and romance have had their will with Franklin. There have even been Chinese pictures of him, with almond-shaped eyes. Though his writing was enriched by long experience abroad, his pages are in the manner of an eighteenth-century American. His letters from 1764 to 1789 are an excellent record of the Revolution, seen through European eyes. And he had time also for those charming epistles to his English and French friends, for such immortal bits as *The Whistle*.

140   From O. L. Holley, *Life of Benjamin Franklin*, Boston, 1856, from the engraving by Anderson after the drawing by Morgan

141   From the painting, 1909, by Charles E. Mills in the Franklin Union, Boston. © Detroit Publishing Co.

THE RETURN TO AMERICA

THUS the residence abroad of the philosopher and scientist added ease and grace to his prose. When he finally returned to America in 1785 he might well be acclaimed as a man of letters, as well as a statesman. His writing is marked by variety, sincerity, and wisdom; and also by the dignity which comes only from strong thought. Sydney Smith used to threaten his daughter with disinheritance if she refused to admire all the writings of Franklin.

Although still uncollected, his many books include discussions of politics, government, science, and religion. He was regarded as an authority not only on the conduct of life but on literature.

AN EARLY EDITION OF FRANKLIN'S WORKS

THE best of Franklin as a writer is not in the curtailed editions of his *Autobiography*. In the combined *Autobiography and Letters*, 1868, so admirably blended by John Bigelow, may be read specimens of the Franklin who can be grave, gay, pungent, and weighty. Finishing the book, one marvels that from so great an intellect one world, that of the imagination, that of the inward eye, should have remained closed. The *Autobiography* describes with equal detachment Franklin's early life in Boston; his increasing success in Philadelphia; his dissipations in London; and the colonies' development. The book was written only after the exhortation of Franklin's friends, and ends with the year 1757.

DR BENJAMIN FRANKLIN.

142   Frontispiece and title-page of Benjamin Franklin, *Works*, New York, 1794, after the engraving by P. R. Maverick

143   From the painting *Dr. Franklin's Sedan Chair* by J. L. G. Ferris
in Independence Hall, Philadelphia

EFFECT OF THE REVOLUTION ON LITERATURE

THE growth of the nation aided literature in creating for it new ideals of independence, but the actual process was attended by changes so swift, so pitiless, that men born for lives of study were enlisted under the new flag, were tossed into prison ships, or engaged in the futile debates of political recrimination. Essayists became pamphleteers, and lyric poets turned satirists. The background of such men as Trumbull, Dwight, and Barlow is a provincial Connecticut town. The genuine poetical vein of Philip Freneau loses itself in vituperation. Meanwhile any one who can hum a tune writes jingles of "the cruel lords of Britain [or America] who glory in their shame." These were sung on the street corners and in camps or printed in the newspapers.

PATRIOTIC DRAMA

BEFORE, however, we pass from the prose to the poetry of this transitional era, we should glance quickly at the beginnings of American drama with its depiction of redcoats, Tories, Indians, or even of stories of antiquity. *The Patriot Chief*, 1784, by Peter Markoe, *The Battle of Bunker's Hill*, 1776, by Hugh H. Brackenridge, and plays by Andrew Barton, Robert Rogers, and others begin a relatively dull phase of our literary history. In Mercy Warren's *The*

145   Mercy Warren, 1728–1814, from the portrait by John Singleton Copley (1737–1815) in the possession of Winslow Warren, Dedham, Mass.

THE AGED FRANKLIN

ONE can hear his quiet chuckle as he reads Whitefield's letter full of his anxiety for the philosopher's welfare in the future life, and see him note down carefully his practical assurance that all will be well with him. "I wish you the same," he adds pleasantly. This world of ours, so very interesting and reasonably cheerful to the alert man, is fittingly described in the honest, sensible prose of the *Autobiography*.

TOM. GAGE's PROCLAMATION;
Or blustering DENUNCIATION,
(Replete with Defamation,)
Threatning Devastation,
And speedy Jugulation,
Of the New-English Nation.—
Who shall his pious ways shun?

WHEREAS the Rebels hereabout,
Are stubborn still, and still hold out;
Refusing yet to drink their Tea,
In spite of Parliament and Me;
And to maintain their bubble, Right,
Prognosticate a real fight;
Preparing flints, and guns, and ball,
My army and the fleet to maul;
Mounting their guilt to such a pitch,
As to let fly at soldier's breech;
Pretending they design'd a trick,
Tho' order'd not to hurt a chick;
But peaceably, without alarm,
The men of Concord to disarm;
Or, if resisting, to annoy,
And ev'ry magazine destroy:—
All which, tho' long oblig'd to bear,
Thro' want of men, and not of fear;
I'm able now by augmentation,
To give a proper castigation;
For since th' addition to the troops;
Now re-inforc'd as thick as hops;
I can, like *Jemmy* at the *Boyne*,
Look safely on—Fight you *Burgoyne*;
And mowe, like grass, the rebel *Yankees*;
I fancy not these *doodle* dances:—
Yet, e'er I draw the vengeful sword,
I have thought fit to send abroad,
This present gracious Proclamation;
Of purpose mild the demonstration,
That whosoe'er keeps gun or pistol,
I'll spoil the motion of his systole;
Or, whip his breech, or out his weapon,
As haps the measure of his Treason:—
But every one that will lay down
His hanger bright, and muskets brown,
Shall not be beat, nor bruis'd, nor bang'd,
Much less for past offences, hang'd;
But on surrendering his toledo,
Go to and fro unhurt as we do:—
But then I must, out of this plan, lock
Both SAMUEL ADAMS, and JOHN HANCOCK;
For those vile traitors (like debentures)
Must be tuck'd up at all adventures;
As any proffer of a pardon,
Would only tend those rogues to harden:—
But every other mother's son,
The instant he destroys his gun,
(For thus doth run the King's command)
May, if he will, come kiss my hand.—
And to prevent such wicked game, as
Pleading the plea of ignoramus;
Be this my proclamation spread
To every reader that can read:—
And as nor law nor right was known
Since my arrival in this town;
To remedy this fatal flaw,
I hereby publish Martial Law.
Mean while take all, and every one
Who loves his life, forsake his gun;
And all the Council, by mandamus,
Who have been reckoned so infamous,
Return unto their habitation,
Without or let or molestation.—
Thus, graciously, the war I wage,
As witnesseth my hand,————TOM. GAGE.
By command of MOTHER CARY,
THOMAS FLUCKER, Secretary.

144   From *The Pennsylvania Journal,*
June 28, 1775

Adulateur, 1773, five acts of blank verse, Brutus and Cassius impersonate rebels like the Adamses and Hancock. Mrs. Warren, satirist, poetess, and philosopher, was the wife of General James Warren of Plymouth, and a friend of Abigail Adams.

REVOLUTIONARY BALLADS

THE PROGRESS OF SIR JOHN BRAG, one of the countless ballads of the Revolution, intimates by title the nature of this poetical bickering: for every exploit a song, and for every song an antiphonal ballad. This was the glorious day of *Yankee Doodle*. Meanwhile *The King's Own Regulars*, *Bold Hawthorne*, and *Hale in the Bush* were among the best of this patriotic verse. Major John André was the subject of a ballad, *Brave Paulding and the Spy*, and was himself the author of the popular Tory song, *Chevy Chase*. All of these echo the folklore ballads, but show more enthusiasm than mastery of meter.

146 From the engraving by Hopwood, 1808, the portrait after the drawing by Major André

FRANCIS HOPKINSON, 1737–91

SOME of the most popular ballads of the Revolution were by Francis Hopkinson, a lawyer, a signer of the Declaration of Independence, and a lyric poet. Hopkinson was indeed much more; by nature and cultivation he was a clever writer. The plain-dealing John Adams speaks of him in a baffled way as "one of your pretty, little, curious, ingenious men."

147 From the portrait by Robert Edge Pine (1730–88) in the Hopkinson Collection, Historical Society of Pennsylvania

BATTLE OF THE KEGS

HOPKINSON'S turn for satire was nice, as his *A Pretty Story*, 1774, an allegory of the times, indicated. His *Battle of the Kegs*, 1778, roused inextinguishable laughter in Philadelphia at the British troops, who fired cannon and muskets, with fierce shouts for King George, at kegs of gunpowder, set afloat to annoy the British shipping.

BATTLE OF THE KEGS P. 372.

148 From James Thacher, *Military Journal During the Revolutionary War*. Hartford, 1834

JONATHAN ODELL, 1737–1818

THE natural medium for the intellectual patriot or Tory poet was satire. Patriots and patriots' descendants have laughed at the sharp couplets of Freneau and Trumbull, but it is profitable to recall that the most virulent and relentless of these satirists was a Tory, the Reverend Jonathan Odell of New Jersey. Odell cracks his verses, like a slave driver's whip, about the head of the atrocious traitor Washington or the meanest tattered rebel. Of Washington he writes: "Go, wretched author of thy country's grief, Patron of villainy, of villains chief." He likes, he says, to "twinge the proud flesh, and draw the face awry."

149 From Winthrop Sargent, *Loyalist Poetry of the Revolution*, Philadelphia, 1857, extra-illustrated by Emmet

TORY SATIRE

ODELL damns unwearyingly the dirty reptiles, the poltroons, the shirtless, shoeless gangs that will not celebrate the King's birthday. It is easy to understand the zeal of "these rats, who nestle in the lion's den" in running down this bitter Loyalist. They search his friend's house, but Odell is concealed in a secret room, and escapes to abuse: "Bostonian Cooper, with his Hancock joined"; "the lies of Paine"; Livingston, with "Gall in thy heart"; and all the swarming maggots and lice who fight under Washington. Odell never accepted the outcome of the Revolution. He preferred exile, and was probably proud of his reputation as the Churchill of the Revolution.

151   From Phillis Wheatley, *Poems on Various Subjects*, London, 1773

THE CONGRATULATION. A POEM.

Dii boni, boni quid porto? TERENCE.

JOY to great Congrefs, joy an hundred fold,
  The grand cajolers are themfelves cajol'd;
In vain has ——'s artifice been tried,
And Louis fwell'd with treachery, and pride,
Who reigns fupreme in heav'n deception fpurns,
And on the author's head his mifchief turns;
What pains were taken to procure D'Eftaing,
His fleet's difpers'd, and Congrefs may go hang.
  Joy to great Congrefs, joy an hundred fold,
The grand cajolers are themfelves cajol'd:
Heav'ns King fends forth the hurricane, and ftrips
Of all their glory the perfidious fhips.
His Minifters of wrath the ftorm direct,
Nor can the Prince of Air his French protect;
St. George, St. David fhow'd themfelves true hearts,
Saint Andrew and St. Patrick topp'd their parts;
With right Eolian puffs the winds they blew,
Crack went the mafts, the fails to fhivers flew;
Such honeft Saints fhall never be forgot,
Saint Dennis, and Saint Tammany, go rot.
  Joy to great Congrefs, joy an hundred fold,
The grand cajolers are themfelves cajol'd:
Old Satan holds a council in mid-air,
Hear the black Dragon furious rage and fwear;
Are thefe the triumphs of my gallic friends
How will you ward this blow, my trufty fiends?
What remedy for this unlucky job?
What art fhall raife the fpirits of the mob,
Fly fwift, ye fure fupporters of my realm,
E'er this ill news the rebels overwhelm,
Invent, fay any thing to make them mad;
Tell them the King——No, Dev'ls are not fo bad;
The dogs of Congrefs at the King let loofe,
But ye, brave Dev'ls, avoid fuch mean abufe.

  Joy to great Congrefs, joy an hundred fold,
The grand cajolers are themfelves cajoled
Courage my boys, difmifs your chilling fears,
Attend to me, I'll put you in your gears
Come, I'll inftruct you how to advertife,
Your miffing friends, your hide-and-feek allies
O YES!—if any man alive will bring
News of the fquadron of the Chriftian King,
If any man will find out Count D'Eftaing,
With whofe fcrub actions both the Indies rang
If any man will afcertain on oath,
What is become of Monfieur de la Mothe
Whoever thefe important points explains,
Congrefs will nobly pay him for his pains
Of pewter dollars what both hands can hold,
A thimble-full of plate, a mite of gold;
The lands of fome big Tory he fhall get,
And ftrut a famous Col'nel *en* brevet
And laft to honour him (we fcorn to bribe)
We'll make him Chief of the Oneida tribe.

150   Poem by Jonathan Odell, from *Rivington's Royal Gazette*, November 6, 1779

PHILLIS WHEATLEY, 1753?–84

A POETESS of the age, who, according to English admirers, might be prophetic of others to come in America, was Phillis Wheatley Peters, a negro slave, who published in London, in 1773, her *Poems on Various Subjects, Religious and Moral*. If Phillis Peters forecast anything, it was not good poetry from Africans. She is, however, apparently the first of our child-poet prodigies. Perhaps an African-born girl, writing at the age of twelve in Boston in the manner of Pope, would be a prodigy in any age.

JOHN TRUMBULL, 1750–1831

"TRUE WIT," said John Trumbull, in an essay written in boyhood, suggestive of his precocity, "is always accompanied with good nature, politeness, and a fine taste." Trumbull's satires do not always realize this ideal, but in scorpion-like wit not unmixed with a genial humor, they are superior to the billingsgate of Odell. Even the mastery, at an early age, of Watts and the *New England Primer* failed to dull the artist in Trumbull; his love of Steele and Addison must have been a corrective. A lawyer, a judge, and a devoted patriot, he composed often for the love of writing. After

152   From the miniature, 1794, by John Trumbull (1756–1843), in the School of Fine Arts, Yale University

the war he was in politics in Hartford. His *Elegy on the Times* appeared in 1774. Late in life he went west, and died in Detroit in 1831.

153   From John Trumbull, *M'Fingal*, New York, 1795, drawn and engraved by Elkanah Tisdale (1771–?)

The TORY'S Day of JUDGMENT.

M'FINGAL

TRUMBULL'S masterpiece is *M'Fingal*, 1775, a satire on the Tories, a creditable imitation of *Hudibras*, with a perceptible alloy of Trumbull, and incidentally, a stirring picture of that New England town meeting which Adams recommended for Virginia, as typical of the spirit of the age. The Scotch Tory M'Fingal excoriates the discontents, but afterward:

> Forthwith the croud proceed to deck
> With halter'd noose M'Fingal's neck, . . .
> Then lifting high th' pond'rous jar,
> Pour'd o'er his head the smoaking tar . . .
> And spreads him o'er with feathers missive,
> And down upon the tar adhesive: . . .
> Then on the two-wheel'd car of state,
> They rais'd our grand Duumvirate . . .
> And hail'd great Liberty in chorus,
> Or bawl'd, Confusion to the Tories.

So perish the enemies of bonfires and liberty poles!

The PROCESSION

154   From *M'Fingal*, 1795, drawn and engraved by E. Tisdale

The *New-Haven Gazette, and the* Connecticut *Magazine.*

(Vol. I.) Thursday, *December* 28, M.DCC.LXXXVI. (No. 46.)

NON SIBI SED TOTO GENITOS SE CREDERE MUNDO.

NEW-HAVEN: Printed and Published by MEIGS & DANA, in Chapel-Street. Price *Nine Shillings* per Annum.

American Antiquities No. 3

Extracts from the Anarchiad, on Paper Money.

Meſſrs Meigs and Dana,

THE readers of news papers through the ſeveral ſtates, in which the two firſt numbers of *American Antiquities* have been publiſhed, will doubtleſs remember that the ſubject of paper money was more than once mentioned. That ſubject I was ſo beautiful an epiſode in the *Anarchiad* that it would be unpardonable not to make extracts from it. All the epiſodes ought to have ſome reference to the promotion of the principal action,——as the underplots in a regular drama ſhould conſpire to the development of the main plot. Such is the ſuperlative advantages of this very poetical digreſſion. For it will ſcarcely be denied in any part of the United States, that paper money is an unfunded and depreciating condition, is happily calculated to introduce the long expected ſcenes of miſrule; diſhoneſty and perdition. On this point the citizens of the union muſt be conſidered as competent judges, becauſe they are inhabitants of the only country under Heaven, where paper (of that predicament) is by compulſory laws made of equal value with gold and ſilver.

The ſociety of critics and antiquarians, who have ſpared neither expence nor trouble, in recovering theſe valuable remains of antiquity from oblivion, cannot help flattering themſelves that their diſintereſted labours will continue to be rewarded with the plaudits of a grateful public. They are conſcious that the manuſcripts from which they have already given ſpecimens, as well as many other in their poſſeſſion, contain performances in poetry and proſe of a very different complexion from thoſe which commonly appear in American news papers. While they publicly acclaim all title to any merit in theſe productions, except that of antiquity in deciphering and preparing them for publication; they would aſk the ſeveral printers on the continent to peruſe them attentively and to publiſh, at leaſt, ſuch pieces as may be applicable to their particular ſtates. The ſociety, who are will henceforward proſecute their reſearches with redoubled diligence, only think it neceſſary to engage, on their part, that

nothing ſhall appear ſanctioned by them, unfavourable to freedom, literature or morality.

It is to be remarked that the following ſpeech is addreſſed, by the old Anarch, to a council of war, conſiſting of his compeers, his general officers and counſellors of ſtate.

Hail fav'rite ſtate, whoſe nurſing fathers prove,
Their faireſt claim to my paternal love !
Call'd from the deck with pop'lar votes elate,
The mighty *Jackſon* guides the helm of State:
Nurf'd on the waves, in bluſt'ring tempeſts bred,
His heart of marble, and his brains of lead,
My foes ſubdued while knav'ry wins the day,
He rules the ſenate with inglorious ſway,
Proud, *for one year,* my orders to perform,
Sails in the whirlwind and enjoys the ſtorm.
Yet not alone the per'lous watch he keeps,
His mate, great Q----n buſtles while he ſleeps;
There G----d----n ſtand, his head with quibbles fill'd,
His tongue in lies, his hand in forg'ry ſkill'd ;
To him, my darling knave, my lore I teach,
Which he to C----s lends in many a pompous ſpeech.
Oh Roguery ! their being's end and aim,
Fraud, Tendry, Paper-bills, whate'er thy name ;
That medium ſtill, which prompts th' eternal ſigh,
By which pageant villains flouriſh, ſmall ones die.
Plant of infernal ſeed, without hell's heat,
Say in what mortal ſoil thou deign'ſt to cheat ?
Fair from the Gen'ral Court's unpardon'd ſin,
Ap'ſt thou the gold Peruvian mines within;
Wak'd to new life by new creative power,
The preſs thy mint, and dunghill rags thy ore.
Where grows ſt thou not ? if vain the villain's toil,
We ought to blame the culture not the ſoil,

Fix'd to that Iſle, it no where paſſes free,
But fled from Congreſs, C----s dwells with thee.
Hail Realm of Rogues, renown'd for fraud and guile,
All hail, ye knav'ries of yon little Iſl
There prowls the raſcal cloth'd with legal pow'r,
To ſnare the orphan and the poor devour,
The crafty knave his creditor beſets,
And advertiſing paper pays his debts;
Bankrupts their creditors with rage purſue,
No ſtop—no mercy from the debtor crew.
Arm'd with new teſts, the licenſ'd villain bold,
Peſents his bills and robs them of their gold ;
Their ears, though rogues and counterfeiters loſe.
No legal robber fears the gallows-nooſe.
Look through the ſtate, th' unhallow'd ground appears,
A den of dragons, and a cave for bears,
A neſt of vipers mix'd with adders foul,
The ſcreeching night-bird and the greater owl.——
For now unrighteouſneſs, a deluge wide,
Pours round the land an overwhelming tide ;
And dark injuſtice wrapp'd in paper ſheets,
Rolls a dread torrent through the waſted ſtreets.
While net of law th' unwary fry draw in
To damning deeds, and ere they know theyſin :
New paper ſtruck, new teſts, new tenders made,
Inſult mankind and help the thriv ... de.
Each weekly print, new liſts of cheats proclaims,
Proud to enroll their knav'ries and their names;
The wiſer race, the ſnares of law to ſhun,
Like Lot from Sodom, from R---I --- run.
As it is vain to expect a whole epic poem, containing twenty four books, ſhould be republiſhed in a news paper, as it is equally impracticable to inſert all the names of the perſons who were principal actors in it; and as it is the wiſh of the ſociety to avoid the imputation of partiality; they direct me as far as in may be done to gratize no ſuch ſubaltern beings here on earth, by informing the public, that honorable mention is made of Mr. G---- I---- as well as of moſt of the horſe

155   Extracts from *The Anarchiad*, from the *New Haven Gazette and Connecticut Magazine*, December 28, 1786

THE "CONNECTICUT WITS"

THE restraint in Trumbull's satire and its relatively quiet irony are significant. These are hints of a new urbanity in American literature. It is not surprising to find Trumbull after the war in Hartford, meeting with David Humphreys, Joel Barlow, and others of literary tastes, such as Elihu Smith, Lemuel Hopkins, Richard Alsop, and Theodore Dwight. These made up the "Hartford Wits," or the "Connecticut Wits." United by common feelings about the war and postwar politics, they supported the Federalist government. In the *New Haven Gazette*, 1786, appeared extracts from the *Anarchiad*, a satire by Trumbull and his friends.

THE ECHO

LATER the "Connecticut Wits" ridicule the literary affectations of the time in satires which appear under the title of *The Echo*. The writhing victims, we hear, damn the authors and the publisher, but are impotent. They can only learn that these were written in "a moment of literary sportiveness," and that they were "printed at the Porcupine Press by Pasquin Petronius."

CONTEMPORARY SIGNIFICANCE

THE waggery of the "Connecticut Wits" or "Pleiades" has lost its edge, but it is possible to construct a charming picture of the little group that met,

156   From *The Echo*, Hartford, printed at the Porcupine Press by Pasquin Petronius, 1807, engraving by Leney after the drawing by Tisdale

perhaps at the "Black Horse Tavern" in Hartford, or at New Haven, talking of books or planning an issue of *The Echo*. In such small literary circles began an urban influence in American literature.

157   From the portrait drawn by Fournier, Paris, in the Massachusetts Historical Society

JOEL BARLOW, 1754–1812

JOEL BARLOW is one of those men of letters over whose memory the goddess of dullness broods, but whose actual life reads like a romance. In 1778 Barlow won, tradition says, a prize for poetry at Yale, and later was a chaplain in the army. At this point his orthodoxy ceased. He soon became connected with a newspaper, and he managed a printing office. He was, in turn, the agent in Paris for a doubtful land corporation, a political theorist in England with Horne Tooke, a French citizen, an ambassador on a special mission to Algiers, and a diplomatic fencer with Napoleon. Duyckinck mentions, among his services to the French government, assistance in organizing the territory of Savoy in 1793, and later a "memoir" denouncing the system of privateering. In spite of services to his country, there is something ineffectual and pathetic about Barlow's scattered efforts in literature. As he lay dying in a Polish village, on his way to meet Napoleon, he must have heard, this Connecticut Puritan, the uproar of the retreat from Moscow. He had dreamed all his life of political fraternity; perhaps in his delirium he heard the retreating footsteps of his enemies. His final effort in verse was a poem concerned with Napoleon. It was dictated to his secretary, Thomas Barlow, in December, 1812. Duyckinck, who saw the original manuscript, noted that it bore the head of Napoleon, and the words: *Napoleon Empereur des Français et Roi d'Italie.*

158   From *The Echo*, Vol. I, p. 4, engraving by Leney after the drawing by Tisdale

159   From Barlow, *The Columbiad*, 1807, engraving by
Anker Smith after the painting by Smirke

160   From *The Columbiad*, 1807, engraving by
Anker Smith after the painting by Smirke

GRANDILOQUENT VERSE — *THE COLUMBIAD*

BARLOW was a practical man of affairs. Undoubtedly his absurdity is connected with his grandiloquent conception of himself as a poet. He was fond of an endless flow of pentameter between covers of embossed leather. He consecrated poetry to patriotism; obviously a gigantic nation should have a gigantic epic. In college he hints that he is composing a monstrosity. In 1787, part of it appears as the *Vision of Columbus*, an earnest, in nine books, of the stupendous *Columbiad*, 1807. It is easy to ridicule the *Columbiad*. Haw-thorne suggested that it be dramatized with salutes of artillery and thunder and lightning. Certainly no heroism described in the poem is comparable to that of the reader who conquers its ten long books. Hesper, appearing to Columbus in prison, vouchsafes him the vision of Mexico, Peru, New England, and Virginia; the Indian wars, the Revolution, "pikes, muskets, mortars, guns and globes of fire." Columbus looks cheerily into the future, still further, and beholds something like the federation of the world. For this last reason, according to one eulogist, Barlow anticipated Tennyson, and in general power he surpassed Milton. More truly the *Columbiad* was, with its eleven engravings, "the most worthy work which had been published in America." Compared with the earlier *Vision of Columbus*, the *Columbiad* was less religious and more pedantic. Yet Barlow had talent. He could use the couplet, and the "darkness visible" in such pictures as that of the prison ship displays his imagination. The deficiency in Barlow was humorous self-criticism. He dared to believe himself an epic poet. We bless that keeper of the Savoyard inn who brought one day to the homesick New Englander his favorite dessert. *The Hasty Pudding*, 1796, dedicated to Mrs. Washington, is enough to prove that Barlow was a master of mock-heroic verse.

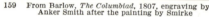

BOOK IV.   COLUMBIAD.   157

Her own resplendent essence. Thence expand
The rays of reason that illume the land;
Thence equal rights proceed, and equal laws,
Thence holy Justice all her reverence draws;   480
Truth with untarnish'd beam descending thence,
Strikes every eye, and quickens every sense,
Bids bright Instruction spread her ample page,
To drive dark dogmas from the inquiring age,
Ope the true treasures of the earth and skies,
And teach the student where his object lies.

 Sun of the moral world! effulgent source
Of man's best wisdom and his steadiest force,
Soul-searching Freedom! here assume thy stand,
And radiate hence to every distant land;   490
Point out and prove how all the scenes of strife,
The shock of states, the impassion'd broils of life,
Spring from unequal sway; and how they fly
Before the splendor of thy peaceful eye;
Unfold at last the genuine social plan,
The mind's full scope, the dignity of man,
Bold nature bursting thro her long disguise,
And nations daring to be just and wise.

161   Page of Joel Barlow, *The Columbiad*, Philadelphia,
1807

TIMOTHY DWIGHT, 1752–1817

ANOTHER epic of patriotic vastness was *The Conquest of Canaan*, 1785, by Timothy Dwight, soldier, farmer, minister, and college president. Again the command of the Muse, "Be thou dull," was obeyed. In vain are the conscientious couplets, in vain the addition of the Revolution amid the wars of Israel. *The Conquest of Canaan* is correct — and boring. This easy inclination by men without genius to the greatest of poetic forms must be ascribed, of course, to the lack of critical standards. Matthew Arnold's rebuke a century later to the lady poet of Ohio is directed toward the same tendency: a poet must have ability as well as patriotism in order to write noble verse. The contemporary interest in epics like Barlow's and Dwight's indicates the absence of general culture, but also the general conviction of the greatness of American destiny.

REV. TIMOTHY DWIGHT, S.T.D. LL.D.

162 From the *Analectic Magazine*, Vol. IX, 1817, engraving by Leney after the painting by Wood

163 Dwight's House in New Haven, from Duyckinck, *Cyclopedia of American Literature*, Vol. I, 1875

THEOLOGY, TRAVELS, AND EPICS

DWIGHT was not, like Barlow, so devoted to the epic; he was the author of narrative and lyric poetry, and a considerable body of prose. It was fitting that a grandson of Jonathan Edwards should publish five volumes of *Theology Explained and Defended*, 1818. The poet Southey liked his *Travels in New England and New York*, 1821–22. On the whole, aside from the stirring lyric, *Columbia*, Dwight's best writing is found in *Greenfield Hill*, 1794. This is bathed in the influences of Denham, Beattie, and Goldsmith. It contains ridiculous lines, but is a pleasant idyl of rural Connecticut.

164   A Southeast View of New Haven in 1786, from the *New Haven Chronicle* of that year

PHILIP FRENEAU, 1752–1832

A SATIRIST rivaling Odell in bitterness was the New Jersey poet, Philip Freneau. A classmate at Princeton of James Madison and Hugh Henry Brackenridge, and later a sea captain, Freneau became known in his own time as the chief gadfly of the Tories. "From an island," he sings of Britain, "that bullies, and hectors, and swears, I send up to heaven my wishes and prayers."

Like most satirists of the time, Freneau had his ears boxed by the Revolution. His eighty years, in spite of quiet days in the West Indies and at his New Jersey country home, were full of change. He was a school-teacher, lawyer, and a clerk under Jefferson. He paid as a penalty for his love of the sea the price of suffering on a British prison ship. Perhaps any one who can command both an American brig and an eighteenth-century periodical through stormy seas may lay claim to versatility, and Freneau's life, like his poetry, evinces this quality. He assisted Brackenridge with *The United States Magazine*, and was editor of the *National Gazette*, of Philadelphia.

165   From an engraved portrait, probably not authentic, in the Boston Athenaeum

ON JONES' "MEMORABLE VICTORY"

APART from the abuse — the fashion of the time — in Freneau's satires, there is a passion which carries him far. Reading the controversial poetry of the Revolution inures one to hearing Cornwallis called a swine or England a dragon's den. Freneau thumped the British and the Loyalists soundly, but his poetry of action, such as that on the victory of Paul Jones, gives us vivid glimpses of the grappling frigates, of sailors swarming over their sides with cutlasses — lets us hear the fierce crackle of the musketry. Freneau bore in many poems the stamp of his eighteenth-century models; he was often commonplace and didactic; but he possessed a lyrical gift. His poems of fancy are few, and when contrasted with similar English poetry of the same time, they appear faint. As productions, however, of the seething Revolutionary period they are unique.

Now Phœbus sought his pearly bed,
But who can tell the scenes of dread,
The horrors of that fatal Night!
Close up these floating castles came
Jones' Victory *page*

166   From Philip Freneau, *Poems Written and Published during the American Revolutionary War*, Philadelphia, 1809, after the drawing by John Eckstein

The Indian Chief who famed of yore,
Saw Europe's sons adventuring here,
Looked sorrowing to the crowded shore,
And sighing dropt a tear!
Prophecy of King Tammany. Page 269.

167   From Philip Freneau, *Poems Written and Published during the American Revolutionary War*. Philadelphia, 1809, after the drawing by John Eckstein

Ease off the curb bridle — give Ranger the whip;

168   Illustration for Freneau's poem, *The New England Sabbath Day Chace,* from *The Cabinet of Momus,*
published by Mathew Carey, Philadelphia, 1809

A PRECURSOR OF LATER TENDENCIES

SOME of Freneau's poetry, such as *The New England Sabbath Day Chace*, has humor. In *The Wild Honeysuckle*, and other poems, Freneau touches, very lightly, the still unworked, vast theme of American nature. The real awakening was not to come till years later, in Bryant. Yet some poems on trees, or plants, or bees are as sympathetic as the later poet's. And in the romantic poem, *The House of Night*, he is a gentle precursor of American literature's connection with the supernatural.

FRENEAU'S SIGNIFICANCE

HISTORICAL significance Freneau certainly has; again and again he hints what American poets may do, if only there may be peace and leisure. Freneau's dignity and strength in lyric poetry appear most clearly in the poem with the noble beginning:

> At Eutaw Springs the valiant died:
> Their limbs with dust are covered o'er;
> Weep on, ye springs, your fearful tide;
> How many heroes are no more!
>
> *   *   *   *   *
>
> They saw their injured country's woe,
> The flaming town, the wasted field;
> Then rushed to meet the insulting foe;
> They took the spear — but left the shield.

From this poem, apparently, Scott drew a line for *Marmion*. "The hunter and the deer, a shade!", a line from the felicitous *Indian Burying-Ground*, is echoed verbatim in Thomas Campbell's *O'Connor's Child*.

The INDIAN BURYING-GROUND

IN ſpite of all the learn'd have ſaid,
I ſtill my old opinion keep;
The poſture, that we give the dead,
Points out the ſoul's eternal ſleep.

Not ſo the ancients of theſe lands—
The Indian, when from life releas'd,
Again is ſeated with his friends,
And ſhares again the joyous feaſt. *

His imag'd birds, and painted bowl,
And ven'ſon, for a journey dreſs'd,
Beſpeak the na ure of the ſoul,
ACTIVITY, that knows no reſt.

His bow, for action ready bent,
And arrows, with a head of ſtone,
Can only mean that life is ſpent,
And not the finer eſſence gone.

Thou, ſtranger, that ſhalt come this way,
No fraud upon the dead commit—
Obſerve the ſwelling turf, and ſay
They do not *lie*, but here they *ſit*.

Here ſtill a lofty rock remains,
On which the curious eye may trace
(Now waſted, half, by wearing rains)
The fancies of a ruder race.

Here ſtill an aged elm aſpires,
Beneath whoſe far-projecting ſhade
(And which the ſhepherd ſtill admires)
The children of the foreſt play'd!

There oft a reſtleſs Indian queen
(Pale *Shebah*, with her braided hair)
And many a barbarous form is ſeen
To chide the man that lingers there.

By midnight moons, o'er moiſtening dews,
In veſtments for the chace array'd,
The hunter ſtill the deer purſues,
The hunter and the deer, a ſhade!

* The North American Indians bury their dead in a ſitting poſture; decorating the corpſe with wampum, the images of birds, quadrupeds, &c: And (if that of a warrior) with bows, arrows, tomahawks, and other military weapons.

169   Facsimile of a part of *The Indian Burying-Ground,* from Freneau,
Poems Written Between 1768 and 1794, Monmouth, 1795

CHAPTER IV

THE ERA OF WASHINGTON AND JEFFERSON

WASHINGTON'S advice to his troops not to huzza at Yorktown might have been given also to America's men of letters. The surrender of Cornwallis meant little to poets. The republic's first quarter of a century was not to be a period of repose, either for the country or for literature. Our population of five million souls was kept uneasy by attempts to stabilize the national debt, by the Indian wars, by the Louisiana purchase, and by wars with Tripoli and England. The old hatred of England flamed high. Yet, as the national danger was less, so the national unity, begotten of expediency during the Revolution, seemed evanescent. Not until Andrew Jackson's victory at New Orleans in 1815 did a wave of real national feeling sweep over the country.

A declaration of independence in politics did not secure freedom in literature. This continued imitative. Loud boasts of emancipation in prose and verse did not conceal our pitiful dependence upon English ideas and English literary forms. In spite of new magazines and larger libraries our culture grew slowly, and the literature of this brief transitory period is a postscript to that of the Revolution. Oration, essay, and poem echo the past: for an Otis, a Randolph; for a Paine, a Rush. Many men of letters, such as Timothy Dwight, write without change of manner in both epochs.

Yet such a view takes too little account of subtle changes. During these years the little urban communities flourished. In 1810 the population of New York numbered nearly one hundred thousand. So cosmopolitan a spirit as Washington Irving found it congenial. Definite traditions of writing had gathered about Philadelphia. Albany, Baltimore, Washington, and Charleston had now distinct associations with literature. Newspapers and magazines were growing rapidly. In 1810 there were three hundred and fifty-nine newspapers. Among the magazines were the *Port Folio*, Philadelphia, 1801–27, and the *Analectic Magazine*, Philadelphia, 1813–20. Nor could the patriotic desire of writers to be free of England in literature be without effect. Sensitive to criticism they were, but pride in native talent, whenever discovered, stimulated in turn original creative writing. One literary master of Charles Brockden Brown, a Philadelphian, was an English novelist, but no Englishman could have created some of the American scenes in Brown's novels. In fact, although we laugh at the patriotic motive in literature, as the inspirer of such leviathans as Barlow's, it must be reckoned with. The admission of five new states into the Union, the prospect of many more, the visions of manifest destiny which now occupied the minds of many thinking Americans created the desire for a great literature. This wish was not granted by a rub of the lamp, but the beginnings of the literature of the republic had their first impetus through this ideal.

This brief era of transition also points forward. If the speeches differ only in celebrating the Fourth of July instead of the Boston Tea Party; if the essays are as commonplace as ever, this is not true of poetry and other forms of literature These have the stir of life: American subjects, American dialect, American ideas.

The chief advance made by the poetry of the era lies in its variety. Satires persist. So do ballads. Perhaps the satires are as vituperative as ever, and perhaps it is fancy to find in *Hail Columbia* and *The Star-Spangled Banner* something finer than exists in the clinking ballads on Burgoyne or Nathan Hale. Possibly the Pope-inspired verse of Robert Treat Paine, and the narrative poems on New Orleans and Niagara might have been written during the Revolution. Even the romantic tales may be echoes of the new voices, Scott or Byron. Yet the vast quantity of lyrics, fanciful, witty, or humorous, the delicacy of verse like Washington Allston's — such phenomena argue something else. This was an increasing sense of a future in literature. The resemblance of *The Country Lovers* by Thomas G. Fessenden to James Russell Lowell's *The Courtin'* is only one instance of American writers beginning to use their materials. "I even journeyed," says a writer who was born about the time of the surrender of Cornwallis, ". . . to the summit of the most distant hill, whence I stretched my eye over many a mile of terra incognita, and was astonished to find how vast a globe I inhabited." This was Washington Irving, and he was writing of American literature.

An unknown land it was, but before 1815 there were explorers. In poetry, in the drama, writers timidly, and not without absurd failures, sought self-reliance. And now, nearly a century after *Robinson Crusoe* and the mighty growth of the English novel, they essayed fiction. The deep-seated Puritan prejudice against novels still prevented a bold use of American material. The scandalous young people in Jonathan Edwards' parish who had dared to read Richardson — such is the story — now had grandchildren who read Byron openly. Yet the old tradition lingered. One by-product of the decline of the rigorous faith was probably the moral tone in literature. It was this which so irritated our early Bohemian, Edgar Allan Poe, and it is this tone which eternally resounds in the early fiction. Our blind spot for native resources in literature was as evident in the early nineteenth century in fiction as it had been in the seventeenth in poetry. Our first great poet dealing with native subjects in poetry was to be Bryant; our first great novelist concerned with American subjects was to be Cooper.

In the writings of Mary Rowlandson or John Williams was the material for thrilling novels, but our first novelists, true to the sentimental type, turned from the near, and longed for the remote. Moreover, this natural sentimental strain was deepened by the prevailing mood of contemporary European literature. What had happened to the English novel since the vigorous realism of Fielding may be realized by comparing *Tom Jones* with Richard Cumberland's imitation of it in *Henry*, 1795, in which the amorous, beef-eating adventurer is become a prig with, says the *Analytical Review*, "a delicacy of honour, a firmness of virtue, and a generosity of sentiment." This was the day of the novel of sentiment, and our early lady novelists, such as Anne Bleecker and Susanna Rowson, were only too eager to perpetuate it.

Yet this fiction, too, is an omen. The tears of Richardson, Sterne, and Mackenzie dampen these pages, and the first American novelist, Charles Brockden Brown, is under the spell of the Gothic school, but often the subjects are American, and sometimes the manner reflects the energy of the new nation. In the seventeenth century excellent descriptions had been written, and during the Revolution fables and allegories had vogue. It was, after all, natural that the first novels should have been imitative. It is significant that they were being written at all, and that here and there were freshness and originality. Brown himself is a promise. His acute sense of the supernatural world, his interest in plot construction, and his glimpses of colonial life prophesy the American novel.

170   From the portrait by James Sharples (1751–1811) in
Independence Hall, Philadelphia

JOHN RANDOLPH, 1773–1833

"Damn George Washington," was once the toast at dinner of the high-strung, passionate John Randolph, in his opposition to the Federalist treaty. The moods of fury and tenderness of this strange statesman entered into his speeches, giving them often a thrilling intensity, and lifting them into the realm of literature. Josiah Quincy said that "the interest of Randolph's speeches was that he simply exposed his intellect and let you see it work." He bitterly opposed the Adamses, he admired Jefferson, though later dubbing him "Sir Thomas of Cantingbury," and he alternately insulted and caressed Daniel Webster.

172   From an extra-illustrated edition of Duyckinck, *Cyclopedia of
American Literature* in the New York Public Library

FISHER AMES, 1758–1808

Meanwhile, on the Federalist side, Fisher Ames, of Massachusetts, cries out: "What is patriotism? Is it a narrow affection for the spot where a man was born? . . . I see no exception to the respect that is paid among nations to the law of good faith. . . . It is observed by barbarians — a whiff of tobacco smoke or a string of beads gives not merely binding force but sanctity to treaties." Ames has less bite than the other orators, but he is a scholar, and can speak a graceful, classical eulogium of Washington. He observes the canons of that Revolutionary oratory which was to die at last with Edward Everett.

171   From the *Portrait Gallery of Distinguished American Citizens*, Hartford, 1846, after a silhouette from life by W. H. Brown

RANDOLPH — ORATOR AND PLANTER

Randolph's production was slight, but his finished malevolence, his culture, and the fire of a few speeches make him a worthy successor of the Revolutionary tradition in literary oratory. His background, too, is picturesque. One cannot see his lean, eccentric figure without thinking of his Virginia estate and its horses and dogs. He led, on the whole, a violent, tortured life, denouncing those whom he believed the enemies of his country in nervous, sinewy prose. An interesting view of him may be had from the *Letters of John Randolph to a Young Relative: embracing a Series of Years, from Early Youth, to Mature Manhood*, a book published in 1834.

EZRA STILES, 1727–95

EZRA STILES, president of Yale College, a writer on politics and religion, became almost a national leader. Learned even among the learned men of his era, he could teach in any department of the college, and he was known as a capable historian.

174 Benjamin Rush, 1745–1813, from the portrait by Charles Willson Peale (1741–1827) in Independence Hall, Philadelphia

MINOR ESSAYISTS

NINIAN PINKNEY describes his travels in Europe. William Ray recounts the story of Tripoli. Benjamin Thompson (Count Rumford) wrote his *Essays, Political, Economical, and Philosophical*, 1798, saying the good works of the celebrated Christian, Mr. Lay, will "exist and bloom forever." It may be. In any case the writings of these essayists will not. Even the later writings of the atheistical Mr. Paine, which appeared about a decade after the Revolution, are far more likely to put on immortality.

EZRA STILES S.T.D. LL.D.

Prefident of Yale College.

173 From Ezra Stiles, *History of Three of the Judges of King Charles I*, Hartford, 1794, engraving by Doolittle after the portrait by R. Moulthrop (1763–1814)

NOAH WEBSTER, 1758–1843

ONE of these universal essayists was Noah Webster. He was a Connecticut Yankee, and, although three years younger than Joel Barlow, was his classmate at Yale, and was later associated with the "Connecticut Wits." Webster's numerous pamphlets and essays lack distinction, but his learning was famous, and Americans read what he said of insurance, teaching, copyright, or the dangers of immorality. His spelling book, of which seventy million copies have been sold, was brought to remote Indian tribes and carried across the plains by immigrants.

175 From Noah Webster, *The Prompter*, Hartford, 1791

WEBSTER'S DICTIONARY

WEBSTER's chief interest was lexicography. Among his Hartford friends he listened quietly to the tongues of flame, but did not reply. He wrote no epics. One wonders what he thought of such amazing use of his beloved English words. He looks down in sculpture, not far from Jonathan Edwards, upon the hurrying undergraduates of his college, who consult, if they must, his Dictionary. Yet it may be truly said that his book is read more often and with more satisfaction than the epics of his friends Barlow and Dwight. His *Speller*, with its fables, appeared in 1783 and his *Dissertations on the English Language* in 1789. The first edition of the Dictionary appeared in 1828, a work of originality and merit. In its present form, however, it would scarcely be recognized by its author.

176 From Webster *An American Dictionary of the English Language*, Springfield, Mass., 1888

177 From the pastel portrait in the possession of Miss Ellen M. Dennie, Cambridge, Mass.

JOSEPH DENNIE, 1768–1812

OUR humble essayists were not without encouragement. Philadelphia, as during the Revolution, was a center of patriotic and political activity, and it also maintained literary traditions. The Irish poet, Thomas Moore, entertained there in 1804, praised excessively its literary coterie. They were, he said, "a sacred few." As we read the writings of these young hierophants, we believe more than ever in Moore's politeness and in his Celtic imagination; and less than ever in the literary value of what these Philadelphians were doing. Their leader was Joseph Dennie, a Harvard graduate, the author of *The Lay Preacher*, 1796, and editor of a weekly magazine, the *Port Folio*.

JOHN QUINCY ADAMS, 1767–1848

PERHAPS Moore admired Dennie's florid dress and large manner. It is difficult to understand how his contemporaries, if they really read the *Farrago* and the continuation of *The Lay Preacher* in the *Port Folio*, could call him, as they did, "the American Addison." The best that can be said of his writing is that it is pleasant and cultivated. As an ally he called in John Quincy Adams, who contributed some letters based on a journey through Silesia. Adams' career included the presidency of the United States and a professorship at Harvard, but even these glories could not snatch the *Port Folio* from dullness.

178 From the *Portrait Gallery of Distinguished American Citizens*, Hartford, 1846, after a silhouette from life by W. H. Brown

WILLIAM WIRT, 1772–1834

WILLIAM WIRT'S *Sketches of the Life and Character of Patrick Henry*, 1817, is an imaginative picture of the eloquent Virginian. Wirt in this book seems less a jurist, like Marshall, than a kindly romancer. One can think of him in the thriving city of Richmond; or listening to Jefferson's stories of Henry, building, as he wrote, the Patrick Henry legend. Wirt knew the life of the middle states at the beginning of the century. Though a Marylander he lived long in Virginia, and attained literary fame in the little Richmond circle, which was cultured, but like all these early groups, provincial. *The Letters of a British Spy*, 1803, and *The Old Bachelor*, 1810, suggest his manner of writing, rhetorical but not without charm.

179 Richmond in 1833, from an aquatint by W. J. Bennett after the painting by G. Cooke in Watts Hall, Union Theological Seminary, Richmond

180 From the *Portrait Gallery of Distinguished American Citizens*, 1846, after a silhouette from life by W. H. Brown

JOHN MARSHALL, 1755–1835

Two or three times only during this period did the talent for miscellaneous writing focus into solid and enduring works of prose. The American mind has always exhibited ability in historical and biographical writing, even before the vast *Magnalia* (No. 35). John Marshall's *Life of George Washington*, 1804–07, in five volumes, is not wholly superseded as a vigorous story of the colonies, the war, and Washington's achievements as president. Marshall had served as a soldier in the Revolution. He was a student of public life, and eventually became Chief Justice of the United States. He wrote that famous biography at the request of Washington.

BALLADS AND OCCASIONAL VERSE

THE days were past when the Rangers marched through a village with the fifes shrilling a popular ballad, while the tramping men sang perdition to King George and the Tories. Yet one type of later poetry was distinctly a survival of these songs. Pride in the new flag, or in the new navy, or old bitterness against the British gave us many a war ditty. Or the Fourth of July inspired a halting ode, or monstrous elegy on the death of Washington. Historians of literature have quoted such lines as those in the *Miscellaneous Poems*, 1801, of Jonathan M. Sewall:

Sage Adams for wisdom, with Pallas may vie,
And Washington equals a Jove!

181 From the painting, *Fourth of July in Center Square, Philadelphia, 1818*, by J. L. Krimmel (1787–1821) in the Historical Society of Pennsylvania

182   From the engraving by John Sartain (1808–97)
after the portrait by Thomas Sully (1783–1872)

JOSEPH HOPKINSON, 1770–1842

IT was, however, the expectation of war with France in 1798 that led Joseph Hopkinson, in this vein of poetry a true son of Francis Hopkinson, to write *Hail Columbia*. No marching men could chant, much less remember, these grandiose words, but the singers at the theaters could, and with the aid of a popular melody the poem resounded throughout the nation.

HAIL COLUMBIA

ALTHOUGH *Hail Columbia* was written in the anxious days when war between France and the United States was almost a certainty, no allusion occurs in the song to the issues in the quarrel. It was the purpose of the author to write a song above personal or political differences. Night after night it was sung by crowds in the streets of the large cities. *Hail Columbia* has long since joined the group of American songs which many commend but few sing.

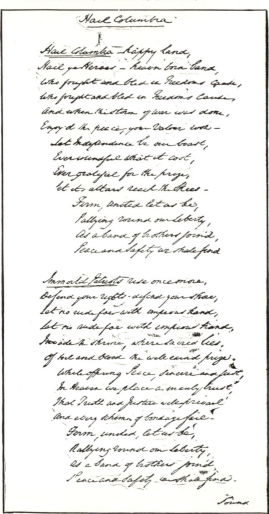

183   From the original Ms. in the Historical Society of Pennsylvania   184   From the original Ms. in the Historical Society of Pennsylvania

FRANCIS SCOTT KEY, 1780–1843

THE STAR SPANGLED BANNER, also, presents a difficult feat for the average voice and memory, but no one may question its sincerity; nor is it without beauty as a poem. This song is hallowed by more than a century of use, and its origin is known to every American. After the anxiety of the night attack on Baltimore in 1814, Francis Scott Key saw "by the dawn's early light" the colors still flying over the ramparts of Fort McHenry. Key's other poems are worthless.

POLITICAL SATIRES

185 From the portrait by Charles Willson Peale (1741–1827) in the Pennsylvania Academy of Fine Arts. © Detroit Publishing Co.

186 From a copy of the first publication in the Yale Collection of American Literature

YET patriotic songs like *The Star Spangled Banner* seem buried under the mass of political abuse. Democrat and Federalist smote one another in satire which, though rough enough, now appears blankly undistinguished. Dust lies heavily on *The Democratiad*, 1795, *The Guillotinad*, 1796, or *The Political Green-House*, 1798, a joint composition by Lemuel Hopkins, Richard Alsop, and Timothy Dwight. This last, a rather clever badgering of Francophile Democrats, is superior to collections like the *Olio*, 1801, or the anonymous satires on the manners of the day.

SOCIETY AT THE CLOSE OF THE EIGHTEENTH CENTURY

AN immigrant to America at about the ending of the century would have found there a picturesque society of ladies of quality, adventurers, Puritans, trappers, and Indians. The romance of all this left little impression on such a newcomer as Mathew Carey, but he thought America a veritable promised land.

187 From the painting *The Christmas Coach*, by J. L. G. Ferris in Independence Hall, Philadelphia

The Gallows rises to his view.
His steps a host of foes pursue;

188   From Mathew Carey, *The Porcupiniad*,
                    Philadelphia, 1799

MATHEW CAREY, 1760–1839

CAREY easily became a representative of an energetic, uncultivated civilization. As an editor and publisher he wrote on various phases of American sociology. For not a single line of this writing, he afterwards boasted, did he receive a cent of money. Carey replied to William Cobbett's slurring *Peter Porcupine* pamphlets in the *Porcupiniad*, 1799, a burlesque whose force raises it somewhat above the level of the ordinary satires of this era. Carey also wrote *Olive Branch*, 1814, *Vindiciae Hibernicae*, 1818, and in 1833–34 published in the *New England Magazine* his autobiography.

THOMAS GREEN FESSENDEN, 1771–1837

THOMAS GREEN FESSENDEN's satire, *Terrible Tractoration*, 1803, modeled on *Hudibras*, advocates the virtues of Perkins' metallic tractors for physicians. Most of Fessenden's poetry, like his life, lacked breeding. He had humor, however, and some of his homely lyrics, notably *The Country Lovers*, made dexterous use of American materials.

189   From Thomas Green Fessenden, *Terrible Tractoration . . . by Christopher Caustic, M.D.*, New York, 1804, engraving after the drawing by A. I. Stansbury

SENTIMENTAL LYRICS

FESSENDEN is one of a number of satirists who wrote poems of sentiment. These bouquets of "pretty" poetry were now to become only too characteristic of American literature. The obvious cause was lack of genius; a contributing factor was the imitation of European poetry. St. George Tucker's graceful poem, *Days of My Youth*, seems like the forerunner of a thousand lyrics on youth, old age, death, and God.

190   St. George Tucker, 1752–1828, from the *St. Memin Collection of Portraits* in the New York Public Library

WILLIAM CLIFFTON,
1772–99

A LEADER of the Philadelphia group was William Cliffton, who sang pleasantly of unclouded days and "chaplets for thy spangled hair." He is a faint, very faint Collins. Cliffton coarsely assailed the democratic spirit of the time in a longer poem called *The Group*, published in 1800.

WASHINGTON ALLSTON,
1779–1843

OR we turn to Washington Allston, a truly artistic spirit with a lyrical gift, a South Carolinian who lived long abroad, and was a pioneer in American painting. Allston had won the regard of Coleridge, whom he mourned in a sonnet as his "most loved, most

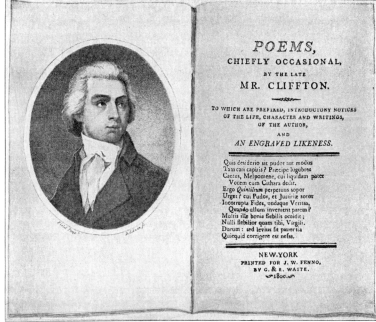

191   Frontispiece and title-page of William Cliffton, *Poems*, New York, 1800, engraving by David Edwin (1776–1841)

honored friend." On his return from Europe he lived in Boston and Cambridgeport, and married a sister of Richard Henry Dana. He continued his studies of art and prepared a course of lectures which were unfinished at his death.

193   From the painting by Washington Allston in the Metropolitan Museum of Art, New York

192   From *The New Mirror*, 1843, drawing by D. C. Johnston (1797–1865)

THE SPANISH GIRL

SUCH poems as *Rosalie* or *The Sylphs of the Seasons*, 1813, are sufficient proofs of Allston's poetical talent. Yet these are tales of little meaning unless we care for the maiden reveries of "gentle Rosalie" or the languid melancholy of Inez, the Spanish girl. His *Monaldi*, 1841, written about 1822, is a melodrama with an Italian background.

GRAY'S ELEGY.

194   From the *New York Magazine*, 1797, engraving by Tanner

THE INFLUENCE OF ENGLISH POETS

THE American poets of this generation were as much affected by the influence of Byron, Scott, and Wordsworth as their ancestors had been by that of Pope. Besides poems of fancy there are tales of adventure. The romantic hero faces death on the wild sea, or in the forest. Or the rural maid tells her simple story of sorrow. The short-lived magazines published pictures under the spell of Gray, Rousseau, and other eighteenth-century Europeans.

195   From the portrait, 1829, painted on wood by George W. Appleton (1805–31) in the Maine Historical Society

JOHN NEAL, 1793–1876

ONE finds tepid solutions of Byron or Wordsworth in the poetry of Sarah Morton, Lucius Sargent, John Linn, or Henry Knight.

196   From R. T. Paine, *Works in Verse and Prose*, Boston, 1812, engraving by E. Tisdale after the portrait by G. Stewart [*sic*]

Collins and Gray and even Pope still had their followers in America. *The Battle of Niagara*, 1818, was perhaps the best, chiefly because of its passages on American scenery, of John Neal's numerous volumes. Neal is an amusing epitome of certain American literary characteristics of this time. He was a "down-easterner" with various occupations, who journeyed to England, where he became a disciple of Jeremy Bentham and a contributor to *Blackwood's Magazine*. His adventurous life is told in his *Wandering Recollections of a Somewhat Busy Life*, 1869.

ROBERT TREAT PAINE, 1773–1811

ONE of the belated followers of Pope, Robert Treat Paine (originally Thomas), had, paradoxically, some of the characteristics of Byronism. His poem for the Phi Beta Kappa Society in 1797, *The Ruling Passion*, is a faithful echo of the eighteenth-century poet, but few Phi Beta Kappa orators have enjoyed so Bohemian a life as Paine. Because of his anxiety not to be confused with the wicked Tom Paine the Massachusetts legislature altered his name, a step, one feels, quite as fortunate for the pamphleteer as for the poet,

ADAMS AND LIBERTY

PAINE's career reminds us of Poe's, except that here is ability instead of genius. He was successively business man, journalist, lawyer, and dramatist. Wit and enthusiastic free-living, combined with facility in verse, were enough to win him a remarkable local reputation in staid Boston. Paine shocked Americans dreadfully, but he became a legend. Both his prose and his verse have life, and the patriotic song *Adams and Liberty*, 1798, although an unconscious satire on the form of the ode, was celebrated.

ALEXANDER WILSON, 1766–1813

NEVERTHELESS, in spite of vagaries, poetry after the Revolution was increasingly concerned with American life, especially with American nature. Alexander Wilson, distinguished by the usual versatility of the time, a pedlar, a weaver, a schoolteacher, and an editor, published in seven volumes *American Ornithology*, 1808–13. Wilson was also a poet, for the most part in the manner of Cowper or Crabbe. His long narrative poem, *The Foresters*, 1809, dwells delightedly on American scenery and American life: Niagara, the mountains in autumn, and humble homes. Such a lyric as *The Bluebird* is sentimental, but is genuine in feeling and keen in observation.

198   The Foresters, from the *Port Folio*, Vol. II, 1809

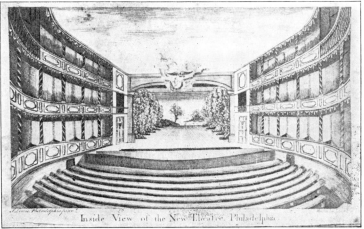

197   From the broadside, 1798, in the Genealogical Society of Pennsylvania

BEGINNINGS OF AMERICAN DRAMA

THE increased liberty in literature induced interest in the drama. This had had its beginnings in Revolutionary days, but the frowns of Puritans and Quakers, as well as the lack of culture, had delayed development. By 1760, however, there were theaters in New York and Philadelphia. Magazines allude repeatedly to the drama. At the former place in 1787 appeared the first play from the pen of an American, acted by professionals. (Thomas Godfrey's *The Prince of Parthia* had been acted in 1767 by amateurs.)

199   From the *New York Magazine*, 1794, engraving after the painting by S. Lewis

200   From Royall Tyler, *The Contrast*, Philadelphia, 1790, engraving
after the drawing by William Dunlap

202   From the portrait by Charles Ingham (1797–1863) in the
National Academy of Design, New York

THE CONTRAST

THIS drama was *The Contrast*, by Royall Tyler (1757–1826), a graduate of Harvard and finally Chief Justice of Vermont.   The subject was — how modern it sounds! — the difference between the traveler veneered by European society and the rustic American — a thin and conventional play.   In it, however, is the Yankee servant, Jonathan, who delivers his jokes with a New England twang.

201   From William Dunlap, *Rinaldo Rinaldini*, New York,
1810, engraving by J. Kennedy

WILLIAM DUNLAP, 1766–1839

MORE noteworthy, both as a man and a dramatist, was William Dunlap, author of *The Father*, 1789, *Leicester*, 1794, *André*, 1798, and of prose works valuable to-day as sources: *A History of the American Theatre*, 1832, and the lives of *George Frederick Cooke*, 1813, and *Charles Brockden Brown*, 1815. Dunlap also translated from Kotzebue and other sentimental dramatists.   He includes in his plays the Yankee type, a fact which is significant; and his technique has a certain cleverness.   Taken together, Tyler and Dunlap suggest the advance made in the drama since the wooden episodes of Mrs. Mercy Warren.

203   From the portrait by Henry Sargent (1770–1845)
in the Massachusetts Historical Society

204 From Jeremy Belknap, *The Foresters*, Boston, 1792, after
an engraving by Seymour

JEREMY BELKNAP, 1744–98

THE unique contribution of these years was fiction. Gothic romance, the novel of sentiment, the redskin, and other elements are strangely jumbled, but the fact remains that there are novels, and occasionally one that rewards the reading. Jeremy Belknap's *The Foresters*, 1792, describes in allegory form the clearing out of John Bull's wilderness, and, incidentally, of John Bull himself from America. This parable is a survival of a fictional form popular during the Revolution. Belknap, who was one of the founders of the Massachusetts Historical Society, wrote a *History of New Hampshire*, 1784, and two volumes of *American Biographies*, 1794–98.

AMERICAN NOVELS

LACHRYMOSE novels abound, such as Mrs. Ann Eliza Bleecker's *The Story of Henry and Anne*, 1793, and John B. Linn's euphoniously named *History of Elvira* and *Augustus and Aurelian*, but, as a balance to these, are the rough, thumping novels — modeled particularly on Smollett, but also on Swift, Rabelais, and Cervantes. These are imitative, but in this raw country a real sympathy exists between the shin-kicking sailor of Smollett and the rough-and-ready American of 1800. Dr. Updike Underhill in Royall Tyler's *The Algerine Captive*, 1799, is a lively ship's surgeon.

The greatest prose of this *genre* came from Washington Irving in 1809, and will be noticed later. The background for some of these novels is the American city, Philadelphia, or old Boston.

205   Mrs. Bleecker, from *The Posthumous Works of
Ann Eliza Bleecker*, New York, 1793

206 From Hugh Henry Brackenridge, *Modern Chivalry*, Philadelphia, 1846, after a drawing by F. O. C. Darley (1822–88)

208 From Brackenridge, *Modern Chivalry*, 1846, after a drawing by F. O. C. Darley

SENTIMENTALITY BURLESQUED

THE merriest of these early novelists, apart from Irving, was Hugh Henry Brackenridge, 1748–1816, a classmate of Freneau and the author of the early American drama, *Bunker Hill*, 1776. Captain Farrago's treatment of the bearer of the challenge was not more summary than Brackenridge's booting of sentimentality. The picture might be a symbol of this group of novelists.

207 From Brackenridge, *Modern Chivalry*, 1846, after a drawing by F. O. C. Darley

MODERN CHIVALRY

MODERN CHIVALRY: or, The Adventures of Captain Farrago and Teague O'Ryan, His Servant, 1792–1805, is a wild, rollicking satire on democracy, with side dishes of the author's observation and humor. Carlyle might have enjoyed this *reductio ad absurdum* of the "ballot-box" method. Teague, fresh from the bogs of Ireland, is elected to high office. Grant the premise, not improbable in this America, and Teague's humiliations are suggestive as well as comical. Brackenridge was steeped, he himself says, in Cervantes and Swift. He loved a buffoon. If the satire lacks delicacy, it has vigor. It was published in Pittsburgh in two parts, in 1796 and in 1806. *Modern Chivalry* is far better than Brackenridge's stiff drama, *The Death of General Montgomery*, 1777. Teague's dialect is strange, but he seems to be a real Irishman.

BRACKENRIDGE'S VERSATILITY

BRACKENRIDGE was no less hearty than the rascals he created. He was at various times a teacher, an editor, and a student of divinity. During the Revolution he was an army chaplain, later a member of the Supreme Court of Pennsylvania, and a dabbler in poetry — he wrote, in fact, a masque, in verse-form reminiscent of *Comus*.

209 Hugh Henry Brackenridge, from the portrait, about 1810, by Gilbert Stuart, courtesy of Joseph McKibbon, Minneapolis

210 From Sarah Wentworth Morton, *The Power of Sympathy*, Boston, 1789, after an engraving by Samuel Hill

NOVELS OF SENSIBILITY

ONE wonders, after all, if these slashing burlesques can be called novels. It must be confessed that as novels they are very far from the real narrative interest of *Roderick Random*. The softer mood is more popular. "I love," says Mademoiselle V. in Ann Bleecker's *The History of Maria Kittle*, 1793, "to indulge these divine sensibilities." Mrs. Sarah Morton's *The Power of Sympathy*, 1789, the so-called first American novel, does this, at least. And *The Story of Ophelia* is full of this type of sensibility. Mrs. Morton also wrote *Ouâbi, or The Virtues of Nature*, 1790, an Indian story in verse, and in 1823 a miscellany, *My Mind and Its Thoughts*.

CHARLOTTE TEMPLE

THE lady writers of the American sentimental novel reiterate that their stories are founded on fact. *Charlotte Temple*, 1790, and *Lucy Temple*, 1828, may have a connection with truth, but it is truth through the eyes of the most sentimental of schoolmistresses. Mrs. Rowson, the daughter of a British naval officer and of a Boston lady, began her career as a novelist in England. The design of her first novel *Victoria*, 1786, is, she says: "to improve the morals of the female sex by impressing them with a just sense of the merits of filial piety." In 1793 she opened her school for girls near Boston. *Sarah, The Exemplary Wife*, 1813, with its motto "Do not marry a fool," is reputed to be autobiographical.

211 From Susanna Rowson, *Charlotte Temple, A Tale of Truth*, New York, 1829

ELIZA WHARTON.

212   From Hannah Webster Foster, *The Coquette*,
New York, 1831

FEMALE QUIXOTISM;
Or, the Extravagant Adventures of
DORCASINA SHELDON.
VOL. II.

Page 205.

BOSTON:
Published by J. P. Peaslee.
1825.

213   From Tabitha Tenney, *Female Quixotism*,
New York, 1825

THE COQUETTE

PERHAPS there is more fiber in *The Coquette; or, the History of Eliza Wharton*, 1797, by Mrs. Hannah Webster Foster, 1759–1840. Mrs. Foster was a minister's wife, living in Brighton, Massachusetts. Her correct tales for young ladies were very popular. *The Coquette* is deeply in debt to the novels of Richardson.

FEMALE QUIXOTISM

TABITHA TENNEY in *Female Quixotism*, 1808, tried the interesting — and unsuccessful — experiment of a novel which included the roughness of Smollett but omitted his oaths and improprieties. We may, if we please, denounce Smollett, but let us never expurgate him! To read *Female Quixotism*, and to learn that it was long popular, is to have a depressing notion of the taste of the age.

CHARLES BROCKDEN BROWN, 1771–1810

IN comparison with these writers Charles Brockden Brown, who has been christened the first American novelist, looms up a giant. Brown's novels have the faults of his time: he is heavily in debt to the Gothic romance and to the novel of sentiment, as well as specifically to Godwin, De Quincey, and other Europeans. Yet he possessed the instincts of a true novelist. In his life Brown, like his contemporaries, suffered diversion to the law, to journalism, and to other pursuits. His nature was sweet; it was that primarily of the artist; and in his early death there is the mood of youthful tragedy. Certainly it was a misfortune for American literature. About his story clings the pathos of unfulfilled aspiration.

214   From a miniature, 1806, by William Dunlap (1766–1839),
courtesy of Herbert L. Pratt, New York

THE QUALITY OF BROWN'S WORK

In 1797 appeared the now rare *Alcuin*. Between 1798 and 1804 Brown wrote six novels, and, although *Wieland*, 1798, may still be considered the most imaginative, the others show his accumulative mastery over weaknesses, and his firmer control of the form of the novel. His last book was written when he was less than thirty-five years old. Fancies are useless, but who can help wondering, in consideration of this development, what Brown might have done at the age of fifty? All these novels reflect an interest which amounted to a spiritual passion: the unseen world of darkness and horror. *Clara Howard*, 1801, and *Jane Talbot*, 1801, are of lower quality.

BROWN AND THE LITERATURE OF TERROR

In *Ormond*, 1799, the title character is a sinister and mysterious presence. *Edgar Huntley*, 1799, includes a horrible scene in a pit which is a genuine contribution to the literature of terror. *Arthur Mervyn*, Part I, 1799; Part II, 1800, is like the cold grip of a nightmare with its deliriums, murders, and hideous burials. And no one who reads *Wieland* will forget the religious maniac as he confronts his

215 From the portrait by James Sharples in Independence Hall, Philadelphia

wife, with the divine command to strangle her. This sketch of the novels cannot fail to suggest their crudeness and melodrama. What unfortunately it will not do is to convey the passionate intensity in these scenes which brings them within the domain of true art.

For Brown's intimations of the dreadful forces that lie about us approach those of the mystic. His maniacs and criminals are apt to be, moreover, like those of the English romantics of gloom, men of high endowment. Clara in *Wieland* cannot forget the face of the unhappy, gifted Carwin. Brown, though he is not didactic, is fond of hinting thus at the price which the gods often exact from genius. This is, of course, a concept found often enough in Shelley and Byron, with whom Brown has some affinity.

216 From Charles Brockden Brown, *Jane Talbot*, Philadelphia, 1801, after a drawing by Seymour

WEAKNESS AND POWER

Much of this writing is marred by imperfect technique. Turgid language, anti-climaxes, lack of motivation are merely a few of Brown's faults. The tremendous scenes in *Wieland* lead up to the most absurd of *dénouements*, and it is doubtful if any one is stirred again in reading this novel, after he learns that Wieland has been deceived by a ventriloquist. Brown imitates unwearyingly. He shows us the Indian, and professes to write of Pennsylvania, but, after all, his backgrounds are shadowy. He belongs to the romantics and their dark corner of art, the Gothic novel. Yet he has something more. He has lived with these; they are his masters; but he is himself. The first novelist of America impresses us with the originality of his genius.

217 From the bronze bas-relief by R. Tait McKenzie (1867–) in the Franklin Inn Club, Philadelphia

CHAPTER V

THE KNICKERBOCKER GROUP

BEFORE turning to the Knickerbocker writers it is suggestive to look for a moment at some wider aspects of American life. During the years between 1815 and 1870 the Americans created a nation, and before the latter date they could point to a national literature. What Emerson wished for the country in 1837 was, in greater measure, true of its literature by 1870: "We will walk on our own feet; we will work with our own hands; we will speak our own minds." Socially, politically, and intellectually this period of growth is complex. Two changes in procedure become essential: to follow in less detail the social and political changes underlying this literature; and to abandon, when convenient, a precise chronology. Thus, as one example, the amazing influence of the frontier may be studied, but not the local effects of the land systems; slavery, but not the Missouri Compromise or presidential policies. Similarly, to trace American writers by precedence of birth would be unwise, meaningless indeed, compared with the significance investing them in certain natural groups.

Such groups are at once distinct and overlapping. The Knickerbocker writers, whose leaders were Irving, Cooper, and Bryant, have a unity of their own. Yet if Thoreau and Alcott are unusual in our philosophical literature, they are bound by countless ties to the writers of poetry, fiction, and history, such as Longfellow, Hawthorne, and Parkman. Names like these indicate another emphasis. What is wealth in one age is poverty in another. Fame in the colonial era might well spell mediocrity in this golden age. Charles Brockden Brown is a humble artist beside a Hawthorne or a Poe. This means a general elevation of standards. Americans wrote as busily as ever, and anthologies, collections of nineteenth-century literature, and ever-multiplying magazines overflow with obscure names which cannot be discussed here. The founding in 1815 of the *North American Review* heralded a score of reputable monthlies and quarterlies, among them the *New York Mirror*, 1823–42, the *American Quarterly Review*, 1827–37; the *New England Magazine*, 1831–35; *The Knickerbocker*, 1833–60; the *Southern Literary Messenger*, 1834–64; *Graham's Magazine*, 1840–50; *Harper's Monthly*, 1850–; *Putnam's Magazine*, 1853–57 and 1867–69; and the *Atlantic Monthly*, 1857–. The names of the new writers seem often more obscure because they live in the age of Emerson. For the first time our criterion may resemble more nearly the famous touchstone of Matthew Arnold: the best that has been thought and said in the world — rather than the best written in America.

Affecting all these natural groups are the general factors in American life so often mentioned in this volume: the farm, the sea, the frontier, and the city. The backgrounds of each group will be considered in due place. Just now it is interesting to survey the fifty-five years to 1870 as a whole, in the light of these powerful influences. Two others demand attention, two other influences less tangible, but mighty as molding forces: the influence of Europe, particularly of England; and the peculiar temper of the American mind. During these impressionable years the nation's character was forming. Our special outlook on life has been variously described. It involves the many qualities which, although we share them with other nations, we have come to call "American": resourcefulness, self-reliance, energy, belief in equality, freedom in religion, sense of manifest destiny, — in short, apart from its abused connotations, American idealism.

Hector St. John de Crèvecœur was thankful that it was his lot to be an American farmer. For more than two centuries, whether a stony Vermont pasture, or a vast Virginia estate, the agricultural community was a typical unit of American life. Even in 1800 more than ninety per cent of the total population dwelt outside the cities. Yet neither the early huts of the Puritans nor the colonial mansions of the Tories had inspired genuine literature. Jefferson no more than William Byrd, nor Freneau more than Anne Bradstreet were inclined to think of the rural background as literary material. Crèvecœur's *Letters from an American Farmer* has no parallel in American literature of the eighteenth century.

Now in the nineteenth century that romance which was beginning to settle down over fading adventure included the New England farm. Some New England families had lived for several generations about the same hearthstones. The inevitable traditions of community and home life, of local customs, and even of language had grown up. The modern poetess who sang movingly of "My New England" echoed what was in the hearts of an earlier people who, not knowing, like their fathers, the hills and wolds of England, looked with affection on the stern hills of New Hampshire or the majestic Connecticut River. We begin to hear of the Merrimac country, the Berkshires, the Hudson, and the Susquehanna. There is a marked increase in the appreciation of rural life. Emerson is not happy away from the village of Concord; Lowell writes in the dialect of a Massachusetts Yankee; and Whittier rivals Cowper and Burns in his poems of humble life in New England. The farm became in the nineteenth century important in two ways: its life was a theme for literature, and it led to our first poetry of nature. Bryant was a farmer's boy.

Meanwhile in the South the farm had another story. It is unlikely that William Byrd or John Randolph, as they rode about their huge tracts of land, foresaw the agonizing conflict which this system was to create. Thomas Jefferson thought the slavery in these agricultural communities a passing evil. Yet writing then with an eye of prophecy he might have described the endless fields of cotton and sugar cane, the debarking of blacks for slave labor, the fulminations of the righteous Northerners (who did not need slave labor), the semi-feudal communities with culture and poverty side by side, John Brown on his way to execution, Fort Sumter, Gettysburg — and more, much more. The direct influence of the southern communities on literature is less apparent, but their indirect effect was enormous: the writing of a Simms, a Stowe, a Lincoln, or an Everett may be traced to their influence. Remote as all this seems from the stone walls of New England, it is in essence the history of another phase of the American farm.

As the farms multiplied, and the Americans conquered the wilderness, felling forests, building roads, linking waterways, and pushing the frontier back ever farther to the West, another and different sort of frontier continued its challenge to American courage. The first frontier of the Puritans was the sea. Elizabethan seamen made possible the colonies of New England and Virginia. These children of an island nation wrested their first food from the sea. From the frontier of the forest they built the ships to conquer the frontier of the sea. Bradford, Winslow, and Strachey write of the power, the terror, and the beauty of the ocean. Millions of Americans were destined to be inland dwellers, but the history of the battle with the sea of the coast communities of New England, New York, or of California, is as thrilling as those of the maritime empires of Greece, Scandinavia, or Venice. Masefield realizes for us three civilizations in three short stanzas on the quinquireme, the Spanish galleon, and the dirty British coaster; and an equally vivid history of the past stirs the imagination in the names of the West Indian merchantmen, the Nantucket whaler, the Rhode Island slaver, the privateer of 1776 or 1812, "the great ship of Salem," the frigate *Constitution*, the Black Ball packet, or the Baltimore clipper. Much of the wealth, and hence of the aristocracy of America has originated in mastery of the sea, in peace;

and in war the sea has been a factor in both national preservation and national tradition. In the eighteenth century rose and fell the great class of wealthy traders; and in the nineteenth century flourished our new merchant marine. Yet we turned from the sea to river, lake, and prairie; we are essentially an inland people. The sea as a primary interest in our life has been intermittent, but it has always been an important element in national growth.

The influence of the sea on our literature is less important than that of the farm, but it is far from negligible. The call of the running tide, "the clear call that may not be denied," is in our blood. The largest number of admirals come from a tiny state without a seacoast; and many a western farmer's lad has had no peace till he has seen the white clouds flash through the rigging of his tall ship. Cotton Mather tells a good sea-story, in relating the adventures of Sir William Phips against Quebec. Crèvecœur in his *Letters* is aware of the beauty of the ships at Martha's Vineyard. John Paul Jones' blunt narrative lets us see the Yankee man-of-war. America has had no Masefield, but the nineteenth-century poets, like Longfellow, are, however slightly, under the spell of the sea. This life on a narrow strip of Atlantic beach dominates the poetry of a Celia Thaxter. The culmination of this spirit in our literature is in nineteenth-century fiction. Its strength is manifest when so esoteric a genius as Poe attempts a sea-narrative. Richard Henry Dana, Jr., concentrates in a single novel all that Americans have felt of the sea and sea-life: its cruelty, beauty, and romance. And Cooper, like Barlow and Freneau, a man of letters who has been knocked about in the forecastle, can create characters on a lurching, storm-driven vessel, sailing that ship with accuracy enough to convince a modern sailor. Some of these characters possessed a reality which has made them by-words among Europeans.

Cooper was even more sensitive to the conquest of the continent itself. He read of Indians, watched the covered wagons and oxcarts roll westward, and himself a pioneer in spirit, knew both the uses and the mystery of the wilderness. The advance of the American frontier has no exact parallel in history. It represents a unique battle of a practical but romantic race with the unknown. Year after year the ax rang out in the forest. Leatherstockings suddenly broke through the brush into the clearing on the mountain and stared down at new promised lands of valley, river, and the dim blue of mysterious mountains. Up the rivers to their very sources sped canoes, guided by hardy woodsmen. Across the plains rumbled the caravans of New Englanders and southerners. One hears of a fort called Chicago. Mrs. Trollope sails slowly, for seven weeks, up the Mississippi, and in the village of Cincinnati cannot sleep for the trampling of hogs beneath her window. It is the most romantic period in American history. On the frontiers gathered Puritans, adventurers, immigrants, and a hundred different types of humanity.

The actual achievements between 1815 and 1870 were stupendous. By 1820 one third of the population of the United States of nine and a half millions was in the West. The purchase of Louisiana had given the country an area equal to one third of Europe. The great Northwest was opened. Travelers were silent before the hushed beauty of the Canadian Rockies. Canals and roads developed internal commerce. State after state was admitted to the Union. Mechanical inventions hastened the great task: Fulton's first voyage up the Hudson on the *Clermont*, or Mark Twain's up the Mississippi on the *Aleck Scott* or the *Grand Turk* are symbols of the conquest of American rivers. Haste indeed was a watchword. The settler blazed a trail, built a lean-to, and pressed on. Afterwards the railroad burrowed through the mountains, then bridged the great rivers, ever farther west. The effect of this was to leave vast tracts of land unexploited, and by 1870, although there had long been towns on the Pacific coast, there were unsettled regions which well deserved the name of frontier. Not until 1890 did a great historian declare that "the frontier has gone, and with it has closed the first period of American history."

The impression made by the frontier upon writers prior to 1815 need not be reemphasized here.   Cooper was the greatest of all writers of the frontier simply because he expressed the inarticulate feeling of many Americans since Captain John Smith about this tremendous influence in American life.   Most Americans in contact with the frontier have been both realists and romanticists.   The pioneer has killed its Indians and its bison; he has navigated its rivers; and he has cultivated its lands.   Then he has also felt, even when in its relentless grip, that beyond its rim — yes, always just beyond — lay the world of romance, the land of noble savages, of still more fruitful lands and streams.   Moreover, as the passage of time softened the ugly aspects of the frontier, he looked back and wove romance about past perils; King Philip, Massasoit, and the early frontiersmen became heroic.

No one has ever made these deep feelings of the American so articulate as Cooper. Writers, however, so different as Crèvecœur and Charles Brockden Brown had already felt their spell, and in the nineteenth century, besides Cooper, many writers rehearsed the story of the frontier.   James K. Paulding wrote an American *Westward Ho!* and a novel called *The Backwoodsman*, 1818; and Mrs. Trollope found everyone talking about Timothy Flint's *History and Geography of the Mississippi Valley*, 1827.   Bryant sings of the redskin in the mood of romance.   Washington Irving goes west and writes *Astoria*, and Walt Whitman is an urbanite turned frontiersman.   Parkman's histories raise tacitly the issue about the truth of Cooper's pictures of the frontier, and numerous minor writers, such as the ethnologist, Henry Rowe Schoolcraft, tell the story again and again. If, as has been said, the frontier is the most important fact in American history, it is a defensible position to claim a similar place for it in American literature.

Meanwhile, behind the frontier grew up the city.   Between 1820 and 1840 the population of the cities expanded at twice the rate of increase of the country as a whole.   Before the Civil War cities owed their existence to internal and foreign commerce, particularly the latter.   Boston, New York, Philadelphia were the results of the influence of the sea. This increase was due also to a general tendency to seek the centers, and to the opportunities in the public lands, many of which were laid out in city-lots.   Another equally important cause was the increase in home industries.   Puritan thrift had built its own chairs, wagons, and utensils.   With the increase of population it was natural to concentrate this skill in the shop or factory.   The Embargo of 1807, Slater's cotton-spinning machinery, and the invention of the cotton gin imparted stimulus to national manufactures. It became a mark of patriotism to use home products, and Madison's appearance at his inauguration in a coat made from the products of Colonel David Humphreys' farm evoked enthusiastic approval.   A result of the vigorous life on the frontier and in the cities was a new zeal for making large fortunes.   Speculation in land and in manufactures increased the wealth of individuals and of the nation.   Stimulated by this wealth the cities grew in number and in population, till in 1860 sixteen per cent of the total population of the United States lived in the cities.

The effect of such centers upon literature has already been noticed.   The little Connecticut River settlement of Hartford had given a background to Barlow, Dwight, and Trumbull.   Philadelphia had literary traditions.   With the increase of population sprang up the cheerful life of cities: libraries, magazines, and newspapers; clubs and societies. Washington Irving found New York life in the early nineteenth century not unlike that of Addison's London.   In the same city Bryant became the editor of our first great newspaper.   Poe was a magazinist in New York, Philadelphia, and in the southern cities.   All of these men write with more or less urban distinction, and some of them are frankly contemptuous of American rural life.   The easy access to books and good conversation, and the contact with other writers creates a new tone in our literature.

The influence of the city upon American literature between 1815 and 1870 is most definite in the years preceding the Civil War.   In Boston and Cambridge, which now redoubled its old prestige as a university town, a group of scholars, wits, poets, and historians, most of them graduates of New England colleges, answer the charges of crudeness preferred by British visitors. Oliver Wendell Holmes, a physician, is, perhaps, with his pride in Boston, and his distilled wit, the best representative of the manner of this Brahmin caste of New England, which returned the derision of the raw West with cool indifference. All of the group were known favorably abroad. Longfellow and Lowell had reputations as scholars, and Emerson, though a later New England writer sneered at his "Concord" culture, is singularly detached from provincial America. When Emerson is in Liverpool in 1848 Arthur Hugh Clough receives from him "an impression of perfect intellectual cultivation." "This Emerson," Carlyle writes in a recently published letter to John Stuart Mill, "proves to be a very notable man."

Emerson himself, in a letter to Carlyle, speaks of this "great, intelligent, sensual, avaricious America." Yet Emerson was disinclined, like a few of his countrymen, some of the New England Brahmins among them, to seek as a remedy a transfusion of the virus of European culture. His clear voice bids independence. Notwithstanding this, European influence, always an important factor, was regnant between 1815 and 1870. Ships brought over European books — without copyright. Wealth permitted travel, and many cultivated Americans elected to live abroad. Two alternatives seemed possible: servile imitation in art and literature, or a crude independence. Instances of the former are everywhere. It is enough, perhaps, to point out the allusive, reminiscent tone of much worthy prose and, particularly, poetry. In reading Poe, one thinks of the German, Hoffman; in reading Longfellow and Lowell, recur faint indefinable echoes of a dozen poets. The names of praise, however the recipients deplored them, suggest the general temper: Cooper is "the American Scott," and Bryant "the American Wordsworth." Nevertheless, there are signs of emancipation. The Americans are hurt by the comments of "Boz" and Mrs. Trollope, but in the meantime the French are hailing Poe as a genius, and in 1855 came the strong voice (or "barbaric yawp") of Whitman.

Besides these influences of the farm, the sea, the frontier, the city, and the condescension of cultivated Europe, there is another which shaped American literature, less definite still — at once an influence upon literature, and a result of these other factors. We have already called it by the cant name: American idealism. It is, perhaps, nebulous, indefinable. It represents the traits of American thought which in these years attained a certain permanence, and it still seems to most of us an integral part of the American mind. These traits created literature.

One dominant idea of the age was a leveling democracy. All others bring us back to this: Jacksonianism, the struggle against slavery, the creation of the West, the amassing of wealth, even, though he might have denied it, the philosophy of Emerson. Americans wished a government, a society, and a system of education by which men might, so far as possible, start equals in the contests for life's prizes. The world has watched the great experiment and has noted its virtues: energy, ambition, self-reliance. The world, moreover, has not been wholly silent about these virtues, but its vices indeed it has proclaimed to the skies. Not the worst, but the most irritating, was that of "American brag." During this time we hear of this from every visitor. Another is *gemeinheit*, our commonplaceness. "They have begotten," says Carlyle, "with a rapidity beyond recorded example, eighteen million of the greatest bores ever seen in the world before — that hitherto is their feat in History." These last gentry, it must be conceded, are not favorable for the creation of a great literature. But the virtues were. Traveler after traveler noted the earnestness of the Americans. The most hostile felt in this people an overwhelming, almost an absurd hope and faith in the future. Yes, the rude immigrant who built his cabin on the edge of the forest was an idealist. "Manifest destiny," is the name given to one phase of this national feeling. The Americans dreamed dreams. This faith is in Franklin; it is in Paine, Crèvecœur, Jefferson, Daniel Boone, and in millions of humbler men.

All that was needed was literary material. It had always existed, but Americans had been too busy. Now it suddenly became evident. An excellent suggestion of our lack of tradition is afforded by taking the railway journey between London and Edinburgh, and then by traversing the same distance between any two cities in America. Here we see an occasional battle field; there we behold streams, hills, and buildings which cry aloud of the ancestral life of the past. Here no grim castles; no cathedral lifted high above an ancient town with its memories of Norman lord, Scottish chieftain, or British king. No thatched cottages along the quiet, mediæval road. Instead the factory, the wooden house, the glimpse of Main Street. Yet now in the nineteenth century began the change of attitude. We rubbed our eyes and saw the Puritan, the Virginian, the old colonial college, the prairie schooner, the camps of California, the Indian, the unequaled natural scenery of the West and Northwest. These became, as never before, the material for literature. Through the New England farm of Whittier, the Concord bridge of Emerson, the ferryboat of Whitman, the steamboat of Mark Twain, the boarding-house of Holmes, the dour Puritans of Hawthorne, American thought was to express itself in literature. Early in the century the life of the villages and cities in the valley of the Hudson, and the larger life of America that lay to the westward, furnished literary materials for that group which has come to be known as the Knickerbocker writers.

To many the word "Knickerbocker" still means Washington Irving. To others it conjures up our early triumvirate of letters: Irving, the essayist; Cooper, the novelist; Bryant, the poet. Happier still is the reader to whom the word suggests the quaint little city of the nineteenth century, complacent in its coterie of half urban, half Bohemian journalists and poets. Poe and Whitman were New Yorkers, too, if partly by adoption, but we think first of the company of early Knickerbockers — so grave and so gay — who teased the town, who meditated on its ways, and who created its beginnings in poetry.

To the lively village with its gabled architecture and its weighty Dutch families, Irving owed much. He knew fashionable Lower Broadway, Upper Pearl and Nassau Streets, and when he returned from Europe in 1806, pavement had been laid on Broadway as far as City Hall! Fitz-Greene Halleck, it is said, once remarked that nearly all his New Year's calls were made below Canal Street.

Here more than a century ago top-hatted gentlemen, in bottle green, crimson, or purple, escorted their crinolined ladies to their Dutch-built houses, and then, dropping into an inn, chuckled over the *Salmagundi Papers* of this clever young Irving. Do the ladies pass the afternoon reading "the first American novel," *The Power of Sympathy?* That is James K. Paulding entering 17 State Street, the home of William Irving, brother of the essayist. He means, perhaps, to attend a meeting of the wits. To-night there is a party. On the way home one guest falls through a grate, but others have the same misfortune, and there in the cellar they prolong the gayety. In October and November of 1809 literary notices appear concerning the disappearance of the mysterious Father Knickerbocker. Certain respectable Dutch families are sure that Mr. Irving has now gone too far!

In 1815 Irving again sets sail for Europe. When Bryant arrives in 1825 from the Berkshires, he finds still an air of levity about literature. In 1813, the devoted friends Fitz-Greene Halleck and Joseph Rodman Drake, both in young manhood, lounge about their boat, deep in the poems of Thomas Campbell. In a pine grove in Love Lane, now the intersection of Sixth Avenue and Twenty-First Street, the two poets abandon themselves to the delights of stories, verse, and music. In 1823 Cooper is living in Beach Street, and about this time Halleck remarks to General Wilson that "Cooper is the colonel of the literary regiment; Irving lieutenant-colonel; Bryant, the major; while Longfellow,

Whittier, Holmes, Dana, and myself may be considered captains." Some of the New England officers in this company were to outstrip the lieutenant-colonel, but not yet. This was the day of New York in literature, a New York which in the 'thirties sheltered at times Poe, Cooper, and Bryant, besides jaunty "Nat" Willis. It was then, however, no longer a village. Bryant was to live on, and behold it a great city.

Their debt to New York these writers paid in some of the best American prose and poetry. The achievements of Irving, Cooper, and Bryant were very different, but each owed to the growing city friendships, talk, and intercourse of clubs and society, and the consciousness that they were American writers. In the early years of the century, its cultural life was more meager than that of Philadelphia. After 1819 its prestige developed rapidly. Here was a group of intellectual men who might well stimulate a boy from Cummington, Massachusetts, or Guilford, Connecticut. Under its kindly influence Irving and James K. Paulding touched lightly social satire. Nor was it merely the city itself. Father Knickerbocker disappeared in the direction of Albany. It was toward the traditions of the Hudson that Washington Irving turned his eyes; near Sleepy Hollow, in the Catskills, lingered legends which he was to perpetuate in American literature, with pathos, with finished wit. Cooper looked farther west, to the frontier, but in New York he wrote three of his novels. Bryant's fifty-three years in New York, as editor and publicist, were not an unmixed blessing for poetry. Yet we hesitate to think of Bryant without the influence of Father Knickerbocker. In spite of the old Dutch gentleman's unpaid bills, he was a benignant soul; he gave Bryant and Cooper, as well as Irving, his blessing.

218   From the engraving by A. H. Ritchie after the painting by Thomas Hicks, 1866

AUTHORS OF THE UNITED STATES, MID-NINETEENTH CENTURY

Reading from left to right: first row, seated, Miss Sedgwick, Mrs. Sigourney, Mrs. Southworth, Longfellow, Bryant, Halleck, Irving, R. H. Dana, Margaret Fuller, Channing, Mrs. Stowe, Mrs. Kirkland, Whittier. Second row, standing, Kennedy, Holmes, Willis, Mitchell, Morris, Poe, Tuckerman, Hawthorne, Simms, P. Pendleton Cooke, Hoffman, Cooper, Prescott, Bancroft, Parke Godwin, Motley, Beecher, Curtis, Emerson, Lowell, Boker, Bayard Taylor, Saxe. Left staircase, Mrs. Mowatt Ritchie, Prentice, Alice Cary, G. W. Kendall. Right staircase, Cozzens, Gallagher, Stoddard, Mrs. Amelia Welby.

YOUNG WASHINGTON IRVING, 1783–1859

WHILE Cooper was preparing for Yale at the Cooperstown village school, the boy Irving watched from the city pierheads the ships sailing for Europe, or wandered with gun and dog in the Catskills. Romance had already marked him for her own.

SALMAGUNDI

IN 1802, just before the eight-year-old Bryant began to write his first verses, occurred another omen of the future: Irving contributed letters to the *Morning Chronicle*, New York, under the name of Jonathan Oldstyle. Then, a year after his return from Europe, appeared on January 24, 1807, the first number of *Salmagundi*, a periodical in the style of the *Spectator*, on the oddities of the town, among these "The Little Man in Black" and "Launcelot Langstaff, Esq."

219 From a carte de visite after the portrait, 1820, by Gilbert Stuart Newton (1795–1835)

220 From *Salmagundi*, New York, 1820, engraving by Alexander Anderson

221 From *Salmagundi*, New York, 1820, engraving by Alexander Anderson

SATIRICAL PICTURES OF NEW YORK

THE twenty numbers of *Salmagundi*, though halting and tepid when compared with later coruscations from Lowell and Holmes, show that Irving had found a natural medium. His papers are better than those of his collaborators, and they anticipate his later urbanity. "Launcelot Langstaff" is no longer funny, but his sayings amused merry old New York, which took kindly to the authors' proclamation: "Our intention is simply to instruct the young, reform the old, and castigate the age." Today these essays, especially in comparison with Irving's later writings, seem amateurish, but the satirical pictures of New York society, or such a figure as "My Uncle John," forecast Irving's art.

222 From *The Beauties of Washington Irving*, London, 1835, engraving by Thompson after a drawing by George Cruikshank (1792–1878)

FATHER KNICKERBOCKER

In *Salmagundi* was the origin of that "small, brisk-looking old gentleman, dressed in a rusty black coat, a pair of olive velvet breeches, and a small cocked hat," who, vanishing up the Hudson, left a book to pay his bill for lodgings.

This book, dedicated to the New York Historical Society and published in Philadelphia, set up a shout of mirth which echoed from Albany to Abbotsford, where Walter Scott read it aloud to his family and declared: "Our sides have been absolutely sore

223   From Washington Irving, *A History of New York . . . by Diedrich Knickerbocker*, New York, 1812, engraving by Kneass after a drawing by Strickland

with laughing." Scott discerned the hidden satire, realizing that an important target was Thomas Jefferson. In the story of the reign of William Kieft may be discerned many parallels to incidents in the life of the stateman.

DISTRESSING.

. Left his lodgings some time since, and has not since been heard of, A small elderly gentleman, dressed in an old black coat and cocked hat, by the name of KNICKERBOCKER. As there are some reasons for believing he is not entirely in his right mind, and as great anxiety is entertained about him, any information concerning him left either at the Columbian Hotel, Mulberry-street, or at the Office of this paper will be thankfully received.

P. S. Printers of Newspapers would be aiding the cause of humanity, in giving an insertion to the above.

Oct. 26.

224   Preliminary Notice, from the *New York Evening Post*, Oct. 26, 1809

HIS HISTORY OF THE DUTCH DYNASTY

DIEDRICH KNICKERBOCKER'S *A History of New York*, 1809, suggested to Irving and his brother Peter by an old guide book or history of New York, is a well-sustained and robust burlesque of the world's progress from its creation till — Irving intimates a climax — the "end of the Dutch Dynasty" in New York. One by-product of the history is the light it sheds on the wide and varied reading of Irving.

To the Editor of the Evening Post.

SIR,

Having read in your paper of the 25th Oct. last a paragraph respecting an old gentlemen by the name of *Knickerbocker*, who was missing from his lodgings; if it would be any relief to his friends, or furnish them with any clue to discover where he is, you may inform them, that a person answering the description given was seen by the passengers of the Albany Stage early in the morning, about four or five weeks since, resting himself by the side of the road, a little above Kingsbridge—He had in his hand a small bundle tied in a red bandana handkerchief; he appeared to be travelling northward, and was very much fatigued and exhausted.

A TRAVELLER.

225   From the *New York Evening Post*, Nov. 6, 1809

LITERARY NOTICE.

INSKEEP & BRADFORD have in the press, and will shortly publish

A HISTORY OF NEW-YORK,

In 2 vols. duodecimo, price 3 dollars, Containing an account of its discovery and settlement, with its internal policy, manners, customs, wars, &c. &c. while under the Dutch government: furnishing many curious and interesting particulars never before published, and which are gathered from various manuscripts and other authenticated sources, the whole being interspersed with philosophical speculations and moral precepts.

This work was found in the chamber of Mr. DEIDRICH KNICKERBOCKER, the old gentleman whose sudden and mysterious disappearance has been noticed.—It is published in order to discharge certain debts he has left behind.

Nov. 29.

226   From the *New York Evening Post*, Nov. 29, 1809

227   New Amsterdam, about 1640, from *A History of New York . . . by Diedrich Knickerbocker*, Vol. I, first edition, 1809

IRVING AND "FATHER KNICKERBOCKER"

ONE hundred and forty-five years had passed since New Amsterdam had become New York, but Irving's boyhood had known the traditions of the burgomaster and of the proud old Dutch families. The wrath of some of these did not lessen the profane laughter of those who, like Dickens, wore out their "Father Knickerbocker" by carrying him about in their pockets.

THE JUDGMENT OF WOUTER VAN TWILLER

WOUTER VAN TWILLER, whose head was a perfect sphere, and whose body resembled a beer barrel on skids, made his famous decision concerning the two account books, by weighing them nicely (one in either hand), and deciding, out of a vast cloud of tobacco smoke, that in this manner the accounts were equally balanced.

228 From *The Knickerbocker, New York Monthly Magazine*, Vol. III, 1834

229 From an engraving by W. Greatbach after the painting by George H. Boughton (1834–1905)

231 From *Knickerbocker's History of New York*, London, 1836, engraving by Davenport after a drawing by George Cruikshank

MORE TALES OF VAN TWILLER

YET alas! although this great judge slept twelve of the twenty-four hours, and smoked and doubted during the others, indicating at such times the commotion of his mind not by speech but by guttural sounds, he rendered up his life at the very moment when the detested Yankees were assailing him: "His lungs and his pipe having been exhausted together, and his peaceful soul having escaped in the last whiff that curled from his tobacco-pipe." Twiller stood, too, for the best in Dutch traditions, such as the "table of avoirdupoise, that the hand of a Dutchman weighed one pound, and his foot two pounds."

230 From *Knickerbocker's History of New York*, London, 1836, engraving by Davenport after a drawing by George Cruikshank

THE PIPE PLOT.

232 From *Knickerbocker's History of New York*, London, 1836, engraving by Davenport after a drawing by George Cruikshank

PETER STUYVESANT AND THE PIG TAIL.

233 From *Knickerbocker's History of New York*, London, 1836, engraving by Davenport after a drawing by George Cruikshank

234 From *Knickerbocker's History of New York*, London, 1824, engraving by A. W. Warren after the painting by C. R. Leslie

KNICKERBOCKER ANECDOTES

THE entire book has a broad, swashbuckling humor that contrasts vigorously with the light satire of some of Irving's later work. The Dutchmen's phlegm, their fondness for tobacco, their breadth of beam achieve Brobdingnagian proportions. William the Testy's edict against tobacco was in vain. "Take away his pipe?" says Irving, "You might as well take away his nose!" A vast army of Dutchmen sat themselves down before Sir William's castle, all smoking with indescribable violence, to the confusion of Sir William. Nor was the obstinacy of the soldier at all shaken by the orders of Peter Stuyvesant to shear off his queue; in his last breath he ordered a coffin with a hole through which his beloved appendage should project, even in death.

Who can forget the great "Oyster War," and the glorious victory over the vile Yankees? Stoffel Brinkerhoff entered the city in triumph: "Five dried codfish on poles, standards taken from the enemy, were borne before him, and an immense store of oysters and clams, Weathersfield onions, and Yankee 'notions' formed the *spolia opima*." It was then that the trumpet of the jolly, robustious Antony Van Corlear rang out, making the Catskills tremble. Antony was a kind of Dutch Cyrano, beloved by all women — maidens, wives, and widows who dwelt in his "bowerie,"

KNICKERBOCKER HUMOR

Indeed *A History of New York* is a noisy, roaring, slap-stick Iliad. One may tire of it, but such masterpieces as the battle of Christina must take their places not so much, as is often said, with the satires of Swift and Sterne, but rather with the horseplay of Smollett. What should still delight Americans is that the book is our own, one of our very first original masterpieces, even if encumbered by literary debts. It was also a satire upon political contemporaries, among them Thomas Jefferson. In addition, it has, after allowance is made for colossal exaggeration, a modicum of truth. Dutch stolidity in love or in war, it may be whispered, is not wholly mythical.

235 Dutch Courtship, from *Knickerbocker's History of New York*, London, 1824, engraving by C. Rolls after the painting by C. R. Leslie

LAUGHING AT A BURGOMASTER'S JOKE

Irving was afterward to capture the more romantic and more evanescent aspects of the Knickerbocker legends. In his *A History of New York* he created the jolliest grotesque ever conceived of the absurdities of the Dutch character in America.

236 From *Knickerbocker's History of New York*, New York, 1860, after the frontispiece by Washington Allston (1779–1843)

IRVING'S ROOM AT THE RED HORSE, STRATFORD–ON–AVON

In 1815 Irving went abroad for his long stay of seventeen years. The traveler in the room of "Geoffrey Crayon" at Stratford-on-Avon recalls the characteristic moods of Irving abroad: musing in Shakespeare's home; or enjoying Christmas in the old English hall; or strolling in the dim twilight of Westminster Abbey.

237 From a photograph by Macbeth, London

STRATFORD ON AVON

Shakspeare is in the chancel. The place is solemn and sepulchral. Tall elms wave before the pointed windows, and the Avon, which runs at a short distance from the walls, keeps up a low, perpetual murmur. A flat stone marks the spot where

238 From *The Sketch Book of Geoffrey Crayon, Gent.*, New York, 1865, engraving on wood after a drawing by McDonough

THE FIRST MAN OF LETTERS

HE is clearly a romanticist, dwelling with tender sentiment on the past, writing for the most part only when the mood bids him, and so with sincerity; and writing also with all the grace natural to him as a man, and as a finished essayist. For this he now was. Reading, conversation, leisure, travel had made Irving, in the larger sense, our first man of letters. So he was regarded in England.

239 From the painting by John F. Kensett (1818–72) in the Metropolitan Museum of Art, New York

THE HUDSON RIVER BACKGROUND OF *THE SKETCH BOOK*

THUS *The Sketch Book of Geoffrey Crayon, Gent.*, 1819–20, is a result of our own urban influences and those of Europe upon an American. The mood of pensive romance has proved less enduring than the portions of the book which dealt once more with the Knickerbocker legends. The Van Winkles, of whom the immortal Rip was a descendant, had fought under Peter Stuyvesant. Sleepy Hollow was a glen in the river country discovered by Master Hendrick Hudson.

RIP VAN WINKLE

THESE two stories, more than dreamy meditations on widows, wives, broken hearts, rural churches, and poets' homes, have made Irving's fame secure. Rip was skilled in hunting, in idleness, and in the good graces of Wolf, his dog. He was beloved by little children, and all the wives of the village — save his own.

240 From *Illustrations of Rip Van Winkle*, designed and etched by F. O. C. Darley, New York, 1848

241   From *Illustrations of Rip Van Winkle*, New York, 1848, by F. O. C. Darley

RIP VAN WINKLE AND HIS FRIENDS

THE story has the tone of the "long lazy summer's day," so frequent in Rip's and Irving's life. The lovable reprobate listens, free just now from Dame Van Winkle, to the schoolmaster, Derrick Van Bummel, reading learnedly from an old newspaper. Meanwhile the patriarch of the village smokes as tranquilly and incessantly as ever did Wouter Van Twiller.

RIP'S REAPPEARANCE

ON the mountain, far above the blue Hudson, Rip hears the distant cry: "Rip Van Winkle!"; he sees the lazy crow in flight; and he has his strange sleep of twenty years. Then awakened, down he goes

into the village, to find the inn of ruddy "King George" now that of "Gen. Washington." Van Bummel is gone; Wolf has disappeared; all are vanished, even, lamentably, Dame Van Winkle! Rip lights his pipe. At night the villagers hear Hendrick Hudson and his crew at their game of ninepins in the Catskills. But Rip smokes on — peacefully. Irving's perpetuation of Dutch tradition is now different from that in *A History of New York.* Its subtlety reflects the maturing influence of the decade between 1809 and 1819.

242 From the *Columbian Lady's and Gentleman's Magazine*, Vol. V, 1846, engraving after a painting by T. H. Matteson (1813–84)

243 From a photograph by Sarony in the Yale University Library

JEFFERSON AS RIP VAN WINKLE

THE years have not blunted us to the charm of this Dutch-American legend. It has won a place in American drama. Of course, it is true; it is, as Irving says, "a posthumous writing of Diedrich Knickerbocker"!

244 From a photograph by Sarony in the Yale University Library

THE LEGEND OF SLEEPY HOLLOW

THE LEGEND OF SLEEPY HOLLOW has less of Irving's sentiment, and more of his humor. The story is less delicate; its pictures done in fresher colors. Old Baltus Van Tassel, with his teeming barn, his hearty cheer, and his buxom red-and-white daughter, Katrina, is the personification of Dutch prosperity, just as the devil-may-care Brom Bones is obviously her natural mate. And Ichabod Crane, with his ramrod body, his anaconda stomach, and his egotism, is doomed to be a butt as surely as his Yankee compeers in *A History of New York*, the renowned Habakkuk Nutter and Zerubbabel Fisk. Ichabod, the Yankee schoolmaster, eked out a slender living from his Dutch urchins. He aided the farmers; he sang in the church; and he was a welcome guest at social gatherings.

245	From *Illustrations of the Legend of Sleepy Hollow*, designed and etched by F. O. C. Darley, New York, 1849

246   From *Illustrations of the Legend of Sleepy Hollow*, 1849, by F. O. C. Darley

ICHABOD AND KATRINA AT VAN TASSEL'S BALL

At Van Tassel's ball Ichabod's hopes of better fortune — and of Katrina — rise high. All aquiver, like Lochinvar, or rather St. Vitus, he leads Katrina in the dance, to the discomfiture of Brom, who sulks in a corner.

ICHABOD AND THE HEADLESS HORSEMAN

The climax of the "headless horseman" has rendered Ichabod's wild ride almost as famous as those of John Gilpin or Mazeppa. For Ichabod had read credulously the dark superstitions of Cotton Mather; he was not one to delay at the sight of a devil. As the headless horseman (Brom Bones, after his marriage to Katrina, was seen to wink at references to a shattered pumpkin) threw his head at the agonized schoolmaster, the glory of Ichabod once more departed.

247   From *Illustrations of the Legend of Sleepy Hollow*, 1849, by F. O. C. Darley

248   *Old Christmas*, from *The Sketch Book*, London, 1876, engraving after a
drawing by R. Caldecott

IRVING'S AFFECTION FOR ENGLAND

Bracebridge Hall and *Tales of a Traveller*, 1824, were, for the
most part, further expressions of Irving's romantic affection for
old England. Her castles, her cottages, her customs, her flowers,
her birds were but the realities of his boyhood dreams. "I
traversed England," he says, "a grown-up child, delighted by
every object, great
and small." *The
Hall, Family Ser-
vants, Falconry, St.
Mark's Eve, May-
Day Customs, Vil-
lage Worthies,*
recount in brief
essay form the
charm of England
and English life.

250   From *Bracebridge Hall*, 1858, after a drawing
by C. H. Schmolze

EUROPEAN REPUTATION OF *THE SKETCH BOOK*

The Sketch Book won for Irving a European reputation. The English reviews at
first expressed amazement, then explained
the mystery by Irving's residence in Great
Britain. Irving himself was amused by this
psychology. "It has," he says in his introduction to *Bracebridge Hall*, 1822, "been a
matter of marvel, to my European readers,
that a man from the wilds of America should
express himself in tolerable English. I was
looked upon as something new and strange
in literature; a kind of demi-savage, with a
feather in his hand instead of on his head."

Ready Money Jack

249   From *Bracebridge Hall*, New York, 1858, after
a drawing by C. H. Schmolze (1823–59)

The thrush sings from the hawthorn as Julia passes, leaning on
her lover's arm. She is fond of flowers, she has studied under
Lady Lillycraft, and she can sing — not the modern bravura of
Mozart — but the simple old melodies of Herrick.

"READY–MONEY–JACK"

Through the pages of this larger sketch book move English
characters native to the manor or the village. Ready-Money-
Jack has always a hundred or two pounds of gold with him, and
never leaves a debt unpaid. He frequents fairs, loves rustic
sports. He is distinguished by his strength, gravity, and by his
dress: a coat of dark green, a waistcoat of figured chintz, stockings of blue, with just a glimpse of a scarlet garter. He is a
solid English yeoman.

MAY-DAY

In the essay *May-Day*, Geoffrey Crayon is roused from a half dream, half reverie, in the English countryside, by the village musicians under the leadership of the tailor, an aspirant on the clarionet. *Bracebridge Hall* is playful, whimsical, wistful. It is also somewhat tepid. Irving may have been conscious of this: he included the long sketch of *The Student of Salamanca*, besides *Dolph Heyliger*, an old Dutch story, and the delightful skit of *The Stout Gentleman*.

251   From *Bracebridge Hall*, 1858, after a drawing
by Schmolze

THE ALHAMBRA

252   From *The Alhambra*, New York, 1860, engraving
after a drawing by James D. Smillie

IRVING'S BOOKS ON SPAIN

This spirit of mild, romantic adventure had even freer play during Irving's three years' stay in Spain (1826–29), where he was to live again from 1842 to 1846. *The Life and Voyages of Columbus, The Conquest of Granada, The Companions of Columbus*, and *The Alhambra* all appeared during the years 1828–1832. The book on Columbus and *The Conquest of Granada* indicate Irving's limitations as a historian. Although not inaccurate, he is more concerned with tone than with fact. *The Alhambra*, essays and semi-narratives of old Spain, is important in two ways: in writing of Moorish castles, moonlit minarets, and haunted dungeons, Irving's romantic mood attains luxuriance; and this book represents the first great influence of Spain upon American literature, thus establishing a tradition to be carried on by Bryant, Longfellow, and others.

IRVING'S LATER WORK

Irving's best literary work was now finished. He was to write his biography of *Oliver Goldsmith*, 1849, *Astoria*, 1836, a record of his journey to the West, the *Life of George Washington*, 1855–59, and miscellaneous books, but these merely enhanced his reputation as a man of letters and of the world. He lived on, with interruptions of travel, until 1859 in the scenes he loved, at

253   Sunnyside, the Home of Washington Irving, engraving after a drawing by W. R. Miller

Sunnyside, near Tarrytown, on the Hudson. Lovers of Irving have fancied a symbolism in his cottage covered with ivy brought from Melrose Abbey. Irving, our first man of letters, owed much to Europe.

254   From a photograph by Rockwood

UNITY OF IRVING'S LIFE AND WORK

IRVING'S life and work have a singular unity. Aside from the great sorrow of his youth in the loss of his betrothed, Matilda Hoffman, his life was usually as happy as one of his own reveries, and as merry as a Dutch host. He was, however, sensitive, and suffered more than is generally supposed from depression. One side of his nature was practical and robust. His urbanity was that of a truly kind and highly cultivated man. It may be guessed that his personal example accomplished as much as his writing in encouraging a *rapprochement* between irritated British and Americans. The evenness of his work is born of a fine artistic sense. Irving is never sublime; he never exalts or inspires. In fact, his power lies in his consciousness that he cannot do this. In his writing as in his life, Irving never strains, is always himself.

AMERICAN ESSAYIST AND SHORT STORY WRITER

THUS, if he never attains heights, he is never absurd, and within his limits he has power: to amuse with playful humor, to enchant the fancy; and to give pleasure through excellence of form. He is our first gifted essayist. This suggests his historical importance: he is first, too, in the field of the short story, though his tales are shadowy, essays rather than narratives. Irving's life spans the era between the two great wars, but his published writings reflect relatively little of the life of his time. He loved America. He gave us the Knickerbocker legend, and he bequeathed to our excited literature a mood of dreams and quiet breathing. Yet Irving was far more than a dreamer. His story has not been told completely. In it lie deep connections with the life of America and Europe during the first half of the nineteenth century.

255   The Road at Sleepy Hollow. © Keystone View Co.

JAMES KIRKE PAULDING, 1778–1860

AMONG the Knickerbockers who listened eagerly for the echoes of the whimwhams of *Salmagundi* was James K. Paulding (No. 256), co-author with Irving in their production. Paulding was five years Irving's senior, became Secretary of the Navy under President Van Buren, and was a controversialist in literary disputes with England. He was a rather heavy-handed satirist, and wrote endlessly in this form, in biography, and in fiction. Not even poetry escaped. *The Diverting History of John Bull and Brother Jonathan*, 1812, an allegory in the manner of Arbuthnot, hardly rescues him from the past.

256 From W. I. Paulding, *Literary Life of James K. Paulding*, New York, 1867

257 From James K. Paulding, *The Diverting History of John Bull and Brother Jonathan*, by Hector Bull-us, Philadelphia, 1827

258 Engraving, about 1835, after the portrait of Drake by Nathaniel Rogers (1788-1844)

PAULDING'S NOVELS

NOR are his mediocre novels read to-day. *The Backwoodsman*, 1818, links Paulding with Cooper, whom he resembled in his robustness of mind. The oft-quoted couplet of Halleck is entire truth:

> Homer was well enough; but would he ever
> Have written, think ye, *The Backwoodsman?* Never!

Westward Ho!, 1832, is a cry from the Kentucky frontier, and depicts Bashfield, a rough hunter who, Leatherstocking might have said, had his "gifts." On the other side, Paulding is closer to Irving in his satiric vein and in his love of Knickerbocker tradition, which he portrayed in *The Dutchman's Fireside*, 1831, a novel which ran through six editions within a year. Paulding was also a poet, and parodied *The Lay of the Last Minstrel* in *The Lay of the Scottish Fiddle*, 1813.

JOSEPH RODMAN DRAKE, 1795–1820

QUITE different from this man of affairs is Joseph Rodman Drake, who is touched with romance and pathos by reason of his talented poetry, his friendship with Fitz-Greene Halleck, his personal graces, and his early death at the age of twenty-five. "Oh, Halleck," he cries out, as they revise together the *Croaker Papers*, 1819, the gay satires on manners, "isn't this happiness?" These were such good-humored, facile stanzas as those on the painter Trumbull:

> The Titian of a table cloth!
> The Guido of a pair of breeches

or on life itself in the merry town of New York. Drake worked hard to support himself. Poetry was usually incidental to necessary tasks: business, the study of medicine, the management of a drug store.

THE CULPRIT FAY

BESIDES the days of idleness with Halleck on Long Island or in the mountains, Drake had others when he wrote such poetry as *The Culprit Fay and Other Poems*, 1835, completed, it is supposed, in his twenty-first year. This poem describes a fairy who loved a mortal and was compelled to atone for the sin.

THE CULPRIT FAY 43

He bridled her mouth with a silkweed twist,
He lashed her sides with an osier thong;
And now through evening's dewy mist,
With leap and spring they bound along,
Till the mountain's magic verge is past,
And the beach of sand is reached at last.

259 From Joseph Rodman Drake, *The Culprit Fay*, New York, 1875, drawing by Arthur Lumley

THE AMERICAN FLAG

DRAKE, though imitative, urged literary independence, and his poetry has glimpses of American nature. The theme of *The Culprit Fay* was inspired, it is said, by an argument with Cooper and Halleck about the value of the Hudson highlands as material for poetry. Queen Mab had been with Drake: his poetry of the fairies, Poe to the contrary, is delicately imaginative. The lyric, *The American Flag*, beginning, "When Freedom, from her mountain height," excels, as poetry, the verse of Hopkinson.

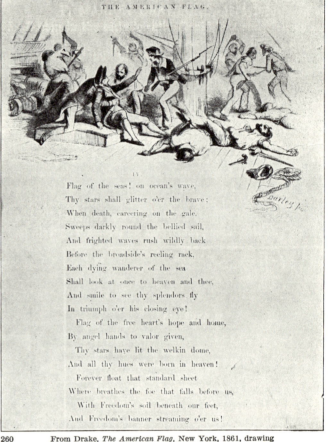

THE AMERICAN FLAG.

IV.

Flag of the seas! on ocean's wave,
Thy stars shall glitter o'er the brave;
When death, careering on the gale,
Sweeps darkly round the bellied sail,
And frighted waves rush wildly back
Before the broadside's reeling rack,
Each dying wanderer of the sea
Shall look at once to heaven and thee,
And smile to see thy splendors fly
In triumph o'er his closing eye!

    Flag of the free heart's hope and home,
By angel hands to valor given,
    Thy stars have lit the welkin dome,
And all thy hues were born in heaven!
    Forever float that standard sheet
Where breathes the foe that falls before us,
    With Freedom's soil beneath our feet,
And Freedom's banner streaming o'er us!

261   From the portrait, 1828, by Henry Inman
(1801–46) in the New York Historical Society

260   From Drake, *The American Flag*, New York, 1861, drawing
                    by F. O. C. Darley

FITZ–GREENE HALLECK. 1790–1867

THE friendship between Drake and Fitz-Greene Halleck began in 1813. Like Drake, Halleck came of Puritan ancestry; unlike him, he was destined for a long apprenticeship in the business world: six years as a clerk in the Connecticut town of Guilford, where he had been born; twenty in the counting-house of Jacob Barker in New York; and sixteen in the office of John Jacob Astor.

Yet he found time for the rambles with Drake and for their partnership which resulted in such "wincing and shrinking at 'The Croakers,' that every person was on tenterhooks." *The Croakers*, 1819, were satirical papers in verse on the foibles of the age, and appeared in the New York *Evening Post*.

262   From the *Columbian Lady's and Gentleman's Magazine*, 1847,
engraving by W. J. Jackman after the painting by J. H. Beard
(1812–93) illustrating a scene from *Fanny*

FANNY

COLEMAN, of the *Evening Post*, may have exclaimed of *The Croakers*, 1819, "My God! I had no idea we had such talents in America!" But he could not have said it of *Fanny*, 1819, Halleck's satire, reminiscent of Byron, and so suggestive of the low ebb, just now, of original poetry in America. In 1877, a decade after his death, a bronze statue of Halleck was dedicated in Central Park by the President of the United States.

MARCO BOZZARIS

HALLECK's poetry as a whole is bronze rather than gold. His *Marco Bozzaris* had the fame among schoolboys enjoyed by Macaulay's *Lays of Ancient Rome*, and the glitter of declamation is in every stanza. Halleck was too deeply immersed in the conventions of Campbell and Byron.

263   From Fitz-Greene Halleck, *Poetical Works*, New York, 1847

264   From *American Melodies*, edited by G. P. Morris, New York, 1841

"GREEN BE THE TURF ABOVE THEE"

YET Halleck could feel deeply and write simply. His poem, *Burns*, moved the sister of the poet. And his lament for the bright and beautiful Drake, 1825, is still fresh:

> Green be the turf above thee,
> Friend of my better days!
> None knew thee but to love thee,
> Nor named thee but to praise.

ALNWICK CASTLE

HALLECK, though he dwelt long in New York and wrote a poem called *Connecticut*, was spiritually neither a Knickerbocker nor a New Englander. He drew poetic life from the wells of romanticism; he never tired of its battle songs, its castles, and its pageantry. *Alnwick Castle*, 1827, ends with a note of humorous satire, but Halleck loves none the less the rude tale of Hotspur and his gentle Kate and "the ruins wild and hoary."

HALLECK'S LAST YEARS

HALLECK was Knickerbocker only by adoption; he spent the last nineteen years of his life at Guilford. On his monument there are written his own lines to Drake. At his death he was still a well-known person

265   From Halleck, *Poetical Works*, 1847

among the literati of New York. Among those who paid him tribute were Holmes and Whittier. His name is now linked with those of Drake, Paulding, and Cooper. Of his poetry little has survived save a few lyrics.

266   From a carte de visite by Charles D. Fredricks

267   From the portrait, 1822, by John W. Jarvis (1780–1840)
in the possession of James Fenimore Cooper, Cooperstown,
New York

JAMES FENIMORE COOPER, 1789–1851

IT must have been during the days when Irving was writing *The Sketch Book* that James Fenimore Cooper laid down, one evening, the book he was reading, and said to his wife: "I believe I could write a better story myself." Mrs. Cooper answered according to the traditions of wives, and in 1820 appeared *Precaution*, the first of more than thirty novels. Some of these were to prove worthless, but others were to be translated into a score of tongues, making the names of Harvey Birch, Leatherstocking, and Uncas bywords in obscure corners of the globe. Cooper's fame grew swiftly. Sir Walter Scott records in his *Journal* in 1826, a scant six years after Cooper's petulant remark to his wife, his meeting with the already famous novelist in Paris: "So," he says, "the Scotch and American lions took the field together." The abounding vitality in Cooper's writing has a parallel in his life. Besides the writing of novels, in which he exceeded Walter Scott's quota, he served as seaman in the navy, consul at Lyons, France, and had a career of libels and lawsuits more stormy than that of Walter Savage Landor. This robustness of body and mind and certain influences of his youth were responsible for his success in literature. In other respects he was ill prepared for writing. His education was sketchy; he lacked literary taste; meditation was not in him.

268   Cooper's Birthplace at Burlington. N. J., from a photograph in the Burlington County Historical Society

COOPER'S YOUTH

HIS youth was steeped in two great elements of American life: the frontier and the sea. One year after his birth his family moved from Burlington, New Jersey, to Cooperstown, New York. Here became his forever the reality and the romance of the wilderness. Not only did he read much concerning the frontier and Indians, mastering the lore of the forest, but his nature stirred with the beauty of sunset on mountain and lake, or the silences of these trackless kingdoms. When thirteen, Cooper entered Yale College, but in his sophomore year he was dismissed for an escapade. He served as a sailor on a foreign bound ship, and later as a midshipman in the navy. After his marriage he resigned.

269   Cooperstown on Otsego Lake, New York, from an engraving, 1860, by J. I. Pease,
in the New York Public Library

FIRST NOVELS

AT about the same time Scott was talking to Highlanders and borderers. Scott, however, was denied dismissal from college and consequent service in the navy, before the mast in a merchant-vessel and as a midshipman on the Great Lakes. Cooper was not to be a struggling writer in an American Grub Street. From the time of his marriage in 1811 his life was his own, with leisure for writing, travel, and litigation. That dull novel, *Precaution*, written when he was thirty, led to *The Spy*, 1821, *The Pioneers*, 1823; in brief, to the greatest American novels of adventure.

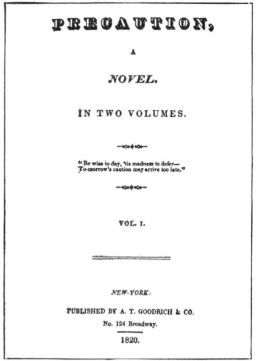

PRECAUTION,

A

NOVEL.

IN TWO VOLUMES.

"Be wise to day, 'tis madness to defer—
To-morrow's caution may arrive too late."

VOL. I.

NEW-YORK:

PUBLISHED BY A. T. GOODRICH & CO.
No. 124 Broadway.

1820.

270   Title-page of the original issue in the New York Public Library

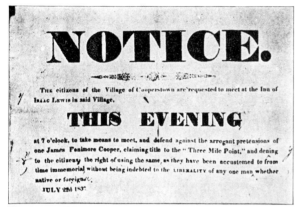

271   From Ralph Birdsall, *Story of Cooperstown*, Cooperstown, N. Y., 1917, from the printer's original proof

CRITICISMS AND LITIGATIONS

BETWEEN 1822 and 1826 Cooper might have been seen often in New York, particularly at meetings of "The Bread and Cheese Club," to which Halleck and Bryant also belonged. Later in France and Italy we hear of him defending America against the abusive criticisms of Europeans. In 1833 he is back, now as belligerently criticizing crude America. However patriotic Cooper's motives, he was tactless. He prodded irascibly our busy ant hills, and soon the insects were nipping his ankles. Then began the famous spectacle of Cooper against America, an absurd, yet impressive display of Cooper's character: its obstinacy and independence. For every assault upon him, inspired by his criticisms, he conducted a libel suit, till no editor dared bark at him. It was an amazing, if somewhat futile performance.

LAST YEARS

DURING these tempests Cooper contrived to write two of his best novels. His last years were peaceful and were accompanied in America by the feeling that justice had not been done him. We see him at the last in his "Chalet," a farm on the eastern shore of Lake Otsego.

272   Otsego Hall, from an engraving by H. B. Hall (1808–84) after a daguerreotype

273   From J. Fenimore Cooper, *The Pilot*, New York, 1859,
engraving by C. Rost after a drawing by F. O. C. Darley

LESSER NOVELS

MORE than half, perhaps three fourths, of Cooper's novels, are ineffectual. Novels like *The Monikins*, 1835, are insufferable, and even such a story as *Afloat and Ashore*, 1844, which appeared within three and four years, respectively, of *The Deerslayer*, 1841, and *The Pathfinder*, 1840, reveals its exciting incidents only after the weary reader has traveled far. Cooper's forte is narrative. When this becomes didactic or prolix, his writing is a land of sand and thorns.

274   From J. Fenimore Cooper, *Afloat and Ashore*, New York, 1861,
engraving by F. Girsch, after a drawing by F. O. C. Darley

COOPER'S REPUTATION

YET after Cooper's reputation was established even the mediocre novels had an audience. Morse, the electrician, quoted by Professor H. A. Beers, says: "They are published, as soon as he produces them, in thirty-four different places in Europe. They have been seen by American travelers in the languages of Turkey and Persia, in Constantinople, in Egypt, at Jerusalem, at Ispahan." To-day Cooper's fame, as he himself foresaw, rests upon the *Leatherstocking Tales*, and upon one or two novels of the sea, notably *The Pilot*, 1823.

275   From J. Fenimore Cooper, *The Pilot*, 1859, engraving by
John Wrightson after a drawing by F. O. C. Darley

For American readers of a century ago, Cooper's stories of the sea had an even greater novelty than those of the frontier. It is difficult for a reader of modern fiction to realize that writers then regarded accurate depiction of sea life as a dangerous business. Two scenes apropos of writing *The Pilot* have interest: Cooper arguing at a dinner party that the author of *The Pirate* must have been a landsman; and his reading of his manuscript to an old seaman. As the frigate maneuvered up the narrow channel through the tempest, the old salt was carried away by excitement. "It's all very well," he cried, "but you have let your jib stand too long, my fine fellow."

THE SPY

Cooper corrected the detail, but the illusion of the sailor was evidence enough that he could rely on his experience. When *The Pilot* appeared, Cooper had created the novel of the sea. Incidentally he had given American literature a picture, in the pilot, of John Paul Jones. Other novels of the sea followed, among them *The Red Rover*, 1828, whose first edition of five thousand copies was sold almost at once. Two years before *The Pilot*, in the year of Scott's *The Pirate* and *Kenilworth*, and of Bryant's early *Poems*, Cooper had published *The Spy*, 1821.

276   From *The Token*, Boston, 1836, engraving by James D. Smillie after the painting by Robert Weir (1803–89)

277   From the *Columbian Lady's and Gentleman's Magazine*, 1846, engraving by Charles Burt after a drawing by T. H. Matteson

"HARVEY BIRCH"

The Spy was a novel of Westchester County, New York, during the Revolution. Among other weaknesses was a dim George Washington. The English editors flayed the book mercilessly. Nevertheless, the breathless adventures of Harvey Birch, the spy, laid the foundations of Cooper's fame in England, in America, and in such remote places as Nicaragua.

LEATHERSTOCKING TALES

Cooper loved the sea but he was closer to the frontier. Turning to it now, he must have been conscious of his power to arrest it in literature. It was not love of writing but love of the frontier in America which called forth the *Leatherstocking Tales*. The first in actual chronology and the next to the last in the history of Natty Bumpo, was *The Pioneers*, 1823. The faithful reread the tales in this order: *The Deerslayer*, 1841; *The Last of the Mohicans*, 1826; *The Pathfinder*, 1840; *The Pioneers*; and *The Prairie*, 1827. This is the true epic of American fiction, with a hero who may be called America's single great contribution to the world's literature of picturesque character. With his dog and his long carabine, Leatherstocking moves against the real-imaginative background of the American frontier. Through his eyes we see the mysterious recesses of the forest, the flush of dawn on the mountain lake. With him we brace ourselves for fierce battle, as the war cry breaks the silences. He is the incarnation of the American frontiersman. Yet Leatherstocking has seemed to some critics duplicated in Long Tom Coffin. Lowell in *A Fable for Critics* says:

And his very Long Toms are the same useful Nat,
Rigged up in duck pants and a sou'-wester hat.

"A series of masterly and rapid evolutions with the horses now commenced."   The Prairie, p. 157.

278   From Cooper, *The Prairie*, New York, 1873, engraving by W. H. Morse after a drawing by F. O. C. Darley

279   From Cooper, *The Pioneers*, New York, 1859, engraving by
John Wrightson after a drawing by F. O. C. Darley

THE LAST OF THE MOHICANS

IN *The Last of the Mohicans* Leatherstocking is himself, resourceful, a master of wood lore, tender to the
weak, a character
not without a cer-
tain daily beauty
in his life. More-
over, he is the
friend of Chin-
gachgook and
Uncas, and the
enemy of the

281   From tne statue of Leatherstocking by
Launitz on the Cooper Monument, in Lake-
wood Cemetery, Cooperstown, N. Y.

THE PIONEERS

THE PIONEERS shows Leatherstocking restless under
the encroachments on the frontier. He has lived his
best days, and interest in him centers in his philosophy, developed by life under the sky, in the forest,
and by contact with primitive men. What *The Pioneers* lacks is clear-cut, exciting narrative. Cooper
reminisces too obviously and too often. The book is
almost a series of pictures: the hunt, the trials of
marksmanship, the forest fire, the brilliant winter
scenery.

280   From Cooper, *The Last of the Mohicans*, New York, 1859, engraving by James D. Smillie after a drawing by F. O. C. Darley

black-hearted Renard Subtil. Never does the blood of a reader congeal
as in this thrilling story, when the bushes part slowly to reveal the faces
of Indians in war paint; or when he hears the dull splash in the pond
of the murdered sentry; or watches the slaughter of women and babes
by Montcalm's Indians.

THE PRAIRIE

IN *The Prairie* Leatherstocking's dismay at the victories of civilization
has driven him to the West, where the squatter lives free from the stifling
air of cities and land titles. Leatherstocking's petulance has yielded, in
The Pioneers, to resignation. His old age and death are peaceful, and
his reverence for God as manifested in nature has deepened. This book
is quieter in tone, and the passages on nature approach the sublime.
These two novels are perhaps the least effective of the famous series.
The Prairie depicts a Natty Bumpo who is no longer young, and *The
Pioneers* is slow in movement and generally prolix.

THE PATHFINDER

THE PATHFINDER and *The Deerslayer* are products of Cooper's mature powers. In these novels his tiresome faults are checked, his genius for narrative is in full play, and his descriptions of nature are best. *The Pathfinder*, concerned with the country on the shores of Lake Ontario, combines the two frontiers of water and forest.

Old Cap and Leatherstocking are repetitious, and Mabel is more like "the delicate females" than the spirited Judith of *Deerslayer*, but one understands (with reservations) Balzac's enthusiasm: "It is beautiful, it is grand. . . . I know no one in the world, save Walter Scott, who has risen to that grandeur and serenity of colors."

"Pathfinder!—Oh! this is worse than I could have imagined—take my hand, excellent Pathfinder, and let me see that you do not hate me."

The Pathfinder, p. 121.

282   From Cooper, *The Pathfinder*, New York, 1873, after a drawing by F. O. C. Darley

" Deerslayer raised the Indian in his arms, and carried him to the lake. Here he first helped him to take an attitude in which he could appease his burning thirst." Page 115.

283   From Cooper, *The Deerslayer*, Boston, 1876, engraving by James D. Smillie after a drawing by F. O. C. Darley

THE DEERSLAYER

IN like manner *The Deerslayer* portrays lake and stream. Here Leatherstocking is youthful. His friendship with Chingachgook, and his devotion to Hutter's daughters interest not only the arrogant Judith, but the overcritical reader.

The pictures of the Indian maiden, Hist, have become evidence in the arraignment of Cooper's idealized Indians. Yet who will forget the wooing or the dramatic rescue by her Indian lover?

COOPER'S FAULTS

COOPER'S faults as a writer have been proclaimed repeatedly. His moralizing, his prolixity, his hit-or-miss diction, petty critics have fastened upon eagerly. These are the carelessnesses of a writer interested in life first, and art hardly at all. They have kept him out of the magic circle of correct literature. Men laugh at him, too, for his plaster of paris characters, his minor figures, his silly women, his noble Indians, his prejudices against Yankees, and his other eccentricities. Hetty, Major Heyward, and his psalm-singing David Gamut are bores. Mark Twain has exploited Cooper as silly.

284   From a daguerreotype, 1850, by Brady in the possession of James Fenimore Cooper, Cooperstown

285 Indian Hunter, marking the site of Otsego Hall, Cooperstown, replica of the statue by J. Q. A. Ward (1830–1910) in Central Park, New York

COOPER'S VITALITY

WELL, let it be so. The answer is merely that Cooper lives. There is Leatherstocking, there is the fight on the island in *The Last of the Mohicans*, there are the descriptions of the lake in *The Deerslayer*, pages thumbed in every library volume of this book. The vitality of this frontiersman is unexhausted. Cooper gathered up the traditions of his people. The awe of the hunter in the forest — his romance; the struggles of the settler with his ax or rifle — his realism; all were in the souls of the nation set down before the sea and the forest. Many an inarticulate woodsman felt them to be enemies yet friends; terrible yet divine. To these confused feelings Cooper gave a voice.

LESSER KNICKERBOCKERS

To name the years between 1815 and 1870 the "Golden Age" of American literature makes a phrase pretty enough to describe its sentimental tone. The adjective does not, however, do justice to other metals of the era. We observed that Americans were not slow to write, even in Colonial and Revolutionary days. Imagine then the floods of print in this time of increased wealth and larger libraries. As one turns the pages of the old English reviews, there are the countless names of the hopeful copyists of Sir Walter Scott — forgotten, all. In America, it was likewise. For

286 New York from Weehawken, from Jacques Gérard Milbert, *Itinéraire Pittoresque du Fleuve Hudson*, etc., Paris, 1828–29

our Irving, Cooper, and Bryant we paid heavily in sentimental essays, feeble frontier tales, and weak nature poetry. When Drake and Halleck won in New York their tiny successes through the *Croaker Papers*, the *Evening Post* was straightway inundated with imitations. English travelers were amazed at the hordes of poets in America. So Lowell rhymed:

In a country where scarcely a village is found
That has not its author sublime and profound.

287 Broadway from the Bowling Green, from the original, about 1826, drawn and engraved by William J. Bennett in the Emmet Collection, New York Public Library

KNICKERBOCKER "ELEGANCE"

IN New York the simplicity of the picturesque old town which Irving loved in the first decade gave way to a sophistication without genius. It was the day of the *Knickerbocker*, of "elegant" literature, of steel engravings, gift books, letters from European society, and sugary poetry. Honest, rough literature hid its head; "inspiration and water" had its day. Down Broadway walked the American Leigh Hunts and Lyttons.

N. P. WILLIS, 1806–67

By far the most striking representative of this school was Nathaniel Parker Willis, born in Portland, Maine, a year before Longfellow, reared in what was left of Boston orthodoxy, and destined to become a darling of European and American society; to fight a duel; to write a novel, a satire in the manner of *Don Juan*, and countless light essays. His training in Park Street Church, Andover, and Yale was all very well, but, aside from paraphrases of Scripture stories, Willis doffed it easily: "Mon Dieu," said a French visitor, "Willis is a poet!"

288   From the portrait, 1833, by William A. Wall (1801–85) in the New York Historical Society

289   From *Graham's Magazine*, Vol. 24, 1844, engraving by A. L. Dick, after the drawing by G. W. Flagg (1816–97)

WILLIS' MAGAZINE VENTURES

He was a magazinist, too, a family tradition which clung to him; his father had founded *The Youth's Companion*. Soon after graduation he was supervising a gift book, *The Token*, and had started the *American Monthly Magazine*. In the early 'forties he was co-editor with G. P. Morris (No. 299) of the *Evening Mirror*, New York.

290   Willis and Morris devoting their time to the *Mirror*, from the *Broadway Journal*, New York, 1845

291   From a carte de visite by Charles D. Fredricks

WILLIS' PROSE

His prose is fluent, witty, polished, and covered with fretwork. He wants simplicity. Lowell in calling him "jaunty and gay" absorbs the favorite adjectives of critics. *Pencillings by the Way*, 1835, 1844, and *Letters from under a Bridge*, 1840, with glimpses of country life outside New England, have the grace which made Willis one of the most popular writers of his day.

WILLIS ABROAD AND AT HOME

Morris sent Willis abroad with a small stipend and letters of introduction, to write letters back to the magazine. Willis met every one; knew everybody. He was loved by ladies, he married, and he returned to live, with much literary labor, in various romantic villas, "Glenmary" and "Idlewild." These adventures he often capitalized in journalistic writing.

292   From N. P. Willis, *Letters from under a bridge and Poems*, London, 1840, engraving after a drawing by W. H. Bartlett

AT IDLEWILD

A caller at "Idlewild" toward the close of his life found him "a tall and elegant figure, with rosy cheeks and a luxuriance of clustering hair." And Oliver Wendell Holmes declared him "something between a remembrance of Count d'Orsay and an anticipation of Oscar Wilde." Willis was not a *poseur*, nor merely a sentimentalist. He was at bottom a journalist.

POEMS

Willis could clothe his sentiment and humor in facile verse. *Parrhasius* deserves perhaps to ring out from schoolboy lips as well as *Marco Bozzaris;* and Poe and Halleck admired *Unseen Spirits*, a poem in which Willis' sentiment is less shallow, though bordering upon melodrama:

The shadows lay along Broadway —
'Twas near the twilight tide —
And slowly there a lady fair
    Was walking in her pride.

293   From a photograph by Rockwood

294   From Willis, *Poems*, Philadelphia, 1854, engraving after a drawing by Emanuel Leutze (1816–68)

A villain with a black mustache and a red waistcoat is obviously lurking at the corner. Willis has historical importance. He encouraged the writing of essays and fiction. It is impossible to omit him from a history of the Knickerbockers. "It is comfortable," says Thackeray, "that there should have been a Willis."

295   From Rev. Henry W. Bellows, *Address at the Funeral of Mr. Henry T. Tuckerman*, New York, 1872

GULIAN C. VERPLANCK, 1786–1870

To guests at "Idlewild" Nathaniel Willis used to point out on the opposite bank of the Hudson the home of Gulian C. Verplanck, who, says Bryant, while Irving, Paulding, and Kemble were frolicking in Cockloft Hall, was held up by older men "as an example of steady, studious, and spot-

CONTEMPORARIES OF WILLIS

AT Newport is a cedar and ebony chest in which repose the works of Henry Theodore Tuckerman, author of an *Italian Sketch Book*, 1835, and various books on Italy and the poets. In no less distinguished darkness rest the writings of other contemporaries of Willis, the illustrious obscure of the Knickerbockers: Robert C. Sands, essayist, poet, and friend of Dana and Bryant; Alfred B. Street; Park Benjamin; and Ralph Hoyt. Street, who wrote the poem *Frontenac*, was, Longfellow thought, an admirable painter of forest scenery, and Bryant praised his poetry.

296   From the portrait, about 1830, by Charles C. Ingham (1797–1863) in the New York Historical Society

less youth." Verplanck was that strange blend, a Congressman and a scholar. His addresses were famous, and he was a contributor and a collaborator in *The Talisman*, together with Sands and Bryant. Verplanck dictated his prose, seated comfortably in Sands' library. In 1847 appeared his illustrated edition of Shakespeare.

SAMUEL WOODWORTH, 1785–1842

ONE of the haunts of Verplanck and Cooper was the house, on Duane Street, of Samuel Woodworth, historian, essayist, and founder, with G. P. Morris, of the *New York Mirror*. Woodworth's operatic pieces are as completely forgotten as everything else about his blameless life. One lyric is occasionally drawn from the well of oblivion, his *Old Oaken Bucket*, 1817. A historian of literature describes the bucket as "embalmed in undying verse," and many modern writers would concede the first adjective, while omitting the prefix of the second.

297   From *The Poems, Odes, Songs and other Metrical Effusions of Samuel Woodworth*, New York, 1818, engraving by Gimbrede after a drawing by Freeman

298 An "Old Oaken Bucket" House, from a photograph. © A. S. Burbank, Plymouth, Mass.

ORIGIN OF *THE OLD OAKEN BUCKET*

WE may weep or laugh according to temperament at the scene in Mallory's hotel. Most of us are likely to regard the incident as an echo of the sentimental Knickerbockers. The unregenerate poet had declared a glass of port better than anything he had ever tasted. Then another present said: "No . . . the draught of pure, fresh spring water, that we used to drink from the *old oaken bucket that hung in the well*." This was too much for Woodworth; tears gleamed in his eyes. In less than half an hour he had written the poem.

GEORGE P. MORRIS, 1802–64

ANOTHER single-song man was George Perkins Morris — journalist and dramatist. With Woodworth he founded *The Mirror*, and with Willis, the *Evening Mirror*. Among his editings were *The Song-Writers of America*, and, with Willis, the modestly entitled *Prose and Poetry of America*, 1845. Songs such as *Near the Lake where drooped the Willow*, and *My Mother's Bible* have been survived by *Woodman, spare that Tree!*

300   From G. P. Morris, *American Melodies*, 1841

299   From the painting by Charles Loring Elliott (1812–68) in the New York Historical Society

WOODMAN, *SPARE THAT TREE!*

MORRIS had his idea from an old gentleman who prevented a woodman from cutting down a tree where he had played as a boy. The ax was ready, the tree was resigned, but the old gentleman, choked with emotion, gave the executioner a ten-dollar note, and received a written bond for the tree's safety. The twentieth century does not weep over this song, but it still remembers its opening stanza.

JOHN HOWARD PAYNE, 1792–1852

A PERSON of more distinction and depth of feeling was John Howard Payne, the author of *Home, Sweet Home*. Payne was an actor, a playwright of some merit, and a natural lover of the theater. As early as 1805 he had edited a dramatic journal. His most creditable play was *Brutus, or the Fall of Tarquin*, 1819. In his wandering, loneliness, death at Tunis, and friendships with great men, he appears as a somewhat romantic figure. His first rôle on the New York stage was "young Norval." Later he acted at Drury Lane in London, and in Paris. The famous poem was in a play written abroad, *Clari; or, The Maid of Milan*, 1823.

301   From the portrait of Payne as *Hamlet*, by Charles Robert Leslie (1794-1859) in the Boston Museum of Fine Arts

302   From the Yale Collection of American Literature, dated 1830

HOME, SWEET HOME

WHILE in England Payne was a friend of Lamb and Coleridge. In Paris he stayed often with Washington Irving. At the Palais Royal is the room which Payne once pointed out to Irving as the place where the song had been written.

THE PAYNE HOMESTEAD, EASTHAMPTON, LONG ISLAND

IN fits of homesickness Payne's thoughts were wont to travel back to his childhood days. He was the sixth of a family of nine children who lived at 33 Pearl Street in New York, but the formative years of his life were passed at Easthampton, Long Island. Here his father was principal of an academy, and here may be seen his "home, sweet home," much as it was in the poet's youth. At his reinterment in Washington in 1883, a great chorus of voices sang his song.

303   From an engraving by John Sartain after the painting by W. H. Willcox

304   From the portrait by Cephas G. Thompson (1775–1856)
in the New York Historical Society

WILLIAM CULLEN BRYANT,
1794–1878

IRVING was a Knickerbocker by birth, Bryant by long association. A direct descendant of John Alden, the son of a physician, he was born in Cummington, Massachusetts. His early educa-

CHARLES FENNO HOFFMAN, 1806–84

THE real founder of the *Knickerbocker*, a means of expression for so many New Yorkers, was Charles Fenno Hoffman, a poet who had the knack of writing songs which were sung and whistled everywhere: *Rosalie Clare; 'Tis Hard to Share Her Smiles With Many; Room, Boys, Room;* and others. Hoffman died after a long period of insanity. In a few lyrics he revealed real power. His *Sparkling and Bright* and *Monterey* are still good reading.

305   Bryant's Birthplace at Cummington, Mass., from M. J. Lamb,
The Homes of America, 1879

tion included Latin and Greek, and he became in boyhood a zealous reader. In his father's library and elsewhere he read, in early years, Homer, Pope, Byron, Scott, and Henry Kirke White. He had a poet's precocity, publishing the political satire, *The Embargo,* at the age of fourteen. In 1817 he amazed the readers of the *North American Review* with *Thanatopsis* (No. 317), possibly his best-known poem. Wordsworth is said to have committed it to memory. Six months after the death of Cooper a memorial meeting was held in New York. Near Daniel Webster, who directed the service, sat Washington Irving. At the close of Webster's address, it was the most distinguished poet of the Knickerbockers, William Cullen Bryant, who rose to pay tribute to their novelist.

306   From a miniature, 1819, by Stibble in the
New York Historical Society

307   From a photograph of a sketch by Daniel Huntington (1816–1906)
made at the Cooper Commemoration, 1852

AMERICA'S FIRST POET OF NATURE

IN the same number was the beautiful *Inscription for the Entrance to a Wood.* Two years earlier as he walked the bleak Berkshire road at sunset he saw a waterfowl in flight against the sky, and wrote, thinking of his own loneliness and uncertain future, the poem *To a Waterfowl.* Thus he unconsciously heralded the meaning of his life. He was to be, above all else, America's first poet of nature, destined to write not of the English larch or oak, but of the pine, the maple, the birch.

EDITOR OF THE NEW YORK
EVENING POST

BY 1825 Bryant had had a year at Williams College, had been a lawyer, had studied widely, had read *The Ages* before the Harvard Phi Beta Kappa Society, and had married. In this year he began, as editor of the *New York Review and Atheneum Magazine,* his half century in New York. Here his ability as a publicist and editor developed, and for many years the New York *Evening Post* meant William Cullen Bryant.

308   From *Graham's Magazine,* Vol. 23, 1843, after a drawing by C. G. Thompson

AN IMPRESSIVE FIGURE AMONG
HIS CONTEMPORARIES

THE year 1828 found him editor-in-chief of the *Post.* From 1834 to 1836 he was abroad. His dignified and thoughtful editorials definitely influenced American thought. He became toward the end of his fourscore years a venerable figure in New York streets. He was known as a traveler, lecturer, editor, and as a poet of nature, but—alas! —the years in New York had checked the flow of poetry. He continued to write, but poetry was now incidental to a distinguished public career. He wrote editorials which for a generation helped to shape American

310   From a carte de visite after a Brady negative

309   From *The Bryant Homestead Book,* New York, 1870, after a cartoon by Thomas Nast (1840–1902)

thought, especially during the Civil War. A revaluation of his life must include a study of his prose.

311   From *Scribner's Monthly*, Vol. XVI, 1878

BRYANT'S LAST YEARS

In his last years, which he divided between the homestead at Cummington and his country estate, Cedarmere, at Roslyn, Long Island, Bryant was a noble and impressive American. In these days his prose, in essay, editorial, or lecture, was well known. He had published some of his articles in *The Talisman*. Among these was his study *On Trisyllabic Feet in Iambic Measure*. Bryant's prose has the clarity of his poetry. "Its truthfulness, in accuracy of thought and diction," says a contemporary, "is a constant charm to those who know the value of words." A citizen of New York or of the world in his thinking, he was still in his appearance and in his severe inner life a New England Puritan. Recalling his boyhood studies, he sought a mental refuge, after the death of his wife, in a translation of Homer.

Hawthorne found Bryant, as others have found his poetry, cold; and he failed to interest the Brownings. Something of the chill of thirty winters in the Berkshires lingered in his blood. Bryant's prose is clear, forceful, and matter-of-fact. His poetry of nature has more fiber than that of the later New Englanders. To trace his poetic development is difficult. The late verse has possibly more fancy, but between such a poem as *The Yellow Violet* and *Robert O'Lincoln* there is actually little difference.

POEMS

BY

WILLIAM CULLEN BRYANT,

AN AMERICAN.

EDITED BY

WASHINGTON IRVING.

LONDON:

J. ANDREWS, 167, NEW BOND STREET.

M DCCC.XXXII.

313   Title-page of Bryant, *Poems*, London, 1832

312   Bryant's Summer Home, Cedarmere, Roslyn, L. I., from M. J. Lamb,
The Homes of America, 1879

POEMS, 1832

After the youthful poetry the most important volume was that of 1832, with the *Forest Hymn*, *The Rivulet*, *Monument Mountain*, *Song of Marion's Men*, *Summer Wind*, *A Winter Piece*, *Oh fairest of the rural maids*, *To the fringed Gentian*, *The Death of the Flowers*, and other characteristic lyrics. This volume was introduced abroad by Washington Irving.

OTHER THEMES

IT was natural for the first great American journalist to write in his poetry of other themes than nature. The influence of foreign ideas is apparent. Bryant, too, was far enough from the red man to depict him romantically, and *Monument Mountain*, with its tale of the Indian maiden who died for love, creates a mood continued by Longfellow.

314   *Monument Mountain*, from Bryant, *Poems*, Philadelphia, 1849, engraving after a drawing by Emanuel Leutze

315   Illustration for *The Death of the Flowers*, from *In the Woods with Bryant, Longfellow, and Halleck*, New York, 1863, engraving after a drawing by John A. Hows (1831–74)

POETRY OF AUTUMN

ALTHOUGH Bryant writes gently of the Indian, he can give us a rousing battle lyric, like the *Song of Marion's Men*. His famous line on Truth is in a poem on war. Yet, after all, Bryant is the American poet of nature — nay, aside from delight in its particular aspects, of one mood in American nature. He is the poet of autumn. He loves the freezing stream and the darkening November land-scape.

BRYANT'S ATTITUDE TOWARD NATURE

NATURE fills him with awe. He connects it less with joy than with the eternal flow of things. Though a thousand

316   Illustration for *To a Waterfowl*, from *American Melodies*, 1841

springs, he said, gushed up in his heart when he first read the *Lyrical Ballads*, yet Bryant's nature is not God, or the garment of God, but rather His temple. "Father, thy hand hath reared these venerable columns," he sings of the forest. And *The Rivulet* suggests not so much the joy of nature as the transiency of man. Thus the wild fowl is but one of God's symbols in nature for guidance in life.

His harm to compass, and his good oppose?
No; one alone, the hapless being spares,
Wages no war, and no resistance dares.
    Yes, earth, kind earth, her new-born son beholds,
Spreads a soft shelter, in her robe enfolds,
Still, like a mother kind, her love retains,
Cheers by her sweetness, with her food sustains,
Paints her fair flow'rs to wake her infant smile,
Spreads out her fruits to sooth his hour of toil,
Renews her prospects, versatile and gay,
To charm his eye, and cheat his cares away,
And if her roseate buds, a thorn conceal,
If some sharp sting the roving hand should feel,
A med'cine kind, the sweet physician sends,
And where her poison wounds, her balm defends.
    But, when at last, her drooping charge declines,
When the dear lamp of life no longer shines,
When o'er its broken idol, friendship mourns,
And love, in horrour, from its object turns,
E'en while affection shudders, as it grieves,
She to her arms, her mould'ring son receives,
Sings a low requiem, to her darling birth,
'Return' thou lov'd one, to thy parent earth.'
Safe in her bosom, the deposit keeps,
Until the flame that dries the watry deeps,
Spreads o'er me parching skies its quenchless blaze,
Reddens her features, on her vitals preys.
Then struggling in her last, convulsive throes,
She wakes her treasure from his deep repose,
Stays her last groan, amid dissolving fires,
Resigns him to his Maker, and expires.

Thanatopsis.

Not that from life, and all its woes
The hand of death shall set me free;
Not that this head, shall then repose
In the low vale most peacefully.

Ah, when I touch time's farthest brink,
A kinder solace must attend;
It chills my very soul, to think
On that dread hour when life must end.

In vain the flatt'ring verse may breathe,
Of ease from pain, and rest from strife,

There is a sacred dread of death
Inwoven with the strings of life.

This bitter cup at first was given
When angry *justice* frown'd severe,
And 'tis the eternal doom of heaven
That man must view the grave with fear.

      —— Yet a few days, and thee,
The all-beholding sun, shall see no more,
In all his course; nor yet in the cold ground,
Where thy pale form was laid, with many tears,
Nor in th' embrace of ocean shall exist
Thy image. Earth, that nourished thee, shall claim
Thy growth, to be resolv'd to earth again;
And, lost each human trace, surrend'ring up
Thine individual being, shalt thou go
To mix forever with the elements,
To be a brother to th' insensible rock
And to the sluggish clod, which the rude swain
Turns with his share, and treads upon. The oak
Shall send his roots abroad, and pierce thy mould.
Yet not to thy eternal resting place
Shalt thou retire alone—nor couldst thou wish
Couch more magnificent. Thou shalt lie down
With patriarchs of the infant world—with kings
The powerful of the earth—the wise, the good,
Fair forms, and hoary seers of ages past,
All in one mighty sepulchre.—The hills,
Rock-ribb'd and ancient as the sun,—the vales
Stretching in pensive quietness between;
The venerable woods—the floods that move
In majesty,—and the complaining brooks,
That wind among the meads, and make them green,
Are but the solemn decorations all,
Of the great tomb of man.—The golden sun,
The planets, all the infinite host of heaven
Are glowing on the sad abodes of death,
Through the still lapse of ages. All that tread
The globe are but a handful to the tribes
That slumber in its bosom.—Take the wings
Of morning—and the Borean desert pierce—
Or lose thyself in the continuous woods
That veil Oregan, where he hears no sound
Save his own dashings—yet—the dead are there,
And millions in those solitudes, since first

317   From the *North American Review*, September, 1817, written by Bryant in 1811

DIDACTICISM

Such "moral interpretation of nature" often becomes frankly didactic, and this fault has injured Bryant's fame more than his limited range, his lack of dramatic sense, his echoes of Campbell, Blair, and Cowper, or his dearth of humor. This conception of nature is joined to his attitude toward death, a central concept in his poetry, which, appearing first in the rhetorical *Thanatopsis*, is always severe, dignified, and free from sentimentality, even in such a poem as *The Fountain*.

BRYANT'S INNER LIFE

Putting together these characteristics of Bryant: his rather orthodox view of God and nature, his sense of the passage of the years and the majesty of death, his meditative cast of mind, his luminous directness, his sternness — all evident in such poems as *The Flood of Years*, *The Ages*, or others already mentioned — we understand more clearly the inner springs of his mind.

318   From a carte de visite by A. A. Turner, New York

319   Illustration for *The Fountain*, from Bryant, *Poems*, 1849, engraving after a drawing by Emanuel Leutze

320   From the portrait by Wyatt Eaton (1849–96) in the Brooklyn Museum

A BELATED PURITAN

BRYANT was a belated Puritan, turning at last, after two centuries, to the nature of his ancestors. Gone is his belief in a Calvinistic future — he is a Unitarian — but here still, as in many of us, centuries later, are the same convictions that life is brief, that death is certain, and that man's lot is full of darkness. As Bryant feels beneath the arches of the forest, so many of his Puritan ancestors had felt before him. As Cooper, our first novelist, draws together the unspoken thoughts of men concerning the frontier, so Bryant sums up their moods toward nature.

One other phase of his nature poetry has been underemphasized, in the mad attempt to compare him with the giant Wordsworth. This is something which is peculiarly his own, and beautiful: his closeness to the earth and things of the earth.

Endowed neither with the natural magic of Keats, nor the profound philosophy of Wordsworth, he cannot appeal to either highly imaginative or highly intellectual men. But the yellow violet, the fringed gentian, the American tree, the winds of autumn — sights, sounds, smells of the soil for their own sake — these Bryant can offer, really for the first time in American literature.

CHAPTER VI

THE TRANSCENDENTALISTS

WHILE the Knickerbockers were caricaturing the Yankees as psalm-singers, traders, and schoolmasters, the deeper thought of the Puritan states was unfolding into a new intellectual life, so virile that it may be justly called "The Renaissance of New England." This movement of revolt against the outworn in religious, social, and political thought began in the 'thirties, and ended only in the strife of the Civil War. Its origins were confused: an accumulation of liberal thought after the downfall of Calvinism; democracy; revolutionary thought abroad; European speculative philosophy. For thirty years this tendency made New England supreme in American thought. Among its voices were those of the Channings, Parker, Margaret Fuller, Alcott, Thoreau. Above all, men heard "a clear and pure voice," says Matthew Arnold, "which for my ear, . . . brought a strain as new, and moving, and unforgettable, as the strain of Newman, or Carlyle, or Goethe." To our generation the resurgence of New England means Emerson. Before him the movement is linked with Unitarianism, in him with transcendentalism, and after him with the great humanitarian reforms.

In one sense Puritan New England had remained unchanged. Its traders and its seamen were everywhere, but the people of Jonathan Edwards and the Mathers still brooded on the unseen world. (Emerson himself was the product of several generations of clergymen.) New England was still a hotbed of religious discussion. We should remember that there had always been liberals — such as Jonathan Mayhew — among the Puritans. Free thought received impetus from the reaction against dogmatism which followed hard on the Great Awakening of 1734–44. The most important aspect of this reaction was emphasis upon the individual's relation to God: his power to assist in his own redemption, to commune directly with God without recourse to doctrines like that of the Trinity. The Unitarians, as they came to be called, throve; in 1819 Channing preached a sermon in Baltimore which was a signal gun for an active and powerful warfare upon the old orthodoxy.

To the Unitarians Emerson owed much, but mainly in an indirect way. They were not mystics, but they were conservative in thought, cultured, and intellectual. "The literature on their tables," says one of them, "represented a wide mental activity. Their libraries contained authors never found before on ministerial shelves." Thus Unitarianism stimulated reading and freedom of thought. Moreover, the Unitarians' denial of the essential depravity of man, so fundamental in Calvin, suited both the righteousness of a New England community — when contrasted with the great European cities for which Calvinism was designed — and the disposition of the forward-looking Americans. Especially did this hopefulness seem a natural garment for such a temperament as Emerson's. To the end of his life the philosophy of Emerson taught that man was not innately bad, but instinctively good. If the individual is basically good, he may trust himself. If he does this, he will find the invisible world speaking to him in the depths of his heart, perhaps under the old guises of God, but, more likely, under those which the speculative, philosophical thought of the time suggests to him. Since he believes in the dignity of the soul, he will adhere easily to the doctrine of innate ideas, transmitted from Kant, Fichte, and Schelling, through Coleridge and Carlyle, and interpreted by French philosophers. He will come to credit that which transcends experience, in the reason, or the soul which unites with God, rather than the understanding which analyzes, and even disputes the evidence of the soul. He will do this the more easily because the contemporary thinkers of England are revolutionary.

And since the New Englander is less a metaphysician than a practical man (perhaps because he is an American), he will try to put his beliefs into practice in new creeds: we hear of Universalists, Adventists, and Come-outers. He will experiment with his intellectual freedom; establish a Brook Farm, found a *Dial*, conduct antislavery campaigns, go in for mesmerism, and become mildly queer.

As we study transcendentalism to-day we hear most distinctly the serene voice of Emerson. When he speaks of man's communion with "the oversoul" he says: "From within or from behind, the light shines through us upon things, and makes us aware that we are nothing, but the light is all." Or: "The sun shines to-day also . . . There are new lands, new men, new thoughts." But in the 'thirties and 'forties there was a babel of other voices; the concept of the oversoul was for some minds a dim and perilous way. Alcott was once asked by a lady whether omnipotence abnegated attribute. Alcott's *Orphic Sayings*, oracles in the *Dial*, discussions of "Harmonic Unity," vegetarianism — all proclaimed the day of the crank. On October 30, 1840, Emerson wrote to Carlyle: "We are a little wild here with numberless projects of social reform; not a reading man but has a draft of a new Community in his waistcoat pocket. I am gently mad myself."

The most famous of the projects was that of the Brook Farm community, which took form in 1841, at West Roxbury, Massachusetts. Here gathered for coöperative work men and women either Transcendentalists or in sympathy with this philosophy. They were restrained Fourierists, living in comradeship, drawing inspiration from nature, and wooing refinement and culture. Their organ of expression was the *Harbinger*, and many of them were contributors to the *Dial*. George Ripley, the leader, Charles A. Dana, Margaret Fuller, and even Hawthorne were prominent in the New England Utopia. To the *Harbinger* also contributed F. H. Hedge, Horace Greeley, G. W. Curtis, and T. W. Higginson. Hawthorne was keenly sensitive to the aspirations and also to the little absurdities of his friends. The best pictures of Brook Farm may be found in his *Note-Books* and — idealized — in *The Blithedale Romance*, in which the heroine Zenobia is presumably an adumbration of Margaret Fuller. Of the cows on the farm Hawthorne writes: "The number is now increased by a transcendental heifer belonging to Miss Margaret Fuller. She is very fractious, I believe, and apt to kick over the milk-pail. . . . April 16th. I have milked a cow!!!"

Brook Farm continued until 1847, the *Harbinger* for two years more. With this microcosm both the hard-headed and the mockers have had much fun, as with the *Dial*, a quarterly edited first by Margaret Fuller, later by Emerson. The pages of the *Dial* include inscrutable nonsense worthy of its motto: "Energise about the Hecatic sphere." Its contributors numbered, besides most of the Transcendentalists mentioned, James Freeman Clarke, John S. Dwight, Christopher P. Cranch, Francis G. Shaw, and William Ellery Channing, Jr. Yet in the *Dial* was such significant writing as a translation of an important lecture of Schelling; reviews of Landor and of Carlyle's *Past and Present;* translations of the sacred writings of the Eastern Races, the "Ethnical Scriptures"; and some of Emerson's best poetry. Nebulous much of this experimenting is, touched with provincialism and solemn eccentricity, but beautiful it is, too: in its high faith, in its purity of temper. Even Jonathan Edwards in the next world, freed of his dark delusions, might approve of the moral idealism of these later Puritans.

Emerson's description of the crusaders, which appeared in the *Dial*, is long, but unrivaled: "No one," he says, "can converse much with different classes of society in

New England without remarking the progress of a revolution. Those who share in it have no external organization, no badge, no creed, no name. They do not vote, or print, or even meet together. They do not know each other's faces or names. They are united only in a common love of truth, and love of its work. They are of all conditions and constitutions. Of these acolytes, if some are happily born and well bred, many are no doubt ill dressed, ill placed, ill made —with as many scars of hereditary vice as other men. Without pomp, without trumpet, in lonely and obscure places, in solitude, in servitude, in compunctions and privations, trudging beside the team in the dusty road, or drudging as hireling in other men's cornfields, schoolmasters, who teach a few children rudiments for a pittance, ministers of small parishes of the obscurer sects, lone women in dependent condition, matrons and young maidens, rich and poor, beautiful and hard-favored, without concert or proclamation of any kind, they have silently given in their several adherence to a new hope, and in all companies do signify a greater trust in the nature and resources of man, than the laws or the popular opinions will well allow."

In all this Emerson himself was at once a leader and onlooker. He overrated men like Alcott, but he was aware of the incoherences of his followers, alluding in his essays to "Arcadian fanaticism." He refused steadily to be drawn into controversy, saying he could not argue. Returning from his pilgrimage to the thinkers of Europe, he was convinced that he was truly returning to himself. One's self and the unseen were, after all, the only realities. We can think of him visiting Brook Farm and editing the *Dial* and interested in antislavery reforms, but less easily than we imagine him walking alone, reading, writing in the growing *Journal*, molding these thoughts into the aphorisms for his essays or lectures — solitary. Yet a cardinal principle of his philosophy forbade condemnation of the vagaries of his disciples. They, too, were practising self-reliance. "The riddle of the age," he says in *Fate*, "has for each a private solution." Emerson's own writings are not without haze. The notion of the "Universal Being," that the soul is "part and particle of God," is given to us in fragments. It is never a system, and sometimes the poet's ecstasy wraps it in a cloud, golden but none the less a cloud. This, however, illuminates still more his integrity. He has the dreamer's indifference to consistency or to the by-products of the search for truth. Emerson is the leader of the Transcendentalists, but it is the leadership of the seer, never of the reformer. Brook Farm, the *Dial* passed, and transcendentalism became for many the humanitarian movement. For Emerson it remained "the firmament of the soul."

In transcendentalism itself then Emerson is unique. In its results, however, he shares honors with his followers. The whole spiritual life of the nation was affected by Emerson's high pitch, but men's activity took form under the practical efforts of the lesser men. Hawthorne feels, I think, the influence of Emerson himself; Whittier, the currents of reforming thought which he set in motion. Taking the spiritual and the practical sides together there is hardly a New England writer unaffected by transcendentalism, — Longfellow, Holmes, Lowell. All this was a growth from the past. There is transcendentalism in Peter Bulkeley, Emerson's ancestor. Edwards is full of it. The "Renaissance of England" was the supreme flowering of Puritan idealism.

321   A View on Boston Common, after an aquatint,
about 1813, by J. Kidder

RALPH WALDO EMERSON, 1803–82

RALPH WALDO EMERSON, more than any other American writer, is detached from locality. We place his essays on the shelf with Montaigne's, and feel no disparity. Yet Emerson is peculiarly ours. He was, in the words of the reiterated pun, a lover of Concord; one strain in his nature is pure New England. There is homespun simplicity in his talk of crops and weather, and many of his metaphors are flowers of his native soil. Emerson's serenity began in boyhood: "A spiritual-looking boy," says Cabot in his *Memoir of Emerson*, ". . . whose image, more than any other's, is deeply stamped upon my mind." After the death, in 1811, of his father, the cultivated pastor of the First Church in Boston, he was under the care of his mother and "Aunt Mary Moody" Emerson, mentors not likely to weaken his character.

PASTORATE OF THE SECOND CHURCH

IN 1821, the year of Emerson's graduation from Harvard, Carlyle in far-off Galloway was being delivered from

322   From a miniature, about 1829, by Miss Goodrich in possession of Mrs. William H. Forbes, Milton, Mass.

"miserable doubts and speculations" by Goethe's *Wilhelm Meister*. There was little indeed in these years to indicate the coupling of Emerson's name with Carlyle's: at the college he ranked, in a class of fifty-nine, thirtieth. Then followed teaching and preaching days, saddened, in 1831, by the loss of his wife. In such a career we must find our drama in the moral crises of the great man. In the life of a Newman it may be a "Tract 90"; in that of an Emerson a sermon on the Lord's Supper, his last as minister of the Second Church. Sentences in this suggest that the revelation of genius was imminent; they are like fearless passages in the *Essays*: ". . . It is my desire, in the office of a Christian minister, to do nothing which I cannot do with my whole heart. Having said this, I have said all. I have no hostility to this institution; I am only stating my want of sympathy with it. . . . I am not interested in it. I am content that it stand to the end of the world, if it please man and please Heaven. . . ."

323   From a miniature, 1845, by Mrs. Robert Hildreth in possession of Mrs. William H. Forbes, Milton, Mass.

EMERSON AND CARLYLE

THIS is clearly the first step beyond Unitarianism. "I never could make much of Unitarians," growled Carlyle in a letter to Mill, in 1832, the year in which Emerson left Concord for Europe. On September 10, 1833, Carlyle again wrote his correspondent: "Emerson, your Presentee, rolled up hither, one still Sunday afternoon, while we sat at dinner." "Hither" was lonely Craigen-

324   Carlyle's Home at Craigenputtock, from a photograph by Robert Dinwiddie, Dumfries, Scotland, courtesy of Stanley T. Williams

puttock. Who that has traveled the long road over the silent moors has not thought of this scene? "A most gentle, recommendable, amiable, whole-hearted man; . . . A good 'Socinian' understanding, the clearest heart; above all," Carlyle adds, "what I loved in the man was his health, his unity with himself."

325   From John Warner Barber, *Historical Collections of Massachusetts*, Worcester, 1839, engraving after
a drawing by J. W. Barber

EMERSON'S LIFE AT CONCORD

He was at unity with himself. Back at Concord in 1833 his work had begun. He had seen the men of whom he had dreamed: Carlyle, Coleridge, Landor, and Wordsworth; and he returned now to meditation. In 1836 appeared *Nature*, the sesame to so much in Emerson; in 1837, the address before the Harvard Phi Beta Kappa Society, which Carlyle read with admiration; and in 1838, the challenge to the Divinity School at Cambridge. From now on, save for family sorrows, peace and distinction came to him in his home at Concord. There was travel abroad, lecturing in New England and in the West. Then quietly appeared the *Essays*, 1841, 1844; the *Poems*, 1847; *Representative Men*, 1850; *English Traits*, 1856; *Conduct of Life*, 1860; and *Society and Solitude*, 1870.

EMERSON'S CONCORD HOME

Even the tragedy of the failing mind from about 1870 to the end in 1882 was softened by the affection of his friends, and by the unchanging sweetness of his nature. The destruction of his house by fire brought him a practical and moving proof of the regard of his fellow-townsmen, who insisted upon rebuilding it for him.

326   From an original drawing by E. J. Meeker

327   From a photograph in the Harvard
College Library

LAST DAYS

Emerson's pathetic illness weakened his memory: "I can't tell its name," he said of an umbrella, not without a touch of Yankee humor, "but I can tell its history: strangers take it away." Toward the end he looked at pictures in books like a child, and at Longfellow's funeral he said: "That gentleman was a sweet, beautiful soul, but I have entirely forgotten his name." The final story is as thrilling in what it suggests as the last letters between Carlyle and John Sterling. For at the last, he saw near him a picture of Carlyle, and whispered: "That is that man, my man."

IDEAS IN *NATURE*

LIKE Carlyle, Emerson develops a few recurrent ideas. In *Nature*, which Oliver Wendell Holmes rightly calls "a reflective prose poem," are the principles of the later essays and poems. That the only reality is Mind: "A noble doubt perpetually suggests itself, whether this end [discipline] be not the Final Cause of the Universe; and whether nature outwardly exists." That the expression of the Mind is an all-pervading beauty: "Beauty in its largest and profoundest sense

328   Emerson's Study, Concord.   © Halliday Historic Photograph Co.

is the expression for the Universe." That Nature educates the moral nature and the intellect: "The moral law lies at the center of Nature . . ."

Thus, Emerson says, "we behold the real higher law." As he meditates he sometimes rises into rhapsody: "Standing on the bare ground, — my head bathed by the blithe air, and uplifted into infinite space, — all mean egotism vanishes. I become a transparent eyeball; I am nothing; I see all; the currents of the Universal Being circulate through me; I am part and particle of God." Passages like this may be found in Fichte, Carlyle, and in all the Transcendentalists.

EMERSONIAN EPIGRAMS

THESE epigrams make, apart from his philosophy, a literature in themselves. For all men, he says: "the unremitting retention of simple and high sentiments in obscure duties"; for the doubter: "Trust thyself! every heart vibrates to that iron string"; for himself: "Give me health and a day, and I will make the pomp of emperors ridiculous"; for worship: "Let us be silent, — so we may hear the whisper of the gods"; for the hesitant: "Hitch your wagon to a star," and "Every man has a call to do something unique"; for independence: "What attracts my attention shall have it"; and the famous appeal to America: "We have listened too long to the courtly muses of Europe. . . . We will walk on our own feet; we will work with our own hands; we will speak our own minds." But it was Emerson's feat to bring philosophy down to New England soil. As in all life he discovers unity in variety, so may we find this transcendental light-fountain bathing all his humbler themes: art, experience, manners, domestic life, compensation, books. The power of Emerson is that we turn to him in daily needs: for problems of society, of politics, of art, and for individual difficulties. His ideas he expressed in aphorisms, the polished products of his *Journal*.

329   From a photograph, 1854, in possession of Mrs. William H. Forbes, Milton, Mass.

330   From a photograph, 1873, in possession of Mrs. William H. Forbes, Milton, Mass.

EMERSON'S POETRY

TIME has borne out Arnold's statement before a ruffled audience, that Emerson was not a great poet. A few lyrics, like *The Snowstorm*, portray simply the landscape of New England, but Emerson's poetry is, for the most part, like that of Arnold, concerned with the idea, the idea touched with emotion.

"LAPIDARY" STYLE

SUCH familiar quotations taken from essays on all types of subjects suggest what he himself called his "lapidary" style, "each sentence an infinitely repellent particle." Fault as this is, it serves him well in the moral maxims. It is surprising how effective it is also in the clear-cut biographical sketches in *Representative Men*, or in the addresses, or even in his only work of sustained observation for its own sake, *English Traits*. In all Emerson's writing, besides the vision of the seer, the rapture of the poet, there is the sharp eye of the Yankee. His terse sentences jerk, if we read him for long periods, but in paragraphs, for meditation, as he doubtless meant them to be read, they are, as Matthew Arnold said, "tonic indeed."

331   Illustration for *The Snowstorm*, from *Poets and Etchers*, Boston, 1882, drawing by Smillie

On this green bank, by this soft stream,
We set today a votive stone;
That memory may their deed redeem
When, like our sires, our sons are gone.

Spirit that made those heroes dare
To die, and leave their children free,
Bid Time and Nature gently spare
The shaft we raise to them and Thee.

By the rude bridge that arched the flood,
Their flag to April's breeze unfurled,
Here, once the embattled farmers stood,
And fired the shot heard round the world.

The foe long since in silence slept;
Alike the Conqueror silent sleeps;
And Time the ruined bridge has swept
Down the dark stream which seaward creeps.

332   From *Harper's New Monthly Magazine*, May, 1875

THE *CONCORD HYMN*

THE *Concord Hymn*, with its beautiful homage to "the embattled farmers" of the Revolution, is one of the few exceptions to Emerson's usual metaphysical mood in poetry. Some of its lines have passed into the speech of men, but they do not echo the deepest thought of the sage of Concord.

333   Model in Harvard College Library for the statue of Emerson in the Concord Public Library, made in 1912 by Daniel Chester French

INDIRECTNESS OF EXPRESSION

FEW of Emerson's poems are as direct in expression as the *Concord Hymn*. He is often as stiff in manner as he is profound in thought; his turn for the oracular is apt to bring with it incoherence. He violates, too, traditions of verse: there are strange inversions, rambling structure, uneven rhymes, even clumsy grammar. Yet *The Sphinx*, *The Rhodora*, *Brahma*, *Days*, and other poems may live. They have, like the prose, piercing insight into life, and are alight with Emerson's serenity.

334 "The rude bridge that arched the flood." © Halliday Historic Photograph Co.

HIS LIMITATIONS AND HIS POWER

NEARLY a century has passed since the Carlyles divined that Emerson had genius. Now it is clear that much of his writing is independent of time and place. One needs to know nothing of America to comprehend Emerson. His faults are obvious: he was not learned; he undervalued science; and he was deficient æsthetically. In his philosophical idealism was much exaggeration. Yet in liberal thought he is still a force. Part of his power is bound up in the sweetness and elevation of his life. He is very different from John Stuart Mill, but Gladstone's name for the Englishman, "the saint of rationalism," might apply, with strong reservations, to Emerson.

335 Emerson's Grave. © Halliday Historic Photograph Co.

EMERSON THE MYSTIC

FUNDAMENTALLY, of course, Emerson is not a rationalist, but a philosopher, a mystic, and a poet. In the stillness of the heart, with the doors of the mortal mind closed, he hears, as clearly as Newman in boyhood beheld the angels, the voice of that which no man can name. Then in words with meaning for the humblest man he declares to us his intuitions. Again Matthew Arnold must be quoted. He wrote in his copy of the *Essays:*

> The seeds of godlike power are in us still;
> Gods are we, bards, saints, heroes, if we will.

Yet this word of Arnold's on Emerson is less than his enduring phrase: Emerson is "the friend and aider of those who would live in the spirit."

336   From a photograph by Elliott and Fry, London

MARGARET FULLER, 1810–50

337   From the portrait, done at Rome, 1847, by
Thomas Hicks (1823–90)

On August 8, 1836, Emerson wrote his brother William: "An accomplished lady is staying with Lidian now, Miss Margaret Fuller. She is quite an extraordinary person for her apprehensiveness, her acquisitions, and her power of conversation." He added that under the influence of her intellect: "you stretch your limbs and dilate to your utmost size." Later Emerson was to long to stretch his limbs for another purpose: to escape from the "repulsions" she occasionally inspired in him — this devotee of the Concord sage, this lecturer in the manner of Socrates, this lady whose favorite studies were demonology and mythology.

No one has ever caught successfully the likeness of "Margaret." She was learned, in some respects masculine, aggressive, somewhat of a mystic, personally unattractive. These characteristics are evident, but for the most part, in spite of the impression she made in New England, her real nature is as difficult to grasp as the surface of a sphere. Even as a young woman she was an accomplished linguist. She taught in Providence and Boston, her classes for women in the latter city becoming famous. She was deeply concerned with sociology, and she made full use of her opportunities for European travel. She was a member of the Brook Farm community, an editor of the *Dial*, 1840–42, and literary editor for Horace Greeley on the New York *Tribune*. After a secret marriage in Italy she set sail for America with her husband, Marquis Ossoli, and their child, only to perish with them by shipwreck, near Fire Island, in 1850. There is something ridiculous about Margaret Fuller's egotism, and her insistent friendship with "Waldo." She wishes, she writes, to "make him the full-fledged angel," by less emphasis on thought. Emerson's reserve would not countenance this translation, or the desired personal intimacy which is the key to his remark in the *Journal:* "She ever seems to crave somewhat I have not, or have not for her."

There is an echo of her aspiration — not unamusing — in the first lines of her frantic *Dryad Song:*

I am immortal! I know it! I feel it!
Hope floods my heart with delight!
Running on air, mad with life, dizzy, reeling,
Upward I mount, — . . .

"Such a determination," says Carlyle, "to *eat* this huge universe!" Her writings are, for the most part, forgotten, save perhaps *Summer on the Lakes*, 1844; *Woman in the Nineteenth Century*, 1844; and *Papers on Literature and Art*, 1846. Margaret Fuller lives chiefly through her literary associations.

AMOS BRONSON ALCOTT, 1799–1888

An admirable proof of the common sense of Emerson is his balance amid the queer, high-minded cranks about him in Concord. In a moment of boredom Emerson christened Amos Bronson Alcott, of Orchard House, "a tedious archangel," but the little Connecticut pedlar with his three or four dreamy, metaphysical ideas, usually delighted him, giving his mind free play, and leading him to call Alcott "the most extraordinary man, and the highest genius of his time." Free play, indeed! Carlyle has two thumbnail sketches of Alcott, the first well known, the second just published. "The good Alcott," he writes, "with his long, lean face and figure, with his gray worn temples and mild radiant eyes; all bent on saving the world by a return to acorns and the golden age; he comes before one like a venerable Don Quixote, whom nobody can laugh at without loving."

338   From a photograph by Warren, Boston

"THE POTATO QUIXOTE"

CARLYLE described him even better in a letter to Sterling. He had been entertained during two meetings. But "the Potato Quixote and I have come to rupture, after our third interview; on my asking him, 'When shall I see you again?' his answer was, 'Never, I guess!' A worthy man; but one of the absurdest I have ever seen." There were excellent qualities in this philosopher, but it is difficult to forget stories like this: "You write," he said to Emerson, "on the genius of Plato, of Pythagoras, of Jesus; why do you not write of me?" Alcott anticipated some of the questions in the pedagogy of to-day. Some of these ideas may be found in *Observations on the Principles and Methods of Infant Instruction*, 1830.

339   Alcott in his Study, from Alcott, *Ralph W. Emerson*, Boston, 1882, after a photograph

QUARTER CARD OF DISCIPLINE AND STUDIES IN MR. ALCOTT'S SCHOOL FOR THE WINTER TERM CURRENT 1837.

THE TUITION AND DISCIPLINE ARE ADDRESSED IN DUE PROPORTION TO THE THREEFOLD NATURE OF MAN.

THE SPIRITUAL FACULTY.	THE IMAGINATIVE FACULTY.	THE RATIONAL FACULTY.
MEANS OF ITS DIRECT CULTURE.	MEANS OF ITS DIRECT CULTURE.	MEANS OF ITS DIRECT CULTURE.
Listening to Sacred Readings on Sunday Morning. Conversations on the GOSPELS. Keeping Journals. Self-Analysis and Self-Discipline. Conversations on Study and Behavior. Government of the School.	Spelling and Reading. Writing and Sketching Maps. Picturesque Geography. Writing Journals, Epistles, and Paraphrases. Illustrating Words. Conversations and Amusements.	Defining Words. Analyzing Speech. Self-Inspection and Self-Analysis. Demonstrations in Arithmetic. Reasonings on Conduct and Discipline. Review of Conduct and Study.

The Subjects of Study and Means of Discipline are disposed through the Week in the following general Order.

TIME.	SUNDAY.	MONDAY.	TUESDAY.	WEDNESDAY.	THURSDAY.	FRIDAY.	SATURDAY.
IX	SACRED READINGS,	WRITING JOURNALS and Studying Lessons.	WRITING JOURNALS and Studying Lessons.	WRITING JOURNALS and Studying Lessons.	WRITING JOURNALS and Studying Lessons.	WRITING JOURNALS and Studying Lessons.	PREPARING JOURNALS AND BOOKS For Examination.
X / XI	with CONVERSATIONS on the TEXT, (BEFORE CHURCH) with	SPELLING with ILLUSTRATIVE CONVERSATIONS on the MEANING AND USE of WORDS.	RECITATIONS in GEOGRAPHY, with CONVERSATIONS and ILLUSTRATIONS.	CONVERSATIONS on the GOSPELS as a MEANS of Spiritual Growth.	ANALYZING SPEECH WRITTEN AND VOCAL with CONVERSATIONS on the PRINCIPLES OF GRAMMAR.	RECITATIONS in ARITHMETIC with DEMONSTRATIONS WRITTEN and MENTAL.	CONVERSATIONS on STUDY and BEHAVIOR as means of PERSONAL IMPROVEMENT.
		RECREATION ON THE COMMON OR IN THE ANTE ROOM.					
X	READINGS and CONVERSATIONS at HOME.	READINGS from CLASS-BOOKS.	WRITING PARAPHRASES.	CONVERSATIONS on NATURE.	WRITING EPISTLES.	READINGS from CLASS-BOOKS.	REVIEW of Studies and Conduct.
		INTERMISSION FOR REFRESHMENT AND RECREATION.					
III / IV	at HOME.	STUDYING LATIN LESSONS with Recitations.	STUDYING FRENCH LESSON with Recitations.	RECREATIONS and DUTIES At Home.	STUDYING LATIN with Recitations.	STUDYING FRENCH with Recitations.	RECREATIONS and DUTIES At Home.

. CONVERSATIONS ON SPIRITUAL CULTURE on Friday Evening of each week, at the School Room No. 7, in the Temple; commencing at 7 o'clock. Teachers of Classes in Sunday Schools, parents, and others interested in Spiritual Culture, are respectfully invited to attend. *Children of both sexes, between the ages of four and fourteen, are admitted to the exercises of the School.*

453   Programme.   1843]

340   From the *Dial*, April, 1843

ALCOTT'S TRANSCENDENTAL SCHOOL

ALCOTT had direct relations with heaven, and never shared the doubts of amused observers concerning his genius. His transcendental school in Boston, where, to compensate for a wrongdoing by a child, he used to flog himself, broke up when he introduced colored students. Some of the results of his teaching he published in 1836–37 as *Conversations with Children on the Gospels*. A year later he was ready with a rhapsody, *Psyche, or the Breath of Childhood*, but it never appeared. It is not culpable merely to mention his verse, *Sonnets and Canzonets*, 1882, and *New Connecticut*, 1881, an autobiographical poem. The prose, *Concord Days*, 1887, or *Tablets*, 1868, or *Table Talk*, 1877, is better. All of these were published during the last twenty years of Alcott's life.

341   Alcott's Home, Concord, from Martha J. Lamb, *The Homes of America*, 1879

342   Brook Farm, from G. H. Gordon, *Brook Farm to Cedar Mountain*, Boston, 1883

TRANSCENDENTAL EXPERIMENTS

ALCOTT overwhelmed Margaret Fuller's *Dial* with Orphic Sayings; he established Fruitlands, a Utopian experiment; he helped at Brook Farm; and he founded the Concord School of Philosophy. He is a delightful example of New England transcendentalism undefiled by a speck of everyday judgment.

343   From Jones Very, *Poems*, Boston, 1886, courtesy
         of Houghton Mifflin Company

JONES VERY, 1813–80

AMONG other Transcendentalists, such as Christopher P. Cranch, William Ellery Channing, Jr., James Freeman Clarke, John S. Dwight, and Orestes A. Brownson, perhaps the most truly literary and artistic was Jones Very. Cranch, by birth a Virginian, lived for a time among the Transcendentalists, and was afterward a student of art abroad. Channing, a nephew of the elder William Ellery Channing, was a brother-in-law of Margaret Fuller, became an editor, and wrote a life of Thoreau. James Freeman Clarke, a distinguished Unitarian clergyman, was known for his zeal as a reformer, and his books on theology, notably *Ten Great Religions*. Brownson had a strange career as Presbyterian, Universalist, Unitarian, and Roman Catholic. He was a politician, and his writings include not merely theological works, but *The Spirit Rapper: an Autobiography*, 1854, and a novel, *Charles Elwood, or The Infidel Converted*, 1840. Emerson found Very "a treasure of a companion," but understated the popular view when he said Very might be insane. He was for a time imprisoned as a lunatic. His poems and essays reveal his intense life of the spirit. Very was a genuine poet. The following lines from *The Old Road* suggest his affinity with the Transcendentalists:

> . . . Learn to go.
> Obey the spirit's gentle force,
> Nor ask thee where the stream may flow.

HENRY DAVID THOREAU, 1817–62

THE real individualist of the Concord group, aside from Emerson, was Henry David Thoreau, poet, naturalist, mystic, humanitarian. Thoreau was born (on the paternal side of French descent, on the maternal of New Englanders) in 1817, the year in which Emerson entered Harvard. He himself was graduated from the college in the year of Emerson's address before the Phi Beta Kappa Society, an unsocial member of the class of 1837. During his life in Concord he was externally school-teacher, pencil-maker, lecturer, and writer, especially for the *Dial*. But the real Thoreau was an idealist, a dreamer, a lover of nature, a fearless and practical interpreter of the transcendental view of life. He was the tireless seeker of the unseen through communion with nature. He died in 1862 murmuring the words: "moose" and "Indian."

344 From a photograph of the crayon drawing, 1854, by Samuel W. Rouse (1822–1901) in the Concord Public Library

345 Thoreau's desk and couch, from the hut at Walden Pond.
© Halliday Historic Photograph Co.

THOREAU'S ORIGINALITY

CERTAIN influences focus in Thoreau. Possibly his French ancestry plays a part in his romantic love of nature. His wide reading brought him the news of European individualism. Beginning in 1841 he lived for two years in Emerson's home. The natives of Concord, and Thoreau himself, thought he echoed the greater man's very tones and gestures. But Thoreau was original, not merely as the villagers thought in his seclusion for two years in the hut at Walden Pond, or in his refusal to pay the poll tax, or in his vegetarianism, but, as later Americans have realized, in his reasoned and independent bearing toward life.

THE OBSERVER AND LOVER OF LIFE

HE was not a curiosity, as Stevenson seemed to think, nor a skulker, nor afflicted with "moral shyness." He was a lover of life, and a shrewd observer of the truth that many human beings make patchwork of it. "I went to the woods," he says, in a passage of typical candor, "because I wished to live deliberately, to front only the essential facts of life . . . I did not wish to live what was not life, living is so dear; . . . I wanted to live deep and suck out all the marrow of life . . . to cut a broad swath and shave close, to drive life into a corner, and reduce it to its lowest terms." He wished to avoid the ordinary routine experience of man. "For," he says, "the mass of men live lives of quiet desperation. . . . From the desperate city you go into the desperate country."

346 Thoreau's home in Concord, from a photograph by Clifton Johnson

347   From Thoreau, *Walden*, Boston, 1871, enlargement
       of vignette on the title-page

THE HUT AT WALDEN POND

THESE were the reasons for the famous sojourn at Walden Pond (1845–47); for the fact that he never gave hostages to fortune in wife and child; for his willingness to suffer imprisonment for the abolitionist cause; for his courageous defense of John Brown. Thoreau's fame arrived too late for him to enjoy it. *The Maine Woods*, 1864, *Cape Cod*, 1865, *A Yankee in Canada*, 1866 — which Stevenson thought so dull — appeared after his death. Much of his unique work was given to the world earlier: *A Week on the Concord and Merrimac Rivers*, 1849, and *Excursions*, 1863, with the remarkable essays *Walking, Night and Moonlight*, and *Wild Apples*. *Walden*, 1854, remains the most enduring record of his adventure with nature. Thoreau's life at the little pond, a mile and a half from Concord, was not so barbarous as has been represented. The borrowing of the ax from Alcott to make the clearing is a symbol of Thoreau's proximity to civilization. From his cabin he heard the shriek of the locomotive, and some evenings found him in the village listening to the day's gossip.

348   From a photograph by Clifton Johnson

THE COVE, WALDEN POND, THE SITE OF THOREAU'S HUT

WALDEN chronicles a bold experiment in living. Here Thoreau worked out the problem of man's self-sufficiency. He planted, repaired his cabin, cooked his own food. His living cost him nine cents a day. Then he watched the animals and birds, and looked out through the pines and hickories to the other shore of the little New England lake. At times he meditated on his reading and writing, or just idled. Occasionally there comes over him a sense of mystery; he hears the elusive voice he is seeking. He does not, like Emerson, become a "transparent eyeball," but he is, in homelier fashion, the mystic. Very homely, indeed: "In *me*," he says, "is the sucker that I see."

349   The Concord Meadows, Nawshawtuck Hill in the distance, from a photograph by Clifton Johnson

THOREAU THE LITERARY ARTIST

YET, whether he realized it or not, Thoreau was primarily a writer. More than a dozen volumes are enough for any anchorite. Stevenson was much interested in his methods of composition, and any reader may enjoy the beauty of his style. In this respect he far excels Emerson. He is too fond of digressions, but he can state a telling opinion. He transcribes his intense love of nature, and he has a sense of rhythm. Certain passages in *Walden*, or *A Week on the Concord and Merrimac Rivers*, are the work of a literary artist. The latter describes Thoreau's happy journey with his brother.

THOREAU'S BELIEFS

IN some ways Thoreau is the high-water mark of New England transcendentalism. Faith in the oversoul, belief in nature as the garment of the "open secret," trust in oneself, renunciation of the sensuous and the way of the crowd can hardly go further practically than in Thoreau. Walden in winter is perhaps a hint of a certain frostiness in this New England version of the world-wide movement of individualism. Thoreau partook of this bleakness. A friend said: "I love Henry, but I cannot like him; and as for taking his arm, I should as soon think of taking the arm of an elm tree." Yet the seer Emerson and the "poet-naturalist" Thoreau, and their strange brethren, have stirred posterity. They pitched life high, and they belong to us; they are American.

350   Walden Pond in Winter, from a photograph by Clifton Johnson

CHAPTER VII

NINETEENTH–CENTURY POETS AND NOVELISTS

AN eavesdropper on the quiet walks taken by Henry Thoreau and Nathaniel Hawthorne might have found the novelist reserved on certain points of conversation. Listening to Thoreau, Hawthorne said, was "like hearing the wind among the boughs of a forest tree." By transcendentalism Hawthorne was deeply influenced. He had been at Brook Farm, he revered Emerson, and the mystery of the soul was his obsession. But of his friends' extremes he was critical. His shy spirit lived in another world, of which all the writers considered in the present chapter were, in greater or lesser degree, denizens: the world of literature for its own sake. Far more than the philosopher Emerson, or the poet Bryant, or the essayist Irving, or the novelist Cooper, Hawthorne, Poe, Longfellow, Whittier, Lowell, and Holmes cared for creative writing. Whitman as a creative writer is an exception only in his strange themes and in the vigor of his art. Poe, as the Europeans at once discovered, possessed the artist's temperament, without alloy.

The grouping is purely for convenience. Hawthorne is close to the Concord writers, and Longfellow, Whittier, Lowell, and Holmes are often called the Cambridge scholars and poets. Poe and Whitman are bound by literary ties to most of these. In respect to environment the farm affects most distinctly Whittier; the city Longfellow, Lowell, Holmes, Poe, and Whitman, who was also affected by the sea and the frontier. European thought leaves its mark on them all, but most distinctly on Longfellow, Lowell, Holmes, and Poe. Yet they are akin in this, that they weave into romance and poetry, far more than previous poets, movements of thought or the life about them, for artistic purposes.

Poe's tales, with their elaborate workmanship, mark an epoch. Irving had literary conscience, but in fiction he contented himself with beginning the American short-story form. Poe's anathemas against the sentimental, moral novel, the absurd comments on his own stories, and the didactic trash in the periodicals indicate that with most critics and readers the artistic ideal was secondary. Cooper himself by word and example openly flouted the importance of this. No novel prior to *The Scarlet Letter*, 1850, had striven for permanence through finish and beauty of form. In poetry Bryant, by self-cultivation, had developed theories of poetry. Lesser poets like Drake, Halleck, or even Freneau had created a poetry of beauty. Yet one has only to open the portentous anthologies (from some of which Poe is omitted) to encounter the watery taste of the time. The remarkable fact about the Cambridge poets was their conviction that poetry was rich in intellectual pleasure.

More remarkable, however, was the emphasis by some of these poets upon the humble facts of American life. Bryant paints American nature, but seems somewhat to lessen the realism by his formal verse. Where, indeed, are the plow, the wind-swept farm-house, the farmer's boy? All these, however, are in Whittier's poetry, and the scholar and diplomat, Lowell, does not hesitate to describe them in frank Yankee dialect. Holmes' *vers de société* has a New England twang, and Lowell's lyric *The Courtin'* is realism. Long-fellow sees humble folk through his study-window, but the backwoodsman Lincoln weeps when he hears *The Ship of State*. Poe, of course, shuns all this, but Whitman with new subjects and new rhythms announces himself as the poet of democracy.

Apart from the inexplicable portent of Whitman, the increased interest in literature for its own sake is traceable to increased culture. This accounts partly for the freer use of American materials. The perfectly bred Bostonian could afford to be humorous about Yankee backgrounds. The Cambridge writers were sure of themselves. This was the most brilliant and distinguished coterie of literary men which has existed in America. In the 'twenties and 'thirties there were living near Boston: Holmes, Sumner, Motley, Phillips, Emerson, Hale, Lowell, Thoreau. During the 'forties Emerson, in Concord, was publish-ing essays and poems; Hawthorne was living in "The Old Manse" and writing *The Scarlet Letter;* Whittier was at Amesbury; Lowell was practicing law and writing *The Vision of Sir Launfal, A Fable for Critics*, and *The Biglow Papers;* Holmes was teaching in the Harvard Medical School; and later Longfellow and Lowell were successively pro-fessors of modern languages at the same university. "Boston State-house," said Holmes, "is the hub of the Solar System." Not quite that, but at no great distance from the Charles River were the *literati* of America. "These are," said a foreign critic, "*tiny* men of letters." Yet dining with them, one may hear good conversation. There are theaters, clubs, the university. From time to time some of the notables are absent in Europe, not unwelcome there. At close range these are cultivated, delightful men, and talented. It becomes easier to understand their interest in literature as an art.

Farther south Poe is finding a less academic and freer intellectual life in New York, Philadelphia, Baltimore, and Richmond. Here journalism is a fascinating game. It is the age of the magazinist and *littérateur*. Bryant and Halleck are writing. The journals publish stolen versions of the latest English novels. Literature becomes more distinctly a profession in itself, and it is less strange that an artistic nature, like Poe's, derives some inspiration from the city. In both New England and in the middle and southern states between 1830 and 1870 conditions are more favorable than ever before for the creation of romance and poetry.

351 Old Corner Bookstore, Boston, from Win-sor, *Memorial History of Boston*, Vol. II, 1886

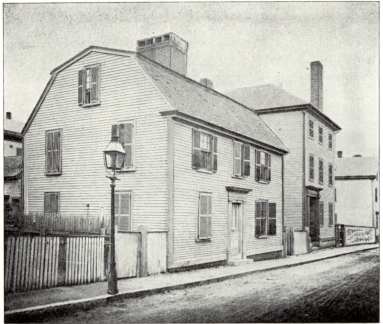

352   Birthplace of Hawthorne, Salem, Mass.

NATHANIEL HAW-THORNE, 1804–64

IN 1804, in Salem, was born, of seafaring Puritan ancestors, our first great master of prose romance, Nathaniel Hawthorne. After his father's death in 1808 began a period of solitude, interrupted by the years at Bowdoin College (1821–25) and by stays at his grandfather's farm in Maine, but resumed for thirteen consecutive years. Solitary, shy, meditative Hawthorne was, even after his happy engagement in 1838. Biographers have dwelt upon these years apart as a cause of his sensitiveness to the problems of sorrow and conscience. From this solitude comes much of the richness and repose of his thought, but Hawthorne was rightly amused at

pictures of himself as delicately morbid.

353   From the painting by C. W. Jefferys (1869–)
            in possession of the publishers

SURVEYOR OF CUSTOMS, SALEM

HE wandered, musing, a picturesque figure, alone, through the streets of the old seaport town. In company he was reserved. He himself says of the influence upon him of this isolation: "Living in solitude till the fulness of time was come, I still kept the dew of my youth and the freshness of my heart." Yet he was merry at college; he was noted for his strength and attractiveness; he was once engaged to fight a duel; and as surveyor of customs he could be a terror to insolent sea captains.

HAWTHORNE AND HIS PUBLISHERS

IN these years Hawthorne had already written much and had been an editor, but he was still, as he used to say, "the obscurest man of letters in America." His two years (1839–41) as a weigher in the Boston custom house ended suddenly. He then entered, though with

354   James T. Fields, Hawthorne, and William D. Ticknor, from a carte de visite in the Harvard College Library

mental reservations, the Brook Farm community. He was not slow to realize that for him at least this commitment was an error: "Is it," he asks, "a praiseworthy matter that I have spent five golden months in providing food for cows and horses? It is not so."

AT HOME IN THE OLD MANSE, CONCORD

AFTER his marriage in 1842 Hawthorne settled down in the Old Manse for four years, in the very study where Emerson had written *Nature*. Here New England Puritans had composed their sermons, and from the windows of this house, one clergyman had seen his parishioners oppose the British on the opposite side of the river: "He awaited in an agony of suspense the rattle of the musketry. It came, and there needed but a gentle wind to sweep the battle smoke around this quiet house." It was a house of memories, of gloom and sunshine, a house fit to shelter Nathaniel Hawthorne.

In Concord, Hawthorne was a detached member of the transcendentalist group. Meanwhile, he mixed on easy terms with farmers, sea captains, and humble men. He became, in 1846, surveyor of customs at Salem, for three years. He lived afterward at Lenox, at West Newton, and again in Concord, at the "Wayside." In 1853 his intimate friend, President Franklin Pierce, appointed him United States consul at Liverpool. In England he knew few men of letters, but later drank deeply of the art and beauty of Italy. He died in the White Mountains in 1864, on a holiday journey with his classmate, Pierce.

355   From May Alcott, *Concord Sketches*, Boston, 1869, in the Yale Collection of American Literature

EARLY WORK OF HAWTHORNE

FANSHAWE, 1828, had failed, but after the publication of *Twice-Told Tales*, 1837, and *Mosses from an Old Manse*, 1846, Poe wrote that in "capability of doing" Hawthorne resembled Coleridge in England at an earlier time. Actually Hawthorne's achievement meant more than this. Sketches like *Young Goodman Brown* or *The Snow Image* first unveiled his dark luxuriance of imagination.

356   Part of the first page of the Ms. of Hawthorne's *The Old Manse*, in the New York Public Library

357   From *Compositions in Outline from Hawthorne's Scarlet Letter*, by F. O. C. Darley, Boston, 1879

THE SCARLET LETTER

THEN in the year 1850, that memorable year for both English and American literature, he read to his wife — the story is, perhaps, apocryphal — in a voice swelling with emotion, the manuscript of *The Scarlet Letter*. In this novel Hawthorne's emotional unity with the somber Puritans' lives, with their anguishing conception of sin, as well as his power as an artist, reach their full expression. In the dark-tinted tapestry are four figures: the minister Dimmesdale, clutching at his heart as the letter burns into his soul, or flames in the heavens; the wronged Chillingworth; Pearl, Hester Prynne's child, like a gleam of sunshine in the New England forest; and Hester herself in her serenity.

PURITANISM IN *THE SCARLET LETTER*

AT later readings we may pause over Hawthorne's technique: the contrast, the symbolism, the slow unfolding; we may even smile at certain provincialisms. But the first impression is abiding: this world of spiritual realities in which these four and their Creator move. Puritanism seems to resemble the ancient necessity of the Greeks or the blind force of Thomas Hardy, making sport with human lives. The vitality of sin and of the avenging moral law blots out, as we read, lighter philosophies of life, and we shudder. Yet, though this heart-broken novel rings true, we feel Hawthorne's revulsion from the ideals of his fathers: Whose fault was all this? "Never, never," whispered Hester Prynne, "what we did had a consecration of its own." For, from the beginning we may trace in Hawthorne's interest in the problem of sin an apostasy from the assurance of the early Puritans that sin confers only injury on the soul. Even in *Twice-Told Tales* the novelist was concerned not merely with sin, but with its mysterious processes of regeneration. Hester Prynne is not unconscious of a purgation of her spirit, a deepening of her nature which would have been unachieved without the sin. It is profitable to compare this facing of reality in the working out of moral law with the somewhat cavalier disposition of sin by such optimists as Emerson and Alcott.

358   Hester Prynne, from an engraving by C. F. Slocumbe after the painting by George H. Boughton

THE HOUSE OF THE SEVEN GABLES

THE baffling complexities of life are less evident in the novel of a year later, *The House of the Seven Gables*, 1851. The background is Puritan superstition, and the mystery of the Pyncheons has a rational ending. The real mystery, however, that of moral law, challenges us again, less movingly, but with pathos in the life of Hepzibah; and with irony in Judge Pyncheon. As a searcher of the soul Hawthorne is here less penetrating than in *The Scarlet Letter*, for he is dealing with a less profound aspect of New England life. In charm *The House of the Seven Gables* is superior: the Pyncheons are the

359   From a photograph, courtesy of the Essex Institute

descendants of the Puritans, still clouded by the gloom of the past, but they live not without cheer in a type of community which every New Englander will recognize.

THE MARBLE FAUN, AND LESSER WRITINGS

HAWTHORNE'S power was to continue until almost the end of his life, though with emphasis upon his more fanciful side. *The Blithedale Romance*, 1852, includes the picture of Brook Farm, and of Zenobia, sketched, the world has always insisted, from Margaret Fuller. *The Marble Faun*, 1860, showed Donatello, and although concerned with sin, had the half-playful symbolism which was interfused with Hawthorne's imagination. Hawthorne's lesser writings have been overshadowed by his two or three supreme efforts. Children, however, remind us of his delight in their stories, such as *Tanglewood Tales*, 1853. He partly repaid his debt to Franklin Pierce by a biography, 1852, and there are touches of the great stylist in his *American Notebooks*, 1868, *Our Old Home*, 1863, and even in the ineffectual novel, *Doctor Grimshaw's Secret*, 1883. One sees more and more the sable in Hawthorne's nature. In another tale, *The Gentle Boy*, the Puritans watch joyful children at play and wonder why, with such a beginning, man's later years become so sorrowful.

360   From *The Gentle Boy*, 1839, illustration by Sophia Peabody

361   Title-page of *Tanglewood Tales*, 1854

362   From a photograph, 1860, by Mayall, London

THE INFLUENCE OF PURITANISM

As a writer Hawthorne, like Bryant, is a proof of the tremendous influence of Puritanism upon writers who personally did not accept spent doctrines. The problem of evil, the Puritan temper of mind, and moral earnestness Hawthorne used — at a time, it is said, when he would not enter a church — for artistic purposes.

HAWTHORNE THE NOVELIST

FOR him the ethical enthusiasms of the Transcendentalists were secondary, or hardly that. Nor was he concerned with the temporal issues in America. As an artist he was first of all interested in the enigma of life; and as a novelist his concern was with character. His weaknesses arose from his parochial environment. After reading of Donatello, one wonders what Hawthorne would have been, had the years of solitude been passed in Italy! By nature a romanticist, he turned to the supernaturalism of Puritan New England.

363   From the portrait, 1835, by Henry Inman (1801–1846) in the Essex Institute, Salem

ANALYST OF THE HUMAN SOUL

HAWTHORNE'S sense of the romantic supernatural suggests Charles Brockden Brown and Edgar Allan Poe. He lacks and would probably have scorned the former's mastery of thrilling but mechanical incident. He is inferior to Poe in intense presentation of the unearthly. But he is superior to the melodramatic Brown in subtle transitions from normal to abnormal, and to Poe in humanity. Obviously he rises far above both writers in his analysis of the human soul, in a psychology with roots not merely in the unseen world but in the secret life of moral law. How keenly he felt its mystery, its cruelty! This understanding, it should be added, he clothed in a style of great beauty: rich, fastidious, tender, unhurried, poetic, — full of the strength of a meditative mind.

364   Hawthorne's Grave, Sleepy Hollow, Concord

HENRY WADSWORTH LONGFELLOW,
1807-82

THE peaceful life story of Hawthorne's classmate at Bowdoin, Henry Wadsworth Longfellow, has become almost a tradition. He was born in Portland, Maine, the "beautiful town that is seated by the sea." His boyhood was happy, in a family of some culture, and his years at the college, then only a score of years old, foretold the serenity of the poet's life. Scholarly, gentle, somewhat apart, he had already written verses for periodicals. He had no eccentric distaste for the curriculum, but found the lectures "very interesting," except some on chemical affinity. "The fact is," he wrote his father, "I most eagerly aspire after future eminence in literature." He ranked fourth in a class of thirty-eight.

LONGFELLOW THE TEACHER

AT graduation the college trustees proposed "informally" to Longfellow that he prepare himself for a new chair of modern languages at Bowdoin, by travel and study abroad. During three years he was a scholarly and sentimental pilgrim on the continent and in England. When he

365 From a portrait, about 1840, by G. P. Healy (1813-94), owned by A. Otis Muller, Geneva, Switzerland. © Detroit Publishing Co.

was fully prepared, it seemed best to the trustees, in their infinite wisdom, to offer him instead of the professorship, an instructorship. This being declined with warmth, he received, true to academic tradition, a professor's appointment — minus two hundred dollars. The next six years (1829–1835) were happy through his marriage, his lectures, and his writing for magazines.

366 From a carte de visite, taken when a Harvard professor

PREPARATION FOR CAMBRIDGE

IN 1836 he succeeded George Ticknor as professor of modern languages at Harvard, and again went to Europe, this time to study the northern tongues. In London, thanks to Emerson, Carlyle called on him.

367 Cambridge in 1831, lithograph after a drawing by J. Kidder in the Society for the Preservation of New England Antiquities, Boston

In Stockholm he noted that the clergymen were smoking in the streets, and in Upsala that the professors were being paid in corn. Sorrow was at hand: in Rotterdam his first wife died. For relief Longfellow turned to intense study. In this period of grief was the turning point of his life.

368   Longfellow's Garden, Cambridge, from *The Mentor*, Vol. 4, No. 9

LIFE IN CRAIGIE HOUSE

AFTER his return to Harvard in December, 1836, his life flowed on peacefully as a teacher and poet. In 1850 he gave up teaching to devote himself to writing. In 1868–69 he was again abroad. Memories cluster about his Cambridge life. One terrible tragedy befell him. In 1861, with unspeakable anguish he beheld his wife, whom he had married eighteen years before, burned to death. Only one bitter cry escaped him: to a visitor's Christian comfort he replied, "*Bear* the cross, yes; but what if one is stretched upon it?" From that year (1861), Longfellow's publications were numerous. *Tales of a Wayside Inn* appeared in 1863, and the remaining nineteen years witnessed nearly a dozen titles. Among these were: *Three Books of Song*, 1872; *The Masque of Pandora and Other Poems*, 1875; *Keramos and Other Poems*, 1878; and *Ultima Thule*, 1880.

369 Pencil sketch of Longfellow, 1847, in
Craigie House, Cambridge

LONGFELLOW'S FRIENDSHIPS

AFTER his wife's death, in the depths of his heart was loneliness, but there was some happiness, too. His friendships with Lowell, Hawthorne, Holmes, Emerson, Prescott, and others; his tranquil life near the Charles; his poetry — all attest his inner faith. That Bowdoin classmate judged him well who said: "Such was his temperament, that it appeared easy for him to avoid the unworthy."

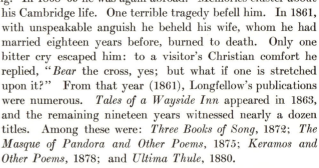

370 Longfellow in his Study, Craigie House. © Halliday Historic
Photograph Co.

LONGFELLOW'S PROSE

LONGFELLOW's prose lacks distinction. *Outre-Mer*, 1833–34, and *Hyperion*, 1839, are sentimental sketches of European scenes. *Kavanagh*, 1849, limns delicately backgrounds of New England. Longfellow as a writer of prose is evidently an imitator of Washington Irving, whom he admired and loved.

371 Longfellow and his daughter Edith on the steps of Craigie House, from a photograph in Craigie House

THE WRECK OF THE HESPERUS

LONGFELLOW'S characteristic writing began in 1839 with *Voices of the Night*, a volume of ballads and lyrics. In his *Journal*, in the same year, he shudders at a wreck of a schooner, the "Hesperus," on a reef "called Norman's Woe." *The Skeleton in Armor* is also taking form in his mind. *The Wreck of the Hesperus* was written in three hours, "with hardly an effort." These are the first two lyrics in *Ballads and Other Poems*, 1841. The last in the volume was *Excelsior*. Longfellow was to write popular narrative poems, dramas, and translations. Poems like *The Psalm of Life*, *The Village Blacksmith*, and *Excelsior* soon suffered parody.

372 Illustration for *Excelsior*, from Longfellow, *Poems*, Philadelphia, 1845, after a drawing by Daniel Huntington

WRECK OF THE HESPERUS.

373 From Longfellow, *Poems*, Philadelphia, 1845, after a drawing by Daniel Huntington

374   Sketch by Longfellow of the "spreading chestnut tree" and the village smithy,
      from a copy in Craigie House of the original drawing

THE CHILDREN'S HOUR

THIS is the "stuff" of Longfellow to which sophisticated modern critics allude. One may doubt the credit in satire at the expense of this verse — it is so easy. His poems on love of children and other emotions, which still have a place in some natures, have been called tepid, feminine, and worse. Somehow they still remain interwoven with the memories of American life.

376   From the painting *Evangeline*, by J. L. G. Ferris in
        Independence Hall, Philadelphia

POPULAR POEMS

YET he was always to continue this poetry of sympathy. Introspection, the poet's frenzy, subtlety of idea or form are absent. In *The Rainy Day*, *The Village Blacksmith*, *God's Acre*, *Maidenhood*, *The Arsenal at Springfield*, *The Old Clock on the Stairs*, *Resignation*, *Day is Done*, Longfellow sang gently of faith, peace, parting, the domestic affections, and God's presence.

375 "Grave Alice, and laughing Allegra, and Edith with golden hair," from a carte de visite of the painting, 1859, by Thomas F. Buchanan Read (1822–72) in Craigie House

EVANGELINE

IN 1848 Arthur Hugh Clough in England writes a long hexameter poem, *The Bothie of Tober-na-Vuolich*, and sends word to Longfellow through Emerson that one source of inspiration "was a reading of his *Evangeline* aloud to my mother and sister." Longfellow's use of hexameter will always be a point of interest in the history of English verse, in spite of such lines as: "Children's children rode on his knee, and heard his great watch tick." The legend of *Evangeline*, 1847, with its moral lessons of love, suffering, and patience, was designed for the poetic taste of the generation. "Everybody likes it," wrote Hawthorne.

LONGFELLOW'S ACADIA

IT chanced to be one of Hawthorne's friends, who told Longfellow the story of the Acadian maiden's separation from her lover, Gabriel, during the dispersion of her people by the British. Longfellow, not troubling to visit Nova Scotia, read Haliburton's stories of Grand-Pré, and books on Louisiana and Philadelphia. His pictures of the northern land have created sentimental interest for many literary pilgrims, who dream over the poet's pictures of the French community before the expulsion.

377   From Noah Porter, *Evangeline: The Place, the Story, and the Poem*, New York, London & Paris, 1882, after a drawing by Frank Dicksee (1853–)

Soon the game was begun. In friendly contention the old men
Laughed at each lucky hit, or unsuccessful manœuvre,
Laughed when a man was crowned, or a breach was made in the king-row.
Meanwhile apart, in the twilight gloom of a window's embrasure,
Sat the lovers, and whispered together, beholding the moon rise
Over the pallid sea and the silvery mist of the meadows.

SCENES OF PARTING

THERE is real pathos in the cruel partings of the Acadians, and in the wanderings of the maiden. We forgive also the vague pictures, in the second part, of the great West and South, chiefly because of Longfellow's sincere portrayal of Evangeline's simple nature. At the beginning of the exile Evangeline tries to comfort the old man.

378   From Noah Porter, *Evangeline*, etc., 1882, after a drawing by Frank Dicksee

Vainly Evangeline strove with words and caresses to cheer him,
Vainly offered him food; yet he moved not, he looked not, he spake not,
But, with a vacant stare, ever gazed at the flickering fire-light.
"*Benedicite!*" murmured the priest, in tones of compassion.
More he fain would have said, but his heart was full, and his accents
Faltered and paused on his lips, as the feet of a child on a threshold,
Hushed by the scene he beholds, and the awful presence of sorrow.

THE POPULARITY OF EVANGELINE

379 From Noah Porter, *Evangeline*, etc., 1882,
after a drawing by Frank Dicksee

Thus many years she lived as a Sister of Mercy; frequenting
Lonely and wretched roofs in the crowded lanes of the city.

THE final meeting of the lovers in the Philadelphia hospital, as Evangeline pursues her works of mercy as a nurse, has been duplicated too often in an art more recent, and cheaper than literature. Yet Longfellow's correspondents spoke of the poem's "sublime moral," and Evangeline's "constancy" became a byword. *Evangeline* is now a popular text in the schools, where, probably, it belongs. Smile, if you will, at the age which acclaimed such a poem. Six weeks after its publication, Longfellow recorded in his journal: "The third thousand of Evangeline." The success of *Evangeline* was due in large measure to the skillful use of hexameters; and, in particular, to the adventures of the lovers, and the descriptions of the then little known land of Nova Scotia.

380 From the painting *Minnehaha*, by J. L. G. Ferris
in Independence Hall, Philadelphia

381 From the painting *Hiawatha's Wedding Journey*, by J. L. G. Ferris in Independence Hall, Philadelphia

HIAWATHA

ALTHOUGH *Evangeline* was proclaimed "American," it is clear that it is a bookish poem. So was *Hiawatha*, 1855, even if it dealt with the American Indian. Nothing like the bloodcurdling yell of Magua is heard in this romantic narrative of Minnehaha and her Indian lover. "I have at length," says Longfellow in the *Journal* of June 22, 1854, "hit upon a plan for a poem on the American Indians . . . I have hit upon a measure, too . . ." *Hiawatha* is an idealized love story based upon the more poetic legends of the Indians.

THE INDIAN ROMANTICIZED

LONGFELLOW's playful tales of the Indians indicate, even more than certain poems of Bryant's, the tendency, as time passes, to regard the hated enemy of the white man as a romantic figure. "It is," the poet himself says of *Hiawatha*, "purely in the realm of fancy." The poem was read everywhere. On the fifteenth of December of the year of publication it was in its eleventh thousand. "Sweet and wholesome as maize," says Emerson.

THE METER OF *HIAWATHA*

IF the interest in these poems of the study is significant, so is the excitement in England and America over the trochaic meter of *Hiawatha*. Again Longfellow had proved that he was a successful experimenter in unusual forms of verse. "A hubbub," said Prescott; "the greatest pother," declared T. W. Parsons. In America Poe was deep in argument. "Are you not chuckling," wrote a friend from London, "over the

382   From the painting *The Death of Minnehaha*, by William L. Dodge (1867–)
in the possession of Jacob Heyl, Buffalo, N. Y.

war which is waging in the *Athenæum* about the measure of *Hiawatha?*" The dainty trochaic measure Longfellow had taken from *Kalevala*, an epic of the Finns. Some of the uproar centered about his failure to acknowledge his debt to this poem.

383   From the painting *Priscilla and John Alden*, 1884, by C. Y. Turner (1850–1918)
in the possession of Mrs. A. Kay Womrathe, Mentone, France

THE COURTSHIP OF *MILES STANDISH*

LONGFELLOW's most even and best sustained poem on early New England is *The Courtship of Miles Standish*, 1858. His own ancestor, John Alden, is the hero, a modest lover, with a Puritan conscience. His errand to Priscilla to plead for her love, in behalf of his friend, Standish, is one of the famous legends of New England. "Why don't you speak for yourself, John?" is still a living sentence.

THE RETURN OF THE *MAYFLOWER*

THE passages of the poem concerning the hardships of the little colony we remember. The Indian wars, the Puritan wedding, the return of the *Mayflower* might not be recognized by the participants in these affairs, but they fixed in American literature the elusive spirit of their romance. For, in some such manner, these people must have bade farewell to the ship:

Then from their houses in haste came forth the
    Pilgrims of Plymouth,
Men and women and children, all hurrying down
    to the sea-shore,
Eager, with tearful eyes, to say farewell to the
    Mayflower,
Homeward bound o'er the sea and leaving them
    here in the desert.

384   From the engraving after the painting by George H. Boughton

Took the wind on her quarter, and stood for the open Atlantic,
Borne on the send of the sea, and the swelling hearts of the Pilgrims
Long in silence they watched the receding sail of the vessel,
Much endeared to them all, as something living and human.

385   From the painting by C. Y. Turner in the Metropolitan Museum of Art, New York

THE WEDDING OF PRISCILLA AND JOHN ALDEN

MEMORABLE, too, is the mighty little Captain, Miles Standish.   John Alden is loyal; Priscilla is womanly; and the warrior lends to the mild tale a touch of fire.   Released at last from his bond by the report of his friend's death, John is betrothed to Priscilla.   "Raghorn, the snow-white bull," bears her to the wedding.

386   From the painting by J. L. G. Ferris in Independence Hall, Philadelphia

THE RETURN OF MILES STANDISH

THEN at the ceremony:

> Lo! when the service was ended, a form appeared on the threshold,
> Clad in armor of steel, a sombre and sorrowful figure!

It was he — Captain Standish, a Puritan and punctual Enoch Arden! But the Netherlands fighter has a soul as generous as Alden's.   John keeps his Priscilla.

THE TIMES OF JOHN ALDEN

So the descendant of the Pilgrims tells the story "of the good old times of John Alden." Puritan life in its deepest currents is not here, but in the feeling for landscape, for idealized mood, for delicacy, *The Courtship of Miles Standish* will retain its hold on New England minds.

THE TALES OF A WAYSIDE INN

I⊤ is certain that Longfellow had the gift of telling a story. *Tales of a Wayside Inn*, 1863, may not rank with the *Canterbury Tales* or *The Earthly Paradise*, but something may

be said for narratives like that of *Paul Revere's Ride*. Longfellow, like Irving, loves a strain of retrospective romance.

In the old inn at Sudbury where Washington dined, where Lafayette stayed, where Daniel Webster meditated, Longfellow loved to look back into the past, and let the ghostly travelers tell their tales.

388 Illustration for *Paul Revere's Ride*, from Longfellow, *Poetical Works*, Boston, 1870

387 From an engraving after the painting *A Puritan Thanksgiving—On the Way to Church*, by George H. Boughton

THE WAYSIDE INN, SUDBURY, MASSACHUSETTS

LONGFELLOW chose as his room the parlor with the fireplace of red brick:

One Autumn night, in Sudbury town,
Across the meadows bare and brown,
The windows of the wayside inn
Gleamed red with fire-light through the leaves
Of woodbine . . .

389 Title-page of *Tales of a Wayside Inn*, Boston, 1863

390   From a photograph by Frank Cousins

391   Charles Sumner and Henry W. Longfellow

DRAMATIC POEMS

LONGFELLOW was not, like Irving, sensible of his limitations. His interest in contemporary political questions which belonged rightly to statesmen led him into some dubious verse. His mistaken notion that he could write drama has saddled us with some halting plays: *The Divine Tragedy*, 1871, *New England Tragedies*, 1868, and others. Such dramatic poems as *The Golden Legend*, 1851, praised by Ruskin, and *The Spanish Student*, 1843, are more natural to his talents, as are some of his numerous translations from continental literatures. The third scene of *The Spanish Student* contains the beautiful *Stars of the Summer Night*. It has often been said that Longfellow's translation in poetry of the *Divina Commedia*, 1867, is his signal achievement. The *Journal* records how he turned to this work, when depressed, as to a rock in a weary

392   Marble Bust of Longfellow by Sir Thomas Brock (1847–) in Westminster Abbey. © Underwood & Underwood

land. On the whole, this was the most successful of Longfellow's translations from European literature, but it does not achieve in any degree the strength of the original.

393   Longfellow Memorial, Cambridge, by Daniel Chester French (1850–)

LONGFELLOW TO-DAY

IN an age which not only disregards, but insults the past, it is natural that Longfellow's poetry should suffer heavily. The story is abroad that Tennyson's friends could bring him to terms with the remark: "Don't do that, Alfred; people will think you are Longfellow." His gentle voice is drowned out in the noise of motors and modern poetry. He has been called, not kindly, the professor poet, the children's poet, and, by Margaret Fuller,

"a dandy Pindar." True, he is sedative. One feels that he did not think enough; that scholarship, romance, and simple faith satisfied him. He depends too much on conventional ideas. He is too didactic. And he is never sublime. Yet he sometimes surprises by his subtlety as in *The Fire of Driftwood*, and by his occasional strength, as in his sonnets, and in the enduring translation of Dante. Nor must we forget his immense service in interpreting European culture to America. To dismiss him with a laugh is a criticism not of him, but of us. He is not a lofty but a pure and refined spirit, and his place is secure.

JOHN GREENLEAF WHITTIER
1807-92

IN East Haverhill, Massachusetts, John Greenleaf Whittier was born. Whittier entered the world ten months later than Longfellow, but was to remain here, in spite of fragile health, ten years longer. We need only recall Longfellow's story to realize how different was Whittier's life experience in early surroundings, in education, in social position, in the history of the time, and in old age. Yet men link their names; they were alike in serenity and sweetness of temper.

394   Whittier's Birthplace, from a photograph by Frank Cousins in the Essex Institute, Salem, Mass.

SCHOOL DAYS

WHITTIER'S education was founded on the thirty volumes of the family library, about one half the size of the Puritan Governor Dudley's. Of these he made early a verse catalogue. Another humble portal to his later erudition was, of course, "the school-house by the road." A boy of fourteen, he listens enthralled to a Dartmouth student reading from Burns. He and his sister pore by candlelight over a Waverley novel — till the candle gutters, and they are left darkling. In school he had already passed about his verses, written on a slate. One day Garrison, then editor of the Newburyport *Free Press*, jumped out of a carriage before the astonished Whittier, who was working beside a stone wall, to compliment him on a poem he had contributed to the paper. From 1827 to 1829 Whittier was a student at the Haverhill Academy, and also taught school. In the next year he edited the *American Manufacturer*, in Boston, and in 1830 *The Gazette*, in Haverhill. With his residence in Hartford, as editor of the *New England Review*, began his long service as a politician — the greatest he had ever met, thought James G. Blaine. By reason of his Quaker training and his democratic youth, Whittier had developed a deep abhorrence of slavery. This cause, as a practical expression of his innate love of liberty, was now his. To it, for the rest of his life, he rendered a passionate but practical devotion.

395   Kitchen in the Whittier Birthplace, from a photograph in the Public Library, Haverhill, Mass.

396   Brook near the Whittier Birthplace, from a photograph by Frank Cousins in the Essex Institute

THE MERRIMAC COUNTRY

In 1663 Thomas Whittier, of Huguenot origin, built his log house in the Merrimac country. Two centuries later his descendant made this country memorable in poetry. He immortalized, in *Snow-Bound*, the old homestead; and, in many shorter poems, the life on the New England farm: the woodchuck, the snouted mole, the blackberry cone, the sand-rimmed pickerel pond, and, of course, himself, the "barefoot boy." This was a Quaker household. Young Whittier listened to his father's expositions of the Scriptures; perhaps he beheld in the Salem meetings what Charles Lamb saw in London, faces "upon which the dove sate visibly brooding." Perhaps the "perfect silence" sank deep into his soul. At home he heard, too, tales of Indians and witches, and learned to meditate on the lore of nature.

397   From a daguerreotype, about 1850, by permission of Charles Scribner's Sons

WHITTIER AS A NATIONAL FIGURE

As an abolitionist Whittier became a national figure. Although not cosmopolitan, he evidently thought of the issue of slavery broadly as a liberalizing current of nineteenth-century thought. Strangely enough, his abandoning of poetry for politics brought him fame in literature, for it was not long before his verse became a soul-animating trumpet for the cause of emancipation. And with this came the realization of his poetic power. In 1857 he assisted in the founding of the *Atlantic Monthly*. Although he is associated in the history of American literature with the Cambridge and Concord writers, he is somewhat apart. His intimates were rather obscure persons in the towns where he lived. He lived on at Amesbury till his eighty-fifth year, lonely after the death of his sister, for he had remained a bachelor. He continued to study politics and wrote to the last. His worshipers told stories of his quiet laughter, and of the tall, slight figure, with the keen, dark eyes, which resembled those of his kinsman, Webster. No man served America more devotedly in humble paths than Whittier. In him was something of the saint. He died peacefully, murmuring again and again: "Love to all the world."

OTHER POEMS

WHITTIER'S work is uneven. The early poems on Indian subjects, *Mogg Megone*, 1836; the poems on slavery; the later work such as *Among the Hills*, 1868, *The Tent on the Beach*, 1867, and *The Pennsylvania Pilgrim*, 1872, are already forgotten. *Cassandra Southwick* was an omen, and in *Voices of Freedom*, 1849, *The Panorama*, 1856, *In War Time*, 1863, and even in *Poems written during the Progress of the Abolition Question*, 1837, are lines hot with his incandescent wrath.

398   From Whittier, *Poems*, Boston, 1849, engraving after a drawing by H. Billings, illustrating *Voices of Freedom*

399   Illustration for *A Sabbath Scene*, from Whittier, *Complete Poetical Works*, Boston, 1876

WHITTIER'S MELODRAMA

THE fault of these poems is their melodrama. They declaim too fiercely on "woman's shriek beneath the lash, and manhood's wild despair." In their violence they remind us of the poetry of Ebenezer Elliott, the Corn-Law Rhymer. We read, always with capital letters, of Oppression or Moloch, "cups of human blood," and "woman's shrinking flesh." Yet Whittier's voice is that of an avenging angel. His indignation is withering, and though there are occasional absurd lines, some poems have a fiery restraint and a deep pathos. Such a poem is *The Farewell of a Virginia Slave Mother*.

400   From the painting by Will H. Low (1853-) in the Albany Institute of History and Art

SKIPPER IRESON'S RIDE

WHITTIER likes, too, homely stories of New England life. These he tells briefly in ballad form. In *Skipper Ireson's Ride* we hear the rattle of the coward's cart, and the jeers of the women of Marblehead for the man who had dishonored the traditions of the Massachusetts seafaring race. The fragrance of the New England clover breathes from the poem of sorrow, *Telling the Bees*, and such lyrics as *In School Days* and *The Barefoot Boy* retell memories of a poet's youth. "How hardly effaced," he says in a prose passage, "are the impressions of childhood!"

401   From the bronze tablet on the Barbara Frietchie monument
at Frederick, Md.

BARBARA FRIETCHIE

THIS type of simple, emotional ballad became Whittier's usual medium. His lines linger in the mind. Historical evidence is slight for the "blush of shame" on Stonewall Jackson's face or his picturesque threat to his troops in *Barbara Frietchie*, but Americans have remembered the poem, and *Ichabod*, the almost biblical lament, elicited by Daniel Webster's Seventh of March speech. The lines in *Barbara Frietchie* outlive their parodies:

> A shade of sadness, a blush of shame,
> Over the face of the leader came;
> The nobler nature within him stirred
> To life at that woman's deed and word:
> "Who touches a hair of yon gray head
> Dies like a dog! March on!" he said.

MAUD MULLER

WHITTIER knew poverty. The injustices under the social laws are often present in his poetry, though usually in gentle mood. Thus *Maud Muller* is a poem of dreams that die out in the light of common day; of buried hopes for the maiden, and for the Judge who found her so fair as she worked in the meadow. *Maud Muller* has kinship with the poetry of Victorian England, and is no less sentimental. "For," so runs the famous couplet, albeit with a New England accent,

> . . . of all sad words of tongue or pen,
> The saddest are these: "It might have been!"

MABEL MARTIN.

How pleasantly the rising moon,

Between the shadow of the mows,

Looked on them through the great elm-boughs!

On sturdy boyhood, sun-embrowned,

On girlhood with its solid curves

Of healthful strength and painless nerves!

403   From Whittier, *Mabel Martin*, Boston, 1876, drawing
by Mary H. Hallock

MAUD MULLER.

MAUD MULLER, on a summer's day,
Raked the meadow sweet with hay.

Beneath her torn hat glowed the wealth
Of simple beauty and rustic health.

Singing, she wrought, and her merry glee
The mock-bird echoed from his tree.

402   From Whittier, *Maud Muller*, Boston, 1866, after a
drawing by W. J. Hennessy (1839–)

MABEL MARTIN

IN *Mabel Martin*, first published as *The Witch's Daughter*, the poet's story is more specific, and has never been popular. Yet the spirit of New England, though sentimentalized, rings true in the young people's songs — those sung by their fathers in Yorkshire and Derbyshire — in the superstitious dread of the daughter of the witch; and in the passage descriptive of the youthful merrymakings.

WHITTIER, THE QUAKER

THE moral fervor in Whittier's poetry sprang from a religious life whose beginnings we observed among the Friends. This spirit never entirely deserted Whittier. He was less sensitive to the doubts of the age than Lowell, perhaps more so than Longfellow. Poems like *My Soul and I* and *Questions of Life* show his bewilderment in the face of the old riddle. He had little power of abstract thought, and fell back, abandoning question, upon the secret trust of the heart. In his *Eternal Goodness* the well-known stanza is typical:

> I know not where His islands lift
> Their fronded palms in air;
> I only know I cannot drift
> Beyond His love and care.

SNOW–BOUND

WHEN nearing threescore Whittier wrote his great idyl, *Snow-Bound*. In it are blended his love, his understanding, and all his memories of the New England people. Cowper's *Task* is more polished — there are doddering lines in *Snow-Bound* — and Burns' *Cotter's Saturday Night* more impassioned, but the poem has the mood of benediction; it is as beautiful as the sound of sleigh bells in the winter night, or the snow-wrapt New England hills. We overlook, for this reason, the occasional weak rhymes and a certain monotony of tone. Most striking, perhaps, are the portraits of the New England father and mother in their home.

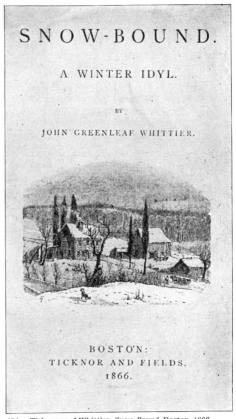

404   Title-page of Whittier, *Snow-Bound*, Boston, 1866

405   Desk upon which *Snow-Bound* and other poems were written; by permission of the Whittier Home Association, Amesbury

406   Whittier's Study at "Oak Knoll." © Halliday Historic Photograph Co.

407   Curson's Bowery Mill (*June on the Merrimac*), courtesy of the Public Library, Haverhill, Mass.

THE WHITTIER COUNTRY

It is difficult to overemphasize Whittier's complete immersion in the sights and sounds of his own corner of New England. He described without effort the brook, the meadow, the rocks, the huckleberry bushes, or the old mill at the turn of the road. He was, says Pickard, "wise in the traditions of the family and neighborhood . . ." He knew "marvelous stories of the denizens of the forest and stream, traditions of witchcraft, and tales of strange happenings."

"THE LAUREATE OF NEW ENGLAND"

In such poetry was Whittier's true utterance as a poet. Critics have had sport with his obvious lacks: he falls into sentimental fluency, and, in spite of much reading, culture passed him by. Nevertheless, he has been called our greatest master of the ballad, and the "Laureate of New England." Tennyson thought that Whittier's descriptions of scenery and flowers ranked with those of Wordsworth. Much of his verse printed in newspapers was improvisation, and is worthless.

408   "Oak Knoll," Danvers, Mass., where Whittier spent his last years. © Halliday Historic Photograph Co.

POET OF THE SOIL

Whittier's simplicity endeared him to his countrymen. Compared with his, the poems of Longfellow and Lowell on men and things of the soil seem distillations of the scholar. Whittier was an Essex County Quaker farmer. He dug in the fields. He heard, a few miles away, the boom of the ocean storms, a sound known to the Puritan. He tramped the valley of the Merrimac. In him was the spirit of the New England landscape: the pine trees, the dusty road, the shambling stone walls, the little ponds. He could write of these, and of the thoughts they bred in New England minds. He is their poet; the poet of the humbler New England people.

409   From a photograph, about 1880, by Sarony

JAMES RUSSELL LOWELL, 1819–91

IN 1819 at Elmwood, in the old house forever associated with his name, was born James Russell Lowell. In Lowell's ancestry were the conflicting strains of race and blood which made his nature so strange a compound of moral earnestness, levity, hard sense, and mysticism. His father, Charles Lowell, was a New England minister; his mother traced her lineage to an ancient family of the Orkney Islands — to Patrick Spence, Lowell used to say whimsically. His earliest books were those in his father's library and those, too, less exactly, of the woods and fields about Cambridge. In his boyish imagination figures from the *Faerie Queen* moved against the landscapes of New England. At college in the alcoves of Harvard Hall he read deeply in Montaigne, and in bards in fealty to Apollo, notably Milton. He was touched by the sentimental fever of the day, writing to a friend: "Pity me, I am in love," but was cured by a characteristic burst of high spirits. One bit of humor indeed led to a rustication at Concord, an exile illumined by glimpses of Emerson. The undelivered class poem was privately printed, and indicates a surprising mastery of meters. For the first few years after his graduation from Harvard he was uncertain about his future, but finally decided upon the law.

409   From a carte de visite, about 1860

MARIA WHITE LOWELL

410   From Maria Lowell, *Poems*, Cambridge, 1855

LOWELL'S quip in a letter to a friend that he would be Chief Justice of the United States gives no hint of his restlessness during the first two years after graduation. The study of the law could not content him, nor his writing for magazines. But with his engagement, at the age of twenty-one, to Maria White, a rare and poetic spirit, new springs of endeavor surged up in him. With her, and with "the band," a group of literary, transcendental young people, came a quickening of his wit, and of his literary and humanitarian impulses.

THE PIONEER

AFTER a volume of youthful verse (*A Year's Life*, 1841) Lowell began his career as an editor with *The Pioneer*, designed, he says, in forceful writing, "to furnish the intelligent and reflecting portion of the Reading Public with a rational substitute for the enormous quantity of thrice-diluted trash . . . which is monthly poured out to them by many of our popular magazines." This frank comment on American sentimentalism in the form of "Ladies' Books" and "Tokens" was fortified on the magazine's cover by a tart admonition from Bacon.

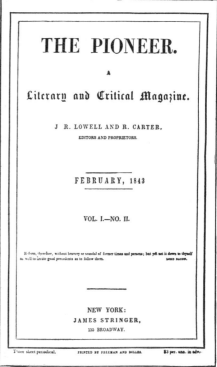

THE PIONEER.

A

Literary and Critical Magazine.

J R. LOWELL AND R. CARTER,
EDITORS AND PROPRIETORS.

FEBRUARY, 1843

VOL. I.—NO. II.

It-form, therefore, without bravery or scandal of former times and persons; but yet set it down to thyself as well to create good precedents as to follow them.   LORD BACON.

NEW YORK:
JAMES STRINGER,
155 BROADWAY.

Three sheet periodical.   PRINTED BY FREEMAN AND BOLLES. $3 per. ann. in adv.

412   Title-page of the second number, Feb. 1843

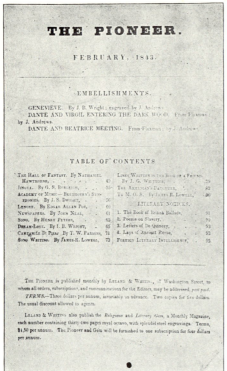

THE PIONEER.

FEBRUARY, 1843.

EMBELLISHMENTS.

GENEVIEVE. By J. B. Wright; engraved by J. Andrews.
DANTE AND VIRGIL ENTERING THE DARK WOOD. From Flaxman;
by J. Andrews.
DANTE AND BEATRICE MEETING. From Flaxman, by J. Andrews.

TABLE OF CONTENTS

THE PIONEER is published monthly by LELAND & WHITING, 37 Washington Street, to
whom all orders, subscriptions, and communications for the Editors, may be addressed, post paid.
TERMS.—Three dollars per annum, invariably in advance. Two copies for five dollars.
The usual discount allowed to agents.

LELAND & WHITING also publish the Religious and Literary Gem, a Monthly Magazine,
each number containing thirty-two pages royal octavo, with splendid steel engravings. Terms,
$1.50 per annum. The Pioneer and Gem will be furnished at one subscription for four dollars
per annum.

413   Table of Contents, from the second number

TEACHER, SCHOLAR, EDITOR, AND POET

LOWELL was not committed to a literary life.

CONTRIBUTORS TO *THE PIONEER*

WHEN the first issue of *The Pioneer* appeared in January, 1843, Lowell's enthusiasm was at high pitch. The list of some early contributors (in another issue, Mrs. Browning) shows that he had not been idle. When there followed, almost immediately, serious trouble with his eyes, consequent discontinuation of the magazine, and difficulty with the publishers, Lowell was bitterly disappointed.

414   Tremont Street, Boston, in 1860. © Halliday Historic Photograph Co.

He was an abolitionist and became a contributor to the *Anti-Slavery Standard*. He traveled in Europe (1851–52), returning to America on a ship with Thackeray and Clough. In Europe, however, he had lost his son, a grief followed by the death of his wife in 1853. From this terrible blow he sought solace in work. After a series of memorable lectures before the Lowell Institute he succeeded Longfellow in the professorship of modern languages at Harvard (1856–77). From now on Lowell assumes the personality which is familiar.

415   From a photograph, about 1875, by Conly, Boston

At one period of his life Leslie Stephen found him a "complete specimen of the literary recluse," but this mood did not last. He married again; he directed the *Atlantic Monthly* and *North American Review;* and he was, successively, minister to Spain and to England. In the rôle of diplomat abroad and that of critic at home Lowell was distinctly an international figure. His interest in national issues was intense, and his patriotism wise as well as stanch. From Spain he wrote, in 1878: "I like America better every day." He is still mentioned as an incarnation of the best kind of Americanism.

416   From *Vanity Fair*, London, 1880

LOWELL'S VERSATILITY

IN the last years he is at Southborough. At Elmwood he watches, he says, the moon rise behind the same trees through which he saw it seventy years ago. The years had brought him fame as a publicist, editor, essayist, poet, humorist, and man. Yet if his mind was strengthened and enriched, it was also, as we see it in his last letters, the same restless, ardent, versatile mind which both baffles and delights his readers.

417　Lowell in his study, from *Harper's Weekly*, March 5, 1887, drawing by T. Blake Wirgman

THE VISION OF SIR LAUNFAL

THE different strains in Lowell's mind are evident in his poetry. The earlier poems stir in us half-forgotten tones of Tennyson, Landor, Keats, and other nineteenth-century poets. In his *annus mirabilis*, 1848, appeared *The Vision of Sir Launfal*, with its blend of haunting mysticism and literalness; *A Fable for Critics*, with its rattling satire; and *The Biglow Papers*, a rollicking New England poem, with many a shrewd moral. "One half of me," says Lowell in a letter, "is clear mystic and enthusiast, and the other humorist."

418　From Lowell, *The Vision of Sir Launfal*, Boston, 1867, in the Harvard College Library, drawing by S. Eytinge, Jr.

A FABLE FOR CRITICS

A FABLE FOR CRITICS is an acute, good-humored satirical survey in verse of contemporary American writers including Lowell himself. Even now it is a stimulating fusillade of wit and sense directed against jingoism, sentimentality, and bad taste in literature. Lowell used to plead for a *natural*, not a *national* literature. His scholarship had given him touchstones of criticism which the satire suggested implicitly, and whose application left no sting. Oliver Wendell Holmes thought it "capital," "crammed full and rammed down hard — powder (lots of it) shot — slugs — very little wadding, and that is gun-cotton — all crowded into a rusty-looking sort of blunderbuss barrel."

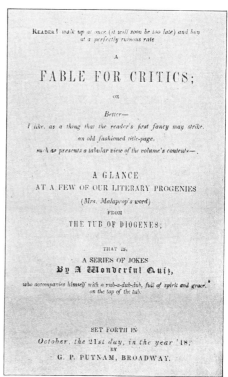

READER ! *walk up at once (it will soon be too late) and buy at a perfectly ruinous rate*

A

FABLE FOR CRITICS;

OR

Better —

I like, as a thing that the reader's first fancy may strike, an old fashioned title-page, such as presents a tabular view of the volume's contents —

A GLANCE

AT A FEW OF OUR LITERARY PROGENIES

(*Mrs. Malaprop's word*)

FROM

THE TUB OF DIOGENES;

THAT IS,

A SERIES OF JOKES

By A Wonderful Quiz,

who accompanies himself with a rub-a-dub-dub, full of spirit and grace, on the top of the tub.

SET FORTH IN

October, the 21st day, in the year '18,

BY

G. P. PUTNAM, BROADWAY.

419　Title-page of the first issue of the first edition, New York, 1848, in the New York Public Library

Birdofredom Sawin, with
only One leg to stand upon.

420   From *The Biglow Papers*, London, 1859,
drawing by George Cruikshank

THE BIGLOW PAPERS, 1848

WITH *The Biglow Papers*, inspired by the Mexican War, Lowell set the whole country laughing, and came into his own as a humorist. Here in Hosea Biglow and Parson Homer Wilbur, A.M., Pastor of the First Church in Jalaam, was the Yankee himself, a shrewd idealist in homespun. "A sort of squib," said Lowell. So "vote fer Guvener B," "Birdofredom Sawin," and other phrases, quoted everywhere, show how deftly Lowell had penetrated not merely the nation's sense of humor, but also its earnestness, in his mocking exposure of shams, whether of war or of politics. "*The Biglow Papers*," says Henry A. Beers, "are Lowell's most original contribution to American literature."

But glory is a kin' o' thing I shant pursue no furder.

421   From *The Biglow Papers*, London, 1865,
drawing by George Cruikshank

The country here is swarmin with the most alarmin kind o' varmin

422   From *The Biglow Papers*, London, 1865, drawing by George Cruikshank

THE SECOND SERIES

THE second series of *The Biglow Papers*, 1867, dealing with Civil War issues, was less exuberant, but deeper in spirit. In these indeed: "There you hev it, plain an' flat." These satires are different from the Revolutionary diatribes in their keen wit and lightness of touch, and, most of all, in their fixing in some sort of permanent type one American character of the time, the Yankee. The following is typical of the fervor of *The Biglow Papers*:

Wut's words to them whose faith an'
    truth
On war's red techstone rang true
    metal,
Who ventered life an' love an' youth
For the gret prize o' death in battle?

THE COURTIN'

YET even in these backwoods idyls another Lowell is heard. In *The Courtin'* learning, satire, altruism are absent. In their place, though in the same racy vernacular, is poetry of simple, tender emotion, not unlike that in such lyrics as *The First Snow-Fall* or *After the Burial*.

423   From *The Courtin'*, Boston, 1874, silhouette
by Winslow Homer (1836–1910)

REFLECTIVE POETRY

LOWELL's poems to his first wife had shown this sincerity in writing of human feeling. This mood was continued to the end, though often unexpressed: for nearly a score of years Lowell published no verse. Often, however, as in *The Cathedral* Lowell is speculative, and the intellectual content of this poem, with its doubt and longing in the face of the revelations of a scientific age, suggests the gray poetry of Arnold and Clough. Lowell's reflective poetry such as his *Ode*, 1865, at a Harvard commencement, with its magnificent stanzas to Lincoln and to America, is profound and noble. Of the faults in this poetry Lowell himself was conscious: its overelaboration of thought, its lack of directness.

ODE

RECITED AT THE

COMMEMORATION

OF

THE LIVING AND DEAD SOLDIERS
OF HARVARD UNIVERSITY,

July 21, 1865.

BY JAMES RUSSELL LOWELL.

CAMBRIDGE
PRIVATELY PRINTED.
1865.

424   Title-page of a copy in the Harvard College Library

425   From *Harper's Weekly,* August 22, 1891

POETRY OF NATURE

STILL another side of Lowell appears in his poetry of nature. Thinking of the science which awoke his musings in *The Cathedral,* he cries out: "I hate it as a savage does writing." His love of nature was sensuous, half pagan. Lying on the warm earth:

> . . . Thought ceased
> Or was transfused in something to which thought
> Is coarse and dull of sense. Myself was lost,
> Gone from me like an ache and what remained
> Became a part of the universal joy.
> My soul went forth, and mingling with the tree,
> Danced in the leaves.

Much of Lowell's delight in nature is connected with his love for the trees and flowers at Elmwood. *To the Dandelion, Under the Willows, Pictures from Appledore, An Indian-Summer Reverie,* and the preludes of *The Vision of Sir Launfal* show his friendly joy in nature, and of course, his happiness, especially, in the sights and sounds of June.

LOWELL AS A CRITIC OF LITERATURE

FROM his first boyish letter on "gumbiles" Lowell wrote interesting prose. His good things in talk came up, said Leslie Stephen, like "bubbles in a spring," and his letters suggest the pleasure of evenings by his fireside. In his literary criticism, perhaps, this spontaneity accounts for a fault, his looseness of weave; such writing becomes often, in spite of the solid foundation of scholarship, just excellent talk about books. One may like or dislike his discursiveness, his love of parallel passages, his wit, his paradox. Yet he is our greatest literary critic. He has learning, even wisdom, and imagination. Beginning with *Conversations on Some of the Old Poets,* 1844, he wrote essays on books which may outlive his poetry. *On A Certain Condescension in Foreigners* is an instance of his observation and his urbanity of manner, as *My Study Windows,* 1871, and *Among My Books,* 1870–76, attest his conscience in literary criticism.

426   Leslie Stephen and Lowell, from a photograph, 1890, taken at Elmwood, in the Harvard College Library

427   Lowell when Minister to England, from a photo-
         graph by Elliott and Fry, London

LOWELL'S COMPLEX NATURE

MANY critics of Lowell have attempted to name the dominant impulse in his many-sided nature. Complex he was, yet transparent; liberal but in moral earnestness a Puritan. And, like overtones, one finds a hundred other qualities: his laughter, his pity, his common sense, his dreams. He was well-rounded, but the formative elements jarred within him. We admire, and we re-read his poetry. It is, therefore, with a start that we discover how easily we forget it. Even with intellectual readers it does not catch hold. In the last analysis the prose is better. Here we are on a sure footing. Good American critics are few, and Lowell will always be consulted, though possibly his best judgments are concerning English literature.

OLIVER WENDELL HOLMES, 1809–94

WHEN Lowell became, in 1857, editor of the *Atlantic Monthly*, he stipulated that the first contributor should be Oliver Wendell Holmes. With this engagement was to begin the doctor's reputation as a man of letters. Holmes would probably dislike any account of him which ignored his "Brahmin" ancestry. His father was the Reverend Abiel Holmes, whose ancestors settled in Woodstock, Connecticut, and who contrived, in spite of Calvinism, to be known as a sunny old man. In his youth he was so handsome that the girls at Cambridge used to say: "There goes Holmes — look!" On the mother's side was "Dorothy Q.," of the Quincys, and Anne Bradstreet. One wonders what Anne would have thought of the Autocrat!

428   From the portrait of Dorothy Quincy which hung in Dr. Holmes'
         study, courtesy of Justice Oliver Wendell Holmes

BIRTH AND BOYHOOD

As if this ancestry were not enough, Holmes managed to be born in the stellar year of 1809 in the house where the Committee of Safety had planned the battle of Bunker Hill. About the cradle hovered the shades of Ward, Warren, and Washington. After a boyhood in this old gambrel-roofed Cambridge house Holmes was exposed to the ministerial influences of Phillips-Andover. He might, he says, have been a minister himself if the clergyman had not looked and talked so like an undertaker. He eventually became a Unitarian.

429   Holmes' Birthplace, Cambridge.   © Halliday Historic Photograph Co.

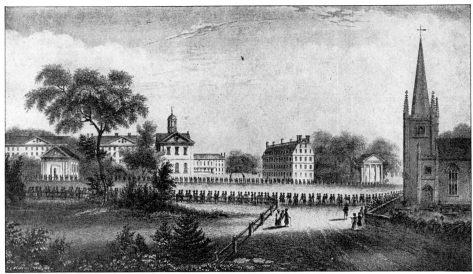

430   Harvard College with the Procession of the Alumni, Sept. 8, 1836, from Josiah Quincy, *History of Harvard University,* Cambridge, 1840

CLASS POET AT HARVARD

INDEED a precocious examination of Calvinism, a peep through a telescope on Boston Common, and omnivorous reading weaned Holmes early from orthodoxy, though not, he says, without some cramps in his mental machinery.   He read Bryant, Percival, Drake, and Halleck, lights "twinkling to the best of their ability," but had a strange preference for Pope's Homer.   At Harvard College (1825–29) he became class poet, for the "Boys," then and in perpetuity.   Finally, in 1830, came a hint that he was to escape the usual oblivion of college poets.   The fiery poem, *Old Ironsides*, written on a scrap of paper, became popular throughout America.

PREPARATION FOR *THE AUTOCRAT*

AFTER a year at the law, Holmes studied medicine in Boston, and later in Paris (1833–35), where he lived a full life, diversified by travel.   He practiced in Boston;   taught in Dartmouth College;   married and had children;   and became professor and Dean in the Harvard Medical School.   All this was before *The Autocrat of the Breakfast Table*, 1858, began: "I was just going to say, when I was interrupted, that . . . " Already a wit and diner-out, Holmes was now to be at the tables of thousands of Americans — and Englishmen — who had never seen the steeples of Boston.

431   From a carte de visite, about 1860, by Silsbee, Case & Co., Boston

THE CHAMBERED NAUTILUS

WHEN *The Autocrat* appeared Holmes was nearly fifty years old.   He was to live thirty-seven years more, but there is little to describe save his enjoyment of life; other, though lesser, literary successes; and honors from Harvard, Oxford, and Cambridge.   In the fourth chapter of *The Autocrat* had appeared the poem declared by Whittier to be immortal, *The Chambered Nautilus*.   In later life this author of an authoritative work on puerperal fever was distinguished as a wit, a poet, and a novelist.

432   From *Vanity Fair*, London, 1886, caricature by "Spy"

433   From Donald G. Mitchell, *American Lands and Letters*, 1899; after a photograph, 1894. taken by Arthur Dexter,
by permission of Charles Scribner's Sons

LAST YEARS

In 1886 Holmes went abroad again, his first and last visit after the sojourn as a medical student. He was lionized, and he bore his honors without displeasure, even when Cambridge undergraduates ventured a song: "*Holmes*, Sweet Holmes." "He is enjoying himself immensely . . . " said Lowell. "Everybody is charmed with him, as it is natural they should be." He lived on at Beverly Farms till 1891, his last years shadowed somewhat by griefs and his threatened blindness. He had, he remarked characteristically, "a cataract in the kitten stage of development." One cannot help observing how prophetic now seemed his poem, *The Last Leaf.*

434 Holmes Leaving his house on Beacon Street, from a photograph, 1893, courtesy of Houghton Mifflin Company

,435 From Holmes, *The Autocrat of the Breakfast Table*, Boston, 1868

THE AUTOCRAT OF THE BREAKFAST TABLE

THE first sentence of *The Autocrat* had a meaning. Holmes *had* been "interrupted." During the early 'thirties, in the *New England Magazine*, he had published two papers with this general plan. "It would be," he thought, "a curious experiment to shake the same bough again, and see if the ripe fruit were better or worse than the early windfalls." Windfalls, in spite of their apparently haphazard form, these wise and witty observations on life were not. As humor *The Autocrat* has been compared to the *Essays of Elia* and to the *Noctes Ambrosianæ.*

CHARACTERS IN *THE AUTOCRAT*

THEY were rather reflections on life comparable to those in the noblest essays in English literature, but conveyed in unique monologues, or semidialogues. The *mise-en-scène* is the breakfast table of a New England boarding house, and the actors individuals known to every dweller in Yankee land: the divinity student, the professor, the schoolmistress, the landlady. With these and others, like the landlady's son ("Benjamin Franklin"), "the old gentleman opposite," and "the Scarabæus," Holmes created an outline narrative, and a romance which makes portions of the book not unlike a novel.

CONVERSATIONAL QUALITY OF *THE AUTOCRAT*

BREAKFAST at this table is breakfast with the Autocrat. It is his mind and eloquence we remember. It is his flow of reminiscence which makes the book almost a collection of essays, though his fellow boarders' in-

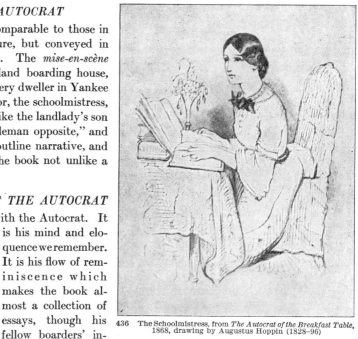

436   The Schoolmistress, from *The Autocrat of the Breakfast Table,* 1868, drawing by Augustus Hoppin (1828-96)

terjections bring it close to the dialogue form. The net result is as near living chat as can well be found in the mute leaves of a book. His topics? Well, who would catalogue in the conversation of a friend the puns, the gossip, the tender recollection, the flashes of insight? It is enough to notice the Autocrat's memories of Paris, his love of books, his valiant pity for suffering, and his maniacal passion for old Boston.

437   The Landlady's Daughter, from *The Autocrat of the Breakfast Table*, 1868, drawing by Augustus Hoppin

OTHER BOOKS OF THE BREAKFAST TABLE

EDMUND GOSSE, who should be a judge, says that Holmes' talk was "an illuminated cascade of fancy and humor and repartee." Later the cascade flowed on over the lesser falls of *The Professor at the Breakfast Table*, 1860, and *The Poet at the Breakfast Table*, 1872. *Over the Teacups*, 1890, brought forth the last genial, if fainter, sallies of the old man. Good things are said at the breakfasts with the professor and poet, and the stories of both books are more definite, but talk at breakfast should be random — if indeed there must be conversation.

438   Holmes' Summer Home, Beverly Farms, Beverly, Mass.   © Halliday Historic Photograph Co.

439   Dr. Holmes in his study, from a photograph, 1888,
       by Notman in the Harvard College Library

THE NOVELS

IN fact Holmes was preparing to be a novelist. In *The Professor at the Breakfast Table* is the origin of *Elsie Venner*, 1861, a tale rather heavily scented with the aroma of the doctor's office. By all means, let us surrender the themes of snake influence to the romantic verse of Keats and Coleridge. One sees here the doctor prodding his captive reptile, and tabulating results. *The Guardian Angel*, 1867, is, even with the character of the scholar, Byles Gridley, still less happy, and one hesitates to mention *A Mortal Antipathy*, 1885. In all these novels Holmes is weighted by the message concerning heredity. Medical science with an ethical purpose is not a healthy graft on the novel. Nor had Holmes the other gifts of a novelist.

440   The Deacon, from *The Autocrat of the Breakfast Table*, 1868, drawing by Hoppin

THE ONE–HOSS SHAY

A MERRY Cambridge undergraduate, during the ovation in England, asked Holmes if he came thither in the *One-Hoss Shay*. And it must be confessed that his arrival at Parnassus was in this vehicle, or else in *The Chambered Nautilus*. The poet's rapture was not his. Instead he possessed sharpness of outline, ease, sparkle, and occasionally, as in *The Chambered Nautilus* and *The Last Leaf*, human aspiration or sadness.

441   From a photograph by Notman

OCCASIONAL POETRY

YET we are told that Holmes longed to be known as a poet. Few scribblers ever broke into anapest or heroic couplets more easily than this octogenarian class poet. Professor Henry A. Beers has a half-humorous list of the score or more types of occasions which elicited verse from him: ". . . inaugurations . . . dedications of cemeteries . . . rural festivals and city fairs . . . jubilees . . . dinners of welcome or farewell to Dickens . . . Farragut, the Grand Duke Alexis, the Chinese Embassy, and what not." Though generally indifferent to public affairs, Holmes wrote poetry in behalf of the Union. He seems the most prolific of occasional poets, and many poems like *The Height of the Ridiculous, Rip Van Winkle, M.D.*, still keep their effervescence. "The muse of Holmes," says Duyckinck, "is a foe to humbug. There is among his poems 'a professional ballad — *The Stethoscope Song*,' descriptive of the practices of a young physician from Paris, who went about knocking the wind out of old ladies, and terrifying young ones, mistaking, all the while, a buzzing fly in the instrument for a frightful array of diseases expressed in a variety of terrible French appellations,"

442   Retouched enlargement of a photograph in the Boston Athenæum

EMERSON AND HOLMES IN THE PUBLIC GARDEN, BOSTON

HOLMES' verse has a sound eighteenth-century flavor. He wrote, in spite of his later appreciative biography of Emerson, only briary jingles on the vagaries of the Transcendentalists, and his poetry seldom dwelt on the unknown. Yet *The Last Leaf* was beloved by Lincoln. Poe copied it in his own hand. In it Holmes' drollery softens into the pathos which sprang from his sympathy with human life.

HOLMES, THE BOSTONIAN

In the final reckoning Oliver Wendell Holmes cannot be declared a great man of letters. Only *The Autocrat* and a few poems survive. Historically, however, he is significant. Intensely local, with his adoration of Boston Common, he is still an excellent representative of our growing cosmopolitanism — of the influence of the city. Holmes had not genius but talent. That the education, the conversation, and the contacts of his day could produce such a man of talent as Holmes is proof enough of our growing culture.

443   "The Long Path," Boston Common, celebrated in *The Autocrat*.   ⓒ Halliday Historic Photograph Co.

444   A water-color portrait attributed to J. C. McDougall,
location not known

EDGAR ALLAN POE, 1809–49

ON the list of contributors to Lowell's ill-fated *Pioneer* (No. 413) was the name of Edgar Allan Poe. While Emerson and Holmes were in Paris, and Longfellow was teaching at Bowdoin, young Poe, born, like Holmes, in 1809 (and in Boston!), was writing for the magazines in the South. He represents the growing intellectual life of the southern cities. But his life story is like a drama fashioned from his own dark dreams.

445   Interior of Poe's Room, University of Virginia,
courtesy of Mary Louise Dinwiddie

EARLY YEARS

POE's grandfather was old David Poe, of Revolutionary fame. His father won success in the rôle of "The Wild Gallant," on the stage, and, apparently, in life. His mother, a gifted actress, played with John Howard Payne. At her death, two years after Poe's birth, he was adopted by John Allan, a native of Ayr and a merchant of Richmond. At first the precocious, beautiful child was loved by the Allans, not wisely but too well, perhaps; we hear of him declaiming *The Lay of the Last Minstrel* before a crowded drawing-room. With the Allans, Poe spent five years at the Manor-House School, near London, a place rich with the past of England. Such years could hardly help becoming for Poe a romantic and shadowy memory. In 1826 he entered the University of Virginia at Charlottesville.

446   Doorway of Poe's Room, University of
Virginia, courtesy of Mary Louise Dinwiddie

447   The Arcade, University of Virginia, courtesy of Mary Louise Dinwiddie

448   The Drill at West Point, about 1828, from J. G. Milbert, *Itinéraire Pittoresque du Fleuve Hudson*, etc., Paris, 1828–29

AT WEST POINT

AT the university he was interested in languages, but also in peach-and-honey, and to this first step, Puritan monitors have not been slow to suggest, Poe owed a life of dissipation.   In 1827 he broke with the Allans, enlisted in the army, and published his first volume, *Tamerlane and other Poems*.   By the spring of 1831 he had been appointed to a cadetship and had been court-martialed and discharged from West Point.

EARLY TALES

Now follows the age-old story of the artist's struggle with the world and with himself.   Poe was wayward, imperious, perverse; subject, even in days of success, to anguish of mind.   Upon such a temperament, poverty and stimulants preyed heavily, and, judged by conventional standards, his career is a wretched tale of failure and weakness. Yet one always feels

449   Reduction from the Ms. of *Annabel Lee, A Ballad*, in the J. Pierpont Morgan Library, New York

in the letters and dim records of this time, besides personal charm, the burning fire of his genius.   In 1833 he achieved some recognition by winning a prize for the *Ms. found in a Bottle*, a forerunner of tales like *The Gold Bug*.   Between 1835 and 1844 he was connected with *The Southern Literary Messenger* in Richmond; and also with *Burton's Gentleman's Magazine*, and *Graham's Magazine*, both of Philadelphia.

450   Title-page of the copy in the New York Public Library

451   The Poe Cottage at Fordham, N. Y., where he lived after his marriage in 1835

VIRGINIA CLEMM

An interlude in the gloom, but hardly less singular than the rest of his life, was Poe's engagement and presumably secret marriage to his cousin, Virginia Clemm, thirteen years old. Poe's real literary partner in a sort of triangular union was the girl's mother, Mrs. Clemm, who gave him understanding and sympathy in his work.

Life in the cottage at Fordham with the delicate, devoted child-wife lifted Poe for a time into sunshine. It is daring to claim in a life like Poe's, as some have, that Virginia Clemm was the only woman he ever truly loved, but her death was a tragedy for the eccentric genius, not less so that she died (1847) in miserable poverty.

452   From a photograph of a water-color portrait; artist, early history, and present location unknown, courtesy of J. H. Whitty, Richmond

POE AND HELEN WHITMAN

But two years before a glimpse and a description of the mind of Sarah Helen Whitman had deeply moved Poe's nature. "A profound sympathy," he later says, "took immediate possession of my soul. . . . From that hour I loved you." Poe, in spite of grief for Virginia, is not especially attractive in these years, holding, as they sit by the fire, the hand of Annie, "a dear friend." This Platonic affair is in keeping with his "divinely beautiful" letters to other ladies. Between himself and Mrs. Whitman existed a strong sympathy, with its roots, perhaps, in their love of the romantic and occult. She promised to marry him, but at the last moment broke off the match, for reasons made clear in her

453   From the portrait, 1838, by Cephas G. Thompson, in the Athenæum, Providence, R. I.

later correspondence. In a recently published letter she says: "I bade him farewell with feelings of profound commiseration for his fate — of intense sorrow thus to part from one whose sweet and gracious nature had endeared him to me beyond expression. . . ."

LAST DAYS

LAST scene of all before the final silence is in Baltimore. Having severed relations with the *Evening Mirror* and *Broadway Journal* of New York, Poe had drifted. After the debacle with Mrs. Whitman he suffered from alcoholism at Philadelphia and Richmond, and finally died in extreme wretchedness in a Baltimore hospital.

454 From *Graham's Magazine*, 1845, after a drawn portrait by A. C. Smith

455 Page of Poe's Ms. of *The Murders in the Rue Morgue* in the New York Public Library, transcript of the original owned by the Drexel Institute, Philadelphia

TALES OF RATIOCINATION

POE'S prose tales have variety, but in them may be easily discovered two dominant interests. One is a passion for analysis, the other tense imagination. At West Point Poe had shown his aptitude for mathematics. Any puzzle delighted him: as an editor he successfully challenged readers to baffle him with cryptograms, and he amazed Dickens and the world by foretelling the end of *Barnaby Rudge*. Stories like *The Gold Bug* or *The Murders in the Rue Morgue* he loved to call "tales of ratiocination." They are superb detective stories.

TALES OF HORROR

IN these Poe is scrupulously realistic, even when, as in *A Descent into the Maelstrom*, horrible imaginings lift him into poetic rapture. Realism and imagination become repulsive in such stories of ghastly adventure as *Arthur Gordon Pym* or *The Pit and the Pendulum*. It is a morbid scene: the swish of the deadly pendulum and the gnawing vermin. In *The Adventures of One Hans Pfall* and similar stories he rivals Defoe in scientific accuracy concerning details which never could exist.

456 The Pit and the Pendulum, from Edgar Allan Poe, *Prose Tales of Mystery and Imagination*, New York, 1903, after a drawing by Alice B. Woodward. © Howard Wilford Bell

457   The Black Cat, from Aubrey Beardsley, *Drawings to Illustrate the Tales of Poe*, the Colonial Co., New York, 1898

THE TERRORS OF CONSCIENCE

POE's imagination flamed with a fierce light on the mystery of conscience. In the spiritual or ethical significance of this, in contrast to Hawthorne, he has hardly a passing interest. But he revels in the murderer's terror at the sound of the symbolical beating heart. And in *The Black Cat*, with its horrible cyclopean eye, or in *William Wilson*, he probes remorselessly the torture which conscience can inflict.

458   From *Dix Contes d'Edgar Poe*, translated by Charles Baudelaire, Paris, engraving by Eugene Dété after a drawing by Martin van Maële

THE FALL OF THE HOUSE OF USHER

THOUGH still a technician in such a story as *The Fall of the House of Usher*, Poe visioned beauty and made it permanent in art. In the countless details of sound and color, in the intense unity of mood, the story is merely skillful, but the strangeness in the proportions of beauty, its curious exaltation ally it to Poe's poetry. It is the beauty of the poet's dream inverted, the beauty of the palace of dim night.

ROMANTIC GLOOM

IT is this almost mystic communion with the unseen, terrible, but harmonious world of darkness which makes Poe, in a few tales, so supreme. He wrote goblin stories, which were impostures, stories designed only to titillate the nerves, or else satires, but in *The Fall of the House of Usher*, in *Ligeia*, and in a few others, there rises to the surface his whole inner life of romantic gloom.

459   From *The Art Journal*, London, February, 1904, after a drawing by E. J. Sullivan

MORELLA

THESE stories became an imperishable part of the literature of the darker side of romanticism. He is with De Quincey or James Thomson. "Holy was the grave to him; lovely was its darkness; saintly its corruption." As the husband lingered by Morella, his strange, mystical wife, "joy suddenly faded into horror, and the most beautiful became the most hideous, as Hinnon became Ge-Henna."

461   Page from *Dix Contes d'Edgar Poe*, translated by Charles Baudelaire, Paris, after a drawing by Martin van Maële

460   After a drawing by Alberto Martini, courtesy of J. H. Whitty

POE'S CONTINENTAL REPUTATION

IT is suggestive to realize that at first Poe could not sell his stories. He had an odd habit of sending his tales to all sorts of people, and the letters in reply record the amazement at the tales of the arabesque and grotesque. The chief objection was, of course, in the America of Longfellow, the lack of moral. Once when Harper's declined to publish for him, Paulding wrote: "Most especially they object that there is a degree of obscurity in their application, which will prevent ordinary readers from comprehending their drift, and consequently from enjoying the fine satire they convey." But Continental critics were more tolerant.

FOREIGN TRANSLATIONS

POE'S genius in such a country as America Europeans could not explain, but genius they knew it to be. His stories were speedily translated into French and other European languages. A homely proof of Poe's audience abroad may be had by turning over library card-catalogues under the names of other distinguished American writers, and then under that of Poe. He definitely influenced a few French writers.

462   The Murders in the Rue Morgue, from Edgar Allan Poe, *Fantastiscke Novelle*, Paa Dansk ved Hermann Petersen, after a drawing by Sofus Jürgensen

463   From *The Raven*, New York, 1884, engraving after a drawing
by Gustave Doré (1833–83)

POE'S VERSE

POE had published three volumes of verse before he was famous as a short-story writer, but his poetic output was relatively slight. His speculative mind is evident even in verse, but particularly in his rather superficial poetics, *The Rationale of Verse*, 1843, *The Poetic Principle*, 1850, *The Philosophy of Composition*, 1846, and *Eureka*, 1848, a daring flight into the spiritual universe. Yet, as in the few great tales, Poe's power as a poet, apart from technique, lies in the ecstatic moment of terror.

THE RAVEN

IN the earlier poems the mood of lurid darkness recurs, as in *The City by the Sea*. Such a poem as *To Helen* with "the glory that was Greece and the grandeur that was Rome," has a simplicity of feeling too seldom found in Poe's poetry. He must have smiled a little — others have later — at the success of his mechanically musical *Raven*, which appeared in the New York *Evening Mirror* for February, 1845. The sentimental public softly quoted "Nevermore," and we hear of Poe declaiming the poem — the audience still as death "as his weird, musical voice filled the hall." Few have thought Poe's account of the composition of *The Raven* ingenuous, though we subscribe readily enough to its conscious artistry. *The Raven* is falsetto. "A cold poem," sums up a general judgment.

ULALUME

POE'S poetry is full of obvious tricks in meter. He is, as Emerson said gravely, "the jingle man." In *Ulalume* he toys with refrains until the poem is very nearly funny. He likes, also, as in the earlier *Al Aaraaf*, to introduce melodious names, the products of a learning that is none too deep. After roaming through "Alleys Titanic" with Psyche, the lover's heart is "volcanic," like — unhappy rhymes! — "the sulphurous currents down Yaanek." Physical exhaustion, which, critics allege, accounts for the passion of this poem, may also explain its ridiculous lines. Yet *Ulalume*, like *Israfel*, is a sigh from the depths.

464   From *The Illustrated London News*, June 19, 1852,
after a painting by E. H. Wehnert

ULALUME

Then my heart it grew ashen and sober
As the leaves that were crisped and sere—

As the leaves that were withering and sere,
And I cried—"It was surely October

465   From *The Poetical Works of Edgar Allan Poe*,
New York, 1857, engraving by W. J. Linton
after a drawing by F. R. Pickersgill

THE BELLS

TRADITIONS have gathered about Poe. New York and Baltimore contend for the origin of *The Bells*. On a winter night in the southern city, so one legend runs, Poe heard in the tinkling of sleigh bells the cadences of the poem. He gained admittance to a house, where he was a stranger, procured paper, and without more ceremony wrote the stanzas which form, perhaps, his most popular lyric. *The Bells* illustrates alphabetically Poe's theory of poetry, *pleasure;* and his delight in sound for its own sake.

THE BELLS.

HEAR the sledges with the bells—
Silver bells!
What a world of merriment their melody foretells!
How they tinkle, tinkle, tinkle,
In the icy air of night!

466   From *The Poetical Works of Edgar Allan Poe*, New York, 1858, engraving after a drawing by F. O. C. Darley

467   From the portrait by Samuel S. Osgood (1798–1885) in the New York Historical Society

POE IN AMERICAN LITERATURE

YET to call Poe insincere is to be concerned with surface values. His narrowness of range enhances his intensity. Historically he is forever linked with the short story and with true literary criticism. His greatness lies in his dedication, in materialistic, sentimental America, to art, a corner of art, but none the less art. "My life," he wrote sadly, "has been *whim* — impulse — passion." Fitfully, with wavering splendor through darkness pass his dreams of beauty. These visions he has made lasting in a few stories and poems. Extravagant as these are, they may prove to be our chief contribution to romantic poetry. One finishes a study of Poe with a desire to point out his faults — a desire which, for many critics, has proved as overmastering as it is easy to indulge. Lowell's verdict has the sting of truth:

> There comes Poe with his Raven, like Barnaby Rudge,
> Three-fifths of him genius, and two-fifths sheer fudge.

Americans have never forgiven Poe's lack of message to his age. More serious to some seems a certain thinness in his nature. His serious thought is superficial, and in art he is apt to play the harlequin.

468   The Poe Memorial, erected by the actors of New York, in the Metropolitan Museum of Art

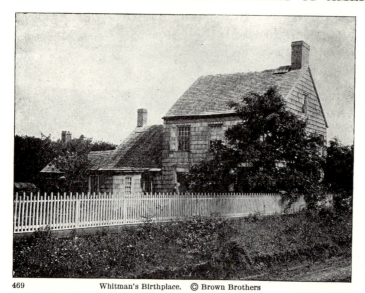

469   Whitman's Birthplace. © Brown Brothers

WALT WHITMAN, 1819–92

SIX years after Poe's death Thoreau heard "an alarum or trumpet note ringing through the American camp." The trumpeter, Walter (Walt) Whitman was born in 1819, at West Hills, Long Island, on a farm within sound of the sea, whose roar he was later to answer with declamations from ancient literatures. In his veins flowed English, Dutch, and Welsh blood. Not merely Homer and Sophocles supplied the place of an education, but the *Arabian Nights* and the poetry of Scott. Whitman falls into this chapter, but he lived on into the last decade of the century, and in many ways is more typical of the age after the Civil War than that which preceded it.

WHITMAN IN YOUTH

IN 1824 the boy's family had moved to Brooklyn, and by the time Whitman was twenty years old he had been printer, school-teacher, and contributor to newspapers. In the next few years he was to write still more: verse, articles, and a novel for a temperance society, composed with a cocktail by his side. Later he was to become the editor of the Brooklyn *Eagle*. These were the years of those early loves, the omnibus and the ferry-boat. Charles Lamb never poked about London more lovingly than Whitman about his beloved New York. Then at Coney Island was that "long, bare, unfrequented shore, which I had all to myself, and where I loved, after bathing, to race up and down the hard sand, and declaim Homer or Shakespeare to the surf and sea-gulls by the hour."

470   From *Leaves of Grass*, Brooklyn, 1855, engraving by Samuel Hollyer after a daguerreotype by Gabriel Harrison

WANDERJAHRE

FROM boyhood increased Whitman's craving for deeper experiences. He sought, half unconsciously, to drink life to the lees. This was the meaning of his idle, observing, zestful friendliness with the New York pilots and omnibus drivers. Now in 1849, through a newspaper connection in New Orleans, he wandered through the South and West, returning with a comprehension of millions of humble Americans. His hands were now busy with his carpenter's tools, but his mind was forming from his experiences his staggering book, the book of himself and of America. He had now traveled; he had read widely in English literature; and he knew the life of the American city.

471   From a daguerreotype, about 1850, courtesy of David McKay, Philadelphia

Leaves

of

Grass.

⸺

Brooklyn, New York:
1855.

472 Title-page of the original edition in the
New York Public Library

LEAVES OF GRASS

LEAVES OF GRASS, 1855, which Whitman set up in type with his own hands, was the product of his own virile reaction to life, but also of the deep currents of the nineteenth century: democracy, science, liberalism, and particularly the American correlations of such thought. For a long time Whitman had carried in his pocket a volume of Emerson.

WHITMAN IN WAR TIME

WHITMAN's simple-hearted passion for his human brothers is noblest in his selfless devotion in the hospitals of the Civil War — "the Good Gray Poet." When he entered a ward, suffering men became quieter. He brought in his knapsack humble gifts, food or reading; he wrote letters for the dying; he consoled the anguished. In this manner he visited between eighty and a hundred thousand soldiers. To this cause he gave his own magnificent health. Some of Whitman's best poetry, from the apostrophes to Lincoln to the laments on the dead, was inspired by the Civil War.

473 From the life portrait, taken in Washington, 1863, given to Horace L. Traubel, Philadelphia

474 Whitman in his Camden, N. J., home, about 1890, from a photograph by Jeanette L. Gilder

INTERNATIONAL FAME

FOR nine years after the close of the war, Whitman was a clerk in Washington, happy with strangely different friends, a John Burroughs, and a Peter Doyle, his loved Irishman. Meanwhile his reputation had established itself. In England Rossetti, Swinburne, and others discuss but do not dispute his genius. At Camden, New Jersey, for the last eighteen years of his life, 1874-92, after a paralytic stroke, he becomes almost a seer. We think of him in his communion with nature; of his meditation on the stars, as, far away, Carlyle lies dying; or of his greeting innumerable pilgrims. And we are inclined to echo Lincoln's phrase concerning him: "Well, *he* looks like a MAN!"

475 Walt Whitman's House on Mickle Street, Camden, N. J.

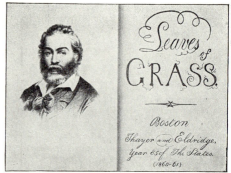

476   Page of the original Ms. of *By Emerson's Grave* in the New York
Public Library

"I CELEBRATE MYSELF"

ALL study of Whitman as a poet reverts to that green volume with its challenging first line: "I celebrate myself." It is true. In it was the full life he had lived. As he contemplates this brave world he is exalted with the bridegroom's exaltation. The heavens, a man's body, or a blade of grass excite him to raptures. All this is himself. For Whitman is a mystic. His "I" often means the average man. He thrills not only in his own power, but in the universal force which permeates all things.

477   From *Leaves of Grass*, third edition, 1860–61

CRITICISM OF *LEAVES* *OF GRASS*

TRANSCENDENTALISM had been a factor in *Leaves of Grass*, and the American leader recognized its significance: "I find it," Emerson wrote him, "the most extraordinary piece of wit and wisdom that America has yet contributed." Yet the book fell flat, and Whittier in destroying, so goes the story, his copy, expressed public opinion. In it many readers saw nothing save conceit and sensuality. "It is," said Thoreau, though he admired *Leaves of Grass*, "as if the beasts spoke."

WHITMAN'S BAD TASTE

CRITICS of this frankness liked to point out also other proofs of Whitman's coarse nature. The modern reader finds these stories rather amusing: how he wrote his own reviews, or how the serene brow of the Concord sage clouded — for once — when he beheld on the back of the second edition of *Leaves of Grass* in large letters his own words, "I Greet You at the Beginning of a Great Career. R. W. Emerson." Most shocking of all was Whitman's indifference to metrical canons. *Leaves of Grass* was "impassioned prose," dependent upon many influences, such as the Bible, or De Quincey, but chiefly, for its rhythmic movement, upon the emotion of the poet.

478   Cover of *Leaves of Grass*, Brooklyn, second edition, 1856.   Copy in
the Harvard College Library

WHITMAN AND THE PARODISTS

THE peculiarities of Whitman were targets for the parodists. Meanwhile *Leaves of Grass* reappeared with other poems, in not less than ten editions during his lifetime. Even if skepticism persisted, recognition of his genius became universal. The barbaric yawp was now really sounded "over the roofs of the world." *Drum Taps*, Civil War poems, with the appended *When Lilacs Last in the Dooryard Bloom'd*, appeared in 1865; *Democratic Vistas* in 1870. From time to time Whitman published poems in which he reverted to old verseforms. *O Captain, My Captain*, written after Lincoln's assassination, and *The Man-of-War Bird* border on the conventional.

479   From *The Bookman*, Vol. 19, 1904, after a cartoon by Max Beerbohm

COUNTER-JUMPS.

A POEMETTINA.—AFTER WALT WHITMAN.

AM the Counter-jumper, weak and effem-
        inate.
    I love to loaf and lie about dry-goods.
    I loaf and invite the Buyer.
I am the essence of retail. The sum and result of small profits
    and quick returns.
The Picayune is part of me, and so is the half cent, and the mill
    only arithmetically appreciable.
The shining, cheap-woven sarsnet is of me, and I am of it.
And the white bobinet,
And the moire antique, thickly webbed and strown with impossible
    flowers,
And the warm, winter gloves lined with fur,
And the delicate summer gloves of silk threads,
And the intermediate ones built of the hide of the Swedish rat,
All these things are of me, and many more also.
For I am the shop, and the counter, and the till,
But particularly the last.
And I explore and rummage the till, and am at home in it.
And I am the shelves on which lie the damaged goods ;
The damaged goods themselves I am,
And I ask what's the damage ?
I am the crate, and the hamper, and the yard-wand, and the box
    of silks fresh from France,
And when I came into the world I paid duty,
And I never did my duty,
And never intend to do it,
For I am the creature of weak depravities ;
I am the Counter-jumper ;
I sound my feeble yelp over the woofs of the World.

480   From *Vanity Fair*, New York, March 17, 1860

PROPHET OF DEMOCRACY

BESIDES the glory of the individual and of the universe Whitman celebrates the glory of these United States. He is the most excited democrat that America has produced, and will long be famous as its prophet. To it he consecrated all his energy, and, some may say, very little thought. The strong men of the West, great leaders, like Lincoln, are enough to convince him that the millennium is approached by the broad road of democracy, marked by the signposts of physical science. Some of this is animal exuberance. One of the ridiculous — or inspiring — qualities of Whitman is that he always talks as if he had just emerged from a cold shower. Yet the roots of Whitman's exaltation were in religion.

WHITMAN AS THE POET OF AMERICA

JUST a century ago Whitman caught his first glimpse of the city whose life he sang. Nearly three quarters of a century have passed since the appearance of *Leaves of Grass*. Yet it sometimes seems as if we were as far as ever from a final evaluation of this bard or prophet. Matthew Arnold thought him a rather unfavorable sign of the spirit of the age, but Swinburne wrote: "O strong-winged soul with prophetic lips —." Whitman's freedoms in speech and metrics no longer astound us. But we are still waiting for the fulfilment of his horoscope that he would be forever the poet of the common people. These have not accepted him. As for more meticulous readers, his faults stand in his way: his easy disposition of all problems of society or of the spirit. Yet true religion is in him. His exultant imagination still stimulates. And the main currents of thought of the young republic may be found in "Walt" Whitman.

481   From a photograph, 1876, by Pearsall, courtesy of Oscar Lion, New York

CHAPTER VIII

SOME WRITERS OF THE NORTH AND SOUTH

INTELLIGENT Europeans who visited America between 1815 and 1870 were amused by the stupendous output of inferior prose and poetry. An Irving, a Cooper, an Emerson, or a Lowell could not help being, in this energetic country, the leaders, even if unconsciously, of an army of writers. The multiplication of newspapers, the spread of education, the growth of cities had created a reading public. The absence of international copyright flooded America with English books, inspiring imitation. It was the age of the annual, the token, the gift-book. Zealous clergymen collected poetry and republished it in huge anthologies. Sentimental ladies wrote refined novels. In fact, Americans embraced writing much as they dealt with their practical affairs — enthusiastically, patriotically.

Nor is all this writing weak. Much of it bears the imprint of Cooper, Emerson, and Longfellow. Donald Grant Mitchell (Ik Marvel) is a Connecticut Irving, and Sylvester Judd of Maine writes transcendental novels. To consider these writers apart suggests the old analogy of *Hamlet* without its protagonist. Yet rereading this literature sympathetically, one understands its influence; encounters, indeed, many an excellent story or poem. English literature of the nineteenth century abounds in prose and poetry which is well-constructed, gifted with ideas, effective in expression, but which is quite, quite dead. We, too, have our Southeys, our Tuppers, and a Felicia Hemans. Yet some of these "minor" authors have talent, and many of them have a flavor which is unique.

"Thus far," wrote, in 1842, the editor of one of the anthologies of poetry, "the chief distinguishing characteristic of American poetry is its moral purity. May it remain so forever." This prayer the Muses seemed likely to grant. So Poe was read sparingly, and Mrs. Sigourney liberally. There were descriptions of nature viewed through a minister's study window, with a copy of Tennyson on the table; tepid romances of the Indians which would have sickened the softest of redskins; and lyrics on snowflakes, young mothers, and funerals. The war brought threnodies, but in general its effect was tonic. Both in the South and North the marching men and the rattle of drums inspired martial ballads, and a few poems, like Brownell's lyrics or Julia Ward Howe's hymn, were to outlive their generation. The center of poetry continued to be New England. Here was still the deepest culture, and poetry in these years, except for Whitman, was a bookish product. Yet Pennsylvania gives us Bayard Taylor, and New England has no minor figure so impressive as William Gilmore Simms or Henry Timrod.

Luckily no anthologies could be made of the novels, and much of the tearful trash died at birth. Yet we are told by a critic in 1870 that the novels of Timothy Flint — who so amused Mrs. Trollope — should be read because "he wrote like a scholar, a man of feeling, and a gentleman"; and in the same breath we hear that Cooper's plots are "commonplace." This critic had in his private library several hundred American novels. Again one thinks of England: of the imitations of Scott, of the diluted Lyttons, and of G. P. R. James. Yet a study of Cooper and Hawthorne by no means includes all readable American novels. Richard Henry Dana's *Two Years Before the Mast* is a magnificent story, and another writer of the sea, Herman Melville, is enjoying a modern revival. *Uncle Tom's Cabin*, Harriet Beecher Stowe's world-famous story of slavery in the South, is an instance of a remarkable narrative not dependent upon the great novelists of the era. The book has the sentimentality, the melodrama, the lack of finish characteristic of the tales of the day, but indicates the increasing tendency of the American novel to identify itself with the history of the country.

As for history itself, no epoch has been more honored. The scholarly Puritans had a knack for writing history; one recalls their tough "annals" and "chronological histories." The intellectual revival in New England spurred men not merely to creative writing, but also to scholarship. History was a natural channel for men of learning, and the literary enthusiasms in the air added a grace which had been absent in the earlier records. Some of our great historians had already tried their hands at literature before they settled down to their life work. The literary flavor in the Massachusetts historians varies from the somewhat formal style of Bancroft to the brilliant writing of Motley. Their subjects, too, are of wide range, suggesting not only the intense interest in the new country as in Sparks' biographies, or Parkman's panoramas of the West, or Bancroft's complete study of the United States, but also the influence of European culture and scholarship in Motley's *Rise of the Dutch Republic* or Prescott's *Reign of Ferdinand and Isabella*. Most significant of all is the fact itself: side by side with the Transcendentalists grew up this group of historians, scientific, patiently industrious, with a philosophic mastery of the past. They, too, were a product of the cities and universities, far-off products, too, of the solid English thought which built the Massachusetts commonwealth. Is it surprising that the historian Parkman, as the story goes, was amused by Cooper's Indians?

Another phase of literature which flourished in these years was oratory. It lacked the literary importance of the Revolutionary speech making — the growth of pure literature prevented that — but for several reasons American literature of the nineteenth century must admit such names as Webster, Clay, and Phillips. When stately periods were infused with the fire of a Webster or an Everett, one might easily be deceived into thinking them literature. Indeed a few surviving passages of this eloquence seem to indicate that it *was* literature. Another reason is that, aside from an occasional war-lyric or a novel like *Uncle Tom's Cabin*, the fierce conflicts of states' rights, slavery, abolition, and other issues on which trembled the fate of the Union, are mirrored in this fervid oratory. The existence of an Emerson must not make us forgetful that this was still the old, turbulent, expanding, excited America. The bombastic style of oratory, however, met its match on that day at Gettysburg in 1863 when Everett spoke in its best vein, and then was dismissed to oblivion by the quiet sentences of an Illinois lawyer. In this oratory one may detect much that is common to the other literature of the period: sentiment, imitation of old forms, patriotism. The forensic mood extended to the church; Channing and Beecher created religious literature of an oratorical cast.

Much of the oratory overflowed into partisan journalism. But the sounds of such shouting have become faint. The chief pleasure in a study of these "minor" writers centers in the more literary persons who described some corner of American life; those who could not write with real distinction, but who deserve our regard for some out-of-the-way virtue: a zest for travel, love of the strange West, humor of the soil. There are the journalists, like Greeley; the students of Shakespeare, such as Hudson; the naturalist, Audubon; the ethnologist, Schoolcraft; Colton and his tales of California; or Fanny Kemble and her journals of the stage.

Not least interesting are our low-life comedians, the heralds of Mark Twain. Lowell and Holmes knew the American vernacular, but this was the American guffaw itself, none too refined, but wholesome, and as genuinely funny as Lincoln's jokes to his Cabinet. We are tempted to invent antecedents: the rough "Cobler of Aggawam," the author of *The Sot-Weed Factor*, the Knickerbocker humorist. Yet, after all, this horseplay was a by-product of democracy, the frontier, and the war. In this writing were the eccentric characters, the slapdash incidents which took the fancy of a quick-witted people. Seba Smith with his "Major Jack Downing"; Robert Henry Newell, with his "Orpheus C. Kerr"; David Ross Locke, with his "Petroleum V. Nasby" of Confederate X Roads, Kentucky; or Thomas C. Haliburton (really a Nova Scotian), with his "Sam Slick," the clock maker — all create a setting for our crude, active life as merry as an inn scene in an Elizabethan comedy. These are interesting bypaths. Less virile, but not without charm, are the minor belletrists, the essayists, and lovers of books. "Peter Parley" and "Ik Marvel" are still known to many Americans, and the prose of George William Curtis, if too restful, retains its grace and breeding. Compared with such men, Cooper, Irving, and Hawthorne appear giants. Yet to know these humbler folk is to gain historical perspective. They are part of the story of American literature.

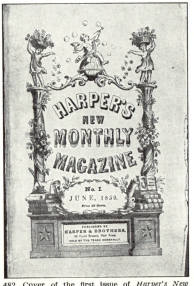

482 Cover of the first issue of *Harper's New Monthly Magazine*, June, 1850, courtesy of Frederick L. Allen

JAMES GATES PERCIVAL, 1795–1856

THE exclusion of Poe's poetry from anthologies is not more amusing, as a hint of erring contemporary judgments, than the picture of James Gates Percival as a central orb for the lesser lights of Bryant and Irving! Percival's story has interest: it is that of the sensitive, egotistic, romantic mind bruised by the world, a very old story indeed, even if its scene happens to be Connecticut. Unusual as his temperament was, his career as an author seems somehow typical of the age. He wandered from one occupation to another — geologist, lawyer, editor, and physician were some of his occupations. Graduated from Yale in 1815, he lectured in botany, was professor of chemistry at West Point, and became a skilled linguist. He wrote voluminously and imitatively; and, for his sentimental verse, he was lionized — much to his alarm, for Percival was instinctively a recluse. Yet even Whittier declared: "God pity the man who does not love the poetry of Percival." If we omitted the lovely poems of *To Seneca Lake* and *The Coral Grove*, we might well accept Whittier's quotation without the negative.

483   From the family portrait in the possession of Katharine Brandegee, Berlin, Conn.

484   From the portrait, artist unknown, in the School of the Fine Arts, Yale University

JAMES ABRAHAM HILLHOUSE, 1789–1841

YET there is in Percival's poetry a vein of gold. This we miss in the verse of his Connecticut *confrères*, that, say, of James Abraham Hillhouse, of whom Halleck sang:

Hillhouse whose music, like his themes,
Lifts earth to heaven.

Hillhouse's sacred drama *Hadad*, 1825, will not save him, Bryant to the contrary, from oblivion.

485   Brainard writing *The Falls of Niagara*, from S. G. Goodrich, *Recollections of a Lifetime*, 1856

JOHN G. C. BRAINARD, 1796–1828

THE Hartford poet, John G. C. Brainard, may be understood from his exceedingly gentle verses on wild Niagara, a scene which he had never beheld. This was a blank verse poem written for a morning newspaper, and has glorified many a school celebration. Brainard, a classmate of Percival at Yale, was a lawyer with a meager but pleasant poetic talent. He was associated with Whittier in newspaper work in Hartford. His verse, like his indolent, though spiritual life, lacked vitality. A characteristic mood may be felt in his best poem: *The dead leaves strew the forest walk.* Brainard died of consumption at the age of thirty-two.

486   From a carte de visite by Brady

LYDIA HUNTLEY SIGOURNEY, 1791–1865

In Hartford Brainard worshiped the "Felicia Hemans of America," Lydia Huntley Sigourney. Even beyond the boundaries of Connecticut this lady was a tradition of Victorian virtue and prolific poetry. Wife and mother, mistress of a girls' school, benefactress, traveler, she yet poured out, beginning at the age of eight, an effortless torrent of prose and verse. Her opening admonition in *Niagara* might have been made to herself: "Flow on, forever..." As she knitted socks she wrote poetry; as she wandered in Europe she wrote poetry; and as she visited tombstones — well, she wrote poetry — forty-six volumes, two thousand articles, and contributions to some three hundred periodicals.

MRS. SIGOURNEY'S POETRY

Her theme is preferably the melancholy, sweet, romantic grave. This was the time of the mezzotint with the sad cypress or willow, and Mrs. Sigourney's titles indicate the tenor of her stimulating message: *Moral Pieces*, 1815; *Letters to Young Ladies*, 1833; *Pocahontas, and Other Poems*, 1841; *The Weeping Willow*, 1846; *Whisper to a Bride*, 1849; *Olive Leaves*, 1851.

487   Title-page of L. H. Sigourney, *Pocahontas, and Other Poems*, New York, 1841

488   From *The Religious Souvenir*, Philadelphia, 1833, drawing by R. Westall for *A Sabbath Evening in the Country*

RELIGIOUS AND ELEGIAC POETRY

In such a world *Water Drops*, in behalf of temperance, failed to provoke the cynical to mirth. Indeed, as the French used to pluck a hair from the mantle of Voltaire, old ladies made pilgrimages to pick a spray of lilac from her garden. She received letters of praise from European royalty, and she was wont to refer graciously to Queen Victoria as "a sister woman." The story has come down of the gentleman who refused to ride in the train with her, lest, in the event of accident, he be made the subject of funeral verses; and a Hartford worthy remarked that her elegiac facility had given death a new terror.

MRS. SIGOURNEY'S SENTIMENT

YET jests of this sort are captious. If we are to find the negative qualities in literature in America — and we are, too often — let them be in a woman as worthy as Mrs. Sigourney. Her poetry is for those who shrink from life, but there is beauty in its cloistered virtue.

Soft tales have lovers told
Into the thrilling ear,
Till midnights witching hour waxed old
Deeming themselves alone while thou wert near.

489 From L. H. Sigourney, *Illustrated Poems*, Philadelphia, 1856. Engraving by Humphreys after the drawing by F. O. C. Darley, illustrating *The Ancient Family Clock*

"Awhile he paused
And set his burden down."

490 From *Illustrated Poems*, engraving by Hinshelwood after the drawing by F. O. C. Darley, illustrating *The Divided Burden*

MARIA GOWEN BROOKS, 1795–1845

A POETESS with stronger pinion was Maria Gowen Brooks, whom Southey called "Maria del Occidente," and whom he described in *The Doctor* as "the most impassioned and most imaginative of all poetesses." *Judith, Esther and other Poems* appeared in 1820. Her *Zophiel, or the Bride of Seven*, 1833, the proof sheets of which Southey corrected, celebrates in Byronic mood a maiden and her demon lover. "It is," said the *London Quarterly Review*, "altogether an extraordinary performance." Mrs. Brooks was well educated and had traveled. She turned to poetry in grief and in the poverty caused by an early widowhood. Not so sublime as Southey believed, though probably in the long run as immortal as himself, she none the less appears, compared with the lukewarm contemporary poetesses in America, a pillar of fire. Much of her passion, however, sounds to-day like grandiloquence. *Idomen*, 1843, is autobiographical.

491 From *Graham's Magazine*, 1848, engraving by Parker after the portrait by Francis Alexander, 1800–80

CHARLES SPRAGUE, 1791–1875

CHARLES SPRAGUE, another Boston poet (and a curious memorial, an ode in the manner of Pope, *Curiosity*, delivered before the Harvard Phi Beta Kappa society, 1829. He wrote also prologues, an ode on Shakespeare, and an essay on drunkenness. Some of his poems on domestic affections, such as *I See Thee Still*, or *The Family Meeting*, are tender and beautiful, and worthy of comparison with Longfellow's lyrics.

JOHN PIERPONT, 1785–1866

EXCELLENCE in one or two performances redeems numerous poets between 1815 and 1870. Thus John Godfrey Saxe, of Vermont, has occasionally some of Holmes' sparkle. It is difficult to read through the eight hundred lines of John Pierpont's *Airs of Palestine*, 1816, 1840, a poem evidently under the spell of Rogers, the banker-poet, and Thomas Campbell. Yet a lyric like *My Child*, in spite of its unrestrained sentiment and orthodox ending, may reserve Pierpont a place in anthologies. A native of Connecticut, he became minister of the Hollis Street Unitarian church in Boston.

493   From a carte de visite by
Warren, Boston

492   Title-page of Charles Sprague, *Poetical and Prose Writings*, Boston, 1850, engraving by Andrews and Rolph after a drawing by H. Billings

494   From Albert Gorton Greene, *Old Grimes*, Providence, R. I., 1867, drawing by Augustus Hoppin

ALBERT GORTON GREENE, 1802–68

ALBERT GORTON GREENE, a Providence lawyer, set an example to other poets by devoting his energies not to the publication of his own verse but to the founding of the "Harris Collection of American Poetry." His contemporaries admired his melodramatic poem, *The Baron's Last Banquet;* and *Old Grimes*, 1820, though rather moth-eaten, sometimes moves among us. Henry H. Brownell, too, of the same state, wrote later his stirring poem on the battle of Mobile Bay, *The Bay Fight*, 1864.

495   From a carte de visite by Case
and Getchell, Boston

THEODORE WINTHROP, 1828–61

THEODORE WINTHROP of New Haven, killed at Great Bethel in 1861, was the first northern officer to perish in the Civil War. "For one moment," says G. W. Curtis, "that brave inspiring form is plainly visible to his whole country, rapt and calm, standing on the log nearest the enemy's battery." He was the author, not without talent, of such novels as *Cecil Dreeme*, 1861, *John Brent*, 1862, and *The Canoe and the Saddle*, 1862.

CHRISTOPHER PEARSE CRANCH, 1813–92

MEANWHILE other poets were influenced by the Concord group. At intervals Christopher Pearse Cranch, artist, musician, and poet, visited Brook Farm. Accompanying himself on the piano or guitar, he sang to these Utopians, or read from his poems, or amazed them with ventriloquism. In spite of a dangerous versatility Cranch, who had been a Unitarian minister and had lived much abroad, was at heart a Transcendentalist. His poetry, often tame, manifests occasionally strong emotion as in *The Bobolinks, The Pines and The Sea*, or in the well-known lines which begin:

> . . . Thought is deeper than all speech,
> Feeling deeper than all thought.

496   From a heliotype about 1860

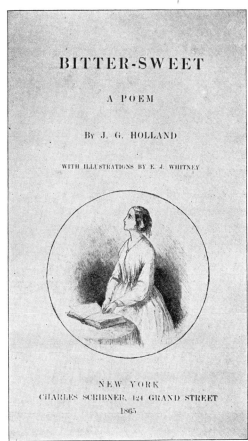

497   Title-page of J. G. Holland, *Bitter-Sweet*, New York, 1865

JOSIAH G. HOLLAND, 1819–81

A POET, novelist, and journalist with an immense contemporary influence was Josiah G. Holland, who developed himself, after miscellaneous trades, into a successful editor. While associated (1849–66), with the *Springfield Republican* he published his *Timothy Titcomb's Letters to Young People*, 1858. He was afterward editor of *Scribner's Monthly*, and widely known as a lyceum lecturer. The dramatic poem, *Bitter-Sweet*, appeared in 1858, followed by *Kathrina, Her Life and Mine*, 1867, and in 1873 by *Arthur Bonnicastle*, one of his many novels. Holland was capable. His writings were known to thousands of Americans, but no better illustration of the adjective "commonplace" could be found in all our literature. Holland is an excellent illustration of the evanescence of "moral" literature, when unendowed with real talent.

498   Holland at fifty years of age, from a carte de visite by Spooner, courtesy of Mrs. John T. Howe, Springfield, Mass.

PERSONS.

ERE dwells the good old farmer, Israel,
In his ancestral home—a Puritan
Who reads his Bible daily, loves his God,

499   From J. G. Holland, *Bitter-Sweet*, drawing
                    by E. J. Whitney

THE BATTLE HYMN OF THE REPUBLIC

IN 1917, at the outbreak of the war with Germany, the New York *Times* printed under a cut of the American flag the words of *The Battle Hymn of the Republic*, written by Julia Ward Howe more than a half century earlier. Perhaps the song will never become universal in America till the memory of other verses, associated with the tune of *John Brown's Body*, is obliterated. Yet it has lived, in spite of its literary character.

501   © 1909, Van der Weyde

HOLLAND'S POETRY OF SENTIMENT

WE understand the secret of Holland's influence in verse like *Babyhood* or *Daniel Gray*, suitable poems for an age of sentiment. Yet these sugarplums show Holland at his very best. We may obtain even now a huge set of his works, and browsing in them, find little else which is not hopelessly banal.

Army Hymn

Mine eyes have seen the glory of the coming of
the Lord;
He is trampling out the vintage where the
grapes of wrath are stored,
He hath loosed the fateful lightning of His
terrible swift sword;
His truth is marching on.

I have seen Him in the watch-fires of an
hundred circling camps;
They have builded Him an altar in the
evening dews and damps,
I can read His righteous sentence by the dim
and flaring lamps;
His day is marching on.

I have read a fiery gospel writ in burnished
rows of steel;
"As ye deal with my contemners, so with you
my grace shall deal;
Let the Hero, born of woman, crush the serpent
with his heel,"
Since God is marching on.

500   From the copy in the J. Pierpont Morgan Library, New York,
            in the handwriting of Julia Ward Howe

JULIA WARD HOWE, 1819–1910

THIS song is Mrs. Howe's sole claim to remembrance as a poetess, in spite of other volumes of poetry, and of books of travel, biography, and social science. Its exaltation of feeling was the climax of a lifetime of devotion to the cause of abolition. Mrs. Howe spent part of her youth in New York, but after her marriage was associated with Boston. Her other miscellaneous writings include: *Passion Flowers*, 1853; *Sex and Education*, 1874, and *Margaret Fuller*, 1883. She was long a writer and lecturer in behalf of abolition as well as co-editor with her husband of *The Commonwealth*, a Boston antislavery paper.

ALICE CARY, 1820–71

IN 1852 came to New York from Ohio the two sisters, Alice and Phoebe Cary, with their sheaves of sentimental poetry. In 1850 they had published together in Philadelphia a volume of verse. A score of years later far different poetry was to be written in the West, but just now the Cary sisters made a slight stir in the artistic and literary life of New York. The two poetesses have been mentioned in the order of importance usually assigned to them. Alice wrote far more than her sister, in both prose and verse, but Phoebe's lovely hymn, *One Sweetly Solemn Thought*, is better known than any poem written by her elder sister.

502 © Gramstorff Bros., Inc.

PHOEBE CARY, 1824–71

LADIES writing lyrical poetry with sentiment and moralizing are not new phenomena in American literature, but we speculate about the aspiration which led to the journey east, and about the contemporary importance of such literature. Interest in the Cary sisters depends, too, on the quality of their work. There are echoes of English poets in both, but the moods of devotion, sadness, and affection for children ring true. Alice Cary, in particular, possessed real talent.

503 From a photograph by Sarony, New York.

BAYARD TAYLOR, THE TRAVELER, 1825–78

THE most distinguished poet of the generation after Longfellow was a native of Pennsylvania, James Bayard Taylor, a farmer's boy of Chester County, born of Quaker and German parentage, in 1825. At the age of seven he had written his first verse, and at nineteen he set out for a two years' journey on foot through Europe, the first of wanderings which took him to almost every corner of the world. After his third tour Taylor remarked to a friend that he had traveled fifty thousand miles.

The two amazing features of Taylor's travels, aside from their extent, were the variety of his hardships and experiences, and the facility with which he transmuted these into books. *Views Afoot*, 1846, the record of the youthful tramp abroad, was the first of his popular series of travel books. In addition, he produced rapidly poetry, dramas, and translations. Taylor's hold on the people was enhanced by his integrity of life, his struggles for success, and his sad romance. He married an old schoolmate knowing that she must die of consumption almost immediately after the wedding.

504 From Bayard Taylor, *Rhymes of Travel, Ballads, and Poems*, New York, 1849, engraving by W. G. Jackson after the painting by T. B. Read (1822–72)

MINISTER TO GERMANY

HE married again in 1857, and four years later cast anchor, though only for a short time, at his home, "Cedarcroft," in his boyhood town. He continued to travel; he saw his literary fame increase; he was secretary to the legation in Russia; in 1878 he was appointed United States Minister to Germany. Yet now his restless energy had consumed him; he died in the same year.

505 Farewell Reception by the Goethe Club, from *The Daily Graphic*, New York, March 23, 1878

506   From Bayard Taylor, *Eldorado, or Adventures in the Path of Empire*, New York, 1850, lithograph by Sarony and Major after the drawing by Bayard Taylor

ELDORADO

BAYARD TAYLOR possessed strange and varied talents of a high order, falling just short of genius. His works of travel such as *Eldorado*, 1850, though distinctly readable to-day, lacked depth, and occasioned the partly justified *mot* that Bayard Taylor had traveled more and seen less than any other man then living. The depressingly long list of titles includes his novels, *Hannah Thurston*, 1863, *John Godfrey's Fortunes*, 1864, and others, all stamped with the seal of mediocrity. Nor was his deep passion to become a poet realized. *California Ballads*, 1848, is a poetical echo of his travels, and though *Lars, A Pastoral of Norway*, 1873, and *The Picture of St. John*, 1866, are eloquent, they are forgotten. *Poems of the Orient*, 1854, is more significant as encouraging a new current in American literature, and as a revelation of the sensuous side of Taylor's nature, which found kinship in the desert and in lonely mountains. No more surprising product has ever come from the Pennsylvania Dutch than the poem, half Shelleyan, half oriental, the beautiful *Bedouin Song*:

> From the desert I come to thee
> On a stallion shod with fire;
> And the winds are left behind
> In the speed of my desire . . .

TAYLOR'S *NATIONAL ODE*

FOR Taylor wrote not only of Norway, and Arabia, but *The Quaker Widow*, 1860, *The Old Pennsylvania Farmer*, 1875, and *The Masque of the Gods*, 1872, to say nothing of a *National Ode* for the Centennial Exposition of 1876. Among his other writings were: *Ximena*, etc., 1844, *A Book of Romances, Lyrics, and Songs*, 1851, *Poems of Home and Travel*, 1855, *Egypt and Iceland*, 1874.

Look up, look forth, and on!
There's light in the dawning sky:
The clouds are parting, the night is gone:

507   From Bayard Taylor, *National Ode*, Boston, 1877, after an engraving by Alfred Fredericks

This is clearly the tragedy of scattered talents, of the artistic nature tossed about, unfocused. Only one strain in Taylor's nature found complete expression, his Germanism, in his splendid translation of Goethe's *Faust*, 1870–71. This is indeed not only an accurate translation but an adequate rendering of the spirit of the poem into English. On this rests Taylor's hope of immortality. In estimating Bayard Taylor, one thinks critically of Oliver Wendell Holmes' words at a memorial service, of "the truly American story of a grand, cheerful, active, self-developing, self-sustaining life." Truly American it was in these respects, but also in its restlessness, its lack of concentration and repose.

508   From a photograph, about 1875, by Mora, New York

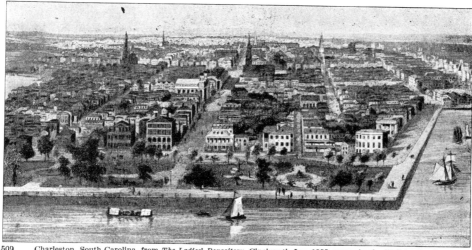

509　Charleston, South Carolina, from *The Ladies' Repository*, Cincinnati, Jan. 1855, engraving by Wellstood and Peters after the drawing by J. W. Hill

POETS OF THE SOUTH

In turning, during these years, to the literary centers of the South, such as Charleston, we are conscious at once of a comparatively slight production in poetry. A more scattered population, a less thorough education, an indifferent attitude toward ballad-mongers are some of the causes. In Maryland is the gallant Edward Coate Pinkney, 1802–28, a naval officer, a soldier, an editor, a professor, and an imitator in his romantic songs of Moore and Byron. In Georgia is Richard Henry Wilde.

510　From the engraving by John Sartain (1808–97) after the portrait by Johnson

RICHARD HENRY WILDE, 1789–1847

Few poets of the South of this time can stand beside, for instance, Bayard Taylor. Yet the Irish-born Richard Henry Wilde was by nature a poet. A lawyer, a congressman from Georgia, he was also a student of Italian literature, and the author of the lyric, *My Life is Like the Summer Rose*.

511　From *Harper's Weekly*, January 5, 1884, drawing by W. L. Sheppard

SONGS OF SOUTHERN LIFE

The South shared the sentimentalism of the day, and also wrote, like the North, its war lyrics. The Africans on American soil had developed a folklore which was to find its best expression later. Just now a Pennsylvanian, Stephen C. Foster (1826–64), used the native themes in verse. Foster's birthplace was Pittsburgh. He lived there and in Cincinnati. He gave up his business to write songs of southern life: *Old Folks at Home, Nelly Was a Lady, Old Black Joe*, and *Old Kentucky Home*. Although not written by negroes, these have long represented to millions of people the laughter and tears of the old southern plantations.

512   From the copy by Stolle of a portrait, artist unknown,
      in the Charleston (S. C.) Museum

WILLIAM GILMORE SIMMS, 1806–70

IN vigor of production, in tragic life, and in measure of talent William Gilmore Simms is the most impressive southern poet and novelist prior to the Civil War. Simms won his spurs through his novels, but he began in verse, and was prominent in the younger generation of poets, which included Henry Timrod and Paul Hamilton Hayne. He was born in Charleston, then the southern literary capital, but, handicapped by scanty education and poverty, had to wrest recognition from that city's aristocratic society. He had been a drug clerk; he visited the western frontier; he became an editor; and in the early thirties he began in New York his friendship with Bryant. He suffered the ardors and humiliations of the secessionists, but when he died in 1870 his writing had an audience throughout America, and even in Europe.

513   From William Gilmore Simms, *The Forayers*,
      New York, 1855

AN INTERPRETER OF SOUTHERN SCENERY

THE long list of Simms' prose works is interspersed with volumes of poetry. The most effective is *Atalantis*, a poem of the sea. Most of this verse is without finish or distinction, though a contemporary critic ventured to think that he described the savannahs and rivers of the South much as Whittier depicted the Merrimac country. The fact that Simms is at this time the best interpreter in verse of southern scenery suggests the sterility of the period. Yet a few of Simms' short poems have lived in collections. Readers may still quicken to *The Swamp Fox*, a ballad of Marion's men.

THE YEMASSEE

SIMMS wrote a biography of Marion, besides others of Captain John Smith, Greene, and Chevalier Bayard. He was the author, too, of hundreds of journalistic articles, contributed to various ephemeral magazines. Yet there was a vital strain of romantic adventure in Simms, and if he owes something to Charles Brockden Brown and Godwin, he is more in debt to Scott. Possibly his real master is Cooper, whom he resembles in slipshod manner, and also in gusto for swift-moving incident. Indeed the best of his novels, such as *The Partisan*, 1835, or *The Yemassee*, 1835, may rank with Cooper's lesser stories.

The failure of so powerful a talent in more than thirty novels, many poems, biographies, and essays to achieve more than a reputation for industry and mild interest indicates once more the limitations of literary America. Simms' life, 1806–70, approximates the period we are studying. Uncongenial environment, poverty, and the Civil War exacted a heavy penalty. Simms will live, but for the most part as the chief southern representative of literature's struggle against such forces.

514   From William Gilmore Simms, *The Yemassee*, New
      York, 1853, drawing by F. O. C. Darley

HENRY TIMROD, 1829–67

SIMMS was a leader in a literary group of which Henry Timrod and Paul Hamilton Hayne, both Charlestonians, were members. Timrod was the son of a poet-bookseller, one of whose poems Poe thought comparable to Moore's. The younger Timrod's life was unlucky. Poverty interrupted his study at the University of Georgia. He was successively a lawyer, tutor, and journalist; and he served with the Confederate army as a war correspondent. Sherman's march through Georgia caused his ruin, and he died in destitution, two years after the close of the Civil War. Timrod's first verse, published in Boston in 1859, secured no recognition, but Hayne's edition of his poetry, 1873, and later study have given him a place in southern literature. In spite of the fierceness of his partisan poetry, Timrod lacks depths of passion.

515   From the portrait by P. P. Carter in the
Charleston (S. C.) Museum

POETRY OF THE CIVIL WAR

THE splendid passage on the Civil War in *The Cotton Boll* hardly counterbalances the halting diffuseness of other parts of this poem. Some of his poetry, like *The Lily Confidante*, is merely saccharine, but there is a fine meditative strain in Timrod's sensitive nature. This mood is variously rendered in *Quatorzain*, *Charleston*, or *At Magnolia Cemetery*.

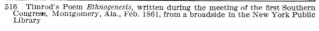

Ode on the Meeting of the Southern Congress.

BY H. TIMROD.

Hath not the morning dawned with added light?
And will not evening call another star
Out of the infinite regions of the night,
To work this day in Heaven? At last, we are
A nation among nations; and the world
Shall soon behold in many a distant part
Another flag unfurled!
Now, come what may, whose favor need we court?
And under God whose thunder need we fear?
Thank Him who placed us here
Beneath so kind a sky—the very sun
Takes part with us: and on our errands run
All breezes of the Ocean; dew and rain
Do noiseless battle for us; and the year,
And all the gentle daughters in her train,
March in our ranks, and in our service wield
Long spears of golden grain!
A yellow blossom as her fairy shield,
June flings our azure banner to the wind,
While in the order of their birth
Her sisters pass, and many an ample field
Grows white beneath their steps, till now behold
Its endless sheafs unfold.
The snow of Southern summers! Let the earth
Rejoice!—beneath those fleeces soft and warm
Our happy land shall sleep
In a repose as deep
As if we lay entrenched behind
Whole leagues of Russian ice and Arctic storm,

And what if mad with wrongs themselves have wrought
In their own treachery caught,
By their own fears made bold,
And leagued with him of old,
Who long since, in the limits of the North,
Set up his evil throne, and warred with God—
What if both mad and blinded in their rage,
Our foes should fling us down their mortal gaze,
And with a hostile step profane our sod!
We shall not shrink, my brothers, but go forth
To meet them, marshalled by the Lord of Hosts,
And overshadowed by the mighty ghosts
Of Moultrie and of Eutaw—who shall foil
Auxiliaries such as these? Nor these alone,
But every stock and stone
Shall help us; but the very soil,
And all the generous wealth it gives to toil,
And all for which we love our noble land,
Shall fight beside, and through us, sea and strand,
The heart of woman, and her hand,
Tree, fruit, and flower, and every influence,
Gentle, or grave, or grand,

The winds in our defence
Shall seem to blow; to us the hills shall lend
Their firmness and their calm;
And in our stiffened sinews we shall blend
The strength of pine and palm.

Look where we will, we cannot find a ground
For any mournful song;
Call up the clashing elements around,
And test the right and wrong!
On one side, pledges broken, creeds that lie,
Religion sunk in vain philosophy,
Empty professions, Pharisaic leaven,
Souls that would sell their birth-right in the sky;
Philanthropists who pass the beggar by,
And laws which controvert the laws of Heaven!
And on the other—first a righteous cause!
Then Honor without flaws,
Truth, Bible reverence, charitable wealth,
And for the poor and humble, laws which give,
Not the mean right to buy the right to live,
But life, and home, and health,
To doubt the issue were distrust in God!
If in His Providence He hath decreed
That to the peace for which we pray,
Through the Red Sea of War must lie our way,
Doubt not, oh brothers, we shall find at need
A Moses with his rod!

But let our fears—if fears we have—be still,
And turn us to the future! Could we climb
Some mighty Alp, and view the coming time,
The rapturous sight would fill
Our eyes with happy tears!
Not only for the glories which the years
Shall bring us; not for lands from sea to sea,
And wealth, and power, and peace, though these shall be,
But far the distant people we shall bless,
And the hushed murmurs of a world's distress;
For to give labor to the poor,
The whole sad planet o'er,
And save from want and crime its humblest human door,
Is one among the many which
God makes us great and rich!
The hour perchance is not yet wholly ripe
When all shall own it, but behold the type
Of what we are and shall be to the rest
Of the broad earth, in our own gulf expressed,
Which through the cold untempered ocean pours
Its genial stream, that far off Arctic shores
May sometime catch upon the softened breeze,
Strange tropic warmth and hints of summer seas!

516   Timrod's Poem *Ethnogenesis*, written during the meeting of the first Southern Congress, Montgomery, Ala., Feb. 1861, from a broadside in the New York Public Library

PAUL HAMILTON HAYNE, 1830–86

TIMROD's friend and biographer, Paul Hamilton Hayne, the nephew of Robert Young Hayne, began his life in prosperity and with distinguished family connections. He studied at the College of South Carolina, and entered the law. He was, however, less fitted for law than for letters, and was soon writing for the Charleston periodicals. Like Timrod, he was overwhelmed by the Civil War. Hayne held a colonelcy in the Confederate army. After the war he lived at Copse Hill, Grovetown, Georgia, until his death.

517   Courtesy of William Hamilton Hayne,
Augusta, Ga.

518   Courtesy of William Hamilton Hayne

COPSE HILL, GEORGIA, HAYNE'S HOME AFTER THE WAR

HAYNE was a bookish man, and it is possible to detect many English influences in his poetry, notably Tennyson's. He had some poetic power, and his sonnets have been deservedly praised. His poems appeared in several editions beginning in 1855. His collected verse appeared in 1882.

HAYNE AND THE NEW ENGLAND POETS

ALTHOUGH incapable of the soul-stirring lyrics of Timrod, Hayne shows a cultivation which entitles some of his work to comparison with that of the greater New England poets. These he visited in 1879, and wrote to them various tributes in poetry.

"That man must die before they fly, or yield to us the field."

519   From Hayne, *Poems*, Boston, 1882, illustration for
       The Battle of King's Mountain

"Have I not followed, followed where she led,
Tracking wild rivers to their fountain head."

520   From *Poems*, Boston, 1882, illustration for *Unveiled*

521 Boston Common, from *The Boston Miscellany of Literature and Fashion*, July-Dec., 1842, engraving by Rolph after the drawing by H. Billings

LESSER NEW ENGLAND AUTHORS

THE lesser novelists between 1815 and 1870 have more individuality than the lesser poets. A novel like *Uncle Tom's Cabin* is far more original than any single poem mentioned in this chapter. In fiction, even more than in poetry, the writers near Boston were more creative, apart from William Gilmore Simms, than those of the South. The best-known novelists in this period were from Massachusetts: Miss Catherine Maria Sedgwick and Mrs. Lydia Maria Child.

CATHERINE MARIA SEDGWICK, 1789–1867

IN 1835 Poe, in praising *The Linwoods*, 1835, remarked of Miss Sedgwick that "of American *female* writers we must consider her the first." The italics are Poe's. "The character of her pen," he said, "is essentially feminine." This is not surprising when we learn that for fifty years she conducted a school for young ladies. Although born in Stockbridge, Massachusetts, she was later associated with Bryant and other New Yorkers.

A SCENE FROM HOPE LESLIE.

523 From *The Columbian Lady's and Gentleman's Magazine*, 1846, engraving by Hinshelwood after the drawing by T. H. Matteson, illustrating *Hope Leslie*

522 From the engraving by A. B. Durand, after the portrait by Charles C. Ingham (1797–1863)

NOVELS OF NEW ENGLAND

REDWOOD, 1824, which Miss Sedgwick dedicated to Bryant, *Hope Leslie*, 1827, and *The Linwoods*, in which appear Putnam, Clinton, Lafayette, and Washington, succeed only in being both moral and patriotic. For the thought of Washington, she says in her preface to *The Linwoods*, filled her with religious awe. Yet, as Poe's approval suggests, Miss Sedgwick could tell a tolerable story. She depicts skillfully early New England life.

524 Lydia Maria Child at the age of twenty;
from the portrait by Francis Alexander (1800–80)
in the Medford (Mass.) Historical Society

LYDIA MARIA CHILD, 1802–80

A DEFINITE fraction, it would seem, of American sentiment and moral enthusiasm is distilled into the long life of Lydia Maria Child, who was widely known for her ardent advocacy of abolition. *An Appeal for that Class of Americans called Africans*, 1833, was fervently admired by philanthropists. Mrs. Child was already a novelist, having published *Hobomok*, 1824, a story of life in early Salem, and *The Rebels: or, Boston before the Revolution*, 1825.

POETICAL ROMANCES

MRS. CHILD's stories are curiosities, but not half so strange to us, at first, as the general excitement about Mrs. Child. Only one instance is Lowell's eulogy of her in *A Fable for Critics*. Much of her fame was due to her didacticism. The titles of her other books need no comments: *The Mother's Book*, 1831, *The Ladies' Family Library*, 1832–35, the series of *Flowers for Children*, 1844, 1846, 1855, *The Progress of Religious Ideas*, 1855, *Autumnal Leaves*, 1856. Yet one understands Poe's amazed pleasure in her poetical romance, *Philothea*, 1836. "We turn," he says, "to these pure and quiet pages with that species of gasping satisfaction with which a drowning man clutches the shore." In Mrs. Child dwelt a tranquil and beautiful spirit.

525   From Lydia Maria Child, *An Appeal for that Class of Americans called Africans*, Boston, 1833

526 From F. O. C. Darley, *Compositions in Outline for Judd's Margaret*, 1856

SYLVESTER JUDD'S *MARGARET*

LOWELL also praised Sylvester Judd, 1813–53, for his novel *Margaret*, 1845,

the first Yankee book
With the *soul* of Down East in't . . .
'T has a smack of pine woods, of bare field and bleak hill,
Such as only the breed of the *Mayflower* could till.

Judd was unquestionably Yankee, a native of Massachusetts, educated in Connecticut (Yale), and for years a Unitarian minister at Augusta, Maine. He was an ambitious spirit, attempting a blank verse tragedy, and publishing, besides *Margaret*, another novel, *Richard Edney*, 1850, and *Philo: an Evangeliad*, 1850.

THE PLOT OF *MARGARET*

SYLVESTER JUDD lives through his first novel. Critics outside New England have been amused by the local devotion to *Margaret*, but have admitted the sincerity and appeal of its interpretation of life there just after the Revolution. The girl Margaret, who communes with the unseen world, finds happiness in a marriage with Mr. Evelyn. With Unitarianism as their guide they found a Utopian community. The latter part of the book is obscured in a fogland of transcendentalism.

527　From F. O. C. Darley, *Compositions in Outline for Judd's Margaret*, New York, 1856

528　After a daguerreotype owned by R. H. Dana, Cambridge, Mass., by permission of Houghton Mifflin Company

RICHARD HENRY DANA, JR., 1815–82

JUDD's poetry and fiction, however, won slight approval compared with the single brilliant novel, *Two Years Before the Mast*, 1840, by Richard Henry Dana, Jr. (No. 528), son of the venerable Knickerbocker poet. The younger Dana, later an abolitionist and an authority on international law, learned the life of the sea on a voyage to California. *Two Years Before the Mast* is little more than a truthful record but it is none the less gripping, and its fidelity gives it a definite superiority over Cooper's sea stories. Dana revealed the life of the forecastle to thousands of Americans.

HARRIET BEECHER STOWE, 1811–96

To be famous as the author of a single book may be the result of writing an occasional novel, like Dana, or, paradoxically, of producing quantities of poetry, fiction, and books of travel. Harriet Beecher Stowe is now remembered, in spite of these other literary ventures, solely as the writer of *Uncle Tom's Cabin*,

529　From an engraving by H. W. Smith after a drawing, 1853, by George Richmond, London, in the Massachusetts Historical Society

530　Harriet Beecher Stowe, Lyman Beecher, and Henry Ward Beecher, from a carte de visite by Brady

1852. The details of Mrs. Stowe's career are interesting: her domestic life as the daughter of Lyman Beecher, the sister of Henry Ward Beecher, and the wife of Calvin Stowe, a biblical scholar, who upheld the traditions of his Christian name; her early reading of *The Arabian Nights* and of Byron; her mastery of Butler's *Analogy;* her keen observation of life in Kentucky, Ohio, and New England; and her simplicity under the test of spectacular fame.

UNCLE TOM SAVING EVA FROM A WATERY GRAVE

"He saw her sink, and was after her in a moment. . . . . He caught her in his arms, and swimming with her to the boat side, handed her up, all dripping, to the grasp of hundreds of hands."—Page 126.

531   From Harriet Beecher Stowe, *Uncle Tom's Cabin,* London, 1852, drawing by George Cruikshank

SENSATIONALISM IN *UNCLE TOM'S CABIN*

SENSATIONALISM was the book's greatest fault, although it is not difficult to point out the stock characters, the eternal mood of weeping, and the rambling structure. The bloodhounds, the escape of Eliza on the ice, Topsy, Little Eva ascending to heaven, have been easy to burlesque.

532   From *Uncle Tom's Cabin,* Boston, 1852, engraving signed "Baker-Smith"

THE CHARACTERS IN *UNCLE TOM'S CABIN*

THE book's popularity is a truer *Key to Uncle Tom's Cabin* than the book of that title written in 1853 by Mrs. Stowe to justify her statements concerning slavery. In many cases Mrs. Stowe documented the incidents in her story. Such proof was hardly needed to convey the reality of the characters. Through their vitality *Uncle Tom's Cabin* lives. Uncle Tom, Simon Legree, and some of the other personages now belong to the traditions of our literature.

Eliza comes to tell Uncle Tom that he is sold, and that she is running away to save her child. Page 92.

533   'From *Uncle Tom's Cabin,* Boston, 1852, engraving by W. J. Baker

THE BOOK'S INFLUENCE

IT has often been said that *Uncle Tom's Cabin* hastened the overthrow of slavery. At least it exerted immense influence on American thought. When Mrs. Stowe's children wept at her reading of the death scenes, they were the first of thousands of readers to feel through this book the blight of slavery.

MRS. STOWE'S ATTITUDE TOWARD SLAVERY

THE secret of the book's effect upon the issue of slavery was less the story, or its descriptive power, than its sincerity. Mrs. Stowe never said that Simon Legrees were common, but it was enough for Americans that under slavery one Simon Legree could exist. In her later life in the South Mrs. Stowe proved that she was not a fanatic; her convictions about reconstruction were liberal. What she wrote was fiction, but the essence of what she said of slavery was truth. The book was conceived in a moment of emotion, and Mrs. Stowe used to ascribe its existence to God.

GEORGE SHELBY GIVING LIBERTY TO HIS SLAVES

"He appeared among them with a bundle of papers in his hand, containing a certificate of freedom to every one on the place, which he read successively, and presented, amid the sobs and tears and shouts of all present."—Page 382.

534   From *Uncle Tom's Cabin*, London, 1852, drawing by Cruikshank

MRS. STOWE'S LATER WRITING

AFTER the publication of *Uncle Tom's Cabin*, Mrs. Stowe lived on for forty-four years. Her other writings confirm the impression that she possessed genius, but for obscure reasons she never recaptured the sustained, impassioned mood of *Uncle Tom's Cabin*.   There are tense scenes in *Dred, A Tale of the Great Dismal Swamp*, 1856, which Harriet Martineau thought her greatest book; and Lowell praised unwisely *The Minister's Wooing*, 1859. Other novels like *Agnes of Sorrento*, 1862, *Pink and White Tyranny*, 1871, or *My Wife and I*, 1871, are commonplace. In Lowell's favorite, *The Pearl of Orr's Island*, 1862, and especially in *Oldtown Folks*, 1869, is the same mastery of local — this time New England — life which is so essential a part of *Uncle Tom's Cabin*.

535   From the engraving by A. H. Ritchie, after a daguerreotype about 1853

536   From Raymond M. Weaver, *Herman Melville, Mariner and Mystic*, engraving on wood by L. F. Grant, by permission of George H. Doran Company

HERMAN MELVILLE, 1819–91

ASSOCIATED with New York during the period before the Civil War was that adventurer, mariner, and original spirit, Herman Melville. As a writer of the South Seas, Stevenson thought him — though Melville could not learn the dialects — wonderful enough to call him "a howling cheese." Melville has been too long undervalued, though he is by no means the union of Plato and Smollett, with an admixture of intervening writers, that some modern critics consider him,

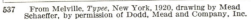

I FOUND HIM RIPE FOR THE ENTERPRISE, AND A VERY FEW WORDS SUFFICED FOR A MUTUAL UNDERSTANDING BETWEEN US

537   From Melville, *Typee*, New York, 1920, drawing by Mead
Schaeffer, by permission of Dodd, Mead and Company, Inc.

FAYAWAY AND I HAD A DELIGHTFUL LITTLE PARTY ON THE LAKE

538   From Melville, *Typee*, New York, 1920, drawing by Mead
Schaeffer, by permission of Dodd, Mead and Company, Inc.

MELVILLE'S *TYPEE*

"A whale-ship," he writes in *Moby Dick*, "was my Yale College and my Harvard." His half humorous fear, conveyed to his friend Hawthorne, was that he should go down to posterity merely as "a man who had lived among the cannibals." For, after desertion from his ship, he had lived with a tribe of South Sea Islanders. Of this experience his first book, *Typee*, 1846, was the fruition.

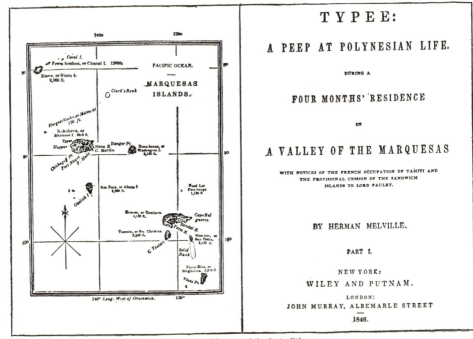

539   Map and title-page of the first edition

MELVILLE'S LATER WORK

O*MOO*, 1847, similar in manner, is concerned with Tahiti. *Red-burn*, 1849, a novel, John Masefield has praised. After *Moby Dick*, 1851, comes the puzzling period of Melville's life, in which he wrote *Pierre*, 1852, *Israel Potter*, 1855, and other stories and poetry — a period which some critics account for as simple decline of power, while subtle devotees find in it an explanation of his mysticism.

MYSTICISM AND MISANTHROPY

FOR Melville was a mystic. He suffered, besides poverty and grief, disillusionment, and a very pretty primer of misanthropy may be culled from his fifteen volumes. The society of men, toward the end of his life, was "hellish," and there are remarks on the futility of the universe and its Deity. Whatever his admirers make of this period as brilliant heterodoxy, they cannot escape the fact that the simplicity of his earlier style has vanished. Carlyle is here, and Thomas Browne, and a host of other mentors, but the old Melville is gone. Melville may not yet have come

"Next instant, the luckless mate was smitten bodily into the air" — *Page 399.*

540 From Melville, *Moby Dick*, Boston, 1922, drawing by A. Burnham Shute, by permission of L. C. Page & Company

541 From a photograph taken at the age of sixty-six, by Rockwood in the Yale University Library

into his own. But if, as the cult says, orthodox America has refused him recognition, neither has Europe accorded it, in the sense that she has recognized our other heretics. *Moby Dick*, allegory or not, of the essential brutality of life, will be read for obvious values: its romance of the perilous game of the sea, and its beauty. In it, says Masefield, "Melville seems to have spoken the very secret of the sea, and to have drawn into his tale all the magic, all the sadness, all the wild joy of many waters."

JOHN PENDLETON KENNEDY, 1795–1870

STRANGELY enough, one of the most remarkable novels descriptive of the South had been written by a Massachusetts woman living in Maine. Southern writers, too, were experimenting in the novel form. In Baltimore, now a literary center, John Pendleton Kennedy, a lawyer, published *Swallow Barn*, in 1832, a series of sketches of Virginia, somewhat under the influence of Irving. Thackeray is said to have admired *Swallow Barn*. Kennedy was a successful politician, a biographer of William Wirt, and a power in the magazine world. He was the devoted friend of Poe. Another novel, *Horse-Shoe Robinson*, 1835, betrays the influence of Cooper, but has originality. It contains a lively description of the battle of King's Mountain. The title-character, a backwoodsman of South Carolina, is a worthy cousin of Leatherstocking. Kennedy's other stories are less convincing.

542 From John Pendleton Kennedy, *Swallow Barn*, New York, 1851, drawing by David H. Strother (1816–88)

543 From a photograph on porcelain, courtesy of Robert Cooke, Front Royal, Va.

JOHN ESTEN COOKE, 1830–86

ANOTHER novelist of the "Old South" was John Esten Cooke, a cousin of John Pendleton Kennedy and a younger brother of the poet, Philip Pendleton Cooke. In 1854 Cooke, who had been a lawyer, published two romances in his favorite setting, pre-Revolutionary Virginia, *Leather Stocking and Silk* and *The Virginia Comedians; Surry of Eagle's Nest*, 1866, and *Justin Harley*, 1874, are typical stories. Most of these are romantic tales of southern society. It is the opinion of several critics that *The Virginia Comedians*, in which an ineffectual Patrick Henry appears, may possibly be the best novel of the South produced before the Civil War. Cooke's impotence after the war, in spite of his abundant writing, sets one thinking about the new school of fiction. Cooke's own comment is suggestive and pathetic: "Mr. Howells," he said, "and the other realists have crowded me out of the popular regard as a novelist, and have brought the kind of fiction I write into general disfavor." He adds: "I do not complain of that, for they are right." — remarks which are omens of the new literature.

JARED SPARKS, 1789–1866

THE growth of the republic brought with it a renewed study of the past. Besides the eminent New Englanders such as Hildreth, Bancroft, Motley, and others, men of lesser talents, like Jared Sparks, prepared the way for wider and sounder historical research. Thus the chief service of Sparks was the collection of materials, as in his *Life and Writings of George Washington*, 1834–38, or his *Diplomatic Correspondence of the American Revolution*, 1829–30. Sparks was a churchman, a professor of history, and president of Harvard (1849–53), and was also editor of the *North American Review*. His *Library of American Biography*, 1834–38; 1844–48, is still a source book. Sparks published more than sixty volumes concerned, for the most part, with American history.

544 From the portrait by Rembrandt Peale (1778–1860) in the Harvard University collection

545 From a carte de visite by Fechner, Berlin

GEORGE BANCROFT, 1800–91

LIKE some of the early Massachusetts writers, George Bancroft was a historian born. Notwithstanding his youthful poetry, his teaching of Greek, and his political and diplomatic career, he was essentially a man with a single great idea. This idea was to write *A History of the United States.*

BANCROFT IN PUBLIC LIFE

BANCROFT'S achievements seem merely an incidental expression of this one absorbing passion. Because of this he studied in Germany, taking his degree at Göttingen in 1820. And because of the intellectual power displayed in the early volumes, together with their patriotism, he was urged to enter politics. Besides minor offices, he held those of Secretary of the Navy, and minister to England and Germany.

546   Bancroft's Birthplace at Worcester, Mass. © Halliday Historic Photograph Co.

HISTORY

OF THE

UNITED STATES,

FROM THE

DISCOVERY OF THE AMERICAN CONTINENT.

BY GEORGE BANCROFT.

VOL. III.

BOSTON:
CHARLES C. LITTLE AND JAMES BROWN.
1840.

547   Title-page of Vol. III of the first edition, 1840

HIS *HISTORY OF THE UNITED STATES*

AMONG his writings is a biography, *Martin Van Buren*, 1889. He also rewrote his beloved history. The revised *A History of the United States* stands on the shelves in six volumes. Sometimes it stands there for long periods. For, though Bancroft's scholarship was sound, his manner does not suit modern taste. He is, as Matthew Arnold remarked of Macaulay, "an honest rhetorician." Eventually Bancroft wearied of his own mood of impassioned democracy, but to it he owed much of the success of the early volumes.

548   Bancroft in his library at Washington, from D. G. Mitchell, *American Lands and Letters*, 1899, courtesy of Charles Scribner's Sons

BANCROFT'S FAITH IN DEMOCRACY

THE true Bancroft is the student in his library, patient, indefatigable. The first volume of *A History of the United States* appeared in 1834. During the next twenty years, six volumes appeared at intervals. Twenty years more, and the scholar had brought his history, in the tenth volume, through the Revolution. Finally, in 1882, he published in two volumes his *History of the Formation of the Constitution of the United States*, a continuation, and for the venerable historian, the conclusion of the story. In spite of Bancroft's solidity, one sees, in reading these pages, the political procession with military band and transparencies. He had unfaltering faith in American democracy, and parts of his history were thorny reading for the Federalists. Although less eloquent than his ancestors concerning a "wonder-working Providence," he is often didactic. Yet this fault cannot dull the dignity of his work. The new era in literature produced not merely poets, but a historian of the nation, a Bancroft. His ideals are traditions in American historical scholarship.

549   From a photograph, about 1855, by Brady

551   From Prescott, *History of the Reign of Ferdinand and Isabella the Catholic*, Boston, 1838, engraving by J. Andrews after the portrait in the Royal Palace, Madrid

WILLIAM HICKLING PRESCOTT, 1796–1859

A HISTORIAN of less weight than Bancroft, but with a style nearly as electric as Macaulay's, was William Hickling Prescott, a grandson of the hero of Bunker Hill. The trivial incident at Harvard College which darkened his life would have interested Thomas Hardy, as an ironical determinant in life. A piece of bread carelessly thrown at table cost him, in effect, his eyesight. But the triumphant courage of the man would not make a good Hardy story.

550   From *The Eclectic Magazine*, 1858, engraving by John Sartain after a photograph

PRESCOTT'S METHOD OF WRITING

WITH his fingers guided by a noctograph, he wrote tirelessly. Apart from the heroism of Prescott, this method of composition has the interest of a new mental discipline. "He was compelled," says Ticknor, "to prepare everything, down to the smallest details, in his memory, and to correct and fashion it all while it was still held there in silent suspense; after which he wrote it down, by means of his noctograph, in the freest and boldest manner, without any opportunity really to change the phraseology as he went along, and with little power to alter or modify it afterwards."

PRESCOTT'S HISTORIES

IN such shadows Prescott envisaged the splendors of Spanish imperialism. In 1837 he published, from materials secured by copyists, his *History of Ferdinand and Isabella*. Washington Irving, with whose romantic love of Spanish subjects Prescott sympathized, had generously yielded him the theme of *The Conquest of Mexico*, 1843. Afterwards appeared *The Conquest of Peru*, in 1847, and *The Reign of Philip II*, 1855–58.

CHARACTERISTICS OF PRESCOTT'S STYLE

PRESCOTT's histories are like great paintings, gorgeous with color, of the pageant of South American history. It is possible to accuse them of an excess of romance, but never to accuse their painter of wilful inaccuracy. In spite of handicaps he was a patient scholar. Kings and conquerors were never so magnificent as Prescott's, nor events so touched with grandeur, but they are alive, and in substance they are true.

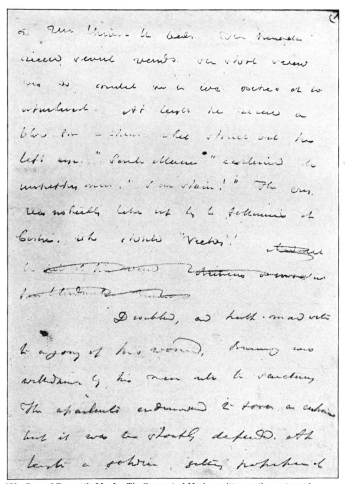

552 Page of Prescott's Ms. for *The Conquest of Mexico*, written on the noctograph, original in the Boston Public Library

553 Home of Prescott, Beacon Street, Boston.
© Halliday Historic Photograph Co.

ROMANTIC SPANISH HISTORY

A MODERN reader finds the colors untarnished, but is sensible of passing a more critical judgment on them than the eager readers of the 'forties, who craved the romantic Spanish traditions. To this craving Irving, Bryant, Longfellow and others were ministering in essay and poem. Prescott gave them Spanish history, not unadorned. In him, as in Francis Parkman, is a literary spirit, a spirit evident, too, in his sketch of Charles Brockden Brown in Jared Sparks' series of biographies.

554 From a photograph by Brady

JOHN LOTHROP MOTLEY, 1814–77

THE most famous of American historians was John Lothrop Motley. He is the subject of a biography by his friend Holmes, and his letters, edited by George William Curtis, tell the story of a strong, richly gifted nature. Motley's life history sweeps us into a full current of events. His universities were Harvard, Göttingen, and Berlin. His early novels, *Morton's Hope*, 1839, and *Merry-Mount*, 1848 (both published anonymously), do not altogether deserve their desuetude. He was successively minister to Austria and to England, and a powerful partisan of the Union.

MOTLEY'S INTEREST IN HISTORY

LIKE Bancroft's, Motley's inner life was consecrated to history. He *had*, he says, to write his books: "My subject had taken me up, drawn me on, and absorbed me into itself." Motley's best work appeared relatively late in his career. It was Prescott who spurred him on to write *The Rise of the Dutch Republic*, 1856. *The History of the United Netherlands*, 1860–68, and his *Life of John of Barneveld*, 1874, are sequels to this history.

THE RISE

OF THE

DUTCH REPUBLIC.

A History.

BY JOHN LOTHROP MOTLEY.

IN THREE VOLUMES.
VOL I.

NEW YORK:
HARPER & BROTHERS,
329 & 331 PEARL STREET.
1856.

556   Title-page of the first American edition, in the
       New York Public Library

THE RISE OF THE DUTCH REPUBLIC

MOTLEY'S power as a historian lies in his singular development of many and different talents. He can analyze like Bancroft, without the smoke of rhetoric; he has the eloquence of Prescott, without his pyrotechnics; and, more even than the latter, he has what Holmes calls "stirring vitality." Some of his biographical sketches, like the famous one of William the Silent, remind one of Carlyle, and they are tempered by scholarly accuracy and by sound judgment.

557   After the portrait, 1861, by George Frederick Watts (1817–1904)

TRIBUTES TO MOTLEY

MOTLEY detested Spaniards and Roman Catholics, at least those of the fifteenth and sixteenth centuries, even as in all centuries he hated persecution. Thus he is open to the charge of partisanship. But he won the tributes not only of his American contemporaries in history and literature, but also those of Froude and Guizot. Motley's *Letters*, full of interest and distinction, appeared in 1877, edited by George William Curtis.

FRANCIS PARKMAN'S *CALIFORNIA AND OREGON TRAIL*

As a boy, Francis Parkman, 1823–93, the youngest of the Massachusetts historians, dreamed of the dark forests of the Northwest. In them, fighting mercilessly for the rule of a continent, he beheld the Jesuit priest, the Indian, the European soldier. The harbinger of his series of histories was the record of his rough western journey which appeared in *The Knickerbocker* in 1847, and which was republished as *The California and Oregon Trail*, 1849.

558 From Francis Parkman, *The California and Oregon Trail*, New York, 1849, drawing by F. O. C. Darley

559 From Francis Parkman, *The Book of Roses*, Boston, 1866

PARKMAN'S NOVEL

By this year Parkman had been graduated from Harvard, had studied law, and had begun the ceaseless battle with eyes and nerves which was to render his histories a memorial of human endurance. Never well, he composed with more difficulty, in a certain sense, than Prescott, and his total product for some days was six lines. There were interludes like the forgotten novel, *Vassall Morton*, 1856, and *The Book of Roses*, 1866, a souvenir of his interest in horticulture, and of his temporary professorship (in this subject) at Harvard.

A HISTORIAN OF FRENCH CANADA

He worked on. There were journeys to France and to remote corners of America. There were fierce struggles of the will, and intense stirs of the mind as the tapestry of history unrolled. And finally other dreaming boys may take down the books from the shelves: *History of the Conspiracy of Pontiac*, 1851; *The Pioneers of France in the New World*, 1865; *The Jesuits in North America in the Seventeenth Century*, 1867; *La Salle; or, The Discovery of the Great West*, 1869; *The Old Régime in Canada*, 1874; *Count Frontenac and New France under Louis XIV*, 1877; *Montcalm and Wolfe*, 1884; *Historic Handbook of the Northern Tour*, 1885; *A Half-Century of Conflict*, 1892.

560 Parkman at twenty-one, from C. H. Farnham, *Life of Francis Parkman*, Boston, 1901, after a daguerreotype, courtesy of Little, Brown & Company

561 Parkman in Later Life. © Gramstorff Bros., Inc.

THEODORE PARKER, 1810–60

IN Boston Music Hall Theodore Parker, inspirer of the "Parkerite Unitarians," preached to enthusiastic audiences on liberal ideas in Christianity, on abolition, and on other topics of the day. Parker, a Lexington blacksmith's son, entered Harvard, but, for the most part, educated himself. He had been deeply influenced by Emerson, and was the fighting man of the Transcendentalists. In spite of his learning and intellectual power, he was a somewhat boisterous crusader. His writings include lectures, sermons, and contributions to magazines, especially to the *Massachusetts Quarterly Review*, which for three years he edited, 1849–52.

PICTURESQUE AND RELIABLE

THE adjective "picturesque" belongs to Parkman's histories, and though a banal word, it is hard to substitute a better. He was a reliable scholar, but he sways us with thrilling incident against the far-flung background of prairie, lake, river, and white-capped mountain. He is personal, vivid. He writes, and we are with him in the romantic wilderness.

WILLIAM ELLERY CHANNING, 1780–1842

MEANWHILE history itself was being made. Baffling questions agitated men's minds, in particular, slavery. In pulpit and forum orators roused the emotions of the people. "We must start in

562   From the engraving in the Bostonian Society, after the portrait by S. Gambardella, 1839

religion from our own souls," wrote William Ellery Channing, leader of the earlier Unitarians. His liberalism struck at orthodoxy, and was the precursor of Emersonian individualism. He was an eloquent preacher, a direct and honest Christian, and a fearless champion of the laws of conscience. His writing has charm, and achieved for him a reputation outside New England, and across the ocean. He was the author of an essay on Milton, 1826.

563   From a portrait in the Lexington Historical Society

HENRY WARD BEECHER, 1813–87

PROBABLY the most popular orator of the church was Henry Ward Beecher, whose humor, easy liberalism, eloquence, and devotion to the Union still keep him on the rim of the fading horizon. His work was con-

564   From a photograph by Falk, New York

nected with Plymouth Church in Brooklyn, but he boldly faced hostile English mobs, and his sermons and essays still have vitality. Not so his novel, *Norwood; or Village Life in New England*, 1868. Beecher's mind was not meditative, and he lacked the literary temperament.

SENATORIAL ORATORY

SECULAR oratory flourished in the Senate or on the public platform. Here Webster, Calhoun, Choate, Clay, Everett, or lesser men like Thomas Hart Benton declaimed, and their breathless audiences thought they were hearing literature. It was not. Who reads now, for example, the heavy volumes of Charles Sumner? John C. Calhoun, 1782–1850, of South Carolina, the foremost orator of the South, began his career of

565 John Caldwell Calhoun, from W. H. Brown, *Portrait Gallery of Distinguished American Citizens,* Hartford, 1846, silhouette from life by W. H. Brown

dialectic by arguing with President Dwight at Yale. Later in the Senate, in advocacy of states rights, slavery, or secession, Calhoun became the model of the intellectual debater, acute, logical, finished, and cold. Unfortunately, his fine mind, in spite of its lofty idealism, was opposed to inevitable events. His subtle defense of nullification, which his enemies called metaphysical, could not stand against two necessities, emancipation and union.

566 Henry Clay, 1777–1852, from a carte de visite by Brady, after a painting

DANIEL WEBSTER, 1782–1852

SURVEYS of American oratory lead always to one name, that of the poor New Hampshire boy who won his way through Dartmouth College, the law, and politics, to his commanding position in the Senate and in the minds of Americans. From 1827 Webster was a prominent member of the Senate, except for two intervals when he was Secretary of State. Although friezes of the silver-tongued, with Webster's head beside those of Demosthenes, Bossuet, Burke, and others, signify little, Daniel Webster was America's greatest orator. Webster had faults as a man and a writer. His large nature harbored strange pettiness, and Websterian diction is too often like the tread of armies, rhythmic, but monotonous.

Henry Clay of Virginia and Kentucky, inferior to Calhoun in intellect, was a demigod to his political followers. Three times a candidate for the Presidency, sponsor of the Missouri Compromise, and a friend of the Union, he declaimed in the resonant rhetoric of the day. Over his pages we smile a little: "And, sir, when you come into the bosom of your family, when you converse with the partner of your fortunes, ... and when in the midst of the common offspring of both of you, she asks you: 'Is there any danger of civil war? ...'" Benton said that Clay's affair with Randolph was the last "high-toned duel" that he witnessed.

567 From the portrait, 1842, by George P. A. Healy (1813–94) in the New York Historical Society

568   Welcome to Webster at Boston, from *Gleason's Pictorial*, May 17, 1851

WEBSTER AS A DEFENDER OF THE CONSTITUTION

On the brow of Webster might be read the passion of his life, a patient, ceaseless devotion to the Union. "I will warrant him," Carlyle writes John Sterling, "one of the stiffest logic-buffers and Parliamentary athletes anywhere to be met with . . . A grim, tall, broadbottomed, yellow-skinned man, with brows like precipitous cliffs . . ." Such a man, though primarily a statesman, could not help producing some literature. His speeches kindle us even now with their glowing periods. We turn most often to the *Reply to Hayne*, 1830, and *The Constitution and the Union*, 1850.

EDWARD EVERETT, 1794–1865

The tendency to cultivate oratory as an art had its supreme expression in the speeches of Edward Everett of Massachusetts, professor, minister, editor, senator, ambassador, and president of Harvard. In his speeches for anniversaries and memorial meetings finished eloquence can go no further; nor, we qualify, can average ability. If Everett's oratory was the culmination of such speech, he himself was also, in a dramatic manner, the last of its heroes. For hardly had his elegant periods died away at Gettysburg, on November 19, 1863, when the gaunt Illinois farmer-lawyer began simply: "Four score and seven years ago . . ."

569   From a photograph by Warren, Boston

WILLIAM LLOYD GARRISON, 1805–79

Besides these orators who wrote were many writers who spoke. Garrison, Phillips, and Sumner were less distinguished in debate than Webster and Calhoun, but wrote unceasingly, and from the lecture platform debated the same questions. Uncompromising to the point of fanaticism was William Lloyd Garrison, who favored, if need be, disunion rather than slavery. One hears still of his fiery abolitionist sheet, *The Liberator*, but more often of his ringing words in his first editorial (January 1, 1831): "I am in earnest! . . . I will not retreat a single inch! . . . And I will be heard!"

570   The Garrison Banner, courtesy of the Massachusetts Historical Society

571   Courtesy of the Yale Collection of American Literature

WENDELL PHILLIPS, 1811–84

WITH all the fervor of Garrison, and some of the elegance of Everett, Wendell Phillips, unmindful of family position or personal consequences, threw himself into the struggle against slavery. The art of such men, like the art of Garrick, cannot be tested. The best speech is by nature ephemeral. Yet tradition pays tribute to the brilliance of Phillips as he moved the people, not without, perhaps, speciousness or recourse to prejudice. He was known, too, for his lecture on *The Lost Arts*.

572   From a carte de visite by Case and Getchell, Boston

573   © L. C. Handy, Washington

CHARLES SUMNER, 1811–74

THE successor of Webster in the Senate as leader of the Abolitionists was Charles Sumner, who endured fierce vituperation, not without adequate response, and a physical assault from "Bully Brooks" of South Carolina. In his most famous speech, *The Crime Against Kansas*, Sumner's friends listened in dismay to his inexcusably violent language. Sumner's *Complete Works*, 1870–83, lifeless now, contain a reasonably complete history of the antislavery movement. He was an idealist, a man of literary tastes, but egocentric and of vehement nature.

HORACE GREELEY, 1811–72

MUCH of the thought of publicists shallowed off into journalism. The lesser writers of this chapter are editors, naturalists, scholars, travelers, essayists. Presently there arrived in New York, carrying a bundle, a poor New Hampshire boy, who was to be the founder of the New York *Tribune*. That bundle of Horace Greeley's contained, apparently, Yankee acuteness, and a genius for building up a great newspaper.

574 Greeley in the woods of Chappaqua, from a photograph taken in 1869, courtesy of Charles Scribner's Sons

575   From *Vanity Fair*, London, 1872

GREELEY AS POLITICIAN AND EDITOR

GREELEY was soon known both in England and America as a politician, preaching from the columns of his newspaper, offering advice to Lincoln, and himself running for president. No one questioned his sincerity or a certain homely power in his personality. He had a knack of interesting and helping literary people, and the contributors to the *Tribune* during his régime included leading Transcendentalists: George Ripley, Margaret Fuller, C. A. Dana, and George William Curtis.

AS JOURNALIST

GREELEY, however, was not infected by the slightest taint of genius. He was, in fact, half educated. Even the *Broadway Journal* noted his flashiness of expression, and called him with some justice a follower of Cobbett and of Macaulay. In literature he is remembered as a liaison officer for greater writers, rather than for such works as *What I Know of Farming*, 1871, or *Recollections of a Busy Life*, 1868.

576   From a photograph by Gurney, New York

THE *GETTYSBURG ADDRESS*

THE greatest of the early statesmen left brief passages of prose which may survive in spite of their consignment to innumerable school editions. Webster's *Reply to Hayne* and *The Constitution and the Union* are full of heavy splendor, and the strong simplicity of Lincoln seems embodied in his *Gettysburg Address*. Lincoln was not a man of letters, but much that is genuine in our literature seems related to him. It is suggestive to learn of his interest in the American humorists, in Whitman's and Longfellow's poetry. Lincoln's prose seems to retain some of the vigor of his life in the West, and perhaps of his study of the Bible and Shakespeare. Both the *Gettysburg Address* and *The Second Inaugural* voiced his force and his emotional depths.

577   Original draft of Lincoln's Gettysburg Address, in the Library of Congress, Washington; the first page written in ink at Washington on White House stationery, the second page written in pencil at Gettysburg, on a larger sheet of paper

JAMES T. FIELDS, 1817–81

JAMES T. FIELDS, whom Dickens affectionately christened "Massachusetts Jemmy," was a Maecenas-publisher for many a New England writer, but, more, he was their friend and inspirer. Like Greeley, he had made his own way from New Hampshire, but had been more successful in filling up gaps in his culture. From 1862 to 1870 he was editor of the *Atlantic Monthly*. *Yesterdays with Authors*, 1872, has irreplaceable chat about the Victorians, but his essays, *Underbrush*, 1877, are less significant. Fields was a literary godfather.

THE

PHILOSOPHY

OF

THE PLAYS OF SHAKSPERE

UNFOLDED.

BY DELIA BACON.

WITH

A PREFACE

BY

NATHANIEL HAWTHORNE,

AUTHOR OF 'THE SCARLET LETTER,' ETC

Aphorisms representing a KNOWLEDGE broken do invite men to inquire further
Jrane Bacon.

You find not the apostrophes, and so miss the accent.
LOVE'S LABOUR'S LOST.

Untie the spell.—PROSPERO.

LONDON:
GROOMBRIDGE AND SONS,
PATERNOSTER ROW.
1857.

579 Title-page of the issue, London, 1857, in the New York Public Library

578 From a photograph by Warren, Boston

MINOR CRITICS AND STUDENTS

ALTHOUGH Lowell is easily the first critic of these years, students of the literature of the past were beginning to write for other students. In 1849 Ticknor had published his *History of Spanish Literature;* Child was collecting ballads; Reed was working on Wordsworth. All this was a tiny balance against the unskilled anthologists Griswold, Duyckinck, and Allibone, but it was a beginning. For the anthologists themselves were pioneers. An amusing *entr'acte* was Delia Bacon's study of Shakespeare, under the patronage of Hawthorne.

SHAKESPEAREAN SCHOLARS

AMONG the students of Shakespeare were Richard Grant White (1822–85), and Henry Norman Hudson. White was aggressive, attacking Collier. He later edited Shakespeare in twelve volumes. Hudson's edition of the plays is not appreciably better, but his career is interesting. A poor youth, and largely self-taught, he became in college an ardent student of Shakespeare, and soon after graduation ranked with the great lyceum leaders as a lecturer in his chosen field.

580 Henry Norman Hudson, 1814–86, courtesy of Ginn and Company, Boston

JOHN JAMES AUDUBON, 1780–1851

ON the fringes of literature other writers were busy. The ornithology of Wilson was supplanted in 1827–38 by John James Audubon's *The Birds of America*. Audubon, a Louisianian, was a scientist, but he spoke often in the tones of literature. Years later the school-teacher John Burroughs chanced on his book: "I took fire at once. It was like bringing together fire and powder."

581 From the painting, about 1841, by John Woodhouse Audubon in the American Museum of Natural History, New York

582   From *The American Portrait Gallery*, New York, 1877, engraving by J. C. Buttre

HENRY ROWE SCHOOLCRAFT, 1793–1864

ANOTHER scientist, this time a geologist, turned ethnologist and wrote of the western Indians. Henry Rowe Schoolcraft was born in New York, but later as a government agent studied the customs of the redskins in the West, recording not only his own travels but Indian folklore. His writing, cool and definite, can hardly be called literature, but it has been the cause of literature in others, notably Longfellow.

MANABOZHO: 135

MANABOZHO:
OR,
THE GREAT INCARNATION OF THE NORTH.
AN ALGIC LEGEND.

Introductory Note.—The accounts which the Indians hand down of a remarkable personage of miraculous birth, who waged a warfare with monsters, performed the most extravagant and heroic feats, underwent a catastrophe like Jonah's, and survived a general deluge, constitute a very prominent portion of their cabin lore. Interwoven with these leading traits are innumerable tales of personal achievement, sagacity, endurance, miracle, and trick, which place him in almost every scene of deep interest that could be imagined, from the competitor on the Indian playground, to a giant-killer, or a mysterious being of stern, all-knowing, superhuman power. Whatever man could do, he could do. He affected all the powers of a necromancer. He wielded the arts of a demon, and had the ubiquity of a god. But in pro-

portion as Manabozho exercises powers and performs exploits wild or wonderful, the chain of narration which connects them is broken or vague. He leaps over extensive regions of country like an ignis fatuus. He appears suddenly like an avater, or saunters over weary wastes a poor and starving hunter. His voice is at one moment deep and sonorous as a thunder-clap, and at another clothed with the softness of feminine supplication. Scarcely any two persons agree in all the minor circumstances of the story, and scarcely any omit the leading traits. The several tribes who speak dialects of the mother language from which the narration is taken, differ, in like manner, from each other in the particulars of his exploits. But he is not presented here as an historical personage, or in any other light than as the native narrators themselves depict him, when they have assembled a group of listeners in the lodge, and begin the story of Manabozho. His birth and parentage are obscure. Story says his grandmother was the daughter of the moon. Having been married but a short time, her rival attracted her to a grapevine swing on the banks of a lake, and by one bold exertion pitched her into its centre, from which she fell through to the earth. Having a daughter, the fruit of her lunar marriage, she was very careful

583   From *Algic Researches*, First Series, *Indian Tales and Legends*, New York, 1839

SCHOOLCRAFT'S STUDIES OF THE INDIANS

To both the *Algic Researches*, 1839, and *The Myth of Hiawatha and other Oral Legends*, 1856, Longfellow was grateful. His comments on Schoolcraft should be considered with reference to *Hiawatha*: "This Indian Edda — if I may so call it — is founded on a tradition prevalent among the North American Indians, of a personage of miraculous birth, who was sent among them to clear their rivers, forests, and fishing-grounds, and to teach them the arts of peace. He was known among different tribes by the several names of Michabou, Chiabo, Manabozo, Tarenyawagon, and Hiawatha. . . . Into this old tradition I have woven other curious Indian legends, drawn chiefly from the various and valuable writings of Mr. Schoolcraft, to whom the literary world is greatly indebted for his indefatigable zeal in rescuing from oblivion so much of the legendary lore of the Indians." The best account of native Indian "literature" may be found in Schoolcraft's *Historical and Statistical Information respecting the History, Condition, and Prospects of the Indian Tribes of the United States*, 1851–57. Schoolcraft was a traveler, a mineralogist, and an expert in lore of the Indians.

584   From Henry Rowe Schoolcraft, *Historical and Statistical Information respecting the History, Condition, and Prospects of the Indian Tribes of the United States*, Philadelphia, 1851–57, engraving after the drawing by Capt. Seth Eastman

SEBA SMITH, 1792-1868

MRS. TROLLOPE and other English visitors found American humor noisy. We have never scorned grinning through a horse collar. The laugh which started in Maine with Seba Smith was characteristic. Smith, a graduate of Bowdoin College, knew Yankee dialect and Yankee shrewdness. Lively newspaper letters began to appear from one "Major Jack Downing, of Downingville." The "Major" soon became, in a New York newspaper, the private adviser of Andrew Jackson. Then he saw service again at the time of the Mexican War, and *Thirty Years of the Senate*, 1859, retells the whole story of this comic character. Smith showed the satirists what could be done. He has a hollow sound to-day, but that is because pupils have excelled the master.

585 From Seba Smith, *Life and Writings of Major Jack Downing of Downingville*, Boston, 1833

Major Jack Downing, of Downingville.

586 From Frederick Swartwout Cozzens, *The Sparrowgrass Papers*, New York, 1857, drawing by F. O. C. Darley

FREDERICK SWARTWOUT COZZENS, 1818-69

TEPID, too, are *The Sparrowgrass Papers*, 1856, supposed experiences of a cockney in America. These were the handicraft of Frederick Swartwout Cozzens, known to Irving and Halleck, and a correspondent of Thackeray. Halleck considered him almost the best humorist of his time, but Halleck thought too hopefully of many Americans.

CHARLES GRAHAM HALPINE, 1829-68

IT is impossible to chronicle all the local humorists, many of whom continued to write after 1870, some obtaining national reputations. Among these are H. J. Finn with his *Comic Annual*, 1831; Augustus B. Longstreet with his *Georgia Scenes*, 1835; William Tappan Thompson, editor and soldier, author of *Major Jones's Courtship*, 1840; George Washington Harris, of Tennessee, a steamboat captain, writer of *Sut Lovengood's Yarns*, 1867; Judge Joseph G. Baldwin with his *Flush Times in Alabama and Mississippi*, 1853; George Prentice of Louisville; Charles Graham Halpine (*alias* "Private" Miles O'Reilly); Benjamin Penhallow Shillaber, with his *Life and Sayings of Mrs. Partington*, 1854. These all differ in dialect and flavor, but are alike in high spirits and mirth at the spectacle of civilizing America. More distinct-

587 Charles Graham Halpine, from a carte de visite by Fredricks, in the Harvard College Library

ive than those on this list, but inferior to David Ross Locke ("Petroleum V. Nasby"), are Robert Henry Newell, of New York, and Charles Henry Smith, of Georgia. Newell was "Orpheus C. Kerr," and Smith "Bill Arp," who wrote tales of the Confederacy. Nasby's letters, which were very popular, were supposed to be written from Kentucky by a waggish, whisky-drinking, office-seeking Democrat. They appeared first in the Toledo *Blade* and are said to have amused Lincoln.

588 David Ross Locke, 1833-88, from a photograph by Warren, Boston

589   From *Harper's Weekly*, November 21, 1868

LOCKE'S "PETROLEUM V. NASBY"

LOCKE, the creator of "Petroleum V. Nasby," was an Ohio newspaper man, who satirized the Copperheads and cheap politicians of his time. His victims seem like perennial types, but the cloud of local issues has obscured Nasby.

CHARLES GODFREY LELAND, 1824–1903

ANOTHER novelty is the dialect verse of Charles Godfrey Leland. *Hans Breitmann's Ballads* appeared in 1871. Americans, until a recent event, have always loved a German-American comedian, and have heard this doggerel recited with unction. Leland was far more than a humorist. A graduate of Princeton, he was an editor, and a persevering student of various topics: gypsy customs, legends of the Algonquins, and the Chinese discovery of America.

590   Page from Charles Godfrey Leland, *Hans Breitmann und his Philosopede*, New York, 1869, drawing by Thomas Francis Beard (1840–1905)

HENRY WHEELER SHAW, "JOSH BILLINGS," 1818–85

SUPERIOR to all these are the subtler (though not too subtle) George Horatio Derby, Henry Wheeler Shaw, and Charles Farrar Browne.

591   From a photograph by Gurney, New York

Derby's *Phoenixiana*, 1855, and *The Squibob Papers*, 1856, are a blend of the humor of the South and the far West. Shaw's *Josh Billings*, 1866, has had longer life because of his racy apothegms, reminiscent of "Poor Richard," his orthography, and his honest common sense. The spelling, ridiculous as it is, provokes a smile even from the dignified. "Flattery," says Josh Billings, "iz like colone water, tew be smelt ov, not swallowed."

592   From a carte de visite by Gurney, New York

CHARLES FARRAR BROWNE, "ARTEMUS WARD," 1834–67

WHAT of Artemus Ward, who delighted the British? He lectured in England and became a contributor to *Punch*. "A Yankee joke," says the English John Nichol, writing of American literature, "is a cracker that, once pulled, has served its turn."

THE GENIAL SHOWMAN

THE fun of Artemus Ward depends on his endless string of such crackers, or, if the desire to analyze humor afflicts us, the chief element is *surprise*. "I've been lingerin by the Tomb of the lamentid Shakspeare," remarks Artemus with imperturbable gravity. "It is a success." Browne's best waggery appeared in the 'sixties: 1862, 1865, 1867, 1869; but he amused Americans long after the Civil War. Much of this humor bridges the war, and belongs partly to the later epoch. The culmination of the laughter was to be in a westerner named Samuel Langhorne Clemens.

THE GENIAL SHOWMAN SURVEYS HIS SHOW.

593   From Edward P. Hingston, *The Genial Showman, Being Reminiscences of the Life of Artemus Ward*, London, 1870, in the Yale Collection of American Literature

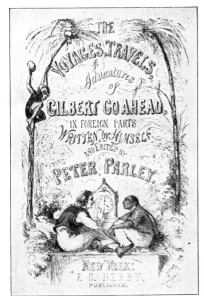

595   Title-page of Peter Parley, *The Voyages, Travels and Adventures of Gilbert Go Ahead*, New York, 1856, design by Benson J. Lossing (1813–91)

FRANCES ANNE KEMBLE, 1809–93

ABOUT the time of Seba Smith's first venture, of Irving's *Alhambra*, and of Emerson's sermon on the Lord's Supper — lest we forget what may happen in America in one year — there came to the United States a young actress, Fanny Kemble, daughter of Charles Kemble. American she was not, nor would American literature claim her drama, *The Star of Seville*, 1837, but we hasten to appropriate the gossipy *Journal of a Residence in America*, 1835. We put it on the shelves with Mrs. Trollope's volume concerning us — for contrast.

594   From the portrait by Thomas Sully, in the Museum of Fine Arts, Boston

SAMUEL GRISWOLD GOODRICH, "PETER PARLEY," 1793–1860

AN ampler record of the first half of the nineteenth century in America is *Recollections of a Lifetime*, 1856, by Samuel Griswold Goodrich, a writer who saw the pioneers go west, watched American literature develop, beheld in fact all that we have studied in this chapter. He himself wrote the "Peter Parley" stories. For Goodrich did not approve of the climax of *Little Red Riding-Hood*, and was scandalized by the morals of *Jack the Giant Killer*.

GOODRICH'S SERVICES TO LITERATURE

THUS Goodrich partook generously of his epoch's sentimentalism.

596   From the engraving by A. H. Ritchie of the medal presented to Goodrich in 1853

Yet he wrote tolerable poetry and good prose. He did yeoman's labor for literature with his anthologies, his editing, and his encouragement of native authors. Thus in the pages of his dusty, prolific *Token* appeared a story called *The Gentle Boy*, and others of the *Twice-Told Tales*. A rumor persists that Hawthorne was not sufficiently grateful for Goodrich's services. Perhaps now the gratitude should be reversed.

597   © Brown Brothers

THOMAS WENTWORTH HIGGINSON, 1823–1911

ANOTHER lieutenant of American literature — a colonel in the Civil War — was Thomas Wentworth Higginson, the friend of the Transcendentalists and the Cambridge scholars, and their survivor by many years. Higginson essayed many kinds of literature without remarkable achievement, but never without a certain grace. His *Cheerful Yesterdays*, 1898, is a memorial of a rich literary life.

DONALD GRANT MITCHELL, "IK MARVEL," 1822–1908

ON the one hundredth anniversary of Washington Irving's birth a memorial service was held at Tarrytown. An oration was delivered by his friend, Donald Grant Mitchell. Bystand-ers whispered to each other that this was "Ik Marvel," author of *Reveries of a Bachelor*, 1850, and *Dream Life*, 1851. They might have added that in literary ideals and in personal temper the younger man was

598   From a photograph about 1880

very like his more gifted friend.

DREAM LIFE AND OTHER WRITINGS

HERE, says Mitchell, speaking of college in *Dream Life*, "you dream first of that very sweet, but very shadowy success, called reputa-

599   From Ik Marvel, *Reveries of a Bachelor*, New York, 1850, drawing by F. O. C. Darley

tion." "Shadowy," it has proved for "Ik Marvel." His later books such as *My Farm of Edgewood*, 1863, *Wet Days at Edgewood*, 1864, or *English Lands, Letters, and Kings*, 1889, are too consciously the books of the literary farmer and the literary traveler. The name "Ik Marvel" now means the mood of youthful reverie.

MITCHELL'S CULTURE

MITCHELL deserves more than this. Born in Norwich, Connecticut, of cultivated family, he was graduated from Yale, and served for a time as United States consul at Venice. The real product of his life, for students of literature, was his culture. At Edgewood he read widely; he had traveled; he loved nature; he was of gentle spirit. Thus his mood is one not too common in America, that of repose and refinement. This found expression in a distinctive style, but it must be admitted that at bottom Mitchell had little to say.

600 From the pen and ink sketch by E. Flohri in the Authors Club, New York

GEORGE WILLIAM CURTIS, 1824–92

AMONG the neophytes at Brook Farm was George William Curtis, later a well-known magazinist and man of letters, though of distinctly second rank. Man of letters Curtis was indeed: novelist, essayist, editor, biographer, and orator. Although he wrote for the New York *Tribune*, managed *Putnam's* and *Harper's Weekly*, we think most of those informal, finished, and idealistic talks from the depths of his "Easy Chair" in the office of *Harper's Monthly*.

601   From a carte de visite, about 1870, by
Fredricks, New York

NOVELS AND BOOKS OF TRAVEL

CURTIS loved the old streets and wharves of his birthplace, Providence, and two years in a New York business house gave him, not love of commerce, but the old bookkeeper, Titbottom, in *Prue and I*, 1856. Brook Farm, that "Age of Reason in a patty-pan," together with years of travel, stored his mind. *Nile Notes of a Howadji*, 1851, and other travel books, with sensuous memories of the East, first made him known as a writer. The *Potiphar Papers*, 1853, contain social satire with a flavor of Thackeray.

602   From George William Curtis, *Prue and I*, New York, 1893, drawing by Albert Sterner, by permission of Harper & Brothers

603   From Curtis, *The Potiphar Papers*, New York, 1853, drawing by Augustus Hoppin

THE "EASY CHAIR"

As essayist, lecturer, and novelist, Curtis may well stand for the best cultivated literary type of the period, without, of course, the gift of genius. He is happily linked with most of the chief New England writers. It was, however, from the pages of his "Easy Chair" that he became present at so many American firesides. In fifteen hundred or more of these little essays, under the guise of very different topics — politics, music, the stage, books — Curtis pleaded, not unlike Matthew Arnold, for more genuine ideals of culture in America.

604   From *Putnam's Magazine*, 1854, engraving by H. B. Hall after the drawing by Samuel Lawrence

CHAPTER IX

LITERATURE OF THE NEW AMERICA

WHEN in 1865 the soldiers of the North and South paused, bruised and breathless, even their leaders understood imperfectly what had happened. Their armies had fought for the old, but they had created the new. As if slavery and other issues of the first half of the century had been dikes, the released energies of the country now flowed into other channels, making a new nation. Easterners had already found their way to the Pacific. The "forty-niner" en route to the California mining camp had passed prairie towns and busy cities. Western regiments had fought in both the Confederate and Union armies. Now, however, the shifting of populations was like the legendary migrations of Asiatic hordes into Europe. These migrations to the West the earlier generations assimilated easily. Travelers noted the vigorous, self-reliant farmer and manufacturer, "the American type."

In the war-torn South there was reconstruction. Bitterness and triumph took their natural human course. Yet in a deeper sense Americans forgot the past. The vast continent thrilled with life. Everything was new: industries, railroads, banking systems, universities. Eleven years after the meeting of Grant and Lee the Centennial could show an impressive record of material prosperity, less suggestive of the hundred years than of these teeming eleven. About four factors studied in this book (the sea, the farm, the city, the frontier) focused the intense ambitions of the American people. By 1900, the seas of the Puritans and of the Oregon Indians were lanes to adjoining continents. The thrifty farms of New England and the estates of Virginia lived again in the huge agricultural establishments of the western states. Chicago and San Francisco were beginning to rival New York, and were themselves rivaled by neighboring cities. Meanwhile the frontier faded into the life of a nation. The transition was accomplished in the thirty years between 1870 and 1900.

In literature the new America was just as startling. Side by side on my shelves stand copies of Willis' *Pencillings by the Way*, 1835, and Mark Twain's *Innocents Abroad*, 1869. What a change is here, toward Europe, toward America, toward life! If I were to duplicate these strange companions, let Longfellow pair with Joaquin Miller; or Hawthorne with Eggleston. The new spirit of literature is evident enough when Mark Twain, speaking before the New England Brahmins, finds his Mississippi jests met with a cold silence.

The essence of the new literature was a freedom from tradition which may be called realism. Emerson's exhortation in the 'forties to "walk on our own feet," was obeyed without reservation in the 'seventies. The actualities of war and of the post-bellum frontier demanded reality in literature. Romance is here, too, but it is a romance born of the soil, the prairie, the mine, the life of the frontier town. Mark Twain, Bret Harte,

Joaquin Miller depict American men and women on the Mississippi, in San Francisco, in the Sierras. Cable, Harris, Page, Craddock, and Allen make permanent in literature southern types. Eggleston, Hay, and Riley in their pictures of Hoosier life tacitly rebuke such artificialities as *Evangeline*. In Drinkwater's *Abraham Lincoln*, the Illinois log splitter kneels before a map of the United States. But the literary map of America was really unfurled only when these writers created literature out of its every corner. The shouts of lumbermen, the curses of steamboat captains, the soft dialect of the negro, the yells of the cowboy and Indian are vocal in these pages. The din was heard in the quiet libraries of poets who wrote of flowers. These closed their windows, but realism had come to stay.

If the years after 1870 have been referred to as "the second discovery of America," it may be as justly said that in these 'seventies, a full century after Jefferson had planned his immortal political document, came the real literary declaration of independence. Americans had written much about self-sufficiency in literature. Meanwhile the poets had quietly imitated Keats, and the novelists, Thackeray and Lytton. Now the mood of emancipation approached insolence. The American traveler who blew out the Vestal Fires with one scornful puff typified the new American attitude. A poet might be influenced, like Joaquin Miller, by Byron, but off with the laurels of any writer who did not communicate something of the liberated vitality of the new nation! All this meant, of course, the decline of New England in literature, the rise of the West and South, and, more important, the creation of a really national spirit in literature.

There is amusement, and food for thought, too, in this young Brobdingnagian striding out into the ocean of literature, without the conventional life belts. Under his tramp the customs of staid old New England trembled. The characteristic writing of these thirty years suggests always realism and the new America. The power of a writer like Mark Twain lay in the fact that he spoke to a country as alive as Elizabethan England, and spoke in its own language. The passion for actual life in literature manifested itself in a thousand ways: in the Pike County literature; in the humor of an Artemus Ward; in the passion for a Dickens; in the published lectures of Ingersoll; in the emphasis on prose; in journalism; in the wider scope of the magazines; in the realistic short story; in revaluations of Emerson, Thoreau, and Whitman; in the interest in scientific literature; or in the fresh study of nature in a Muir or a Burroughs.

In New England itself realism was released. Here it had always lived, though well-guarded. Sylvester Judd, and other novelists, and among the poets even Lowell and Whittier, had inclined toward it. Yet ever it had been diverted by transcendentalism or slavery or Brahmin tradition or the ideals of England. Now it was to be as stark as that of the West. William Dean Howells came to the shrine, but worshiped in his own way. His novels were studies of ordinary New England life. With the passing of conservative Harvard men, like Holmes, the virtue of their literature was also to fade. The realists of New England are inferior to her scholars and philosophers. Mrs. Meynell described this new local literature when she said of Sarah Orne Jewett that she "was saturated with the essence of New England."

The New England realism lacked the bluster and crudeness of the West. Howells is finished, self-contained. Although he mirrors American characters and scenes, we do not feel his approval or disapproval. He is part, too, of a reaction against the exuberance of the first outburst. Poets like Stedman and Aldrich continued to observe the old traditions, and in some the horror of the rough, talkative, red-blooded America never abated. The supreme example of protest against the new Americanism in literature was, of course, Henry James, who depicted the unhappiness of the artist or the cultivated man of letters in such a *milieu*. James finally abandoned a ship which carried such passengers as Joaquin Miller and Jack London. It was he who tried to show us the American as he appeared in Europe.

Realism is indeed a powerful literary impulse in America between 1870 and 1900. Yet, as always in such characterizations, qualifications must be made. It is chiefly the realism of the strong, healthy soul craving life more abundantly; not naturalism, nor the realism of decadence. It is a realism like that attending an eager traveler in new lands. The strange life which he beholds he describes, and he describes it with a glow of joyous feeling. Hence a Whitman, a Mark Twain. There were many echoes of the old literary ideals, but America as a country was growing up. (How out of place in this generation seemed the survivor, Bayard Taylor!) There is enough sentimentality of one kind in America, but the sentimentality of the "Tokens," the poems on lilies, the cypress-shaded graves had received a destructive blow. The day was past when J. G. Holland was to refer reverently to *Maud Muller;* when Mrs. Sigourney was to receive America's crowning tribute in the phrase, "the Felicia Hemans of America." America was to remain in the judgment of many English critics a mixture of crudeness and eccentric culture, but the dominion of such as Nat Willis was over. The story told in this chapter is not primarily of the greatest writers between 1870 and 1900, but of those who best represent the main tendencies of the new era.

605   The Home of the *Atlantic Monthly*, Tremont Street, Boston, about 1875, courtesy of Houghton Mifflin Company

606   Steamboat on the Mississippi, from Basil Hall, *Forty Etchings*, etc., Edinburgh, 1829

SAMUEL LANGHORNE CLEMENS, "MARK TWAIN," 1835–1910

"THE great Mississippi, the majestic, the magnificent Mississippi, rolling its mile-wide tide along, shining in the sun." So Mark Twain wrote of this inspiration of his life, almost half a century after he first knew the river most intimately. Born at Florida, Missouri, he was taken, soon after his birth, to Hannibal, where, lingering on its quay, he passed his boyhood. Later he was really to understand the river, to master its lessons. It is symbolic, perhaps, that he was born on its western bank.

MARK TWAIN'S BOYHOOD

IT was westward, after service as a printer, a steamboat captain, and — for a brief time — a Confederate soldier, that a river vaster than the Mississippi swept him — the current of the westward movement. *Roughing It*, 1872, tells the story. The boy Samuel Clemens, the dreamer, heard the rumbling of the caravans, slept under the stars, dug in a gold mine, set up a timber claim near Lake Tahoe and served on the staff of the San Francisco *Call*. The West was schooling her first great man of letters.

607   Mark Twain's Boyhood Home, Hannibal, Mo.
© Clifton Johnson

EARLY JOURNALISM

PART of the training was a visit to the Sandwich Islands as newspaper correspondent. An omen of the future was his recital in the San Francisco mint to a young Pacific writer, called Bret Harte, of a story, "in a slow rather satirical drawl," says Harte, "which was irresistible." *The Celebrated Jumping Frog of Calaveras County*, 1867, was next to appear in a New York newspaper.

BROOKLYN ACADEMY OF MUSIC, FEB. 7th

Tickets at 244 Fulton St. and 172 Montague St.

608   From a poster advertising a lecture, about 1869, by Mark Twain, in the New York Public Library

609   Twain's home "Stormfield," at Redding, Conn., courtesy of Harper & Brothers

LATER LIFE

THE rest was fulfilment. Clemens went east and explored Europe and the Holy Land. These he beheld through the unabashed eyes of the western newspaper man. He published *The Innocents Abroad*, 1869, thus beginning his long career as a prominent journalist, lecturer, humorist, romancer, and, it may be added, philosopher. Toward the end both Hartford and New York claimed his allegiance. During the last two years of his life he lived on his estate at Redding, Connecticut.

HONORS AT OXFORD

OXFORD conferred upon him the degree of D.C.L., strange largesse to the boy who had thrilled to "S-t-e-a-m-boat a-comin'!" and whose "permanent ambition" had been to stride its decks as captain. In the early years with which this chapter is concerned salesmen might have been seen offering a book, with the recommendation that it was as funny as Artemus Ward. It was, but it was more serious, too. *The Innocents Abroad* was akin to *The Jumping Frog* in solemn sincerity of manner, but in this book, the quick-eyed, blunt-speaking westerner had a subject. No one had ever written about Europe in this way. No one had inquired of the stunned guide: "Is Columbus dead?" Or wept at the tomb of Adam. Mark Twain had donned his suit of motley. From now on he turned out page after page of this nonsense.

610   © Underwood and Underwood

THE INNOCENTS ABROAD

THE INNOCENTS ABROAD is the journal of experience that many an American soldier in the last war might have written if he had owned Mark Twain's gift of expression. Which is perhaps like Lamb's quip that Wordsworth could have written *Hamlet*, if he'd had the *mind*. For the traits in this book are ours. There is the same preference for things American, the same contempt for the lifeless past, the same bewilderment at its importance.

DRIFTING TO STARBOARD.

611   From Mark Twain, *The Innocents Abroad*, Hartford, 1869, drawing
by True Williams

THE JESTER

ANYONE could repeat a dozen anecdotes of the young man's irreverence: the "dull canvas" of the Last Supper; the boring word "Renaissance"; the ascription of the endless bronze statues to Michelangelo. The jests, too, are familiar, in two senses: seasickness; ringing for soap in the French hotel; or "the Interrogation Point," whose tunnel is several hundred feet longer than the hill it pierces. One hears talk like this to-day on every Atlantic liner.

MARK TWAIN IN MIDDLE LIFE

THE INNOCENTS ABROAD represents the early Mark Twain. Much of his ridicule he directs at insincerity. The bitter denunciation of Abelard, uncalled for, suggests the humorist's love of justice, his impatience of sentimentality.

613   From a photograph by Sarony

612   Josh Billings, Mark Twain and Petroleum V. Nasby, from a photograph by G. N. Baker, Boston, 1868, in the American Antiquarian Society, Worcester

MARK TWAIN'S HUMOR

MARK TWAIN's humor depends upon manner: a droll solemnity, exaggeration, impudent good nature. It often flattens into the obvious and cheap, and it lacks universality. No character contributed by Mark Twain will live as many months as "Dogberry" has years. His humor survives chiefly, like Lincoln's, in the flavor of personal anecdotes. In the same way his moral enthusiasm lacks cohesion. His rage at oppression is intense, but its force scatters. Thus *The Man That Corrupted Hadleyburg*, 1899, interests chiefly as a revelation of Mark Twain's own nature.

614   William Dean Howells and Mark Twain, from William Dean Howells, *My Mark Twain*, New York, 1910, courtesy of Harper & Brothers

STORIES OF BOYHOOD

PERHAPS we laugh now a little less at the smoker's rule of only one cigar at a time, or the dollar and the penny in the collection plate, the penny for the heathen, the dollar to get it to him. Unquestionably the books which endure are those creations, from the depths of his romantic spirit, of the pioneer West which has now disappeared. Such are the imperishable stories of boyhood: *The Adventures of Tom Sawyer*, 1876, *The Adventures of Huckleberry Finn*, 1884, and *The Tragedy of Pudd'nhead Wilson*, 1894. *The Gilded Age*, 1874, was written in collaboration with Charles Dudley Warner.

615   From Mark Twain, *The Adventures of Tom Sawyer*, Hartford, 1876, drawing by True Williams

30   *TOM SAWYER*

"Why it's you Ben! I warn't noticing."

"Say—*I'm* going in a swimming, *I* am. Don't you wish you could? But of course you'd druther *work*—wouldn't you? Course you would!"

Tom contemplated the boy a bit, and said:

"What do you call work?"

"Why ain't *that* work?"

Tom resumed his whitewashing, and answered carelessly:

"Well, maybe it is, and maybe it ain't All I know, is, it suits Tom Sawyer."

"Oh come, now, you don't mean to let on that you *like* it?"

The brush continued to move.

"Like it? Well I don't see why I oughtn't to like it. Does a boy get a chance to whitewash a fence every day?"

That put the thing in a new light. Ben stopped nibbling his apple. Tom swept his brush daintily back and forth—stepped back to note the effect—added a touch here and there—criticised the effect again—Ben watching every move and getting more and more interested, more and more absorbed. Presently he said:

"Say, Tom, let *me* whitewash a little."

Tom considered, was about to consent; but he altered his mind:

"No—no—I reckon it wouldn't hardly do, Ben. You see, Aunt Polly's awful particular about this fence—right here on the street, you know—but if it was the back fence I wouldn't mind and *she* wouldn't. Yes, she's awful particular about this fence; it's got to be done very careful; I reckon there ain't one boy in a thousand, maybe two thousand, that can do it the way it's got to be done.

'AIN'T THAT WORK?'

616   From Mark Twain, *The Adventures of Tom Sawyer*, Hartford, 1876, drawing by True Williams

HUCKLEBERRY FINN

HUCKLEBERRY FINN, like *Tom Sawyer*, is often makeshift in incident. Mark Twain loves a wild yarn, and one readily understands his posthumous success in the cinema. Clemens was, in some ways, a sensationalist. More definitely still these books remind us of the rogue novels. Certain rascals of Tobias Smollett would have found congenial company in that journey down the river, among the crowd of rustics, cheats, gulls, and eccentrics!

TOM SAWYER

IN these stories the plot is nothing. In *Tom Sawyer*, however, is the immortal incident of whitewashing the fence, and in *Huckleberry Finn* the uproarious "Royal Nonsuch" episodes with their roots deep in human nature. Most of all, we gaze at the river country of the 'forties and 'fifties, then as romantic as the Scottish border. It unfolds before us as we go down the river on the raft, just as it appeared to the Hannibal urchin, in the golden haze of youth. Many of the adventures of *Huckleberry Finn* and *Tom Sawyer* had their originals in Clemens' life.

HUCKLEBERRY FINN

617   From Mark Twain, *The Adventures of Huckleberry Finn*, New York, 1885, drawing by E. W. Kemble (1861–)

THE PANORAMA OF THE WEST

ONCE more we come to the real value of these books, and of others in similar temper: *The Gilded Age* (with its picture of "Colonel Sellers"), *Life on the Mississippi*, 1883, *Roughing It*, *Pudd'nhead Wilson*. Taken together they are part of the Iliad of the West. Out of the past appear and disappear, like Mark Twain's own "Pony Express," the hunters, miners, trappers, and immigrants. They seem to say: "We lived, we were real, but we no longer exist. We belong to the past like Leatherstocking." And in this spectacle may be seen the magician himself. In their proper order the books are autobiographical.

THE "BATON ROUGE."

618   From Mark Twain, *Life on the Mississippi*, Boston, 1883

619 Mark Twain at sixty, on his way around the world, from Mark Twain, *Following the Equator*, Hartford, 1897.

MARK TWAIN'S OTHER WRITINGS

MARK TWAIN's other writings reflect, with less power, his humor, his hatred of shams, and his love of romance. *A Tramp Abroad*, 1880, and *Following the Equator*, 1897, are less spontaneously funny. Besides the *Prince and the Pauper*, 1882, Clemens wrote also *A Connecticut Yankee at King Arthur's Court*, 1889. He hated Walter Scott and false notions of the Middle Ages. The last book contains sane ridicule of sentimentality, and some good fooling, such as attaching St. Simeon, in his genuflexions, to machinery, but the age of chivalry suggested by the burlesque is as false as the interpretations which Mark Twain attacks. For Clemens was subject to violent prejudices. His glorification of *Joan of Arc*, 1896, is as unsound in principle as his splenetic arraignment of Christian Science, 1907.

TO A MASTER OF HIS ART.

620 From *Punch*, London, June 26, 1907, cartoon by Bernard Partridge

ENGLISH APPRECIATION OF MARK TWAIN

IN the meantime the Mississippi river pilot had attained fame. He was known in every English-speaking country. Two sister lands, *Punch* wrote in 1910, lay beneath the spell of his laughter. That he and Artemus Ward could conquer the readers of *Punch*, if they could not the Brahmins of New England, hints at the contagion of this western laughter.

THE SERIOUS SIDE OF THE HUMORIST

YET the secret of Mark Twain's power does not reside wholly in his mirth. As in many humorists his laughter often welled up from an abiding sense of the sorrow of life. A blunt explanation of his hold upon his generation would be his sincerity. For this directness we love him. His concern with the serious issues of life was sometimes grotesque in expression, but always honest. Toward the close of his life he lost faith, and as the years and personal sorrows laid siege to him, his utterances about life became as black as Schopenhauer's.

621 Dinner Party on his seventieth birthday, from *Harper's Weekly*, Dec. 23, 1905. © Harper & Brothers

MARK TWAIN TOWARD THE END OF HIS LIFE

MODERN criticism is by no means done with the soul of Clemens. Van Wyck Brooks' powerful but oversubtle study is a violent reaction against the conception of Mark Twain as a buffoon. Perhaps he is the lover of beauty crushed by Philistine America, a product of the frontier where, says Albert Bigelow Paine, "women laughed that they might not weep; men when they could no longer swear." Perhaps his laughter is the safety valve for the artist soul repressed. Perhaps, in simpler psychology, he is the poet with the mood of quicksilver, of jesting. In any case, many have felt with Robert Underwood Johnson: "The world has seemed to me very strange without Mark Twain in it."

622 Mark Twain in Bed. © Van der Weyde

623   From a carte de visite, about 1870

FRANCIS BRET HARTE, 1839–1902

"HARTE," wrote Mark Twain of the San Francisco days, "trimmed and trained and schooled me." In mere writing, in the mastery of telling a story, a gift enhanced by the influences of Irving, Poe, and Dickens, Harte excelled Twain. He was an Albany boy of English, German, and Hebrew blood, who came to California at the age of fifteen, in time to see the settlements and mining camps of the Pacific slope altering into cities. In this life he had a part, earning a doubtful living as a teacher, a miner, a printer, a drug clerk. Finally, in the perilous office of express messenger, he escaped the casualties of his predecessor and successor. Yet at his first game of roulette the bearded Californians looked at him curiously. He himself was untouched by the rough life, viewing it consistently through literary eyes.

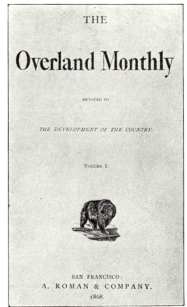

624   Title-page of the original issue in the New York Public Library

BRET HARTE'S LATER LIFE

IN the new West Harte wrote his best stories and poems. He contributed to the weekly *Californian*, and became the first editor of the *Overland Monthly*. Then followed the triumphal journey to the East of this representative of western literature. There developed a rather irresponsible life in New York and watering places as lecturer and writer on the old themes. Finally, came his removal to Europe. Here he served as American consul in the German town of Crefeld and, later, at Glasgow. He remained in England until his death.

THE LUCK OF ROARING CAMP

POSSIBLY the contemporary feeling of the West about *The Luck of Roaring Camp*, 1870, that it represented its people imperfectly, is continued in the lingering conviction that Bret Harte's personality possessed more specious talent than depth. After the first remarkable stories of the California period, his writing, in spite of his profusion, trails away. An unpleasant tradition, too, exists of aimless years at Newport, and of his inability to pay debts. Certainly his power ceased after he set sail for Europe. Despite his many volumes, was his nature profoundly stirred by the life of the West? Was it not rather for him a play, and was he not a kind of actor? He did not, like Mark Twain, grow up with the country. He was less a participant than an observer. His interest in the West was that of a literary journalist.

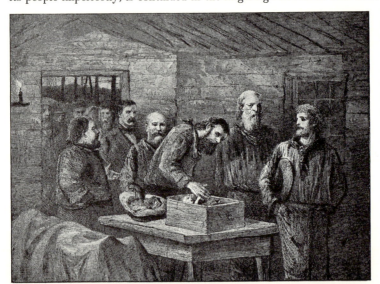

625   From Bret Harte, *The Luck of Roaring Camp and Other Stories*, Boston, 1872, in the Yale Collection of American Literature

BRET HARTE'S EARLY TALES

THE point seems to be that Bret Harte, with his interest in literary technique and picturesque phases of life, was a clever writer who struck it rich. That turn of the wheel which brought before him the shining pile of gold instead of his single coin symbolizes his luck. And the wheel never spun just so again. Among his winnings were *The Luck of Roaring Camp*, *The Outcasts of Poker Flat*, *Miggles*, *Tennessee's Partner*, and tales of the Spanish tradition.

626   Illustration for *Tennessee's Partner*, from *Every Saturday*, January 14, 1871

PLAIN LANGUAGE FROM TRUTHFUL JAMES.   BY BRET HARTE.

AH SIN WAS HIS NAME.

WHICH I wish to remark, —
And my language is plain, —
That for ways that are dark
And for tricks that are vain,
The heathen Chinee is peculiar,
Which the same I would rise to explain.

Ah Sin was his name;
And I shall not deny
In regard to the same
What that name might imply;
But his smile it was pensive and childlike
As I frequent remarked to Bill Nye.

627   From *Every Saturday*, April 20, 1874, drawing by Sol Eytinge, Jr.

LATER WORK

HARTE had written these tales, as well as *Condensed Novels*, 1867, before he came east in 1871. Some thirty books, including *Tales of the Argonauts*, 1875, the unsuccessful novel, *Gabriel Conroy*, 1876, and many poems, appeared after this date, but they come from a different Harte — however unscrupulous the pun on the writer's name. His style is less effective, and self-consciousness creeps in.

POPULAR VERSE

AND for small change there was the poetry — half doggerel, but with the rough vigor and humor of the primitive community. *Truthful James* and *The Heathen Chinee* (*Overland Monthly*, 1870) were welcome guests in many cultivated homes in England and America. Other poetry was frankly sentimental, such as *Her Letter*, or *Dickens in Camp*. Harte had facility, but his mild stanzas hardly equal the worst poetry of his masters, Longfellow or other New Englanders.

628   Illustration for *Miggles*, from *Every Saturday*, June 17, 1871, after the drawing by Sol Eytinge, Jr.

629   From a photograph, about 1875, by Sarony

HARTE'S REALISM

YET if we tend to forget Harte the literary lion, the lecturer, the prolix writer of fiction, we do, nevertheless, keep returning to those earlier tales: to "Flynn of Virginia," who saves his partner's life in the tunnel; to "Yuba Bill," and to "Colonel Starbottle"; to the affecting pathos of "Tennessee's" friend; to "M'liss"; to this whole world, in brief, of red-shirted prospectors, whisky drinkers, and cutthroats. Once more it is the realism of the new nation demanding expression.

630   From *Vanity Fair*, London, 1879, cartoon by Spy

A MASTER OF THE SHORT STORY

HARTE's hero type, so like that of his master, Dickens, is obvious enough. In the terminology of melodrama, beneath the flannel shirts of these outcasts beat hearts of gold. Harte relies upon the elementary forms of incongruity. Yet his characters are alive. Like the English novelist, Dickens, he has the devouring eye for the picturesque in character. Such personalities he places in brief thrilling actions. We tolerate his poetry, but the first great story orients the reader, revealing the truth about Harte; this is not a writer of prose drama — critics to the contrary — or of novels, but of the American short story. Harte has Poe's feeling for the word and for unity of impression. In this form he will continue to enjoy historical importance. His stories influenced Robert Louis Stevenson and Rudyard Kipling.

JOAQUIN MILLER, 1841–1913

ALTHOUGH Bret Harte is the writer of California, his life story leads us eastward, until finally America knows him no more. Not so with the strange poet, Cincinnatus Heine (Joaquin) Miller, who was born, it is said, in a covered wagon, and who ended his life in a cabin above San Francisco, with the earth, sea, and heavens of his beloved West flung out before his worshiping eyes, "the utmost limit of the westmost land." Miller traveled and lived in Europe, but never failed to return to the West.

631   From a photograph, about 1890, by Sarony

MILLER'S ROMANTIC LIFE

MILLER, far more than Mark Twain or Bret Harte, was in the *mêlée* of the new America. His life is a romantic adventure colorful enough to have satisfied his idol, Byron. Stories of his life fascinated Rossetti, as if they had been incidents in a mediæval quest. Miller's eyes opened on the caravan and the frontier. He saw the procession cross the mighty Missouri. He saw the Indians, the alkali plains, and white Shasta. He himself was wounded by a Modoc arrow. He beheld San Francisco in its youth.

632   Mount Shasta with the Sacramento River in the foreground, from a photograph by Gabriel Moulin

633   Miller's Home, the "Heights," Oakland, Cal.
© Brown Brothers

HIS STRANGE POETRY

MILLER's contacts with civilization were equally bizarre. He studied at a humble college in Oregon, and published in 1868 a volume of verse under the title, *Joaquin et al.* He tried the law. In 1871 he was in London vainly offering *Pacific Poems* to John Murray. With the publication of this volume at his own expense commenced his long career of prolific writing, traveling, and posing. When he died in 1913 he had won the admiration of various distinguished men of his time, though some of these were inclined to smile, as did Bret Harte in the early days, at this compound of madness and poetic genius. For in this conventional world of ours the performance of the Sierra poet was distinctly anomalous. He was one of the most original writers America has produced, but he was also a slavish imitator of Byron and Swinburne. He was a child of the plains, yet he bore himself in society like a Spanish grandee. He wrote some poetry as sublime as the Canadian Rockies, yet sixty per cent of his production was rubbish. Much of his poetry is pantheistic. Yet sometimes its dominant strain is Scotch Hebraism.

POET OF THE WESTERN EMPIRE

PART of the rubbish Miller himself consigned to the dustbin. Readers have tacitly eliminated other portions. Even in the remainder one feels the lack of cultivation which Miller asserted too complacently was secondary to the divine impulse. His early line, so true, "I am as one unlearned, uncouth," still describes him. In Miller the old desire of the eighteenth-century Barlows and Dwights seems realized: a poet to express the magnificent vastness of America. This he does, till we behold the vision. In his poetry we hear the tumult of the western empire: Idaho, Montana, California, Oregon,

634   Casting the Ashes of Joaquin Miller into the Fire, from a photograph by Gabriel Moulin

635   From a photograph. © Dassonville,
                          San Francisco

JOHN MUIR, 1838–1914

WHILE Joaquin Miller was apostrophizing the snowcapped mountains, John Muir was climbing over them with a geologist's hammer and notebook. This Scotchman with the eye of a scientist and the soul of a mystic stood before the West with all the freshness and wonder of Twain, Harte, and Miller, but devoted himself not to its people, but to its lakes, plains, and, most of all, to its incredible mountains. "I am," he wrote, "hopelessly and forever a mountaineer."

IN THE MOUNTAINS

A BOY of eleven, Muir was clambering about Dunbar Castle. A few years later he was studying botany and other sciences in the University of Wisconsin. Then came his journey on foot to Florida, his brief glimpse of Cuba, and the turning westward to his paradise — the Sierras, the Yosemite, and Alaska. One would like to dwell on this fine life. Few figures of the time are more vivid: the slight man, with gray beard and gray eyes, looking in the wilderness, says a friend, like John the Baptist. Living only on bread and tea, but all activity, he climbs Mount Tyndall; "up and back," he says, "before breakfast." Classifying the crags with scientific accuracy, he looks down, so runs the story, into the Yosemite, and weeps. "Mon," he says, with a Scotch burr, "can ye see unmoved the glory of the

Almighty?" We pause over his wit and sympathy, forgetting that he is not a man of letters, but an inventor, botanist, geologist, and that his first book did not appear until he was in his fifties.

637 From the bust by Malvina Hoffman, in
     the American Museum of Natural History

636   Muir's Cabin in the Yosemite, from a photograph by George Fiske,
                     courtesy of William F. Badè, Berkeley, Cal.

MUIR ON NATURE

YET his writing has the clarity of a Huxley, and occasionally the emotion of a poet. He can describe in proper temper the contrasting forms of natural life, which interested Emerson philosophically (the squirrel and the mountain), with kindly amusement at the brave chatter of the squirrel, and with awe before the storm in the mountains. Especially will his *My First Summer in the Sierra*, 1911, and *The Story of My Boyhood and Youth*, 1913, remain parts of American literature. Muir continues with wider sweep the new interest in nature which followed Thoreau. Besides the books mentioned above, he wrote: *The Mountains of California*, 1894; *Our National Parks*, 1901; *Stickeen, the Story of a Dog*, 1909,

JOHN BURROUGHS, 1837–1921

MORE of a scientist than Thoreau, more of a man of letters than Muir, John Burroughs was far more complex in mental life than either, but he was less endowed than they with the sense of a divine mystery in nature. In spite of susceptibility to intellectual influences — he was deeply affected at various times by Emerson, Whitman, Wordsworth, and Matthew Arnold—Burroughs never lost the homely atmosphere of his boyhood farm in Roxbury, New York.

639 © Brown Brothers

THE SAGE OF WOODCHUCK LODGE

ALTHOUGH the literary criticism of his later life gives hints of his scanty education, it attests rather the wide reading and intellectual discipline to which he subjected himself. When he was twenty-seven he had begun the work from which he was to steal the hours for his study of nature. For nine years he was in the Treasury Department at Washington. Later he was a bank examiner. It was not until 1884 that he could give himself unreservedly to life in the country. His last years reveal him as a kind of sage at "Woodchuck Lodge." Pilgrims listen to his tranquil talk on literature, science, and nature. Or, quite as often, he gossips of the woods or tells anecdotes of his adventures.

638 From the bust by C. S. Pietro, presented to the American Museum of Natural History by Henry Ford

640 Burroughs at "Slabsides." © Clifton Johnson

HIS LITERARY OUTPUT, 1871–89

BURROUGHS never hurried. His first magazine articles had appeared quietly. These were papers, *From the Back Country*, and were published in the New York *Leader*. The Burroughs we know may be found in some eight books written during a period of less than twenty years, beginning with *Wake-Robin* in 1871, and ending with *Indoor Studies* in 1889. These are books carefully written, exact, sympathetic, but with few intimations of that presence which haunted Thoreau.

641   Burroughs Studying the Birds. © Underwood & Underwood

WAKE–ROBIN

WAKE-ROBIN, with its quest of birds, its intimate talk of the wren, the ovenbird, the vesper sparrow, and its half-poetic tone has been deemed the most pleasing of Burroughs' books. It is youthful, ardent, with less emphasis on the testimony of the microscope. There is meaning in Burroughs' later reiteration of the phrase "sharp eyes." He became increasingly scientific, decreasingly sentimental. One may trace for himself the change through *Winter Sunshine*, 1875, *Locusts and Wild Honey*, 1879, *Fresh Fields*, 1884, *Signs and Seasons*, 1886.

642   Among his Beloved Catskills.   © Brown Brothers

LITERARY INFLUENCES

YET the evolution in the thought of Burroughs toward science was accompanied by struggles with another side of his temperament which may be called intuitional. "There is," he says on one occasion, "much soft rock in my make-up." The influences of Emerson, Whitman, and Wordsworth had done their work. Though he put aside conventional religion, he never quite relinquished the sense of the supernatural. He was touched, too, by the fever and unrest induced by the modern scientific world. Burroughs' understanding of Matthew Arnold seems surprising, unless we remind ourselves of this tendency in him.

THE SCIENTIFIC SPIRIT

YET it is the scientific spirit which gives value to Burroughs' literary criticism in *Notes on Walt Whitman*, 1867, and *Indoor Studies*. This and his freshness of manner are his chief literary qualities. We wonder as we survey his life, subjected to many influences, if the fault was not in those early years, in the absence of a complete education. He saw life steadily, but never whole.

643   Burroughs in his Last Years. © Underwood & Underwood

644   From a photograph, about 1870

JOHN HAY, 1838–1905

ONE of Muir's mountains, Pike's Peak, was named after its discoverer, Lieutenant Zebulon Montgomery Pike. So was Pike County, Missouri, but the lieutenant was to do more. He was to christen indirectly a remarkable school of American realism. Turning the pages of John Hay, the poet, or Edward Eggleston, the novelist, the reader may echo Morse in *Tennessee's Partner*, with perhaps the same amused smile; "Pike — aren't you?" Even if it be true that Bret Harte was the pioneer in this literature (though Mark Twain thought not), John Hay's *Pike County Ballads*, 1871, are the best verse sketches of these pale, rangy, tobacco-chewing natives of Indiana, eastern Ohio, and southern Illinois.

LITTLE BREECHES.—"I want a Chaw of Terbacker."

645   From *Harper's Weekly*, May 20, 1871, after a drawing by Sol Eytinge, Jr.

EARLY TRAINING

JOHN HAY lapsed only once — though this lapse was lucky for his posthumous fame — into the Pike vernacular. As a boy he knew Pike County, Illinois, but at Brown University and in literary circles he adopted the more polite mediums of the age. He became a translator, and an imitator, seemingly, of Longfellow. Back in the West, studying law, he finds the old life crude. Only his continued friendship with Nora Perry revives the poetry in him. Hay became a secretary under Lincoln, and later a diplomat in European capitals. He had, we hear, the good taste and bad judgment to regret the *Pike County Ballads*. Perhaps the famous ambassador to England (1897–98), who preferred to be the author of *The Surrender of Spain*, would not like to retell

How Jimmy Bludso passed in his checks
The night of the Prairie Belle.

Nor would he care for *Little Breeches* as a diplomatic costume. But most Americans still like these better than the finished lyrics of his *Castilian Days*, 1871, or even his *Abraham Lincoln*, 1890 (in collaboration with Nicolay), or his novel, *The Bread-winners*, 1883, published anonymously.

647 Hay as Ambassador, from *Vanity Fair*, London, 1897, after a caricature by Spy

THE MYSTERY OF GILGAL.—"Jest Drap that Whisky-skin."

646 From *Harper's Weekly*, May 20, 1871, after a drawing by Sol Eytinge, Jr.

648   From a photograph by Gutekunst

EDWARD EGGLESTON, 1837–1902

It will be recalled that the answer of Tennessee's Partner was shameless. He said: "I'm from Pike County, Mizzouri." Edward Eggleston dug in the new soil with delight. What he found he included in his seven novels of the larger Pike County. On the substructure of a two years' education he had built up a knowledge of literature sufficient to make him eventually an editor and novelist. Eggleston shares with more gifted realists the consecration of life to the people he describes. He became "a circuit rider." From crude settlements to tiny border towns the parson rode, preaching to his Methodist flocks, and observing the revival meetings and the boorish entertainments and the intimate life of the villages.

SPINNING-WHEEL AND RIFLE.

649   From Edward Eggleston, *The Circuit Rider*, New York, 1875

THE HOOSIER SCHOOLMASTER

The Hoosier Schoolmaster appeared in *Hearth and Home*, 1871. These stories seemed like caricatures. Yet caricature or hyperbole these pages were not, but more or less authentic transcripts of American frontier life. There is less justice in the pages of Mrs. Trollope's *Domestic Manners of the Americans* than in these etchings of Indiana and Ohio.

650   From *Hearth and Home*, September, 1871, drawing by Thomas Francis Beard

LATER WRITINGS

The Hoosier Schoolmaster, 1871, which depicts the locality Eggleston knew best, is characteristic of his method. *Roxy*, 1878, and *The Hoosier Schoolboy*, 1883, complete the picture. *The Graysons*, 1888, includes Abraham Lincoln. The other historical novel, *The Circuit Rider*, 1874, is the most powerful. *The Faith Doctor*, 1891, and the volumes of stories are inferior. Eggleston tells his stories of illiterate school trustees, silly girls, and desperadoes without flinching. Perhaps the unique contribution to our knowledge of America through these novels is contained in the survey of revivalistic religion. Matthew Arnold would have enjoyed these pictures of the "dissidence of dissent and the Protestantism of the Protestant religion." It is hardly necessary to add that Eggleston lacked finish. He was not, like Harte, a student of technique. Yet many pages are human enough to transcend tricks of style.

OLD JACK MEANS, THE SCHOOL TRUSTEE.

651   From *Hearth and Home*, October, 1871, drawing by Thomas Francis Beard (1842–1905)

GEORGE W. CABLE, 1844–1925

ALTHOUGH fiction after the Civil War was realistic, it was touched also, we noticed, with colors of romance. True of Mark Twain and Bret Harte, this is likely to make us forget that in the new southern literature there was much realism. Some of us have had the experience of discovering in a friend, behind a romantic face, a matter-of-fact mind. The mood of languor in the novels of George Washington Cable is equally deceptive. Their characters and scenes have models in the Louisiana descendants of the Acadians, Spaniards, and French. These are romantic stories, but they reflect faithfully "old Creole days." *Scribner's Magazine* compared Cable's faithful reproduction of scenes in New Orleans to Balzac's in Paris.

652   From a photograph by Falk

NEW ORLEANS

THE greater part of Cable's life was spent in New Orleans. Not the Confederate army, the cotton business, newspaper work, illness, nor failure could dim his artistic interest in this mysterious mingling of the aristocracy of Europe with the blacks of Africa.

653   A Creole Courtyard, Royal Street, from *Historical Sketch Book and Guide to New Orleans*, edited by W. H. Coleman, New York, 1885, drawing by C. Spiegle, Jr. approved by Cable

CABLE'S LATER YEARS

CABLE never wearied of meditating on the strange setting of the drama: the magnolia groves, the bayous, and the dark jungles of Louisiana. Later he lived in New England, took the approved cut of literary men, and studied the negro sociologically. Yet his natural gifts were those he manifested early: first, the passionate response to the romantic spectacle; second, the faithful portrayal of what he saw.

654   Cable at seventy-seven. © Underwood & Underwood

OLD CREOLE DAYS

CABLE secured the blessing of J. G. Holland in the early 'seventies, but apparently lived it down. *Old Creole Days* appeared in 1879. *Sieur George*, Cable's first story, had been, says a writer of those days, "a fresh and gentle southwest wind." *Old Creole Days* was another, not so gentle.

655 Père Antoine's Date Palm, from *Historical Sketch Book and Guide to New Orleans*, New York, 1885, drawing by C. Spiegle, Jr. approved by Cable

656 Madame Delphine's, from *Historical Sketch Book*, etc., 1885

"BRAS-COUPÉ" IN *THE GRANDISSIMES*

THE GRANDISSIMES, 1880, with the sinister affair of "Bras-Coupé," revealed fully Cable's talent. It was a book full of beauty, and terror. Yet even *The Grandissimes* lacks genius. Cable was primarily a skillful local colorist. After *Madame Delphine*, 1881, the gods withdrew their favor. It is not necessary to chronicle the novels of the later period — nor the short stories nor the articles. We detect easily Cable's faults, especially in the last years: his crudeness, his formlessness. Yet it is more difficult to record his virtues without falling into the commonplace. His pictures, his people, are haunting — and real. Again in American literature, we encounter the artist stirred deeply, but too briefly, by rare literary material.

657 Chartres Street, *Vieux Carré*, New Orleans. © Detroit Photograph Co.

EARLY PLANTATION DAYS OF THOMAS NELSON PAGE, 1853–1922

THUS in these days flourished the novel of "local color." Writers in particular fields, half-realistic, half-romantic, will be considered in the next chapter. Those studied here are not always more remarkable, but sum up types of literary impulses. Representative of the reawakened interest in the past of the South is the work of Cable and also of Thomas Nelson Page, who wrote of the old aristocracy in the days before 1861. The names of this novelist and poet are significant. On the family

658   Page's Birthplace, Oakland Plantation, Hanover County, Va., from a photograph by H. P. Cook

estates as a boy the patrician life of the old régime, with the pride of the young Virginian braves, and the laughter of their ladies, impressed his imagination ineffaceably. Over these lawns, too, he saw, before he was twelve, the blue-coated Yankees swarm.

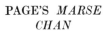

659   From a photograph by Davis & Sanford

A SOUTHERN GENTLEMAN

PAGE's career does honor to the best traditions of the South. He was a student of the classics; he was educated at Washington and Lee and at the University of Virginia; and for nearly twenty years he practiced law in Richmond. Later he served as ambassador to Italy. Known everywhere as a cultivated man of letters, he continued to turn out books until his death in 1922. We hear of him as a diner-out, reading aloud his "funny, darkey stories."

PAGE'S *MARSE CHAN*

THIS trivial echo means something. Page, in spite of other talents and his concern with larger problems, won distinction through his interpretation of the old South and the negro. The dialect of *Marse Chan* was hushed four years in the editorial office of his publisher before, in 1884, it delighted American readers who were interested in the vernaculars of the newly discovered country. With the publication of this and similar stories in the volume, *In Ole Virginia*, 1887, Page's best work was done. From this time on his performance was uneven. The ambitious *Red Rock, A Chronicle of the Reconstruction*, 1898, explains his single success and subsequent failure. For some chapters are touched with the glamour which Cable felt so deeply, and others are claptrap. Page never recaptured his old power.

660 From Thomas Nelson Page, *In Ole Virginia; or Marse Chan and Other Stories*, New York, 1892, etching by W. L. Sheppard by permission of Charles Scribner's Sons

661   From a photograph about 1895

JOEL CHANDLER HARRIS, 1848–1908

PAGE, however, beheld the negro through the moonlit haze of a summer night on the old plantation. The darkey was real, but he was an appendage of an old Virginia family. Cable had shown him as a human being in a bygone age. Others were to reveal his soul. "Others" means primarily Joel Chandler Harris. This Georgian was a journalist, not a man of letters, but his contribution to American literature endures. Uncle Remus is genuine, like Leatherstocking.

HIS CAREER IN JOURNALISM

THE humble life story of Harris has interest: his industry, his modesty, his amazement at his own fame. The fascination of printer's ink began in an association with a prosperous Georgia planter who published a journal at his own expense. As a boy, under his benefactor, Harris learned to manage a newspaper. More important, he learned that he could write. He delved in his employer's books, and at the close of each day he listened to the stories and songs of the negroes. Afterward he served on newspapers a long apprenticeship, and during the last decade of the century he was widely known as the editor of the *Atlanta Constitution*.

"Ef you don't lemme loose I'll knock you agin!"

663   From Joel Chandler Harris, *Uncle Remus: his Songs and his Sayings*, New York, 1908, drawing by A. B. Frost, by permission of D. Appleton and Company

662   Harris in his Georgia Home, from a photograph in the Authors Club, New York

BR'ER RABBIT

IT was early in the 'eighties that Harris threw off a negro-sketch to fill up a gap in the department of an irregular contributor. *Br'er Rabbit* had come out of his burrow! At once other newspapers captured him. The stories had begun which delight children, and which fix in an unusual form the humor and pathos of the African race in America. *Uncle Remus: his Songs and his Sayings, the Folklore of the Old Plantation*, 1880, included thirty-four negro folktales, and other sayings of Uncle Remus. *Nights with Uncle Remus* was published in 1883.

UNCLE REMUS

For Harris' stories recreated the folklore of the negro. Few readers of the saucy lingo took this aspect of his work seriously. Nor did Harris compete with the ethnologists. Yet the truth of the legends, in their half-unconscious symbolism of the tragic, yet not unhappy history of the race, coupled with natural art in their relation, created reality. When Harris visited New Orleans with Mark Twain and Cable, people exclaimed: "Why, he's white!"

"Brer Rabbit ain't see no peace w'atsumever."

664 From Harris, *Uncle Remus: his Songs and his Sayings,* New York, 1908, drawing by A. B. Frost, by permission of D. Appleton and Company

665 The Creator of *Uncle Remus.* © Underwood & Underwood

HARRIS' PLACE IN LITERATURE

Harris wrote too much. If we remember that these stories were by-products in the day of a busy editor his output seems prodigious. Their quality suffered as their author became more conscious of a purpose. Harris' other writings, on the "cracker" white, may be disregarded. Yet his place in American literature is definite. *Uncle Remus* might not be an acceptable comrade to the Pike County man, the miner, the hunter of the West, but he is as vigorous a type in fiction as they.

SIDNEY LANIER, 1842–81

The literature of the West after 1870 was not unlike the pioneer movement in which it originated: ardent, virile, and after the first burst of activity, subsiding into more conventional forms. A study of the magazines during the 'eighties shows the prominence of the literature of the South. Most of this was prose, as suited the temper of the country, but the group of poets centering in Timrod and Hayne had a successor who bridged in poetry the old South and the new. This was Sidney Lanier, a true poet.

666 Lanier at the age of fifteen, courtesy of Henry W. Lanier, New York

667   From the original written by Sidney Lanier. © Henry W. Lanier, New York

LANIER, THE MUSICIAN

LANIER was born in Macon, Georgia, and is associated with this part of the South, though he is also identified with the intellectual life of Baltimore. A detail of ancestry with meaning is that Nicholas Lanier, a court musician, wrote accompaniments for Jonson's masks and the lyrics of Robert Herrick. In a troubled life two lights beckoned Lanier on — music and poetry. For, like the older poets', Lanier's dream of an intellectual life was broken by the Civil War. Four hard years in the Confederate service offered only the scanty solace of his flute, which never left him, and a few books. While in service in Petersburg he contrived to spend some time in the library. Toward the close of the war he was taken prisoner on a blockade runner, and after his release he returned home, broken in health, to try various employments. For a time he taught school. He was a clerk in a hotel. Finally, he tried his father's profession, the law. All these occupations checked the chief interests of his life.

THE YEARS AFTER THE WAR

YET during the years from 1865 to 1873 Lanier was laying the foundations, with much suffering, of a career. He was also breaking with the poetic traditions of his boyhood. In the latter year he announced his determination to give himself unreservedly to music and poetry. In the former, recognition came almost immediately in his success as a flutist in orchestras in Baltimore and New York. Afterward he won distinction through the publication of his poem, *Corn*, 1875, in *Lippincott's Magazine*.

668   Lanier at the age of twenty-eight, courtesy of Henry W. Lanier, New York

SUNRISE, HIS LAST POEM

SIX years remained — "six little years — six drops of time!" The battle was now with the old enemy, consumption, and Lanier's life, never calm, was a fitful fever: he played with guide books, lectures, and juvenile stories. He died with his finest poem, *Sunrise*, barely finished. This haste was characteristic. Lanier's spirit was eager, aspiring, full of an intense longing for beauty, and until the very end he was struggling against relentless circumstance. No one who studies his life can refrain from speculation about his power under a favorable star. It would seem that he never came to full maturity.

I

SUNRISE

IN my sleep I was fain of their fellowship, fain
Of the live-oak, the marsh, and the main.
The little green leaves would not let me alone in my sleep;
Up-breathed from the marshes, a message of range and of sweep,
Interwoven with waftures of wild sea-liberties, drifting,
Came through the lapped leaves sifting, sifting,
Came to the gates of sleep.

[3]

669   From Sidney Lanier, *Hymns of the Marshes*, New York, 1907, photograph by Henry Troth, taken near Brunswick, by permission of Charles Scribner's Sons

IDEALS OF THE NEW SOUTH

IF we consider Lanier's life as a whole, we cannot help feeling how admirably he stands for the thought of the South between 1850 and 1880. Its ideals for war, for learning, and for the new nation were all his. He was a soldier under the Confederacy, a scholar, and a poet. He wrote variously: in the vein of Timrod and Hayne, in dialect, and in a manner which was a strange compound of Victorian masters and his own.

THE MARSHES OF GLYNN

TIGER LILIES, his novel of 1867, is a key to his imperfections as a poet. In it are his elaborate diction and his strained flights of fancy. *Corn*, full of life and melody, is, after all, a confused rhapsody. His notions of poetry, which he set forth in *The Science of Verse*, 1880, did not include, at least practically, revision and structure. But few, save Rossetti and Swinburne,

670 Sidney Lanier's Grave, Baltimore, courtesy of Mrs. Lawrence Turnbull

have caught more clearly than Lanier the suggestion of thought by sound. *The Marshes of Glynn, The Symphony,* and *Sunrise,* and lesser poems have in them a wail of the violins, the boom of the viol, and voices of a symphony of music — the world which Lanier thought reality. After all, there is something of the beautiful and ineffectual angel about Sidney Lanier. He reaches out to the unseen but is rudely thrust back to earth. His poems form a group of lovely fragments. His collected poems were edited and published in 1884.

671 Lanier's Oak, Brunswick, courtesy of the Southern Railway

A PILGRIM TO BOSTON

DURING the years before the war, when Lanier was dreaming of a future in music and poetry, there came from the West to New England, a pilgrim to his holy land, William Dean Howells. Later when this westerner had become — a significant fact — the leader of New England literature, other pilgrims from the prairies were to come to him. For, although Howells' reading and culture made him the natural successor of the Brahmins, his vitality was western. Like the writers of the West, he was to be the vigorous realist, but, unlike them, the realist not of the mining camp, but of the village and city, the realist of commonplace society. Among his intimate friends were the antipodes of the period, **Mark Twain** and Henry James.

672 Louisburg Square, Boston. © Halliday Historic Photograph Co.

673   From a photograph taken at eighteen or twenty,
        courtesy of Miss Mildred Howells

WILLIAM DEAN HOWELLS, 1837–1920

THE boyhood of Howells was passed in Ohio, in his birthplace, Martin's Ferry; in "the boy's town" (Hamilton); and in larger cities, Dayton and Columbus. In few authors more than in Howells does biography depend upon what he called his "literary passions." Though he played at Indian, planted corn and melons, and wrestled with the forests of hickory, he was in love with the immortal dead — with, first of all, Cervantes, Goldsmith, and Irving, then, one after another, with the great Victorians. We guess a meaning in his early preference for Pope over Walter Scott. In *A Boy's Town*, written years later (1890), are memories of the novelist's early life among books and in his father's printing-office.

JOURNALIST AND CONSUL

To continue his reading Howells declined, in 1856, a tempting offer from the *Cincinnati Gazette*, but he was drifting more and more into the journalistic world. Before he was thirty he had served on the *Ohio State Journal;*

674   The Palazza Giustiniani, at left, where Howells lived while in Venice,
        courtesy of Miss Mildred Howells

had published with J. J. Piatt his *Poems of Two Friends*, 1859; and had won the appointment of United States consul at Venice. Before he sailed he had begun his friendship with James Russell Lowell, and with New England.

"THE PUBLISHER SEEMED AWARE OF THE POETIC QUALITY OF THE TRANSACTION"

675   Ticknor Paying Howells for his First Poem, from Howells, *Literary Friends and
        Acquaintances*, New York, 1901, courtesy of Harper & Brothers

VENETIAN LIFE, 1866, AND THE RETURN TO AMERICA

HOWELLS' blissful four years in Italy, during the Civil War, are described, like so many other episodes of his full, happy career, in his own autobiographical prose, in *Venetian Life*, 1866. Seven years after his return he was editor, at the age of thirty-five, of the *Atlantic Monthly*. On his desk lay contributions from the most distinguished American men of letters. It was a brilliant record, yet only a beginning. During the next fifteen years appeared his poetry and his volumes of light prose sketches,

HOWELLS, STUDENT OF MIDDLE-CLASS LIFE IN AMERICA

WHEN in 1881 Howells resigned his editorship to Thomas Bailey Aldrich, he had revealed the character but by no means the scope of his talents. Gradually, the poetry in him, the romantic tendencies, faded. *Their Wedding Journey*, 1871, and the slight novel, *The Lady of the Aroostook*, 1879, had shown his quiet mastery of American life as a thoughtful observer would find it in the middle classes of the 'seventies. Not profound, but with the surface lines so true that the reader to-day has no shock in slipping into the reality of these pages. Already Howells stood for the actuality for which he was to fight. "Ah! poor real life," he says in a frequently quoted passage, "which I love, can I make others share the delight I find in thy foolish and insipid face?"

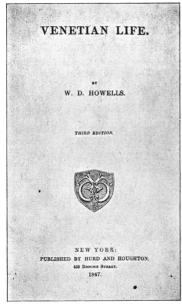

677   Title-page of the third edition

676   Howells at about forty, courtesy of Miss Mildred Howells

INTERPRETER OF THE NEW AMERICA

THUS Howells' novels, *A Modern Instance*, 1882, *The Rise of Silas Lapham*, 1885, *A Hazard of New Fortunes*, 1889, *The Kentons*, 1902, and others less inspired, are the natural culmination of a life steeped in literature and acutely conscious of this American society. As sustained and faithful interpretations of how American people thought, talked, and appeared during the last quarter of the century, they are unparalleled. The years brought also their guerdon of sincere and artistic expression; the style of these novels is almost faultless. For the most part Howells' contracts were now with Harper's. From the *Editor's Study* he challenged the world in behalf of realism. From the *Easy Chair* he chatted of books and things. Yet, Howells said at the celebration of his seventy-fifth birthday, quoting Hawthorne, that there was nothing like recognition to make a man modest. His generous nature never realized how his wise counsels to Mark Twain and Henry James revealed him as, on the whole, the most fully-rounded interpreter of the new America. Whatever we hear of Howells' writing as "classical" or as a "reaction against the romance of the age," we must not forget the mood of youthful feeling in the poems or in the sketches written in early manhood. Though restrained in expression, these share the cheerful freshness of the new era. *Their Wedding Journey* is an example of this mood. The books of travel and the stories of Italian life are all alike in this respect.

678   From Howells, *Their Wedding Journey*, Boston, 1872, drawing by Augustus Hoppin

Apart from this tendency, which dimmed as Howells grew older, the sketches of Italy and Cambridge, or of Bostonians and westerners are like novels without plots. There are pages of painstaking descriptions — of a mode of dress, of a glance, of a young girl's face.

THE RISE OF SILAS LAPHAM

HOWELLS learned how to tell a story. The influences of the sketches of Irving, Hawthorne, Ik Marvel, and Curtis could not detain him in the essay form. The pictures of the Boston to which Marcia Gaylord and Bartley Hubbard flee are characteristic of his comedy of manners, but the weakness of Bartley, the temper of Marcia, as well as the incidents, make an absorbing story. *A Modern Instance* and *The Rise of Silas Lapham* take us beneath the surface of New England life.

OBSERVER AND STYLIST

YET not far beneath. The sad eyes of Hester Prynne and the gesture of Dimmesdale on the scaffold warn us not to be lulled into false judgments. The face of New England he saw, but to the mysteries of its dark, complex soul he remained an outsider. He shows us not the inner

679 The house at 302 Beacon Street, Boston, where Howells wrote *Silas Lapham*, courtesy of Miss Mildred Howells

life of New England but the results of that life upon conventional and everyday intercourse. A "modern instance" or the "rise" of a character Howells can portray; their obscure origins in the spirit are beyond him. Indeed, as matters of art, such problems hardly interest him. For Howells was scientific in method, even as his age was scientific. He was detached from the mystery of life, and his sympathy was that of artistic comprehension, not of deep feeling before the paradoxes of life. He was an observer. Moreover, as in observers, his success is bound up in his medium. Howells was a stylist. Let us note once more that adoring tribute of Mark Twain: "For forty years his English has been to me a continual delight and astonishment. In the sustained exhibition of certain great qualities — clearness, compression, verbal exactness, and unforced and seemingly unconscious felicity of phrasing — he is, in my belief, without peer in the English-speaking world. *Sustained.* I entrench myself behind that protecting word . . ."

680   Howells at seventy. © Van der Weyde

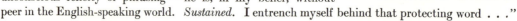

681   From *Harper's Weekly*, March 9, 1912, photograph taken at the dinner in celebration of Howells' seventy-fifth birthday

HENRY JAMES, 1843–1916

HOWELLS' essay in the *Century* in 1882 on Henry James, in which he declared that all the stories had been told, and in which he defended aggressively the new realism, was at once an admission of the temper of the time, and a recognition of its greatest exponent. For some of the best writing of these years was a protest against the earlier romanticism. Henry James, who began with criticism, carried into the novel the analytical faculty in degrees of distilled refinement which leaves even some of his cult in bewilderment. One thinks of Thackeray's exhausted cry as he finished writing a novel; of Hawthorne's breaking down as he finished the *Scarlet Letter,* and then, in amazing contrast, of this deliberate art of James. Not even the gentle glow of Howells lies upon these cold pages.

682   Henry James and his Father, from a daguerreotype, 1854, courtesy of Charles Scribner's Sons

EARLY YEARS

THE few facts in the life of Henry James mean little unless we think of his detachment from rough experience. Even this detachment connotes little, unless we conceive clearly his subtly philosophizing mind, which broods on every sound, sight, color; and transforms them by analysis into an intricate psychology of the nuances of thought and emotion. All this began early. James was of an Albany family but was born in New York, and lived there until he was twelve. He was educated in the usual manner, but perhaps most important were the four years of "impressions" — impressions of old civilizations and the art of London, Geneva, Zürich, Bonn.

THE STORY OF A YEAR.

I.

MY story begins as a great many stories have begun within the last three years, and indeed as a great many have ended ; for, when the hero is despatched, does not the romance come to a stop ?

In early May, two years ago, a young couple I wot of strolled homeward from an evening walk, a long ramble among the peaceful hills which inclosed their rustic home. Into these peaceful hills the young man had brought, not the rumor, (which was an old inhabitant,) but some of the reality of war, — a little whiff of gunpowder, the clanking of a sword ; for, although Mr. John Ford had his campaign still before him, he wore a certain comely air of camp-life which stamped him a very Hector to the steady-going villagers, and a very pretty fellow to Miss Elizabeth Crowe, his companion in this sentimental stroll. And was he not attired in the great brightness of blue and gold which befits a freshly made lieutenant ? This was a strange sight for these happy Northern glades ; for, although the first Revolution had boomed awhile in their

midst, the honest yeomen who defended them were clad in sober homespun, and it is well known that His Majesty's troops wore red.

These young people, I say, had been roaming. It was plain that they had wandered into spots where the brambles were thick and the dews heavy, — nay, into swamps and puddles where the April rains were still undried. Ford's boots and trousers had imbibed a deep foretaste of the Virginia mud ; his companion's skirts were fearfully bedraggled. What great enthusiasm had made our friends so unmindful of their steps ? What blinding ardor had kindled these strange phenomena : a young lieutenant scornful of his first uniform, a well-bred young lady reckless of her stockings ?

Good reader, this narrative is averse to retrospect.

Elizabeth (as I shall not scruple to call her outright) was leaning upon her companion's arm, half moving in concert with him, and half allowing herself to be led, with that instinctive acknowledgment of dependence natural to a young girl who has just received the assurance of lifelong protection. Ford was lounging along with that calm,

684   Page of James' first published story, from the *Atlantic Monthly,* March, 1865

683   James M. Barrie and Henry James.
© Brown Brothers

HIS DEVOTION TO ART

SOON after he returned to America came the crash of southern artillery, but Henry James was not made for war, or even for the Harvard Law School where for a time he studied. On the steamer to Newport after visiting the wounded at Portsmouth Grove, he stirred with a high-strung mood of resolution. He would devote himself to art. From this determination he never wandered. Even during the contacts and friendships of later successful years, he remained the intense, almost mystical devotee of the creation of art through prose fiction.

685   James in his Study at his Home, Rye, England, from a photograph taken in 1900

HENRY JAMES IN THE LATER YEARS

EXTERNALLY he never submitted to the training of this world, but his inner life was intense self-discipline. He read, he wrote, he lived abroad. Finally, he left America never to return, save for brief visits. Then, shortly before his death, during the war with Germany, he became a British subject, to manifest his sympathy for his adopted country — a superfluous sacrifice, some have thought, a proof hardly needed of where his allegiance lay.

THE AMERICAN

IT is easy to understand what had happened in this aloof, gifted mind. . . . "I had," says Clement Searle in *A Passionate Pilgrim*, "the love of old forms and pleasant rites, and I found them nowhere. . . . Sitting here in this old park, in this old country, I feel that I hover on the misty verge of what might have been! I should have been born here and not there." James thought that what Emerson had achieved in the things of culture was summed up in the thought of Concord. *The American* shows Christopher Newman, a wealthy business man, baffled by the older civilization of Europe. When he was twenty-two the *Atlantic Monthly* published James' first story (No. 683), but in this and the other tales or in the early critical sketches was slight promise of the future "international novelist."

686   From *The Academy*, London, 1898, caricature by Max Beerbohm

1876.]   *The American.*   651

THE AMERICAN.

I.

ON a brilliant day in May, in the year 1868, a gentleman was reclining at his ease on the great circular divan which at that period occupied the centre of the Salon Carré, in the Museum of the Louvre. This commodious ottoman has since been removed, to the extreme regret of all weak-kneed lovers of the fine arts; but the gentleman in question had taken serene possession of its softest spot, and, with his head thrown back and his legs outstretched, he was staring at Murillo's beautiful moon-borne Madonna, in profound enjoyment of his posture. He had removed his hat, and flung down beside him a little red guide-book and an opera-glass. The day was warm, he was heated with walking, and he repeatedly passed his handkerchief over his forehead, with a somewhat wearied gesture. And yet he was evidently not a man to whom fatigue was familiar; long, lean, and muscular, he suggested the sort of vigor that is commonly known as "toughness." But his exertions on this particular day had been of an unwonted sort, and he had often performed great physical feats which left him less jaded than his tranquil stroll through the Louvre. He had looked out all the pictures to which an asterisk was affixed in those formidable pages of fine print in his Bädeker; his attention had been strained and his eyes dazzled, and he had sat down with an æsthetic headache. He had looked, moreover, not only at all the pictures, but at all the copies that were going forward around them, in the hands of those innumerable young women in irreproachable toilets who devote themselves, in France, to the propagation of masterpieces; and if the truth must be told, he had often admired the copy much more than the original. His physiognomy would have sufficiently indicated that he was a shrewd and capable fellow, and in

truth he had often sat up all night over a bristling bundle of accounts, and heard the cock crow without a yawn. But Raphael and Titian and Rubens were a new kind of arithmetic, and they inspired our friend, for the first time in his life, with a vague self-mistrust. An observer with anything of an eye for national types would have had no difficulty in determining the local origin of this undeveloped connoisseur, and indeed such an observer might have felt a certain humorous relish of the almost ideal completeness with which he filled out the national mold. The gentleman on the divan was a powerful specimen of an American. But he was not only a fine American; he was in the first place, physically, a fine man. He appeared to possess that kind of health and strength which, when found in perfection, is the most impressive — the physical capital which the owner does nothing to "keep up." If he was a muscular Christian, it was quite without knowing it. If it was necessary to walk to a remote spot, he walked, but he had never known himself to "exercise." He had no theory with regard to cold bathing or the use of Indian clubs; he was neither an oarsman, a rifleman, nor a fencer, — he had never had time for these amusements, — and he was quite unaware that the saddle is recommended for certain forms of indigestion. He was by inclination a temperate man; but he had supped the night before his visit to the Louvre at the Café Anglais, — some one had told him it was an experience not to be omitted, — and he had slept none the less the sleep of the just. His usual attitude and carriage were of a rather relaxed and lounging kind, but when, under a special inspiration, he straightened himself, he looked like a grenadier on parade. He never smoked. He had been assured — such things are said — that cigars were excellent for the health, and he was quite capable of believing it; but he

687   From the *Atlantic Monthly*, June, 1876

688 Daisy Miller leaving New York, from the painting by Henry Bacon (1839–1912). © Gramstorff Brothers, Inc.

INTERNATIONAL NOVELS AND SHORT STORIES

FOR James' first, and possibly his best work showed Europe through the eyes of young Americans, and young Americans through the eyes of Europe. In this cycle are *Roderick Hudson*, 1875, *The American*, 1877, *Daisy Miller*, 1878, *The Europeans*, 1878, a gay story of the visit of well-bred continentals to America. In these novels are the friction of different manners and customs, the encyclopedic dissection of the American visitors, but most of all, here is the autobiography of Henry James. Here are the endless ramifications of his "impressions" of life, formed by the conflict in himself of his American and European points of view. The Americans themselves, the types of wealthy and leisured residents who enjoyed Europe in the nineteenth century, are inexact, except for mannerisms. All are rich, all are provincial, but all are incredibly introspective, refiners of delicate feelings. All, in a word, are Henry James.

He came to understand Americans less and less, and his novels tended to drift away from the international situation. Robert Herrick depicts him on a winter day in Chicago, overcome by the ugliness of it all, and we may imagine a favorite intonation when he remarked, as the tradition goes, that "Niagara Falls were in very good taste." Such individuals as Bartley Hubbard and Marcia, in *A Modern Instance*, James had never penetrated, though he could have painted their dress, deportment, and feelings in the Louvre far better than Howells.

THE STYLE OF HENRY JAMES

AMERICANS continued to be present in the novels, but the vivid contrast between the two civilizations became less central in the writer's mind. Instead, the niceties of feeling increase, as do the filigree and chasing in the novelist's style. For hours of the reader's time characters stand before a fireplace without moving. In *The Bostonians*, 1886, one pauses literally in a vestibule for a prolonged examination of the place. *The Portrait of a Lady*, 1881, with all its thousands of words is just that. In *The Aspern Papers*, 1888, the scientist tests under many lenses the shrunken soul of Juliana Bordereau.

James was a disciple of Flaubert and George Eliot, but he heard whispers of the mind which never touched their ears. No one must think all this affectation. For this art he burns with the zeal of an apostle, and he replies contemptuously to his warm-hearted brother's suggestion that he write what ordinary beings can understand. In 1907–09 were published his complete works with revisions of novels written in his early, simpler manner. A contrast of almost any novel in the two forms for a half dozen pages tells the story. Incidentally the critical prefaces of this edition are at once an ultimatum to critics, and a revelation of his aims in art.

689 © Alice Boughton

II.

"I have adopted a little girl, you know," Roger said, after this, to a number of his friends; but he felt, rather, as if she had adopted him. With the downright sense of paternity he found it somewhat difficult to make his terms. It was indeed an immense satisfaction to feel, as time went on, that there was small danger of his repenting of his bargain. It seemed to him more and more that he had obeyed a divine voice; though indeed he was equally conscious that there was something grotesque in his new condition, — in the sudden assumption of paternal care by a man who had seemed to the world to rejoice so placidly in his sleek and comfortable singleness. But for all this he found himself able to look the world squarely in the face. At first it had been with an effort, a blush, and a deprecating smile that he spoke of his pious venture; but very soon he began to take a robust satisfaction in alluding to it freely, in all companies. There was but one man of whose jocular verdict he thought with some annoyance, — his cousin Hubert Lawrence, namely, who

690   Page of *Watch and Ward*, from the *Atlantic Monthly*, 1871, in James' early style

II

"I HAVE adopted a little girl, you know," Roger said, after this, to a number of his friends; but he felt, rather, as if she had adopted him. He found it somewhat difficult to make his terms with the sense of actual paternity It was indeed an immense satisfaction to feel, as time went on, that there was small danger of his repenting of his bargain. It seemed to him more and more that he had obeyed a divine voice; though indeed he was equally conscious that there was something comical in a sleek young bachelor turning nurse and governess. But for all this he found himself able to look the world squarely in the face. At first it had been with an effort, a blush, and a deprecating smile that he spoke of his pious venture; but very soon he began to take a robust satisfaction in alluding to it freely. There was but one man of whose jocular verdict he thought with some annoyance, — his cousin Hubert Lawrence, namely, who was so terribly clever and trenchant, and who had been through life a commentator formidable to his modesty, though, in the end, always absolved by his good nature. But he made up his mind that, though Hubert might laugh, he himself was serious; and to prove it equally to himself and his friends, he determined on a great move. He withdrew altogether from his profession, and prepared to occupy his house in the country. The latter was

691   Page of *Watch and Ward*, London, 1923.
© The Macmillan Company

CRITICISM OF JAMES

SUCH an attitude toward life could not but provoke wonder and amusement, even among intellectual people. He has been assailed in dozens of kindred ways, as characteristic of critics as they are inessential in a final estimate of Henry James' unique genius. Perhaps James has been least understood when he has praised continental life, as in his descriptions of London or Paris. Missiles which he would have despised are still cast at his memory. One still hears attacks on his passion for London. Another remarks that he failed his country; his expatriation has not been forgiven. We hear that he feared real life, that he shrank into his ivory tower; that he grew increasingly cold; that he was a *poseur;* that, most absurd of all, he himself did not understand what he was trying to do. All these criticisms lead directly to the fane. For the understanding of Henry James rests upon the reflection that here was a human soul that trusted utterly in art as the secret of life, and was from first to last never uncertain about what art should mean to him. In Henry James was a purposefulness that, strangely enough, might have pleased his Puritan ancestors. His strength lay in his absolute conviction about art and his destinies in art.

JAMES' IDEALS OF ART

THAT most of his experience of life was secondhand, he was aware, as he was aware of his self-consciousness, and the other faults incidental to his ideal. The ideal, nevertheless, was the thing! For it he paid, though willingly and with the aid of his temperament, the price of so-called normal life, of which the *Letters* and certain passages in the novels show him to have been entirely capable. Toward the end he wrote of the powers and forces and divinities to whom he had always been loyal and who had never failed him — he meant his ideals of art.

692   © Van der Weyde

CHAPTER X

VARIED TRENDS OF THOUGHT

THE object of this chapter is twofold: First, to complete the survey of the nineteenth century by a consideration of lesser figures concerned with tendencies already mentioned. Second, to discuss other authors: either exponents of attitudes beginning late in the era and extending beyond its limits, like F. Marion Crawford and the new romanticism; or upholders of old traditions, like Edmund Clarence Stedman; or authors who are composites of these influences, like James Whitcomb Riley; or authors who are isolated, like Lafcadio Hearn. Never before has American literature been so kaleidoscopic. Realism, romance, sentimentalism, foreign influences, create through these lesser personalities, between 1870 and 1900, a vast, heterogeneous American literature.

The realism of William Dean Howells, conjoined with the decline of New England literature, was the signal for a general inventory of stock. Elizabeth Stuart Phelps Ward and others reflected the November sun of the New England landscape in studies of character. These writers were descendants of the Puritans. In them was the same intense reaction to the world of the spirit, the same conscience, the same introspection. In reveries their minds were darkened by ancestral Calvinists, Transcendentalists, and reformers. Ghosts which visited Hawthorne appear also to them, but in their veins the blood flows more slowly. They are distilled products, and in their stories of New England life one is conscious of their taut nerves. These younger women — the scepters of the Brahmins had passed to women — describe a changed and changing New England. Externally these novelists depict a different community. The migrations to the West, the surrender of literary supremacy, the dwindling of this section in relative importance had sapped New England vitality. The great period of intellectual growth was past. There were to be no Emersons or Hawthornes, though their thought was to permeate this later literature. It was the epoch of abatement, inevitable after such a fulfillment as that manifested through the Cambridge and Concord groups. Spiritually, literature, like Carlyle's Methodism, was now inclined to fix its eyes too closely on its own center. New England, like Bulwer Lytton as a child, is now always "thinking of its own thoughts."

Thus Elizabeth Stuart Phelps Ward pours out passionately in *The Gates Ajar* the anguish and mystical convictions of the New England soul in the grip of war. Rose Terry Cooke photographs commonplace individuals of the village. Later Sarah Orne Jewett sketches the white farmhouses of the Maine coast in landscapes which are delicate and clear. Mary E. Wilkins Freeman writes with less cheer. Her merciless eye is fastened on the spinster, the miser, the poor man. Her manner has the severe light of a New England living room. Alice Brown is gentler, but she, too, is intensely local. It is significant that all this analysis was roughly synchronous with the exultant literature of

California. The more vigorous members of the American literary family have gone out to the new playgrounds. The intellectuals, inheritors of a bygone age, remain, as it were, indoors, describing faithfully the old home: its inner rooms; what they behold from its narrow panes and its gardens.

Outside of New England many a humorist strives to echo the Mississippi pilot. Bret Harte is said to have inspired most of the Pike County literature. In the South, Lew. Wallace, like Cable, was interested in old Spanish themes. Helen Hunt Jackson wrote in *Ramona*, though she herself was a New Englander, of the Indians and of the missions of California. John Esten Cooke, lingering on after the war, described the new South. Meanwhile Mary Hartwell Catherwood, inspired by Parkman, celebrated the Canadian West. Besides the negroes of Joel Chandler Harris there are the farmers of the Georgian, Richard Malcolm Johnston, the Tennessee folk of Charles Egbert Craddock, and the southerners of the Reconstruction of Constance Fenimore Woolson. The nature tradition, dignified by Muir and Burroughs, was supported by lesser writers like C. C. Abbott and W. H. Gibson.

Although such authors varied individually in romantic or realistic tendencies, there was strong interest in native scenes. Side by side with these, others stoutly maintained Victorian traditions, especially in poetry. The old guard, in spite of a Whitman or a Mark Twain, did not die in 1870, or even surrender. Thousands of Americans thought *Leaves of Grass* idiocy, and turned to Bayard Taylor. Poets like Taylor or Aldrich or Stedman represent writers who never really acknowledged the new literature of America. Taylor published his *Lars* in the very year which brought forth novels by Howells and Eggleston, and poems by Joaquin Miller, John Boyle O'Reilly, and Will Carleton. Like Thomas Buchanan Read and George Boker, Taylor belonged to the past. Stoddard and Stedman, who were associated with New York, never quite recovered from their youthful draft of Keats' vintage, though the Civil War roused Stedman to battle lyrics.

The defense of the old ideals became to Stedman and Stoddard a point of honor. They fought the crude Americanism. Either they carried on a defensive warfare from their palaces of art; or, like Stedman, wrote prose criticism; or fell silent. America was done, though they would not admit it, with adoration of Keats. The story of Thomas Bailey Aldrich differs somewhat, though he, too, never listened to this alien music from beyond the Mississippi and the Sierras. His development in literature was less human than artistic. From the softness of his early mood he became more severe, but this change might have taken place in London. His beautiful lyrics owe hardly more to America than Poe's.

How strong the bookish influences were may be seen from a study of these minor poets who wrote after the Civil War. Not even a Whitman could silence the European echoes of Byron and Shelley and Keats. Thus poetry after 1870, apart from its nature, is less realistic than the prose. Yet compared with the poetry before the war, the realistic note is heard again and again. Sometimes, as in Irwin Russell, it creates characters as real as those in prose. Sometimes it is a blend of actual fact and sentiment, as in Will Carleton or James Whitcomb Riley. Sometimes romance or realism appears successively in different work of the same poets, as in Eugene Field, born in the West, but a child of the East.

In fact a characteristic of the lesser literature of the last quarter of the century is the variety of tones in the choir. Classification is nearly impossible. With the rise of the great monthlies and weeklies writing had become a trade, and the main currents of romance and realism broke up into eddies and cross streams. In the last decade, echoing the revolt of Robert Louis Stevenson, F. Marion Crawford and scores of others wrote swift-moving romances and historical novels, dealing with every colorful period of the past. In Emma Lazarus were both Hebraism and Hellenism. Richard Watson Gilder wrote lyrics in the old manner. The novel, the short story, and essay were of infinite variety. One might read the moral novels of E. P. Roe; the dramatic short stories of Frank Stockton; the local color tales of Kentucky of James Lane Allen; the whimsical essays of Charles Dudley Warner; or the fantasies of Lafcadio Hearn. To all these we are too close for final judgment. The "Prince of Posterity" must decide. One inclines to note certain traits of this writing, such as the gradual disappearance of the serious moral novel before the love of writing for its own sake; the increase in mechanical perfection of the short story; or the greater mastery of the essay. Yet conclusions about these are dangerous. It is all a somewhat tangled, if flourishing shrubbery. And above all rise like giant trees the figures of Mark Twain, William Dean Howells, and Henry James. We had best stick to these as emblems of the era. From them we may learn the significant tendencies of the age between 1870 and 1900.

693 From the original cover design by Stanford White for the first issue of *Scribner's Magazine*, January, 1887, courtesy of Charles Scribner's Sons

694   © Gramstorff Bros., Inc.

MISS ALCOTT'S *LITTLE WOMEN*

THE ineffectual Bronson Alcott his daughter did
not see, but only what the world valued less,
the sweet simplicity of his nature. Her earlier
work such as *Hospital Sketches*, 1863, was commonplace, and her talent was happiest in the
memories of the Concord home. *Little Women*,
1868–69, pictures the daughters of Bronson
Alcott. This book and the others in the series
show us a New England we must not forget: the
village, the home life, and the countryside seen
through the eyes of youth.

696   © Gramstorff Bros., Inc.

LOUISA M. ALCOTT, 1833–88

IN September, 1860, Louisa M. Alcott wrote to a friend in
good New England vernacular: "Our humble place of abode
is perking up." The Alcott household's visitors were Charlotte
Cushman, Miss Stebbins, the actress, and Whittier. The
"humble abode," with its recollections of the older New England, inspired Miss Alcott's most famous novel, and formed
her character as an interpreter of New England life.

"They all drew to the fire, mother in the big chair, with Beth at her feet"
(See page 9) FRONTISPIECE

695   From *Little Women*, Boston, 1896, drawing by F. T. Merrill by
permission of Little, Brown & Company

ELIZABETH STUART PHELPS WARD, 1844–1911

IT is well to begin a study of this New England school with a writer
like Miss Alcott, for soon enough we encounter Puritan nerves.
Born in Andover, Massachusetts, Elizabeth Stuart Phelps, later
Mrs. Ward, contributed when still a girl to the *Youth's Companion*
and *Harper's Monthly*. She is as intense in *The Gates Ajar*, 1868, if
less doctrinal, than the generations of divines of whom she was the
descendant. Bereavement through battle — the death of her brother
— led her spirit beyond the veil. As the shows of this world fade,
she discloses the future life. The anguished certainty of *Gates Ajar* sustained many a bruised heart.
Mrs. Ward's later work is more objective, but in a limited way she is a realist of the New England soul. Her
long list of writings includes, also, *The Struggle for Immortality*, 1889.

697 © Gramstorff Bros., Inc.

MISS JEWETT'S NEW ENGLAND

SARAH ORNE JEWETT, 1849–1909

HARRIET PRESCOTT SPOFFORD, with her *Amber Gods*, 1863, was more romantic, and was, perhaps, influenced by Hawthorne, but realism of another kind appeared in the finished stories of Sarah Orne Jewett. *A Country Doctor*, 1884, shows "the country of the pointed firs," about South Berwick, Maine. Here dwell the old families, the solid farmers, and the young maidens — like Stevenson's, with their quiet eyes — and the physician-father who was her complete friend.

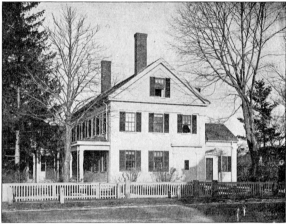

698 Miss Jewett's Home, South Berwick, Me. © Halliday Historic Photograph Co.

THE old New England was passing, but Miss Jewett caught on her canvas its fading colors, touching lightly the by-products of the decline. After *Deephaven*, in 1877, she continued to depict her countryside: its natives, its summer boarders, and its life by the sea. About all her work hovers something like the clear sunshine of Jane Austen.

MARY E. WILKINS FREEMAN, 1862–

MISS JEWETT is in a sense a transition from the interpreters of the old New England, like Mrs. Stowe and Rose Terry Cooke, to those of the new, like Mary E. Wilkins Freeman and Alice Brown. Anyone who knows these northern states can understand the significance of Miss Wilkins' girlhood in Randolph and Brattleboro. In adjacent villages may be found the true aftermath of New England Puritanism. Miss Wilkins knew this life — its meagerness, its rigidity, its inhibi-

tions. Her work and that of Elizabeth Stuart Phelps Ward seem complementary: in one is the external body; in the other the soul. Miss Wilkins is a realist of the French school. *A Humble Romance*, 1887, or *A New England Nun*,

699 From a photograph, about 1890. © Gramstorff Bros., Inc.

1891, reveal her art: as severe and sharp as the bleak trees against a wintry sky line.

ALICE BROWN, 1857–

ALICE BROWN, distinguished to-day as a novelist, and playwright, loves, more than Miss Wilkins, her New England country. She likes to hear the rough dialect, to dream a little over the illusive warmth of the northern summer. In spite of her later successes in other fields, readers will turn to *Tiverton Tales*, 1899, and earlier work.

700 Courtesy of The Macmillan Company

701   From a photograph by Conly, Boston

LEWIS WALLACE, 1827–1905

DEFYING classification, American fiction now becomes miscellaneous. Scores of tendencies do battle, one with another. Boys who wide-eyed beheld the chariot race in *Ben-Hur: A Tale of the Christ*, 1880, by Lew. Wallace, threw down *The Prince of India*, 1893, and his other writings in disappointment. Wallace, a native of Indiana, had returned from service in the Mexican and Civil wars with enthusiasm for the old Spanish dominion. The setting of his first novel, *The Fair God*, 1873, was the conquest of Mexico. In *Ben-Hur*, his best novel, are Wallace's faults: his lack of finish and his melodrama. Yet in it

702   From a photograph by Warren, Boston

also is his strong imagination. A song from *Ben-Hur* is included in some anthologies.

HELEN HUNT JACKSON, 1831–85

THE old régime aroused also Helen Hunt Jackson, a woman of strong ethical feelings. Reared in New England, she married first an army officer, and later William S. Jackson of Colorado Springs. Legends of her survive in Colorado and San Diego, where "Ramona's Home" is visited by tourists. Her attitude toward the Indian in her tract, *A Century of Dishonor*, 1881, and her apostolic zeal for his welfare in the novel, *Ramona*, 1884, are a strange culmination of the Indian's place in our literature. Imagine a tête-à-tête between Mrs. Jackson and James Fenimore Cooper on the redskin! After the loss of her first husband and of her children, the initials "H. H." began to appear in periodicals. Among her vagaries was a passion for anonymity, as reflected in her supposed connection with the mysterious stories signed "Saxe Holm," 1873; and for wandering, as evidenced, in varying degrees, in her books of travel, literary criticism, and poetry.

MRS. JACKSON'S *RAMONA*

MRS. JACKSON reminds us a little of Charles Kingsley in her substitution of emotion for art. Her concern for the wrongs of the Indians reached its climax in *Ramona*, the romance of life in Southern California. Although weighed down by a problem, diffuse, full of inconsistencies, this novel is always passionately sincere, and, occasionally, enthralling

703   East Veranda at Camulos Ranch.   © C. C. Pierce, Los Angeles

RICHARD MALCOLM JOHNSTON, 1822–98

WE turn from the West, with only a glance at the exciting romances of Mary Hartwell Catherwood, of Ohio, who described the St. Lawrence and the Canadian wilderness. Chronologically, Richard Malcolm Johnston of Georgia was a writer of transition. He was born in 1822. Yet his best work was done after he was sixty, and, like Page and Harris and Eggleston, he became an explorer in the newly discovered fields of fiction.

704 From the *Century Magazine*, May–Oct., 1888, engraving after a photograph, courtesy of the Century Co.

SKETCHES OF GEORGIA LIFE

JOHNSTON's precise contribution was the Georgia "cracker," whose more obvious traits he exploited in humorous sketches, essays, and caricatures. While a lawyer and school-teacher Johnston had hobnobbed with these quaint specimens. He lacks depth, but can be amazingly funny. *Dukesborough Tales*, published first in 1871 in the *Southern Magazine*, makes up an album of rural faces and scenes to which a student of the past will turn with amusement, and also with the knowledge that it adds to the gallery of frontier pictures.

705 From R. M. Johnston, *Dukesborough Tales*, New York, 1883, drawing by A. B. Frost, courtesy of Harper & Brothers

MARY NOAILLES MURFREE, "CHARLES EGBERT CRADDOCK," 1850–1922

OTHERS who portrayed various forms of this primitive life were William N. Harben, Harry Stillwell Edwards, and Sarah Barwell Elliott. In Tennessee, on the other side of the ridge which fringed Georgia, was born Mary Noailles Murfree, whose characterization of the "po' white" may prove to be lasting. In the 'seventies stories appeared in *Appleton's Journal*, each signed "Charles Egbert Craddock." Her secret was well guarded. It was with a shock that the editors of the *Atlantic Monthly* looked across their desks at a woman.

706 From a photograph, about 1880, by Soule

707 From *Harper's Weekly*, Dec. 11, 1886, drawing by Frederick Dielman, illustrating Charles Egbert Craddock, *Processioning in Pardee's Land*

TENNESSEE REALISM

MISS MURFREE's first success was *In the Tennessee Mountains*, 1884. Her novels followed swiftly, two in 1885 and seven between 1884 and 1888. A few pages are sufficient to indicate that Miss Murfree was not really a part of what she wrote. Her models were Hardy, and English realists, but she was deeply affected by the scenery of Tennessee and Georgia, and by the pathetic lives of their people, who are, after all, not very different from those described by R. M. Johnston.

708 From Constance Fenimore Woolson, *Two Women: 1862*, New York, 1890, courtesy of D. Appleton & Company

CONSTANCE FENIMORE WOOLSON, 1838–94

LATER Constance Fenimore Woolson, born in New Hampshire (a niece of Cooper), in such books as *Castle Nowhere*, 1875, and *Rodman the Keeper*, 1880, dealt with the post-war South. Mary Hallock Foote wrote of the mining camps. Henry B. Fuller pictured Chicago life.

EDWARD BELLAMY, 1850–98, AND OTHER NOVELISTS

EDWARD BELLAMY wrote *Looking Backward*, 1888. Captain Charles King described army and frontier life. Not without laurels in their own day, but far from immortal now, were Clara Louise Burnham, Frederic Jesup Stimson, Hjalmar H. Boyeson, Robert Grant, Paul Leicester Ford, Harold Frederic, Blanche Willis Howard, and Arthur Sherburne Hardy.

EDWARD PAYSON ROE, 1838–88

709   © Gramstorff Bros., Inc.

710 Tablet on a Bowlder at Roe Park, Cornwall-on-Hudson, N. Y

IN such an army it is difficult to distinguish the soldiers from the camp followers. The output of fiction was enormous, the types heterogeneous. A few leaders emerge. The masters of "moral" fiction were J. G. Holland (No. 498), and Edward Payson Roe, a minister who wrote "preachy" novels. To some modern readers such a sugar-coated tale as *Barriers Burned Away*, 1872, is insufferable, but Roe has popular successors in our own day. His novels enjoyed a huge circulation, and did good, if we except his influence on the imitators. Among his most popular books were *The Opening of a Chestnut Burr*, 1874, and *Near to Nature's Heart*, 1876.

FRANCES HODGSON BURNETT, 1849–1925

MRS. FRANCES HODGSON BURNETT, who was born in England but made her home in America, spoke to the same audience. Her stories were sentimental and often melodramatic, but she wrote skillfully. Stuart P. Sherman believes that her *Little Lord Fauntleroy*, 1887, belongs in the class of Clemens' *The Prince and The Pauper*.

711   From a photograph by Elliott and Fry, London

MRS. BURNETT'S *LITTLE LORD FAUNTLEROY*

WITHIN limits of the conventional novel Mrs. Burnett is versatile. Her first important story, *That Lass o' Lowrie's*, 1877, was a study of Lancashire folk. Other novels treat American themes. In all her career, from the novels of her youth to these last studies of English life, like *Robin*, 1922, she has written nothing so well known as *Little Lord Fauntleroy*, 1887, the delight of children during the last decade of the century.

712   From the photogravure by Goupil & Co., after the drawing by Marcus Simons, courtesy of D. Appleton & Company

SILAS WEIR MITCHELL, 1829–1914

MRS. BURNETT was romantic, and during the last years of the century the romantic impulse was concentrated in the historical novel. Stevenson and Blackmore may have set the new wave in motion; or perhaps it was the far-off wake of Sir Walter Scott's mighty ship. This was the day of the historical novel. Some of its creators were to live on, like Booth Tarkington, to be molded by new forces. About 1900 everyone was reading the historical tales of Paul Leicester Ford, Winston Churchill, and Mary Johnston. The most scholarly and the most skillful of all these writers was Silas Weir Mitchell, a physician, who wrote for the love of literature. Dr. Mitchell was a worthy descendant of the old literary groups of Philadelphia. We still read narratives like *The Adventures of François*, 1898, and *Hugh Wynne*, 1897.

713   From the portrait by Robert Vonnoh (1858–) in the Pennsylvania Academy of Fine Arts, Philadelphia

714   From a photograph by Rockwood, New York

F. MARION CRAWFORD, 1854–1909

In Boston in the early 'eighties Longfellow and Holmes and Julia Ward Howe delayed long over the dinner table, listening to brilliant talk of India life from a young man named F. Marion Crawford. He had been born in Italy and educated at Concord, Cambridge (England), Heidelberg, and Rome. He was destined to live for many years in Italy and to become the most cosmopolitan, save Henry James, of American novelists. Crawford wrote more than two score novels, five sixths of which described foreign civilizations. His *Mr. Isaacs*, 1882, is concerned with India. His novels of America exhibited little understanding of his own country. Crawford was the bitter enemy of the novel of purpose. Although he possessed a gift for realistic portraiture, his talent was inherently romantic. Hugh Walpole has recently made a strong plea for Crawford's art: his high romance, his marvelous knack of telling a story.

---

28   MR. ISAACS.   [CHAP. II.

CHAPTER II.

In India—in the plains—people rise before dawn, and it is not till after some weeks' residence in the cooler atmosphere of the mountains that they return to the pernicious habit of allowing the sun to be before them. The hours of early morning, when one either mopes about in loose flannel clothes, or goes for a gallop on the green *maidán*, are without exception the most delicious of the day. I shall have occasion hereafter to describe the morning's proceedings in the plains. On the day after the events recorded in the last chapter I awoke as usual at five o'clock, and meandered out on to the verandah to have a look at the hills, so novel and delicious a sight after the endless flats of the northwest provinces. It was still nearly dark, but there was a faint light in the east, which rapidly grew as I watched it, till, turning the angle of the house, I distinguished a snow-peak over the tops of the dark rhododendrons, and, while I gazed, the first tinge of distant dawning caught the summit, and the beautiful hill blushed, as a fair woman, at the kiss of the awakening sun. The old story, the heaven wooing the earth with a wondrous shower of gold.

---

715   Page from F. Marion Crawford, *Mr. Isaacs*, New York, 1883

STORIES OF OLD ROME AND OF THE EAST

Crawford knew Rome best. It is difficult to believe that such a trilogy as *Saracinesca*, 1887, *Sant' Ilario*, 1889, and *Don Orsino*, 1892, with their galleries of old Roman characters, will ever be totally forgotten. Yet he writes almost as well of the East, or of other parts of Europe. *Greifenstein*, 1889, *Via Crucis*, 1898, and *The Cigarette Maker's Romance*, 1890, are full of the elements which he said should constitute the novel — clever dialogue, swift action, character — justifying his own theory that the novel should always be "a pocket-drama."

716   From F. Marion Crawford, *Saracinesca*, New York, 1899, drawing by Orson Lowell (1871–), courtesy of The Macmillan Company

STEPHEN CRANE, 1870–1900

STEPHEN CRANE, too, whose intensity and subtlety still command many readers, was romantic, without the conscious strength of Crawford. He was driven by circumstances into a kind of false realism. A journalist, he saw service in the wars between Greece and Turkey, and between Spain and America. Crane knew exaggerated moods, as in his *Red Badge of Courage*, 1895, but in spite of haste and excitability he reveals a fine intelligence, and he was far in advance of his own generation.

717   Courtesy of D. Appleton & Company

F. HOPKINSON SMITH, 1838–1915

MANY more novelists, for example, Margaret Deland and Frank Norris, belong to the last years of the century. Apart from the few leaders, the characteristics of these are as various as their environments. A complicating factor in an appraisal is the devotion of many, such as Stephen Crane and F. Hopkinson Smith, to the short story. Smith, lighthouse builder, novelist, artist, and writer of short stories, was the author of some delightful narratives, notably *Colonel Carter of Cartersville*, 1891, and *Caleb West*, 1898.

718   From a photograph taken at Dives, Normandy, courtesy of the Authors Club, New York

EDWARD EVERETT HALE, 1822–1909

AFTER the Civil War the short story form, since the days of Poe a favorite American venture, became epidemic. One may trace its rise, with many a vicissitude, from Irving to Poe, from Poe to Bret Harte, and from Harte to the modern tale. Poe himself thought this interest due to the nervous, intense spirit of the American—no leisurely Victorian novels for him! After Harte there arose conflict between the careful technique of Henry James and William Dean Howells, and the virile Western sketch. By 1885 the short story was a characteristic product of American literature in the work of men like Stockton, Bunner, or Garland. During the Civil War, however, Edward Everett Hale had published *The Man Without a Country*, 1863, a short story suggestive of the finish which this form had already achieved.

719   From a photograph by G. C. Cox, New York

720 From Hale, *The Man Without a Country*, Boston, 1889, drawing by F. T. Merrill

HALE'S *THE MAN WITHOUT A COUNTRY*

HALE was a Unitarian minister of Boston, and gained distinction as a humanitarian, editor, and writer. As a historian he has not lived, but the dramatic scenes in this story and its unique theme have made Philip Nolan's fate of exile and repentance known to every American.

JAMES LANE ALLEN, 1849–1925

IN the South of the 'eighties there were echoes of the local novel in Grace King's short stories of Creole society, and in the tales of Louisiana by Kate Chopin. Easily the best, however, of the short story writers of the South was James Lane Allen, a thorough student of literature and of the art of writing. Allen loved Kentucky, and its Blue Grass regions were symbols of his spiritual quest. He was an idealist. *The Choir Invisible*, 1897, *A Kentucky Cardinal*, 1895, *The Mettle of the Pasture*, 1903, *The Reign of Law*, 1900, are records of his questionings about life.

721   © Brown Brothers

FRANK R. STOCKTON, 1834–1902

FRANK R. STOCKTON, however, whose tales Robert Louis Stevenson worshiped, was in quest of fun. When asked whether it was *The Lady or the Tiger?*, 1884, he used to reply gravely: "I don't know." And husbands and wives of his generation have never, in their discussions, arrived at a better answer. Stockton was born in Philadelphia, where he was for a time engaged in newspaper work. His first volume of stories, 1869, received scant attention.

722   © Brown Brothers

STOCKTON'S *RUDDER GRANGE*

YET such stories as *The Lady or the Tiger?* or those in *Rudder Grange*, 1879, evinced Stockton's comprehension of human nature. He was primarily a whimsical soul, naming his chickens Richard Watson Gilder and Mary Mapes Dodge, and depending for his effects in fiction on similar absurdities. Stockton was a New York magazinist and an incurable writer of juvenile tales, whose traits often intruded into his stories for adults. His more serious work, such as *The Late Mrs. Null*, 1886, and *The Hundredth Man*, 1887, has gone the way of all commonplace novels. He published some forty volumes.

723 From Stockton, *Rudder Grange*, New York, 1885, after the drawing by A. B. Frost, by permission of Charles Scribner's Sons

724 © Jarvis White Art Company

ALICE FRENCH, "OCTAVE THANET," 1850–

SOMEWHAT later appeared the stories of the West, by Alice French, or "Octave Thanet." Her work was uneven, and a *penchant* for sociology finally smothered a moderate talent for the short story. Her best writing was done after observation of rural life in Arkansas, where she has spent a large part of her life. She is the author of *Knitters in the Sun*, 1887, *Otto the Knight, and Other Trans-Mississippi Stories*, 1891, *We All*, 1891, *Stories of a Western Town*, 1892; *And The Captain Answered*, 1917.

HAMLIN GARLAND, 1860–

725 From a photograph by permission of Hamlin Garland

YET what realistic power Alice French has might serve as a foil to the greater talent of Hamlin Garland. Rowland E. Robinson writing of Vermont, or Philander Deming describing the Adirondack country, and many others, deserve only casual mention beside certain merciless pictures of life in Dakota, Minnesota, and Wisconsin, from Hamlin Garland. Learning of Garland's life, one is not surprised that he was influenced by the naturalistic school. Born on a Wisconsin farm, his boyhood was a series of migrations westward. One memorable day in reading *Hearth and Home*, he stumbled on *The Hoosier Schoolmaster*. His years in Boston as student and teacher meant a final breaking with the old life. From this time on he was to describe it ruthlessly, often with a bitterness that we can understand but not always condone.

726 From a photograph by permission of Hamlin Garland

GARLAND'S EARLY TALES OF THE WEST

THE hard realism in Garland's early work has softened. He has written numerous stories and novels — these are less effective — not only of the West of his youth, but of more remote regions. Altogether he has told many a good tale, but we recall sympathetically Marion Crawford's distaste for moral enthusiasm in the novel. Garland is too ready to teach us something. Aside from a novel like *The Captain of the Gray Horse Troop*, 1902, or the remarkable autobiography, *A Son of the Middle Border*, 1917, we turn for his best work to those books of the 'nineties: *Main-Travelled Roads*, 1890, or *Prairie Folks*, 1892.

727 © Brown Brothers

728   © Brown Brothers

RICHARD HARDING DAVIS, 1864–1916

IN the same years the short story was being cheapened by scores of magazines. It became a journalistic feature. We have seen that men like Stephen Crane were aware of this opportunity. It now remains to mention a master of the plated theatrical short story, a form that has, apparently, come to stay in American journalism. Richard Harding Davis has no title to creative literature. He was a type. He merely did better than anyone else what scores of clever young newspaper cubs were attempting. He knew, and could describe for his morning paper, any corner of the known world. Wars were his pastime. All through his work, from *Gallegher and Other Stories*, 1891, to the later *Somewhere in France*, 1915, we hear the anxious clatter of the printing press. Davis had a mechanical mastery of the short story, and belongs to the school of O. Henry.

HENRY CUYLER BUNNER, 1855–96

OMITTING Ambrose Bierce, who has often been compared with Poe, we may pause briefly at Henry Cuyler Bunner, a journalist, too, and long editor of *Puck*, but blessed with a strain of the romancer. In some respects his *Story of a New York House*, 1887,

729   No. 7 State Street, New York, Scene of Bunner's *Story of a New York House*. © Keystone View Co.

with its characterization of humble city dwellers, is an index to his interests. His short stories, especially *Short Sixes*, 1890, and *More Short Sixes*, 1894, are alive with the tricks of American journalism, but they have also restraint and condensation, born perhaps of the French school.

CHARLES DUDLEY WARNER, 1829–1900

LOOKING back at the years since 1870 the student of American literature may feel momentarily that repose vanished with the Civil War. This seems particularly true of prose forms other than fiction. There were histories, and innumerable articles, but the old sentimental essay of travel, of dreamy reminiscence, of men and manners had died away. Only Charles Dudley Warner and a few others renew the Irving tradition kept on through Ik Marvel and George William Curtis. He collaborated with Mark Twain in *The Gilded Age*, and succeeded Curtis in the "Easy Chair" of *Harper's Weekly*.

730   Charles Dudley Warner, from a photograph by Rockwood, New York

WARNER'S ESSAYS

WARNER was born in Massachusetts, and was educated at Hamilton College and at the University of Pennsylvania. After four years as a Chicago lawyer, he came east to engage in journalism. He wrote abundantly, always without a hint of genius, but his mood of kindly, humorous observation created good books for the fireside: *My Summer in a Garden*, 1870; *Backlog Studies*, 1872; *Being a Boy*, 1877; and reminiscences of his journeys. His appeal resides in his naturalness of manner, and his lovable simplicity.

731 Warner's Boyhood Home, Charlemont, Mass., the scene of *Being a Boy*.
© Clifton Johnson

LAFCADIO HEARN, 1850–1904

THE variety in prose writing is suggested by two such opposites as Charles Dudley Warner and Lafcadio Hearn. Between the conventional New Englander and this romantic product of Irish, Greek, Japanese, and American

732 From Yone Noguchi, *Lafcadio Hearn in Japan*, Yokohama, 1911, after the drawing by Shoshu Saito

influences are all the prose impulses of the period. After his education in France and England, Hearn set out on the wanderings which took him to New York, New Orleans, Cincinnati, and, finally, to Japan, where he founded his household, and dreamed his intense dreams of art.

Compared with the prolific Japanese period, Hearn's early writings seem fragmentary. Yet in them are his passion for color, and his strange exotic moods, without parallel in American literature. *Gombo Zhêbes*, 1885, was a book of proverbs from the Creole. *Chita*, 1889, pictured feverishly the life of old New Orleans, and *Two Years in the French West Indies*, 1890, described another languorous pause in his odyssey.

733 From a photograph, courtesy of Houghton Mifflin Company

A CITIZEN OF JAPAN

AFTER 1894 numerous volumes appeared, steeped in oriental life, oriental religion, and, especially, far-eastern art. The bright color and strained feeling in some of these passes belief. Never did the East and West meet more fervidly than in Lafcadio Hearn. He became a Japanese citizen, married a Japanese, and was buried with Buddhist rites.

734 Funeral of Lafcadio Hearn. © Brown Brothers

JOHN FISKE, 1842–1901

IN history no one appeared to rival the achievements of the Cambridge group. John Hay and John Fiske were capable historians, but not Bancrofts or Parkmans. Hubert Howe Bancroft had begun the chronicles of the new West in his *Native Races of the Pacific States*, 1874–76, and the *History of the Pacific States of North America*, 1882–90. John Fiske, born at Hartford, a graduate of Harvard, and long a resident of Cambridge, was less an expert scholar than an interpreter of history and science. He lectured widely on subjects which received fuller expression in his books, such as *The Unseen World*, 1876, *Darwinism*, 1879, *American Political Ideas*, 1885, *The American Revolution*, 1891, and *The Beginnings of New England*, 1889. The last book still retains an influence upon our generation.

735   © Brown Brothers

736   Horace Howard Furness.
          © Gutekunst

HORACE HOWARD FURNESS, 1833–1912, SHAKESPEAREAN SCHOLAR

SCHOLARSHIP, however, was both wider and deeper than in the earlier era. Besides the aggressive Shakespearean quarrels of Richard Grant White, editor, satirist, and novelist, there was the monumental *Variorum* edition of Shakespeare by Horace Howard Furness.

737   Charles Eliot Norton, 1827–1908, courtesy
          of Houghton Mifflin Company

CHARLES ELIOT NORTON AND EDWIN P. WHIPPLE

LITERARY scholarship and criticism recall the cultivated personality of Charles Eliot Norton, professor at Harvard, editor, among other books, of the letters of Carlyle and Emerson, translator of Dante, and intimate of the Cambridge group. We puzzle over the reputation of the critic, Edwin Percy Whipple, with his didactic strain and his occasional absurdities. Wrongly, however. His *Essays and Reviews*, 1848, if we except Lowell's work, was, for this time, a relatively remarkable book of criticism. There are, moreover, good things in much of Whipple's later work, such as *Literature of the Age of Elizabeth*, 1869, or *American Literature, and Other Papers*, 1887.

738   E. P. Whipple, 1817–86, courtesy of
               Houghton Mifflin Company

RICHARD HENRY STODDARD, 1825–1903

AMONG the lesser poets of the age was a disciple of the old tradition who lived on into the twentieth century quite immune from the vital forces around him. This was Richard Henry Stoddard, during the latter part of his life a literary celebrity. Stoddard was almost wholly self-educated, and besides other humble employments had shod horses and painted carriages. He had secured a position in the New York customhouse (1853–70) through the influence of Whipple and Hawthorne. While earning his living in various ways, Stoddard also wrote for the New York *World*. Later, he served on the *Mail and Express*, "the mule in distress," as he called it — one of the ghosts of his wit which questions the justice of his reputation as a talker. His prose is trivial. Only his poetry lifts Stoddard above mediocrity.

739   From Richard Henry Stoddard, *Songs of Summers*, Boston, 1857, engraving by Capewell & Kummel

740   R. H. Stoddard and Elizabeth Barstow Stoddard from a photograph by Rockwood, in the possession of the Authors Club, New York

A WRITER OF LYRICS

IN all of Stoddard's lyrics is a shade of self-consciousness. Perhaps there is meaning in his remark to a friend: "Well, now I am going home, and I am going to sit down and write one of the damnedest, sweetest, little religious poems you have ever read." Yet this is unfair. His prose is stuffy, and the man is self-important, but write lyrics he could and did — lyrics free from all moralizing and excesses of language. Many of them betray their origins — the poets of England — but they have also the melody and polish of their masters, and, besides, Stoddard's personal feeling, as in *The Flight of Youth:*

We are stronger, and are better,
Under manhood's sterner reign:
Still we feel that something sweet
Followed youth with flying feet,
And will never come again.

Something beautiful is vanished,
And we sigh for it in vain:
We behold it everywhere,
On the earth, and in the air,
But it never comes again.

EDMUND CLARENCE STEDMAN, 1833–1908

STODDARD remained true to the poetic ideals of the good Queen's time, but Edmund Clarence Stedman, though he never deserted, wavered. When Lowell disapproved of his orthodox poem, *Alectryon*, Stedman finally agreed with his critic who said, with characteristic vigor: "I don't believe in these modern antiques, — no . . . not in any of 'em . . . the material you work in is dead." Under the impact of the Civil War Stedman ended his poetry of conventional art. For he was capable of feeling the realities of the new poetry though he would not write it. He turned for self-expression to literary criticism, in which he was perhaps the most useful craftsman of the century.

741   Stedman at fifty, from a photograph by Mora

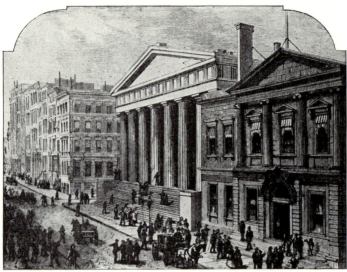

742   From *The Union of American Poetry and Art*, edited by John Jones Platt,
Cincinnati, 1880

PAN IN WALL STREET

STEDMAN was a New Englander. Born in Hartford, Connecticut, he enjoyed a merry but brief sojourn at Yale. After experiments in business and newspaper work he became a New York broker, later earning the nickname which he detested, "the banker-poet." It is a little startling to discover that these lyrics were written by a member of the Stock Exchange. *Pan in Wall Street* indeed! Stedman was sincere in his assertion that literature was his real interest. In 1900 he retired to devote to it his remaining years.

Just where the Treasury's marble front
  Looks over Wall Street's mingled nations;
Where Jews and Gentiles most are wont
  To throng for trade and last quotations;
Where, hour by hour, the rates of gold
  Outrival, in the ears of people,
The quarter-chimes, serenely tolled
  From Trinity's undaunted steeple,

Even there I heard a strange, wild strain
  Sound high above the modern clamor,
Above the cries of greed and gain,
  The curbstone war, the auction's hammer;
And swift, on Music's misty ways,
  It led, from all this strife for millions,
To ancient, sweet-do-nothing days
  Among the kirtle-robed Sicilians.

743   Stedman at seventy, from a photograph

STEDMAN AS CRITIC AND POET

As a critic Stedman is interesting and, except for a few idiosyncrasies of taste, reliable. Yet for a modern reader he starts few new trains of thought. He was right in thinking that his best work was on Poe, whose works he edited with George Woodberry. In *Victorian Poets*, 1875, *Poets of America*, 1885, and *The Nature and Elements of Poetry*, 1892, may be found the bulk of his sane criticism. In American literature Stedman's name is omnipresent as a critic, and his services as editor were basic. His *A Library of American Literature*, 1887–90, done in collaboration with Ellen M. Hutchinson, is still a valuable reference book, and *An American Anthology*, 1900, though somewhat clumsy in arrangement and, of course, not abreast of our time, must be consulted for the lesser poets. As a poet Stedman lacks the delicacy of Stoddard, but when once free from the Tennysonian strain his verse has manly strength and sincerity. *Kearny at Seven Pines* and the battle songs set the heart beating, and there is passion in the lyric: *Thou art mine, thou hast given thy word*. It is credible that when Stedman's criticism and anthologies have been superseded, his memory may live in these few lyrics.

744   From Stedman, *The Star Bearer*, Boston, 1888

THOMAS BAILEY ALDRICH, 1836–1907

A WRITER linked with Stoddard and Stedman during his early years, but far more important, was Thomas Bailey Aldrich, a poet as significant as some mentioned in the preceding chapter, but not representative of a new tendency. He was inferior to Longfellow, whose influence over him never ceased, and whose poetry, he said, spoke to him "like a human voice." He shut his eyes to the new America. "Whitman's manner," he declared with absurd sincerity, "is a hollow affectation, and represents neither the man nor the time."

745 Aldrich at the age of nineteen, from a photograph by permission of Mrs. Thomas Bailey Aldrich

EARLY YEARS

A STUDY of Aldrich's active, happy life makes an admirable approach to the more conservative aspects of American literature. *The Story of a Bad Boy*, 1869, not only reflects Aldrich's humor and deeper feeling, but also sketches accurately his early years in Portsmouth, New Hampshire, and New Orleans. At the age of sixteen he entered business in New York. Seven years later he was well-known as a poet and man of letters, besides being accepted personally by Willis, Stoddard, Taylor, and the New York "Bohemians" of the 'fifties.

746 Aldrich at the age of thirty-two, from a photograph by permission of Mrs. Thomas Bailey Aldrich

BOSTON DAYS

LATER he came to Boston. For the poet it was a momentous removal; it meant an alteration in Aldrich himself. In the New England air the "apricots and dewberries" of his writing, which Oliver Wendell Holmes had deplored, did not flourish. In Aldrich this change of sky seems to have been also a change of mind. His writing became more severe, self-contained. From 1881 to 1890 he was editor of the *Atlantic Monthly*. His life at Ponkapog, and his years of travel show him beloved, and a leader in literature. Aldrich wrote much that has been forgotten, such as *Mercedes, a Drama in Two Acts*, 1895. His *Works* were published in 1896.

747 Aldrich's House at Ponkapog, Mass., from R. H. Stoddard, *Poets' Homes*, Boston, 1877

MARJORIE DAW

748 From W. D. Howells, *Heroines of Fiction*, 1901,
drawing by H. C. Christy, by permission of Harper &
Brothers

ALDRICH'S *MARJORIE DAW*

THE life with his friends at Pfaff's restaurant and about the city had ended suddenly. As editor of the *Saturday Press* and war correspondent, for a short time, in the service of the *Tribune*, he was connected with New York till 1865, when he left for Boston, to edit *Every Saturday*. The magazine office adjoined that of the *Atlantic Monthly*, and in this office was young Howells. Boston readily adopted Aldrich. "Though I am not genuine Boston," he used to say, "I am Boston-plated." Besides personal charm, Aldrich possessed a sense of humor, and some of his letters to Mark Twain might have had the latter's signature. Its best flavor is found in *The Story of a Bad Boy*. His other prose has proved ephemeral, such as *Ponkapog Papers*, 1903, though *Marjorie Daw*, 1873, a technical masterpiece in the short story form, with its surprise ending, was at once translated into other languages.

749 Aldrich at seventy. © Alice Boughton

ALDRICH THE POET

ALDRICH was indeed a man of the world, but, so Whittier thought, first of all he was a poet. His imperfect sympathies with his age have been suggested by his thinking Whitman a charlatan. The fault of his poetry, especially in earlier poems, few of which were included in the last two volumes, is its cloying quality. Hawthorne was kind enough to tell Aldrich that it was "rich, sweet, and magnetic," but the caustic Doctor of the Hub was kinder when he urged him to conquer his "tendency to vanilla-flavored adjectives and patchouli-scented participles." "Your danger," wrote another friend, "is on the sensuous side of the intellect."

750   From Thomas Bailey Aldrich, *The Story of a Bad Boy*, Boston, 1870

THE LITERARY ARTIST

IT was characteristic of Aldrich's ideals that he heeded a warning pertaining to art, and disregarded the threatening storm of the new literature, which he viewed with some contempt. With high standards of art, he came to despise his juvenilia, and expunged with a ruthless hand. Such poems as *Baby Bell*, *The Course of True Love Never Did Run Smooth* are very different from the later poems.

ALDRICH — AN ESTIMATE

SOME have fancied that they found literary forbears for Aldrich in such poets as Herrick, a lyrist he loved, and perhaps there is truth in these imaginings. Not without human feeling, he was, nevertheless, not richly endowed as an interpreter of life. He refines rather in lovely and finished verse the normal moods. Aldrich is first of all a craftsman and literary artist.

751   The Aldrich Memorial, Portsmouth, N. H., courtesy of Rev. Alfred Gooding

GEORGE HENRY BOKER, 1823–90

GEORGE H. BOKER was a wealthy Pennsylvanian who served as United States minister to Russia and Turkey. Boker aimed high, writing numerous romantic tragedies, but these and his short poems have only one merit — enthusiasm.

752   From *The Bryant Festival at "The Century,"* New York, 1865, illustrated edition, after a photograph

RICHARD WATSON GILDER, 1844–1909

IN later years the minor poetry either followed the old laws so dear to Aldrich, as in Richard Watson Gilder; or succumbed to the new influence, as in Irwin Russell; or struggled between the two, as in the work of James Whitcomb Riley. Gilder was a practical altruist in many public causes. He left only verse, most of it collected in *Poems*, 1887. It was his idealism which did so much for *Scribner's Monthly*, and for the *Century Magazine* when he was on their editorial staffs. Writers gathered at the Gilder "studio." The sincerity of Gilder's fine nature is evident now in his verse. He had elegance, too, in his writing but the most devoted friend can hardly assert more.

753   From the portrait of Richard Watson Gilder by Cecilia Beaux in possession of Rodman Gilder, New York

754   From a photograph, courtesy of Houghton Mifflin Company

EDWARD ROWLAND SILL, 1841–87

ONE finds few references, either among the New York or the Boston literary groups, to Edward Rowland Sill, a Connecticut poet of slender, but exquisite talent. Aldrich thought him an "ideal contributor"; Sill's slight output was even in quality. After graduation from Yale in 1861 as class poet, he taught for a time in the University of California. He died in Ohio. Sill's literary ideals were unruffled by the West. He writes of nature; of questions of conscience; and of God as a Puritan might write. His poetry is usually in quiet key, but describes often his struggles of the spirit. His best known poem is *The Fool's Prayer.*

> Our faults no tenderness should ask,
>   The chastening stripes must cleanse them all;
> But for our blunders — oh, in shame
>   Before the eyes of heaven we fall.
>
> Earth bears no balsam for mistakes;
>   Men crown the knave, and scourge the tool
> That did his will; but Thou, O Lord,
>   Be merciful to me, a fool!

EMMA LAZARUS, 1849–87

EMMA LAZARUS, too, was influenced by the thought of New England. She was a friend of Emerson. Possibly her best poem is that addressed to him in *Admetus, and Other Poems,* 1871. Her life, however, was mainly devoted to her race; she had been born of a New York Jewish family. Hence her undying passion for Heine, hence her *Songs of a Semite,* 1882. Her dramas, *The Spagnoletto,* 1876, with a setting of seventeenth-century Italy, *The Dance to Death,* 1882, on the Thuringian Jews, are passable, but inferior to her narrative poems, and both are less effective than a few passionate lyrics such as *The Crowing of the Red Cock, The New Ezekiel,* and *The Banner of the Jew:*

> Oh, for Jerusalem's trumpet now,
>   To blow a blast of shattering power,
> To wake the sleepers high and low,
>   And rouse them to the urgent hour!

Songs of a Semite:

THE DANCE TO DEATH,

AND OTHER POEMS,

BY

EMMA LAZARUS,

AUTHOR OF "ADMETUS, AND OTHER POEMS," "ALIDE," "TRANSLATIONS FROM HEINE," ETC.

—

NEW YORK
OFFICE OF THE AMERICAN HEBREW,
498-500 THIRD AVENUE.
1882.

755   Title-page of the issue, 1882

CELIA THAXTER, 1835–94

MEANWHILE near Portsmouth, Celia Thaxter, the daughter of a lighthouse keeper of the Isles of Shoals, lived and wrote of the sea. Lowell discovered her, and *Among the Isles of Shoals,* 1873, essays, appeared in the *Atlantic Monthly.* Miss Thaxter had not the skill of the city poets nor was she moved by the new impulses. But the sea is hers; she is part of it. In her poems one sees the sweep of sandy shore, with its flitting birds, the white lighthouses, "the close-reefed vessels," and feels the "warm, wild, rainy wind" of May. American poetry will always include *The Sandpiper, Seaward, The Wreck of the Pocahontas.*

756   From a photograph by Warren, Boston

THOMAS BUCHANAN READ, 1822–72

AMONG lesser men who wrote with ideals not dissimilar to Bayard Taylor's and R. H. Stoddard's was Thomas Buchanan Read, sculptor, painter, poet, and prose writer, now remembered only, in spite of fecund pen, for his lyric, *Sheridan's Ride*, 1865.

MADISON CAWEIN, 1865–1914

FROM the South came the opulent poetry of Madison J. Cawein (No. 758), and that of Robert Burns Wilson, not unlike him in temper. Richard Hovey, singer of Dartmouth, was one of the most graceful imitators of Tennyson.

757 © Gramstorff Bros., Inc.

758 From the portrait, 1914, by J. Bernhard Alberts (1886–)

EMILY DICKINSON, 1830–86

OF other poets who clung to the old traditions of poetry one might reread Mary Mapes Dodge, with her verses and stories for children, and her *Minuet;* or the New Englander, Emily Dickinson, with her short, flower-like stanzas; or Edith Matilda Thomas of Ohio. Emily Dickinson was born and lived at Amherst, Massachusetts. Most of her poetry was published posthumously, and her short, penetrating judgments on life in verse have only recently become known and valued at their worth. *Poems by Emily Dickinson*, edited by two of her friends, appeared in 1890.

IRWIN RUSSELL, 1853–79

THE poets who celebrated the new ideas in American literature were less distinguished, and, on the whole, less numerous than the realistic writers of fiction. We should look back once more to the southern group, of which Lanier was the leader, at Irwin Russell, resembling

759 From an early photograph, retouched by Laura Coombs Hills, published in Martha Dickinson Bianchi, *Life and Letters of Emily Dickinson*, Boston, 1924, courtesy of Madame Bianchi and Houghton Mifflin Company

760 From the bust by Elsie Ward, in the Mississippi Hall of Fame

the older poet. Russell's life was almost as active as Lanier's: he moved from city to city, trying various occupations, and he was popular in humble communities because of his banjo. Later the *Century* recognized him as a pioneer in the poetry of negro dialect.

"Balance all!"—now, step out rightly"

761   From Irwin Russell, *Christmas Night in the Quarters and Other Poems*, New York, 1917, drawing by E. W. Kemble, by permission of the Century Company

RUSSELL'S POEMS OF NEGRO LIFE

RUSSELL was widely read. One source of inspiration was Robert Burns. No tale was too humble, no dialect of the negro too crude for his verses. Unquestionably he felt the sentimental appeal of the negro, but he wrote as he saw, and his darkies roll their eyes, croon, and speak their vernacular with distinctness. Joel Chandler Harris in an introduction to Russell's poems, quoted by Professor F. L. Pattee, says: "Irwin Russell was among the first — if not the very first — of southern writers to appreciate the literary possibilities of the negro character, and of the unique relations existing between the two races before the war, and among the first to develop them."

762   © James Notman Studio, Boston

JOHN BOYLE O'REILLY, 1844–90

IN the West John J. Piatt, who had been co-author with Howells, attempted to put rustic subjects into his poetry without breaking from the old conventions. John Boyle O'Reilly wrote his *Songs of the Southern Seas*, 1873. He was an Irishman, brought to Australia for treason, who succeeded in escaping to America. He became editor of the Boston *Pilot*. Among his writings were: *Songs, Legends, and Ballads*, 1878, and *Essays and Sketches*, 1888.

763   From a photograph by Sarony, New York

WILL CARLETON, 1845–1912

IN a sense it is absurd to align Will Carleton with the poets of the new America. He was too deeply influenced by Longfellow. Yet he lacks utterly the finish and artistic ideals of the Aldrich school, and his subjects are, after all, those of humble life. He received his education at Hillsdale College, in Michigan, and later spent twenty years, quite unknown, on a lonely farm in that state. He then led a roving life of journalism. He was connected with newspapers in Detroit, Chicago, and, finally, in Boston and New York. He became a successful lecturer. He came in, as it were, with the ballad, *Betsey and I Are Out*, published in the *Toledo Blade*, 1871.

GONE WITH A HANDSOMER MAN

CARLETON followed up this success with *Farm Ballads*, 1875, and with more poems for the masses, such as *Over the Hill to the Poorhouse*, *Gone with a Handsomer Man*, and *The New Church Organ*.

"WHY, JOHN, WHAT A LITTER HERE! YOU'VE THROWN THINGS ALL AROUND!"

764   From *Harper's Weekly*, July 15, 1871

765   Carleton late in life. © Brown Brothers

POEMS FOR THE PEOPLE

"These poems have been written," says Carleton, ". . . amid the rush and roar of railroad travel . . . and in the editor's sanctum, where the dainty feet of the Muses do not often deign to tread. But," he adds, ". . . The People are, after all, the true critics." Such a confession explains Carleton's point of view.

JAMES WHITCOMB RILEY, 1849–1916

JAMES WHITCOMB RILEY, like Carleton, loves the humble poeple of the new America, and like him, is not quite ingenuous; is, in brief, another sentimentalist. Aldrich disapproved of Riley because, as it seemed to him, he vulgarized the English language. Yet Riley became famous. Nearly every town in Indiana, Riley's native state, has claimed the original of *The Old Swimmin'-Hole.*

766   © Brown Brothers

RILEY'S DIALECT POEMS

RILEY, though a lawyer's son, had wandered about the country, trying his hand at various trades. He finally found his niche as a journalist. Under pseudonyms he won a reputation as a dialect poet and humorist which was to

767   From James Whitcomb Riley, *A Child World*, Indianapolis, 1877, drawing by Will Vawter, by permission of the Bobbs-Merrill Company

last. He was often in demand as a lecturer and reader in American vernacular. "Don't fail to get Riley," said Bunner in preparation for some readings in New York in 1883. Bunner had observed the success of *The Old Swimmin'-Hole and 'Leven More Poems.* Similar volumes followed.

768   The Old Swimmin'-Hole, drawing by Will Vawter, by permission
of the Bobbs-Merrill Company

770   © Brown Brothers

RILEY'S SENTIMENTAL VERSE

RILEY has much to answer for as the begetter or energizer of the newspaper poetry which fills our columns with rippling rhymes. He softens strong old men to tears of sentiment. Yet Aldrich thought there was a finer vein in Riley. When not writing with self-consciousness, he could be genuinely affecting.

769   © Brown Brothers

EUGENE FIELD, RILEY, AND BILL NYE

IN both Carleton and Riley we have noticed a preoccupation with subjects for the people, and conscious sentiment. They represent a characteristic American attitude toward poetry during the last quarter of the century. These tendencies were epitomized with more originality in Eugene Field, who had the same point of view, but far more talent, and a real gift of humor — a humor finer than Bill Nye's, and akin to that of the robust Christopher North.

EUGENE FIELD, 1850-95

FIELD is associated with Chicago, but he was born in St. Louis, and his parents were from New England. His education included stays at a New England college and in the West. He traveled abroad, and served on newspapers in western cities. His career began with *Sharps and Flats,* a column of poetry, quips, and humorous observation in the Chicago *Daily News.* His life was as merry as a musical comedy; he jested with his associates, with the public, and with a congenial spirit of the past, Horace. By the 'eighties Field's books were under way; *The Denver Tribune Primer,* 1882, and *Culture's Garland,* 1887, facetiæ. Afterward he wrote such prose as *A Little Book of Profitable Tales,* 1889, and *Love Songs of Childhood,* 1894. Children still like *Wynken, Blynken, and Nod* and *Seein' Things at Night.* He was primarily a journalist, not a man of letters, but he kept sweet, and his sentiment often rests on an understanding of life.

CHAPTER XI

MODERN AMERICAN LETTERS

AS we look about us to-day we discover what is true of any age, that there are many writers who have outlived their most characteristic work. Although Bryant, for example, lived on till 1878, no one would identify his poetry with the realism or romance of the new literature after 1870. Bryant belongs to the first half of the century. So in our time live distinguished writers whose aims and manner are more typical of the two decades before 1900 than the two which follow. Some men of letters die, like Byron, in the full current of thought and feeling which first inspired them. Others live on, like Landor, and behold the new order. Although we do not cease to honor them, the work of Winston Churchill in fiction or George Woodberry in criticism belongs to the previous generation in American literature. So William Dean Howells lived to see his fickle public forsake him for more daring insurgents than himself. Dreiser, Mencken, Sandburg — these represent more nearly what is new in the spirit of American letters in the twentieth century.

Both groups of writers deserve consideration here, the survivors of the past, and the new authors. Not every writer can be named, but we shall study all, alive or not, who did characteristic work for American literature after 1900, whether in the conventional forms like William Vaughn Moody or through the new impulses, like Edgar Lee Masters. In respect to the meaning and future of such impulses this chapter will necessarily be speculative. And it must be brief.

On the horizon of early twentieth-century literature were certain mirages. One of these was the historical romance. In their easy-chairs, unconscious victims of a Stevenson or, later, of an Anthony Hope Hawkins, Americans lived through the Revolution with Richard Carvel; or fought duels with Monsieur Beaucaire; or won thrones and princesses in mythical Teutonic kingdoms. No period of the glamorous past escaped; no costume, whether powdered wig and rapier or frontier buckskin. Yet this was an illusion, a ribbon of cloud between days of reality. The literalists were not to be waved aside by *Alice of Old Vincennes* or *The Cardinal's Snuffbox* or the romances of Owen Wister or Robert W. Chambers. So in criticism and poetry. Critics who judged books as respectable tailors sample tweeds continued to speak gravely — oracular Whipples. Yet now, in the decade after 1900, original minds were attacking the canons of the past, breaking with them, insulting them. Realism again. Even more shadowy was the mirage of convention and sentimentalism in poetry. More than any other form American poetry was to be individualistic.

Now were evident the consequences of the independence of Emerson, the nationalism of Whitman, the insolence of Mark Twain. Much of this assurance had root in material prosperity, and in our position in the world. It is unnecessary to dwell, like Macaulay in nineteenth-century England, on our railroads, manufactures, and achievements. Yet these do affect a nation's literary consciousness. After all, we are three centuries old. The traditions — they were traditions now — of our frontier, our sea, our farms, were unique among all literatures. And in the cities men could allude to continuous literary backgrounds. This does not imply that our literary consciousness rested on pride in the past, or that our literature was complacent. Precisely because it was realistic and also self-critical it was different from that of the preceding century. We now relied far more on our own judgments. A century earlier we were cocksure of our greatness in every way. As Matthew Arnold observed in the 'eighties, we had not a single doubt. Now the arrogance is not less in material affairs, but to-day every American hears talk of our intellectual shortcomings. About these we speculate rather painfully. This is significant, but so is the fact that we mean to remedy them not by the opinions of Europe, but by our own. It is an age of introspection, but also of self-reliance.

The twentieth-century novel shows the dominance of realism, and indicates the underlying spirit of questioning. These writers seem to say: "This is America. Make what you can of it." Just as certainly they add: "Let us work out our own destiny." After 1900, American themes were a matter of course. Forms and technique of the earlier realism survived. Thus the romantic coloring of realistic material continued to be a popular mode, as in the narratives of brutal, adventurous sea life from Jack London, the most theatrical figure of the early years. The humor and journalization of the short story reached a peak in O. Henry. In Frank Norris realism developed into naturalism. This was during the first decade. In the second the realistic and naturalistic were to assume highly specialized forms, as in the fiction of Sinclair Lewis or Theodore Dreiser or Sherwood Anderson, or in the drama of Eugene O'Neill.

This realism, which may be said to have had its origins in the new literature of the pioneer West, was encouraged by Howells, although he repressed and tamed it. It is easy to trace, through various realists after Howells, its increase in daring, and its expansion into naturalism. Mary E. Wilkins Freeman peered into the corners of New England villages. Hamlin Garland gave the lie to romance in his pictures of the Middle West. Margaret Deland offered her analysis of certain traits of American character. Stephen Crane dealt reticence a smashing blow with such a story as *Maggie*. Frank Norris began an endless series of novels on politics. The transition is obvious to the excitement of Jack London, the fleshly naturalism of Dreiser, or the bitter controversy of Upton Sinclair. With the exception of Crane, who died early, these writers are connected with both the 'nineties and the twentieth century. Yet it was in the twenty years after 1900 that the barriers broke down completely. The realists of to-day regard freedom as a premise. They laugh at the sensations created by Crane or London or Norris.

In fact our modern school is quite fearless, though in them is often the submission of artistic ideals to practical standards: what people will read — and buy. (Lesser American novelists have usually lacked artistic courage.) In general the novels now exhibit honest realism. This expresses itself in various ways. One of these is the photographing of American life in minute detail, with more or less irony, as in the novels of Sinclair Lewis. Another is the tendency, about as new as Sophocles, to find beauty in the ugliness depicted, a more common expression of romance than is usually realized. We must not classify. Yet we think also of writers who study America with prepossessions. Such are, for instance, the psychoanalysts, the devotees of modern psychology, the Sherwood Andersons or the Floyd Dells.

No one can exaggerate the variety in the present realism, or predict its future. Sinclair Lewis, with the merciless scrutiny of a Swift, fastens on one aspect of the village or city. His hard pictures are true, but true to only one side of American life. He writes with an undercurrent of disgust. Booth Tarkington, now far from his early tinsel romances, and Willa Cather show the developing West, but with more body and more warmth. In them is the cheerful life of the Philistine village. Sunshine bathes the western fields and hills. In Edith Wharton, who sees us through European eyes, we pause over the graceful irony, but in Dorothy Canfield Fisher we feel the echo of romance. Her stories analyze, yet play with the feelings. Robert Herrick, the "discouraged idealist," studies character in the American social arrangement. Many of these novelists, admirable in the craft of writing, like Zona Gale and Joseph Hergesheimer, are inclined to find beauty in sordid life. The heroines of *Lulu Bett* and *Java Head* live in a very real America, but over them hovers a light different from the severe clarity of *Main Street* or *The Age of Innocence*. Meanwhile Sherwood Anderson looks beneath the humdrum of ordinary America for manifestations of the unconscious mind, "the beast at the threshold." And James Branch Cabell, incurable romantic at heart, jests at his own fancies and symbolism — somewhat pointlessly ironic. The short story form, too, still fascinates us. Most of these novelists have experimented in it. Apart from them, there are various masters of its technique: Daniel Steele, Edna Ferber, Fannie Hurst, Katherine Fullerton Gerould, and others quite as skillful.

Literary criticism at the beginning of the century maintained our meager but respectable traditions. Since Bryant journalism has flourished. William Allen White and Walter Lippmann are but two of many literary publicists and editors. It has been an age of biography: witness such different studies as those by Henry Adams, William Roscoe Thayer, Edward W. Bok, and Amy Lowell. In criticism the self-examination has overturned a hive of bees that sting right and left: novelists, poets, and one another. Confusion reigns, but the English critic is right: "The history of American criticism appears, even more than that of other departments of literature, to be very mainly a history of the present." American literary criticism prior to 1900 had the orthodoxy of English criticism without its genius. We have never had a Coleridge. Critics like George Woodberry, W. C. Brownell, Brander Matthews, Paul Elmer More, and Bliss Perry have in their several ways perpetuated the tradition of Lowell in criticism. Of the attacks on tradition in various forms of national life and literature, none is so slashing and provocative as those of H. L. Mencken. Between these two positions, as between the host of academic scholars writing for other scholars and the host of reviewers writing for all who will read, there is a middle ground which is the hope of the future. Free-lance critics have quickened our intellectual life, but the indifference to the past of criticism has its dangers. The critic guided by the past, equipped by knowledge and principles — a word hateful to the iconoclasts — hardly exists as in England and France. Our magazines tell the story. In our discussions we no longer care or have time for the old critical essay, a form frequent enough in English periodicals. Criticism has become a brilliant game, a business of reviewing, a contest of clever comment.

We need not trace as in fiction the ancestry of realism in the new poetry. All such study of the relation of the present to the past brings us in the end to the name of Whitman. His assertion that he would be the poet of the future has not been taken seriously by his people of these states, but there are few modern poets who owe nothing to him. Since 1900 there has been sentimental poetry in the manner of the New England school, but it is a whisper compared with the new voices. Perhaps Edwin Markham, Bliss Carman, Richard Hovey, and lesser men than Whitman hastened the change. In the poetry of William Vaughn Moody there is protest. Startling at any rate is the complete revolution in respect to subject and form. The strength of the new movement in American poetry lies in its sincere devotion to actual life. Sara Teasdale declares bravely that the vigorous spirit of America is producing the best poetry which is now being written in English. Such a statement is strong enough, but it may be true. In the poetry appear to be more fervor and literary conscience than in the fiction.

For the central fact about all this poetry is its interest in everyday life. Modern poetry is curious about life, and it is equally curious about the forms of art which shall reveal this life most truly. Hence in the eccentrics we encounter ridiculous subjects and tortured meters, but in the better poets an amazing verisimilitude. Life itself, as we know it to-day, is in their poetry. This passion for truth takes innumerable forms. In Edwin Arlington Robinson we meet the Puritan in his later struggle with his inheritance. After searing self-analysis, he sets forth an intellectual adjustment of the modern man afflicted by such a legacy. Robert Frost shows in more external ways the New England community and scenery. As our consciousness widens, other racial influences appear, as in the realism of Edgar Lee Masters and Carl Sandburg. The latter is an apotheosis of the immigrant.

"The new times," wrote Whitman, "the new People, the new vistas need a tongue accordingly — yes, and what is more they will have such a tongue." I shall attempt no catalogue of the subjects of this new tongue, or of its accents. Masters, in the simplest language, repeats the life histories of village folk buried in a western churchyard. Vachel Lindsay describes in onomatopoetic rhymes a political parade, a negro dance, or California whales. Ezra Pound silhouettes faces in the subway. There are the "imagists," "H. D." and John Gould Fletcher. In various combinations of occult sound and strange theme, we have not merely lyricists, but rhapsodists, expressionists, impressionists, vorticists, and — heaven help us — cerebralists. Possibly the leaders, though not the sponsors, of this new poetry, are those poets mentioned in the preceding paragraph — and Amy Lowell. Her reasoned defenses of imagism and of the new thought, coupled with her own sound performance, helped to give it a hearing.

As to the future, who will hazard a guess? The camp followers build their little fires, as ever when new enterprises stir the human mind. The passers-by smile, and talk of the return to convention or the old-fashioned romance. This alone we know, that never before has literature in America been so distinctive or so intellectually alive.

WINSTON CHURCHILL, 1871–

WINSTON CHURCHILL is the novelist of the patriotic, energetic American. In *Richard Carvel*, 1899, *The Crisis*, 1901, *Coniston*, 1906, or *The Inside of the Cup*, 1913, one may enjoy the picturesque romance of American history. Or the patriotic reader may resolve to perfect still further his American democracy. For Churchill, active in New Hampshire politics, transfers to his novels his moral earnestness. He is clearly influenced by Theodore Roosevelt, whose own performance as a man of letters the next generation will judge. Churchill's books lack subtlety and show no great stylistic power, but represent excellently the democratic and romantic aspirations of a vast number of Americans.

771   Underwood & Underwood

JACK LONDON, 1876–1916

FAR more typical of the early years of the century's literature was Jack London, who bade us prepare for the kingdom of the brute, and who, single-handed, almost throttled sentimentalism. London tasted the dregs of life, and performed incredible sacrifices to enter the University of California. He returned disillusioned, but with literary ambitions, to a life in the Klondike, before the mast, and of wandering over the

772   © Brown Brothers

earth. In the war between Russia and Japan he served as a newspaper correspondent. His life, with its melodramatic struggles and physical exultation, was the real source of his superabundant fiction about hurricanes, fist-fights, wrecks, diseases, and terrors of the night. His ideals in literature were to be assimilated to the point of absurdity by writers such as Rex Beach and Zane Grey.

THE SPIRIT OF HIS NOVELS

INFLUENCED first by Bret Harte and Kipling, London sought stronger teachers in Marx, Nietzsche, and the Russian realists. London's romantic strain carried him beyond these into a nightmare world of supermen and strange heroic countries. He exaggerates, like some primitive writer of early races. Even the dogs in his Aurora-lighted northern climes are like the animals of Norse gods. *The Call of the Wild*, 1903, or *The Sea-Wolf*, 1904, his best novels, suggest his inexhaustible vitality, his lurid sense of the dramatic, as well as his diffuseness, and other weaknesses of style. The autobiographical books such as *Martin Eden*, 1909, or *John Barleycorn*, 1913, reveal best the man himself.

773   © Brown Brothers

774   © Brown Brothers

ETCHINGS OF CRUDE AMERICA

WHAT "Carol Kennicott" beheld as she walked from the station at Gopher Prairie, Minnesota: the garage, the moving-picture palace, the men in shirt sleeves, the linen on the lines, the salesmen whom the successful "Babbitt" knew at his club — these acid etchings of crude, complacent America amused and chagrined us. *Arrowsmith*, 1925, in part a satire on medical training and the life of a physician, is still more powerful and hints that Lewis has not even yet put forth his full strength.

776   © Brown Brothers

SINCLAIR LEWIS, 1885–

IN his excitement Jack London was a little absurd. American realism was to be calmer. Four years after London's death Sinclair Lewis, a young newspaper man, wrote *Main Street*, 1920. In a few months the title was an idiom of current speech. Lewis knew nearly every corner of commonplace America, and he never forgot what he saw. This novel and *Babbitt*, 1922, were at once photography, satire, and caricature.

775 Sinclair Lewis and James Branch Cabell, courtesy of Robert M. McBride & Co.

THEODORE DREISER, 1871–

BY such pictures Hamlin Garland's realism becomes antiquated. Yet it is Theodore Dreiser who refuses to let us draw our own conclusions from sordid American life. He dwells upon it, argues about it, and probes gloomily into biological motives. Had his master, Zola, lived in our day, and in America, so he would have written, though never so clumsily. Dreiser, hopeless student of brutality and animalism, is, nevertheless, our greatest novelist of naturalism. His life gave him the materials for such books as *Sister Carrie*, 1900, *Jennie Gerhardt*, 1911, the brooding novel, *The Genius*, 1915, or, *An American Tragedy*, 1926.

BOOTH TARKINGTON, 1869–

THE propaganda in the novels of Lewis and Dreiser is slight compared with that in the socialist, Upton Sinclair, author of *The Jungle*, 1906, or *The Brass Check*, 1919. No realism could be more different from these than that of Booth Tarkington, who has moved gradually away from the rococo romance of *Monsieur Beaucaire*, 1900, to the wholesome studies of American life in *Alice Adams*, 1921, and *The Midlander*, 1924. Tarkington in Indiana knew the earlier Hoosiers; was the friend of Riley; and he has never lost interest in the political destinies of his state. His abandonment, after the years at Princeton, of the profession of art, symbolizes to some his failure as an unusual craftsman in fiction.

777 © Underwood & Underwood

STORIES OF AMERICAN LIFE

HIS sympathetic interest in adolescence has made the Penrod stories (*Penrod*, 1914; *Penrod and Sam*, 1916; *Seventeen*, 1916) a source of entertainment to all America. They have the lightness of Kate Douglas Wiggin's juvenile stories (*Rebecca of Sunnybrook Farm*, 1903) and are, besides, briskly modern. In political stories like *The Gentleman from Indiana*, 1899, Tarkington shows his mastery of American backgrounds. The later novels make us wonder if he may not possess more than talent. In *Alice Adams*, with its daring and beautiful ending, and in *The Midlander* is much of the actuality of Lewis and the other realists, ennobled by hopeful American virtues. Here is Main Street in sunlight

778 From Booth Tarkington, *Monsieur Beaucaire*, 1902, drawing by C. D. Williams. © Doubleday, Page & Co.

WILLA CATHER, 1875–

MUCH of the same light plays about the stories of the West by Willa Cather, rendering her superior to such writers as Charles G. Norris or his wife Kathleen Norris, the brother and sister-in-law of Frank Norris. *O Pioneers*, 1913, by Miss Cather, proclaimed her interest in the changing life of the frontier. *My Ántonia* (Án'-ton-ee-ah), 1918, is her most powerful novel. The brilliant short stories in the collection *Youth and the Bright Medusa*, 1920, give promise of her art in telling a tale, fulfilled in the admirable picture of western life, *One of Ours*, 1922. Miss Cather's dénouements are likely to be sketchy, as in the half symbolical study of the decadence of the West, *A Lost Lady*, 1923. Mrs. Forrester represents, perhaps, the West, and its surrender to materialism. Miss Cather gives always an impression of reserve and strength. In *The Professor's House*, 1925, she writes again, with symbolism, of the sadness of fulfillment.

779 Courtesy of Alfred A. Knopf, Inc.

780   © Alice Boughton

ZONA GALE, 1874–

THE limitations of American life are more harassing in the novels of Zona Gale, a writer with delicate perceptions, and with a style that challenges the English May Sinclair, though the latter is a far greater novelist. The origin of her career, her manner of writing, and something even of her character are hinted at in her comment on an early event: "I secured a position by attrition. I presented myself every morning at the desk of the city editor. At the end of two weeks the city editor let me write about a flower show. I have never put such emotion into anything else I have written." The emotion in *Lulu Bett*, 1920, the story of the spinster-drudge in the western family, is restrained and harrowing. This and *Faint Perfume*, 1923, an even subtler study of environment, have revived her earlier novel, *Birth*, 1918.

DOROTHY CANFIELD FISHER, 1879–

WITH feelings strong but far less contained, and with a manner too explicit, Dorothy Canfield Fisher has written stories of New England life, such as *Hillsboro People*, 1915. Her later novels, the products of life abroad, blend the European and American scenes. *The Brimming Cup*, 1921, and *Rough-Hewn*, 1922, are studies of courtship and marriage. The later stories, *Home Fires in France*, 1918, *The Day of Glory*, 1919, *Raw Material*, 1923, are inferior to *Hillsboro People*.

EDITH (NEWBOLD JONES) WHARTON, 1862–

THIS influence in modern fiction of European life upon women who have lived long abroad is distinct in Anne Sedgwick, author of *Tante*, 1911, and *Adrienne Toner*, 1922. The supreme instance, however, is Edith Newbold Jones Wharton, who depicts the old New England in *Ethan Frome*, 1911, or the old Manhattan in *The Age of Innocence*, 1920, and *Old New York*, 1924, or

781   © Underwood & Underwood

Europe both old and new in *A Son at the Front*, 1923. Beginning in childhood Mrs. Wharton has spent much time in Europe. She became early a student of languages and of the acknowledged masters of fiction. Her first book, *The Greater Inclination*, 1899, published in her thirty-seventh year, was the first of a series of sophisticated novels of character. Mrs. Wharton was long ago the pupil of Henry James, but now draws essentially nothing from him. She is clear, cool, distantly ironic, and in moments thrillingly intense. Untouched, like more obvious realists, by our rasping life, she yet understands us well, and no better studies of the effect of American environments on character have been written in recent years than *Ethan Frome* and *The Age of Innocence*.

782   Courtesy of D. Appleton & Company

MARGARET DELAND, 1857–

WITH the age of Henry James, too, is associated Margaret Deland. Yet if *John Ward, Preacher*, 1888, and *Old Chester Tales*, 1898, belong to the nineteenth century, nearly a score of Mrs. Deland's stories appeared in the twentieth, among them *Dr. Lavendar's People*, 1903, *The Awakening of Helena Richie*, 1906, *The Iron Woman*, 1911, or *New Friends in Old Chester*, 1924. On the whole her art has grown more powerful and more moving. In the little Pennsylvania town she saw not merely the humble American types; she envisaged and dissected their souls. She is never uncertain in touch when she beholds a human being battling with a great force, such as heredity or religion.

783   © Brown Brothers

JOSEPH HERGESHEIMER, 1880–

ONE of the most thorough investigators of American backgrounds is Joseph Hergesheimer, who will collect, probably not unaided, the material for a *Java Head*, 1919, with the patience of a graduate student. A realist in technique, Hergesheimer is often a colorist, and painter of pictures. His novels are full of scents, sounds, and hues, and are European in point of view. Nor are the colors always untouched by decadence, witness *The Three Black Pennys*, 1917, or the unpleasantly plush *Cytherea*, 1922. He represents our realists who find a certain beauty in the drab. Above all, whether in the earlier novels or *The Bright Shawl*, 1922, Hergesheimer, a theorist in the novel, is a craftsman. We can deny this no more than we can ignore his frequent bad taste.

784   Courtesy of Alfred A. Knopf, Inc.

SHERWOOD ANDERSON, 1876–

FOREMOST among students of America who possess a marked psychological bias is Sherwood Anderson, of humble parentage and meager education, who worked five years as a laborer. His *Winesburg, Ohio*, 1919, is a study of character in a small town. More typical of his original attack on the novel form is his *Many Marriages*, 1923, which strips off the upper layers of consciousness to comprehend the real egos of certain insignificant people, with startling, if sometimes futile, effects. Anderson thinks sex has hitherto received inadequate emphasis in literature. His autobiographical confessional almost restores the balance for all literature; no one can accuse him of leaving sex out of the novel.

785   From a photograph by Alfred Stieglitz, courtesy of Huebsch, Inc.

786 Courtesy of Robert M. McBride & Co.

JAMES BRANCH CABELL, 1879–

A MORE cultivated artist is James Branch Cabell, a southerner, and a romantic; a lyrist in prose, one sharpened with a brier-like irony. *Beyond Life*, 1919, sums up his philosophy of art: it should, he asserts, be based on a dream of life, not on life itself. Hence his fabulous Middle Ages, with excerpts from mythical writers; his assemblage of confused allusion; his flights of fancy. The books with strange titles, *The Cords of Vanity*, 1909, *The Rivet in Grandfather's Neck*, 1915, *The Cream of the Jest*, 1917, embody his dreams, his symbolism, his interest in medieval subjects, such as gallantry, chivalry, and the rest. He is fond of *double entendre*, and *Jurgen*, 1919, is half lyrical and half a shrewd attempt to escape the censor.

WILLIAM SYDNEY PORTER, "O. HENRY," 1862–1910

MANY of the writers considered in this chapter essayed the short story form. It has become, as Poe divined, a characteristic medium of American expression. We must look back at the early years of the century. In William Sydney Porter, with his famous pseudonym of O. Henry, most of its virtues and faults had a glaring emphasis. O. Henry's training in realism was severe. He knew the hard life of the West, vagabondage in Central America, sensationalism in New York newspaperdom, and the human wreckage of a prison where he spent three years. In his innumerable stories meet humor, unscrupulous willingness to please his public, clever technique, and something else. This, due partly to his masters in fiction, such as Kipling or the French writers, is an innate affinity for the right phrase. Pater and Henry James would have scorned O. Henry, but in the midst of buffoonery, anecdote, and cheapness, he occasionally rivals their perfect intuition for the word and the sentence.

787 Courtesy of Doubleday, Page & Co.

GEORGE ADE, 1866–

HUMOR found further expression in journalism in John Kendrick Bangs, who continued to write well on into the twentieth century, and whose most genial and clever compositions were real anticipations of modern humor. The *House Boat on the Styx*, 1895, is still a delightful skit. His successors, Finley Peter Dunne (the *Mr. Dooley* series, 1898 and later) and George Ade, belong more precisely to our own time, particularly Ade, whose *Fables in Slang*, 1900, have sequels at this moment. An interesting and perhaps in one sense a final development of American humor is the newspaper columns of wit and wisdom, conducted by Bert Leston Taylor, Franklin P. Adams (F. P. A.), Don Marquis, and Christopher Morley. The old Civil War humorists would enjoy this laughter. The caricature, the observation, and the dialect are here in twentieth-century dress.

788 Courtesy of Doubleday, Page & Co.

GEORGE EDWARD WOODBERRY, 1855–

But we must hasten from the humorists and from the dramatists, of whom Percy Mackaye, Augustus Thomas, and Eugene O'Neill are representative, to criticism. Here indeed since the days of E. P. Whipple's glory (No. 738) and Matthew Arnold's despair of us, is activity. Henry Van Dyke, poet and essayist, writes gentle criticism in the old manner. George E. Woodberry (No. 789), also a poet, published in 1921 his six volumes of *Collected Essays*. A graduate of Harvard, he was professor of English at the University of Nebraska (1877–78) and of Comparative Literature at Columbia from 1891 to 1904. Since that date he has written much, including criticism of Lamb,

Tennyson, Coleridge, Shelley, and Swinburne. We turn often to these dependable studies of books and men of letters. His *Edgar Allan Poe*, 1885, revised later, is one of the few excellent critical biographies written in America. Bliss Perry, a novelist and critic, carries on the tradition, and typifies the best American critical thought.

789   © Alice Boughton

790   Courtesy of Alfred A. Knopf, Inc.

HENRY LOUIS MENCKEN, 1880–

Strikingly opposed to the old tradition is the group of writers who have sworn death in America to the conventional, the academic, the Puritanical, or the crude. James Gibbons Huneker, musical and dramatic critic, with his *Iconoclasts —
A Book of Dramatists*, 1905, *Ivory Apes and Peacocks*, 1915, or the autobiographical *Steeplejack*, 1919, strives to revitalize our artistic ideals. Among others Henry Louis Mencken in his series of *Prejudices*, 1919, 1920, 1922, 1924, launches himself furiously at every American tradition. He considers himself the gadfly of American thought. He is — although his brilliant sallies against the Philistine have often the flavor of the smart undergraduate.

STUART P. SHERMAN, 1881–1926

Between two such attitudes as those of Woodberry and Mencken — both would enjoy this juxtaposition — have developed critics who have not cut cables with the past, but who are, in varying degrees, a part of this new, nervous, fearless self-criticism. Some of these, like John Erskine, Carl Van Doren, Brander Matthews, William Lyon Phelps, Henry Seidel Canby, Stuart P. Sherman, J. E. Spingarn, Irving Babbitt, or George Santayana, have been allied with the more progressive critical thought of the universities and magazines. Others, like William C. Brownell, or Paul Elmer More do battle in more conservative fashion. Preëminence is not easy to determine. The important fact is the identification of these and such a man of letters and critic as Bliss Perry, not only with American literature and American education, but with American thought as a whole.

791   Courtesy of Charles Scribner's Sons

AGNES REPPLIER, 1858–

ALL of the foregoing are essayists as well as critics. Irving and Charles Dudley Warner would be at home perhaps only in the peaceful meditations of Henry Van Dyke, or Samuel McChord Crothers. In general, the American essay is more tense and sharp-cutting, as in the work of Katherine Fullerton Gerould or the clever papers of Agnes Repplier.

WILLIAM VAUGHN MOODY, 1869–1910

COMPARATIVELY free from the innovations in poetic form, William Vaughn Moody represents none the less the increased independence of

792 © Moffett

the twentieth century. Born in Indiana, a graduate of Harvard, and connected, until his early death, with the University of Chicago, Moody wrote plays, some for the stage like *The Great Divide*, 1906, and the *Faith Healer*, 1910. Others were lyrical dramas. The exact meaning of these last, with their weighty intellectual content, is still doubtful. Moody was shaped by many influences; of these the Greek drama, Shelley, and Whitman are a few. In his proposed triology (only two parts were completed), *The Masque of Judgment*, 1900, and the *Fire-Bringer*, 1904, he sets forth with intense feeling and mysticism the "necessity of God to man and man to God." It is once more the Greek and the Shelleyan conception, this time through the mind of a twentieth-century American.

"The Man With the Hoe."

Written After Seeing Millet's World-Famous Painting Now in This City.

BY EDWIN MARKHAM

BOWED by the weight of centuries he leans
Upon his hoe and gazes on the ground,
The emptiness of ages in his face,
And on his back the burden of the world.
Who made him dead to rapture and despair,
A thing that grieves not and that never hopes,
Stolid and stunned, a brother to the ox?
Who loosened and let down this brutal jaw?
Whose was the hand that slanted back this brow?
Whose breath blew out the light within this brain?

Is this the Thing the Lord God made and gave
To have dominion over sea and land;
To trace the stars and search the heavens for power
To feel the passion of Eternity?
Is this the Dream He dreamed who shaped the suns
And pillared the blue firmament with light?
Down all the stretch of Hell to its last gulf
There is no shape more terrible than this—
More tongued with censure of the world's blind greed—
More filled with signs and portents for the soul—
More fraught with menace to the universe.

What gulfs between him and the seraphim!
Slave of the wheel of labor, what to him
Are Plato and the swing of Pleiades?
What the long reaches of the peaks of song,
The rift of dawn, the reddening of the rose?
Through this dread shape the suffering ages look;
Time's tragedy is in that aching stoop;
Through this dread shape humanity betrayed,
Plundered, profaned and disinherited,
Cries protest to the Judges of the World,
A protest that is also prophecy.

O masters, lords and rulers in all lands,
Is this the handiwork you give to God,
This monstrous thing distorted and soul-quenched?
How will you ever straighten up this shape;
Give back the upward looking and the light;
Rebuild in it the music and the dream;
Touch it again with immortality;
Make right the immemorial infamies,
Perfidious wrongs, immedicable woes?

O masters, lords and rulers in all lands,
How will the Future reckon with this Man?
How answer his brute question in that hour
When whirlwinds of rebellion shake the world?
How will it be with kingdoms and with kings—
With those who shaped him to the thing he is—
When this dumb terror shall reply to God,
After the silence of the centuries?

OAKLAND, CALIFORNIA

794 © Underwood & Underwood

793 © Brown Brothers

CHARLES EDWIN MARKHAM, 1852–

A POETESS of slight intrinsic value, but a reminder of the sentimental newspaper tradition, is Ella Wheeler Wilcox. Mrs. Wilcox, Edgar Guest, Edwin Markham and others have satisfied the children and grandchildren of Josiah G. Holland's readers. In the magazines with a border of heroic figures, or in the literary columns of newspapers these verse-platitudes jingle their way into popular favor, proclaiming with Rufus Griswold that the moral poetry of America shall not die! It was Edwin Markham, author of *The Man With the Hoe* and *Lincoln, the Man of the People*, who was greeted as the creator of "the battle cry of the next thousand years."

EDWIN ARLINGTON ROBINSON, 1869–

EDWIN ARLINGTON ROBINSON, who, Amy Lowell thought, is the most remarkable of living American poets, was born in Maine, studied at Harvard, struggled with poverty in New York, where for a time he worked in the subway, and attracted the attention of Roosevelt through such poetry as *The Children of the Night*, 1897. Since his recognition he has contributed a body of verse which may endure, notably *The Man Against the Sky*, 1916, *Collected Poems*, 1921, and the poetry which reveals his literary preceptors, *Merlin*, 1917, and *Lancelot*, 1919. In Robinson one may study the hard-won victory of modern analysis over Puritan tradition. From it come his hard style, his dark brooding, and his strength and fervor.

796 From the portrait, 1916, by Lilla Cabot Perry- courtesy of the Macmillan Company

797 © Alice Boughton

ROBERT FROST, 1875–

ROBERT FROST'S vignettes of New England landscape and character are bleak and more dispassionate. For, aside from his vagaries of being born in San Francisco, and living for some time in England, he is a sensitive recorder of the life of New England. Here he has worked in a mill, taught in Amherst College, and photographed New England's humble life. Frost has positive but not very clear philosophies of his art. But in *A Boy's Will*, 1913, or in *North of Boston*, 1914, move — perfect in appearance, diction, and mood — the hired man, the New England wife, the old farmer. Here, too, are the straggling stone walls, the white birches, the ice storm, the cow, as "she bellows on a knoll against the sky." *New Hampshire*, 1923, is his latest poetry on the country "back of the mountains."

EDGAR LEE MASTERS, 1868–

IT is strange to hear of a son of the pioneers depicting far more grimly the decadence of the Illinois village, but the *Spoon River Anthology*, 1915, a merciless satire by Edgar Lee Masters, does this. Masters had written thousands of lines, had been a lawyer and politician before he turned, under the influence of the Greek anthologies, to chronicle in free verse the epitaphs of Hod Putt, the Indian trader, Lucinda Matlock, mother of twelve children, and Old Fiddler Jones. His large purpose "to analyze society, to satirize society, to tell a story, to expose the machinery of life, to present a working model of the big world," is all fulfilled in this single book, but hardly so, it is to be feared, in his earlier and later writings.

798 Courtesy of the Macmillan Company

CARL SANDBURG, 1878–

EVEN with such a preparation Carl Sandburg's brutality amazes. In this westerner of Swedish descent every hindrance of conventional thought and form collapses. In so far as possible his poetry registers direct physical contacts with ugly life. Although a college graduate, his hands have done service in a dozen rough occupations, from that of truck-handler or dishwasher to carrying a rifle in the Spanish-American war. His strain of delicate feeling and mysticism hardly tempers his fierce concern with steel mills, hog-butchers, thugs, and prize fighters. In *Chicago Poems*, 1916, *Smoke and Steel*, 1920, or *Slabs of the Sunburnt West*, 1922, is the raw stuff of America: coarse democracy, dirt, and sweat. Yet his cadences haunt: Whitman should be alive to read the verse of this, his most tempestuous progeny. Sandburg's latest tribute to democracy was a bizarre biography of Lincoln, published in 1926.

NICHOLAS VACHEL LINDSAY, 1879–

YET Sandburg is not, like Vachel Lindsay of Springfield, Illinois, a lecturer for the Anti-Saloon League. Lindsay will tell you in any conversation that he is interested chiefly in politics. He is the western Puritan strumming a primitive lyre, partly in behalf of reform. His genius is lyric, and though his themes are daring (the negro, John L. Sullivan, a proletariat heaven), he is primarily a singer. People leave his readings declaring it is good vaudeville, and they never forget the rhythms of *The Congo and Other Poems*, 1914, *The Daniel Jazz and Other Poems*, 1920, *The Golden Book of Springfield*, 1920, or *The Golden Whales of California*, 1920.

AMY LOWELL, 1874–1925

BESIDES the wild men of modern poetry there are others in whom revolt and tradition meet more gracefully. In the variety, intelligence, and beauty of her writing as critic and poet, James Russell Lowell would certainly applaud his kinswoman, Amy Lowell. She owes much to John Keats, whose biography, 1925, claimed years of her life, to French imagists, to Matthew Arnold, to other poets, and to her long period of self-cultivation before she began to write. With this apprenticeship, her interest in the new verse forms has dignity, not less so because she wrote much in the mediums of the past. Imagism, she says, strives to employ the language of ordinary speech; to use the precise word; to make new rhythms; to use any subject whatever; to make poetry which is clear and definite; and to condense. Her partial realization of these ideals may be tested in, among other volumes, *Sword Blades and Poppy Seed*, 1914, or in later work.

"H. D.", 1886–

MISS LOWELL herself found the subtlest and finest exemplification of such tenets in "H. D." Interrupted in her education at Bryn Mawr, "H. D." went abroad in 1911, and found there the natural environment for her love of beauty. Little that is external finds its way into this poetry save as a stimulus to beauty. Her genius reminds one of certain nineteenth-century English poets, a Shelley or a Keats, in its intense inner life. Her brief lyrics in *Sea Garden*, 1921, or *Hymen*, 1921, are delicate stanzas reflecting these perceptions of beauty.

OREAD

Whirl up, sea —
Whirl your pointed
   pines.
Splash your great
   pines
On our rocks.
Hurl your green over
   us —
Cover us with your
   pools of fir.

802   From a photograph by Man Ray, Paris, courtesy of "H. D."

803   Courtesy of the Macmillan Company

JOHN GOULD FLETCHER, 1886–

IN John Gould Fletcher images and rhythms have freer play. Fletcher was born in Little Rock, Arkansas, but has lived much abroad. Multiform influences meet in him: Danish ancestry, for example, and his love of French literature and post-impressionistic painting. In *Irradiations — Sand and Spray*, 1915, and subsequent poems we feel the intensity that distinguishes "H. D.", as well as a mastery of the new forms, but also an abandon to these sense impressions, and experiments in technique. That word used so endlessly is true of Fletcher: he is vivid.

EZRA LOOMIS POUND, 1885–

MORE difficult to analyze is Ezra Pound, a strange child of Idaho, and a shocking relative for Longfellow! Educated here, he has now deserted us for England, whence he sends back jibes, erudition, and singularly poignant poetry. "Poetry," he says, "is a sort of inspired mathematics." The mingled influences of deep learning, observation of European life, and subservience to many English masters have created a poetry which is a mixture of triviality, bitterness, erudition, and power. One must wade through a good deal to reach the best of Pound. This best, however, may not be disregarded. *Umbra*, 1920, and other lyrics, which one constantly encounters in magazines, we reread. "All talk," says Carl Sandburg, "on modern poetry by people who know, ends with dragging in Ezra Pound somewhere."

804   Courtesy of Alfred A. Knopf, Inc.

CONRAD POTTER AIKEN, 1889–

CONRAD AIKEN, a poet with marked intellectual power, is a southerner, born at Savannah, a graduate of Harvard, and has lived much in England. He lacks the audacity of many of our moderns, and his poetry echoes more or less faintly the tones of other

poets. Yet the resulting melody is his own, and is very fine. On the waves of this he carries us off into a borderland of dreams. It is only when he takes Freud and his own self-analysis too seriously that he becomes obscure and rather empty. His best work in poetry — he writes criticism also and stories — is *Punch, the Immortal Liar*, 1921.

806   Courtesy of the Macmillan Company

805   Courtesy of Alfred A. Knopf, Inc.

SARA TEASDALE, 1884–

THE aim in the poetry of Sara Teasdale is not to surprise her readers, but to say what moves her. Her little poems are like pendants or intaglios, lovely and perfect in form. A native of Missouri, Miss Teasdale has traveled widely. From her first volume, *Sonnets to Duse, and Other Poems*, 1907, which won Arthur Symons, to the later *Love Songs*, 1917, or *Flame and Shadow*, 1920, her brief lyrics are always skillfully artless, as it were, and evocative. Her poetry is, however, less subtle metrically than the brilliant, colorful verse of Eleanor Wylie.

807   © Brown Brothers

EDNA ST. VINCENT MILLAY, 1892–

MORE varied, and with a thrilling spiritual intensity, is the work of Edna St. Vincent Millay, whose first notable poetry was written while she was at Vassar College. Miss Millay professes to be a later Elizabethan, but her whimsicalities are modern. We come to watch for the quick turn of her sophisticated wit. More than all else, however, we quicken before the fervor of her feeling. In *The Harp-Weaver, and Other Poems*, 1923, are some of her magnificent sonnets. In the younger singers such as Stephen Benét and Miss Millay is promise for the future of American poetry.

NOTES ON THE PICTURES

1. Only two copies of this publication are known: one in the British Museum; one in the Huntington Library. It has been privately printed several times. The poem relates to the experiences of the voyagers to Bermuda.
2. This and the other engravings in the *Generall Historie* were by John Payne, d. 1647(?), one of the earliest line engravers in England. He made many portraits and title-pages of merit, and was probably an imitator of Simon and William Van de Passe. The engraving is derived from de Bry, as are many of those in John Smith's works. See Vol. I, Nos. 379–385.
4. Engraving is signed "Graven by John Barra." The pictures are a combination of the scenes from the Smith map of Virginia and de Bry's Virginia engravings.
5. Hamor's *True Discourse* gives the first account of the baptism and marriage of Pocahontas.
6. Romney painted "The Tempest" for the proposed Shakespeare gallery started in London in 1786 by Alderman Boydell.
8. Identity of "H. W.", who signed the verse, has not been ascertained.
9. Barber, a Connecticut draftsman, was also a historian. He made engravings, working chiefly on wood and illustrated his own books.
11. See note on this publication in Vol. I, p. 207.
12. According to Bradford's "History of Plimoth Plantation," the Standish party on this occasion included eleven of the Mayflower company; the picture shows but nine.
13. Bradford's Ms. was in Boston until about 1765 and had been often quoted by early writers. It may have been carried off when the British evacuated Boston in 1776, or taken by soldiers from the Old South Church, then occupied as a riding academy. It was located about 1855 in the Palace of the Bishop of London at Fulham. Several attempts to recover it from the English authorities were made by appeal of American Ministers to England. In 1897, after many formalities, the Episcopal Consistorial Court of London issued a decree authorizing the return of the precious document, through the then American Ambassador, Thomas F. Bayard, to the State of Massachusetts. It had been known at Fulham as the "Log of the Mayflower."
16. The cut was probably the earliest figurative representation of America. This Indian *motif* was perpetuated and appeared now and then in English prints and caricatures of the period of the Revolution, persisting into the nineteenth century.
19. The scene is at a point known as "Porter's Rocks."
20. This curious map cut on wood was, as the vignette states, the "first that ever was here cut, and done by the best Pattern that could be had, which being in some places defective, it made the other less exact. . . . The figures that are joyned with the Names of Places are to distinguish such as have been assaulted by the Indians from others." The cut was made by John Foster (1648–81). The date of publication, 1677, places this engraving later than the reputed earliest engraved portrait, that of Richard Mather, also done by Foster. Hubbard's Ms. of this "History of New England" was saved from the mob by the Rev. Dr. Andrew Eliot at the same time as that of Hutchinson's "History of the Province of Massachusetts-Bay." See No. 124.
21. By a noted American illustrator whose historical illustrations are marked by vigor, accuracy, and intelligence. Illustrated many books in mid-nineteenth century. See Vol. XII.
23. Dickenson's "God's Protecting Providence," was the first book printed by Jansen, early Philadelphia printer. Engraving in the Dutch translation has striking resemblance of treatment to the prints in Pieter Van der Aa of Leyden. See Vol. I, pp. 79 and 158.
25. Idealistic conception.
26. By well-known illustrator of his day, representing the visit of Miles Standish and his party from Plymouth to take Morton by force.
29. The book by John Josselyn is a mixture of superstition and scientific information, of cures for agues, cuts, wounds, of love potions, etc., mixed with descriptions of types of American birds, animals, plants, minerals, etc. He identifies among American birds, the humming bird, turkey, goose, buzzard; among animals, the bear, wolf, raccoon, porcupine, beaver, deer; various flowers such as columbine, Solomon's seal, cinquefeuille; various berries; the walnut, filbert, birch and other trees. He lists the vegetables which will grow in America, including cabbage, lettuce and parsnip, as thriving particularly well. He publishes a few recipes and ends with a section devoted to

strange cures which he has heard of in America. Josselyn first came to America in 1638, and paid visits to Winthrop and Cotton. He came again in 1663 and stayed over eight years.

33. Peter Pelham, portrait painter and mezzotint engraver, came from London to Boston in 1726, and produced portraits of leading Boston men and women, also engravings of other character.

40. Williams landed, according to tradition, at What Cheer, Slate Rock, on the bank of the Seekonk. The name was derived from the words of the Indians "What Cheer, Netop" (friend).

41. Picture expresses the spirit of the scene, but architecture and costume are open to criticism.

43-44. The rhymes in the earliest issues of *The New England Primer* are credited to Benjamin Harris, who had a printing house in Boston, 1690 to 1694; he was printer to the Governor and Council, but returned to London.

49. *The Day of Doom* was widely read and often reprinted in the 17th century.

51. Sewall in his *Diary* says of Shepard's funeral: "June 9. The Reverend Mr. Thomas Shepard burial; Governor, Deputy Governor, and magistrates there. . . . It seems there were some Verses, but none pinned on the Herse. Scholars went before the Herse."

53. Example of a "broadside" of an elegiac character. The broadside was adopted from England, where in the 16th century it was used for Royal proclamations, Acts of Parliament, municipal publications, etc., and in political or personal controversy. From the broadside came the newssheet, and from this the newspaper of to-day. The broadside sometimes was used for ballads. The early one here illustrated shows the use of such sheets for elegiac verses. "The funeral verses which were pinned to the pall covering the coffin, represent the earliest personal employment of the broadside." — W. C. Ford, Introductory Note to *Broadsides, Ballads, etc. Printed in Massachusetts, 1639–1800*, The Massachusetts Historical Society, Boston, 1922.

55, 56. These are modifications of de Bry's engravings after John White.

58. Artist a versatile painter and illustrator of American history and life.

62. Pictures of animals probably copied from maps of the 16th century.

65. The lithograph of Penn's landing is not signed. Others in the same book are signed W. L. B., and still others, W. L. Breton.

66. Ferris has painted over fifty canvases on American history of markedly sentimental feeling and rich color effects. See No. 376.

69. Portrait was painted in New York between 1760 and 1764.

76. McRae's engraving reveals the tendency of his day to romanticize American history. The incident is based on tradition.

78. Portrait of Philip is imaginary. Revere, hero of the famous ride, was a goldsmith with a taste for drawing; he designed ornaments, engravings for paper money, designed and executed the engravings of various views and caricatures, and several portraits. Revere often adopted and engraved the designs of others.

82, 87, 88. Smibert (Smybert), born in Scotland, worked first as a house painter, and then as a coach-painter; after copying for dealers he went to Italy and studied under Italian masters. He came to America with Bishop Berkeley, 1728.

86. Kilburn arrived from London in 1754, advertising in the papers soliciting business. Portraits by him are in New York at the present day.

89. Text of the sermon was from Deuteronomy 32:35: "Their foot shall slide in due time."

90. The cut is John Warner Barber's attempt to reconstruct *singing in companies*, which he says "in going and returning from the house of God was a common practice in many congregations during the time of the revival — in literal accordance with the 100th Psalm."

91. A good example of the use of the broadside (see No. 53) in glorification of military success. Of these there are many examples in the 18th century.

101. Although July 4, 1776, is the date of the Declaration, no signatures were attached on that day, except one — that of John Hancock. It was ordered on the 19th to be engrossed on parchment. Most of the signatures were affixed on August 2, but at least two, those of Thomas McKean of Delaware and Matthew Thornton of New Hampshire, were attached later. The latter was not a member of Congress when the Declaration was signed, but obtained permission to sign in November after his election.

103. Blackburn, an Englishman, painted portraits in Boston, Portsmouth, and other New England towns between 1754 and 1761.

105. The Patrick Henry portrait, according to Charles Henry Hart in a paper printed in the *Proceedings of the Numismatic and Antiquarian Society of Philadelphia*, No. 26, 1913, was made from the portrait by Dance of Capt. James Cook, the English explorer, whom Henry resembled. It was painted by Sully for the purpose of being engraved as a frontispiece to William Wirt, *Life of Patrick Henry*, 1817. Hart says the true portrait of Henry is a miniature by Robert Sully, reproduced in Vol. VIII.

106. Crawford was famous in his day for his sculptures. See Vol. XII.

107. The sculptor, Irish-born, was a wood carver before he studied sculpture. Going to Rome he modelled busts of Pope Pius IX, and of several eminent Americans. Other works are soldiers' and sailors' monuments in American cities.

114. Artist a successful painter of historical pictures of the Revolutionary period to the number of thirty or more. See Vol. VI.

116. Paine's *Common Sense* appeared as a pamphlet of 79 pages. It was reprinted again and again throughout New England, in New York, in Charleston, also in London and in Edinburgh. It appeared in French and in German. Over 100,000 copies were sold within a short time.

124. Winsor, *Memorial History of Boston*, Vol. I, says Hutchinson "left the manuscript to its fate, . . . it was saved by the interposition of Rev. Dr. Andrew Eliot, and was not so much injured but that the author readily repaired the loss."

125. The demand for Allen's *Narrative* caused it to be reprinted in various editions under varying titles as late as 1849.

127. The Jersey prison ship was originally a British 64-gun ship, the *Jersey*, dismantled in 1776 and then placed in the Wallabout.

129. See 86.

130. For the original painting of Crèvecœur's farm, see Vol. III, No. 200.

132. The artist, John Gadsby Chapman, born in Virginia, studied in Italy, lived there much of his life, and painted Italian scenes. His *Baptism of Pocahontas* in the capitol at Washington was painted by order of the U. S. Government. A large collection of his paintings, drawings and engravings has been preserved in the Virginia State Library. Chapman's Drawing-Book passed through many editions.

136. Oliver Pelton, born 1798 at Portland, Conn., engraved bank-notes, and did some cuts for books.

137. Franklin's bookshop was near Christ Church in Philadelphia. Appearance of bookshop probably correct.

138. The Duplessis portrait of Franklin painted in France is a copy of the original which is said to be the one in the Boston Public Library. There are several other copies. For other Franklin portraits see Vol. VIII, Chapter IV.

139. Franklin may have met Mirabeau while in France, but the incident pictured is purely an invention. The legend in French reads: "Mirabeau arrives at the Champs Elysées; over his head hovers the spirit of liberty, bearing a banner, 'Free France.' Mirabeau presents a constitutional charter to Rousseau. Franklin places a crown of oak leaves on Mirabeau's brow, while Montesquieu, Voltaire,

Mably and Fénelon come to receive him. In the background Demosthenes and Cicero speak of the French orator as they look upon him. Genii follow him, bearing his works."

140. Picture represents Franklin about to land at the same wharf where sixty-one years before he arrived in Philadelphia as a penniless youth to seek his fortune.

142. Title-page a good example of decorative engraving as used for books of the day, by Peter Ruston Maverick, who was self-taught but an accomplished engraver. Several other Mavericks were known as engravers.

143. Franklin in his later years was a sufferer from gout and it was his habit to ride in a sedan chair, brought by him from France. The scene is the State House yard, Philadelphia. Chief Justice Thomas J. McKean is among those in the company.

144. Gage was frequently satirized at the outbreak of the Revolution.

145. Portrait the work of a noted American painter, born in Boston of Irish parents. Copley painted many of the personalities of the day; he went to England in 1774 and did not return to his native land. For critical estimate of his work see Vol. XII.

146. Engraving is inserted in a copy of *The Cow Chace*, a satirical poem by André. For the portrait of André by himself see Vol. VI.

147. Pine, an Englishman who arrived in Philadelphia in 1784, painted portraits of the leading men of the day, also an unfinished picture of the signing of the Declaration of Independence (*Congress Voting Independence*).

151. Portrait is fictitious.

152. Artist a cousin of Trumbull, the author. Many of his miniatures are in the Yale School of the Fine Arts, besides originals, in oil, of his celebrated military paintings. For these, see Vol. VI.

153, 154. Elkanah Tisdale, born at Lebanon, Conn., probably in 1771, was a designer, engraver and miniature painter. His work also appeared in the *Echo* in 1807. He did many commercial plates in Hartford.

156, 157. See 153.

159. Anker Smith an Englishman as was Smirke. The engraving was probably made for the English edition.

162. By a competent engraver in stipple, born in London of Scotch descent in 1769. He had engraved several huge plates; among them, Rubens' *Descent from The Cross*. He came to America about 1805, and in New York joined Rollinson, the engraver of bank notes.

166, 167. Eckstein, "portrait painter, modeller in clay" was, according to Dunlap, working in Philadelphia in 1796 and as late as 182?; Sully called him a "thorough-going drudge."

168. The illustration depicts the pursuit by the church elders of farmers endeavoring to escape attendance on Sabbath Day services.

170. Sharples, an English painter in pastel, was educated in France; came to America in 1794 and again in 1809. His crayons, finely powdered, were applied with a camel's hair pencil. He made a portrait in two hours, using a thick gray paper softly grained. For these he charged $15 for a profile, $20 for a full face. Of each portrait he made a replica for himself. This collection was purchased in 1876 by the city of Philadelphia. His portraits were very numerous. He visited the larger cities and towns. His pastel portrait of Washington, the last sitting given to a painter, 1796, has been much admired. George W. P. Custis declared it to be the "finest and purest likeness" of the General.

171. Brown, a silhouette artist, born 1808 in Charleston, S. C., specialized in cutting full-length portraits of statesmen. He used the methods of the brilliant French silhouette artist, August Edouart, who worked in the United States from 1839 to 1849, cutting the portraits of many of the most distinguished Americans of that period, when this type of portraiture was in high favor.

173. This crude portrait is by Amos Doolittle, the New Haven engraver, who made the four curious copper plates of the battles of Lexington and Concord. See Vol. VI. It was taken from the Stiles portrait by Reuben Moulthrop in the Yale School of the Fine Arts.

174. Peale a prolific painter of portraits of the Revolutionary period. See Vol. XII.

178. See 171.

179. George Cooke, born in Maryland in 1793, painted in Alexandria and Richmond prior to 1826, then spent five years in Europe. Exhibited in New York after 1830.

180. See 171.

181. Krimmel, born in Germany in 1787, came to Philadelphia in 1810, and acquired local fame for his portraits and landscapes. His painting of the group in Center Square has been said to rival Hogarth in truth and humor. He died in 1821. See also Vol. XII.

182. Sartain, a versatile English artist, came to America and distinguished himself as engraver, painter, architect, and editor. For Sully see Vol. XII.

190. St. Memin, 1770–1850, a French portrait-engraver, made portraits of many Americans during his visit to this country in the period following the Revolution. His method was unique, involving the use of a pantograph to reduce his drawings before he engraved them.

191. The likeness is an engraving by David Edwin, after a miniature by Robert Field. Edwin, an Englishman, born 1776, who worked at Amsterdam, came to Philadelphia in 1797. Made portraits in stipple from original paintings, many of them by Gilbert Stuart. His work was unrivaled at this time for its finish and delicacy.

192. Johnston, born in Philadelphia, made drawings for wood and copper engravers, and drew caricatures, political and theatrical. He was also an actor.

193. Allston, born in South Carolina, was educated in the North and became a noted painter. For a critical estimate of his work see Vol. XII.

194. Benjamin Tanner worked as an engraver in New York in 1792 and later in Philadelphia with his brother, Henry S. Tanner, and as a member of the engraving firm of Tanner, Vallance, Kearney & Co.

195. Appleton was a Boston portrait painter and engraver.

200. Dunlap painted portraits early in life, including one of Washington. Studied in London, 1784, with Benjamin West; later painted a series of large pictures, mostly scriptural, which attracted attention. He was director of the American Academy of Fine Arts, afterward merged with the National Academy of Design.

202. Ingham, born in Dublin, came to New York in 1816; as a painter of portraits marked by richness and harmony of coloring, he had a considerable vogue.

203. For Sargent, see Vol. XII.

206, 207, 208. See 21.

209. See 86.

210. Hill a Boston engraver who made many plates for the *Massachusetts Magazine*, 1789–96.

214. See 200.

216. See 170.

218. Artist a successful portrait painter. See Vol. XII. The engraving by Ritchie was widely sold as a large print.

220, 221. Anderson, born at Jersey City, 1775, produced thousands of wood engravings for books and periodicals of the early nineteenth century. He was self-taught. See Vol. III, *Notes on the Pictures*, No. 142.

222. Cruikshank a noted English caricaturist and illustrator. The satirical illustrations in the "Knickerbocker" series by Cruikshank, Leslie (No. 234), Allston (No. 236) and others have gone far to perpetuate a distorted view of manners and customs of early New Amsterdam.

223. Strickland a well-known architect; also painted portraits and engraved aquatints.

227. Re-engraving from the Visscher map of *Novum Belgium*, 1651–55. See Vol. I, No. 227.

228. Illustration signed "C" possibly by E. W. Clay. Figure of Diedrich Knickerbocker evidently copied from the figure in No. 223.

229. Artist, English-born, noted for sympathetic pictures on the Pilgrims; see Vol. I, Nos. 410, 437, 482.

230, 233. See 222.

239. Kensett a noted painter of the "Hudson River School." See Vol. XII.

240, 241. See No. 21.

242. Matteson, painter of pictures on early American history, has here attempted to visualize the popular notion of the Rip van Winkle legend created by Irving.

245, 246, 247. See 240.

248. Caldecott an English artist and illustrator.

260. See 21.

262. Beard, a New York artist whose later work brought him distinction as a painter of animals.

267. Jarvis was one of the first artists in the United States to give attention to art-anatomy. His portraits are agreeable and natural.

269. Joseph Ives Pease, 1809–83, a Connecticut engraver very skillful in books and bank notes.

273, 274, 275. See 21.

276. Smillie was a pioneer in bank-note engraving, and a landscape engraver of the first rank. Robert Weir is best known by his historical landscapes.

277. See 242.

278, 279, 280, 282, 283. See 21.

286. Milbert was a French naturalist, who visited the United States about 1828, and painted scenery, as well as the fauna and flora of America.

287. W. J. Bennett, died in New York in 1844, was a painter and engraver of English birth, who had wide experience in painting European scenes.

288. Artist born at New Bedford, Mass., studied under Thomas Sully and abroad. The Willis portrait was painted from life while in Italy.

289. Flagg, born at New Haven, Conn., studied under Washington Allston, his uncle, and in London. The New York Historical Society has twelve paintings by him.

292. Bartlett, an English illustrator and author who drew many American scenes. See Vols. I, III and XIII.

294. Leutze, born in Germany, came in boyhood to America, by his early drawings earned enough to enable him to go in 1841 to study in Düsseldorf. Painted many celebrated historical pictures. He worked in this country from 1859 until his death.

296. See 202.

299. Artist born at Scipio, N. Y., became a pupil of Trumbull, and painted portraits early in western New York; opened a studio in New York in 1834; was a member of the National Academy of Design in 1846; is said to have painted more than seven hundred portraits, many eminent men of his day being his sitters.

301. Leslie was born in England and studied under Benjamin West and Washington Allston. For two years, 1831–32, he was Professor of Drawing at West Point. In England he was a Royal Academician in 1845, and painted many pictures, chiefly of historical characters.

304. Thompson, born at Middleboro, Mass., painted portraits at Plymouth, at Providence, R. I., spent seven years in Italy, and in 1860 settled in New York City.

307. Huntington, born in New York, studied under S. F. B. Morse and Henry Inman, and later in Italy. His talent showed great versatility. He painted many portraits of Americans besides landscapes, historical pictures, European and American, and illustrations for books. He was president of the National Academy 1862 to 1869 and again in 1877. See Vol. XII for further notice of his work.

308. See 304.

309. Nast was born in Bavaria and at six years of age came to America, drawing for illustrated journals when he was fifteen. Early in the Civil War he sent drawings of war scenes to *Harper's Weekly*, which attracted attention. Toward the close of the war his talent for caricature was developed and in this field he became noted for many stinging cartoons in exposure of political corruption and demagogues. See Vols. III and IX.

314, 318. See 294.

320. Artist, born in Canada, studied in Paris under Gérome. The Bryant portrait was exhibited in 1878 by the Society of American Artists, the year of the poet's death.

321. Kidder made topographical drawings and engraved aquatints at Boston early in the nineteenth century.

325. See 9.

326. Meeker a contributor to *The Century*, *St. Nicholas* and other illustrated magazines.

331. See 276.

337. Hicks, born at Newtown, Penn., became a noted painter of portraits. Studied in Philadelphia and New York, and from 1845 to 1849 in Italy and Paris.

345. Thoreau's desk, chair and bed are preserved in the Antiquarian Society of Concord.

357. See 21.

358. See 229.

363. Inman was a versatile artist, an engraver as well as a painter. See Vol. XII.

365. G. P. A. Healy, born in Boston, went to Paris at twenty-five to study. He became a popular painter of portraits of which he is said to have executed nearly six hundred. His large canvas in Faneuil Hall, "Webster's Reply to Hayne," completed in 1831, contains 113 portraits. This work shows the influence of his French masters.

372. See 307.

375. Read, born in Chester County, Penn., after a rambling life in his youth, opened a studio in Cincinnati and painted portraits. He was virtually self-taught. He painted several allegorical and mythological subjects. The picture of Longfellow's children caught the popular fancy of the day as did his "Sheridan's Ride." He wrote many poems.

376. Ferris, born in Philadelphia, 1863, studied in Paris under Jean Laurens Gérome, after whom he was named. His collection of over fifty canvases in Independence Hall represent the work of twenty-five years. See *Notes on the Pictures*, Vol. I, No. 409. See also Vol. I., Nos. 425, 469, 486, 498, 598.

377, 378, 379. Dicksee, an English artist, capable and versatile.

380, 381. See 376.

382. Picture is interesting by contrast with Ferris' conception (No. 380) of the Indian maiden.

383. Turner, American artist, studied in Paris as one of the Munkacsy group. His works include mural paintings on historical subjects for public buildings. See Vol. I., Nos. 159, 160, 176, 244.

384. See 229.

335. See 383.

386. See 376.

387. See 229.

388. Who it was that raised the lantern as a signal to Paul Revere was for some time a matter of controversy. Whether it was Robert Newman, the sexton of Christ (or North) Church, or John Pulling, the warden, still remains undecided. A tablet was placed in 1878 on Christ Church in commemoration of the event.

400. Low, a New York artist, studied under Gérome in Paris. See Vol. XII.

402. Hennessy, an Irish artist, worked in New York and London as an illustrator, and painter in oils and water colors, specializing in landscapes.

412–413. The publication was discontinued after three issues.

418. Eytinge a clever illustrator for periodicals.

419. Title-page composed probably by Lowell.

421, 422. The English caricaturist has drawn the marching figures in uniforms of fifty years earlier than the Civil War.

423. Winslow Homer studied lithography as a boy in Boston, and later while making drawings for a New York publishing house obtained instruction in painting at a night school. His pictures had immediate success for their genuine motive, and after a period of study in Paris he achieved distinction as a painter, particularly in marines. His silhouettes testify to his talent in drawing. See Vol. XII.

436, 437, 440. Hoppin a clever and graceful draftsman on wood. Illustrations in books published in the 'sixties and 'seventies, and in *Harper's Weekly*, were noteworthy.

448. See 286.

450. Design is by William E. Burton, actor, who established the magazine (1837–41) and gave his name to it.

453. See 304.

457. Beardsley an English artist and illustrator noted for his originality.

463. Paul Gustave Doré was a French artist who made his greatest reputation for paintings on religious subjects.

465. William J. Linton, born in England in 1812, won success as an engraver and editor before coming to the United States in 1867. He illustrated various works on wood engraving.

466. See 357.

467. Osgood, born at New Haven, painted portraits in Hartford about 1825, later studying in England where he painted British notables.

482. Design was the work of Benson J. Lossing.

494. See 436.

504. See 375.

510. See 182.

511. Artist of southern birth, painted and illustrated many scenes of southern life.

514. See 21.

522. See 202.

523. See 242.

526, 527. See 21.

531. See 222.

542. Strother, born at Martinsburg, W. Va., engraved on wood and was a writer under the name of "Porte Crayon" of clever southern sketches which were published with his own illustrations. Also an illustrator of books.

550. See 182.

558. See 21.

565. See 171.

567. See 365.

581. John Woodhouse Audubon illustrated much of the work of his father, John James Audubon, the naturalist.

584. Capt. Seth Eastman was a graduate of West Point and served on the frontier. Later he taught topographical drawing at the Military Academy, and wrote a treatise on this form of art. See Vol. I.

586. See 21.

590. Artist, known as "Frank" Beard, was illustrator for *Harper's Weekly* during the Civil War, and later for other weeklies; popular as a lecturer ("chalk talks"); professor of æsthetics at Syracuse University, 1881. See 651.

595. Lossing, besides writing and editing many historical works, was an accomplished draftsman and designer. No. 482 also by his hand.

599. See 21.

603. See 436.

606. By an officer of the Royal Navy who traveled in the United States in 1827–28. See Vols. III IV and V.

617. Artist had notable success with his humorous character sketches of negroes.

627, 628. Artist a popular illustrator for weekly publications of his day.

645, 646. See 418.

649. Wood block by Karst, who engraved designs for many publications, 1870 to 1890.

651. See 590.

660. See 511.

663, 664. By a clever and versatile illustrator of rural life and scenes. See Vol. III for other examples of his work.

678. See 436.

705. See 663.

723. See 663.

INDEX

Titles of books under author are in italics; titles of illustrations under producer are in quotation marks.